A Peace History of India

From Ashoka Maurya to Mahatma Gandhi

A Peace History of India

From Ashoka Maurya to Mahatma Gandhi

Klaus Schlichtmann

English language editor Dermot McCann

Vij Books India Pvt Ltd
New Delhi (India)

A Peace History of India: From Ashoka Maurya to Mahatma Gandhi

First Published in India in 2016

Published by

Vij Books India Pvt Ltd
(Publishers, Distributors and Importers)
2/19, Ansari Road
Delhi – 110 002
Phones: 91-11-43596460, 91-11-47340674
Fax: 91-11-47340674
e-mail: vijbooks@rediffmail.com
web : www.vijbooks.com

ISBN: 9789385563386 (Paperback
ISBN: 978-93-85563-52-2 (ebook)

FOUR PRESENTS

I come to you with four presents.
The first present is a lotus flower.
Do you understand?
The second present is a golden net.
Can you recognize it?
My third present is a shepherds' roundelay.
Do your feet know to dance?
My fourth present is a garden
Planted in the wilderness.
Could you work there?
I come to you with four presents.
Do you dare accept them?

(Accorded to the Buddha)

Contents

PART I
Ashoka of the Axial Age, His Time and his Work

PART II

The Palas in India and Abroad

PART III

A Little Axial Age around 1800

PART IV

Modern India, Gandhi and World Peace

Klaus Schlichtmann is author of *Japan in the World, Shidehara Kijuro, Pacifism and the Abolition of War* (2 vols.), Lanham Boulder, New York, Toronto etc., Lexington Books, 2009.

For Irena
Frank and Mark Palok

"Because time, all-powerful and formative, demands at last that ideas be given their fair due and justice, *living in the realm of the ideal* and *living in the world* no longer be thus altogether totally opposed (and divided), which equation, after all, makes for history's meaning and significance."[1]

"History is a set of lies agreed upon." (ascribed to Napoleon Bonaparte)

"There is also an issue of intellectual fairness in dealing with global history..." (Amartya Sen)

"Lead us from the unreal to the real. Lead us from darkness to light. Lead us from death to immortality." (Brihadaranyaka-Upanishad 1.3.28)

---

1 "Denn die allmächtig bildende Zeit will eben, daß die Ideen auch endlich Recht behalten, so daß: *in den Ideen leben,* und *in der Welt leben,* nicht mehr so ganz zweierlei sey, welche Gleichsetzung eben auch der Sinn und die Bedeutung aller Geschichte ist." Erathsrath von Berger, Ueber Volks-Eigenthuemlichkeit und den Gegensatz zwischen mehreren Völkern (About the national characteristics and the contrast between various peoples), *Kieler Blätter*, vol. II, No. 1, Kiel 1916, p. 5.

Foreword

Art and History are always interconnected stories of human development. It is through a diligent study of its artefacts that a culture's development through the ages can be retraced by historians. Conversely, artists study the texts of chroniclers to create their imaginative works. This is a book that traces the history of a people in order to glean from it the many ways in which rulers and scholars have striven to bring peace. The world requires a comprehensive understanding of the growth of humanity so as to underline movements in history which brought about peace.

Man's love for peace is manifest in many ways in the cultural history of India. Peace cannot be achieved by spreading a set of principles by force. If Ashoka could spread Buddhism far and wide, it was because of his generosity. He supplemented conquest with a kind of ethics based on discourse. King Ashoka distributed his wealth generously. The edicts are there for others to follow his example: his generosity, which means generosity in kind, not mere talk.

I find in this book the scholar's uninhibited faith in the unity of humanity. He refers to "the complicated religious ideas and rituals, the scholarly language, the highly developed art forms and the social and political systems to which the earliest inscriptions and other facts give testimony," which had been communicated by the Brahmins. Since the Southeast Asian tribes and kingdoms had themselves already reached a rather civilized state, they welcomed the Indian impetus, which they felt was "an enrichment of their own culture."

One of the devices used by Ashoka for the spread of Buddhist morals was the appointment of religious leaders. They were called *Dharmamahamatras*. They were some kind of dedicated 'comrades', and this included elements of benevolent control as well as faithful adherence to principles of conduct avoiding extremes, in accordance with the Buddha's middle way. The emperor reduced his army. He vowed never again to fight in a battle. He conquered the people's hearts. He spread laws instead, because the state, law and order could not be replaced by *dharma* alone. Similarly, centuries later, under Dharmapala northern India appears to have been unified from the east coast to the west; between the ports of both coasts there existed periods of close economic cooperation. Through this network, art grew many styles. The old Indian myths and epics were added and blended with indigenous themes.

Buddhism is one of the greatest propagators of peace. In Buddhist practice, there are monks, scholars, *bhikshus* and teachers. A religious class of 'priests' as such did not exist. Gautam Buddha was classless. He renounced a world that was full of contradictions. One such contradiction was the division into rich and poor classes. After his Enlightenment, which he achieved by meditation, he came back to the world of men to exhort people to seek a religion of their own. The spread of Buddhism has therefore been free from conflict. Mind Training is practiced to achieve compassion and wisdom. It is neither an imposition of 'law and order' to bring about social justice, nor is it an 'administration' of rights and duties to punish an offender. Buddhist practices assume one big humanism among all. Meditation can bring inner peace and resolve all inner conflicts –*ashanti*–and strife–*dwesh* – that cause violence. Buddhism eschewed Nationalism which is a western concept. From Nalanda, through Bengal, to the Malayan islands as well as to Tibet and China, Buddhism spread beyond India's boundaries. There was nothing like a missionary conquest to spread a religion.

Scriptures like the Buddhist Dharma aimed at individual perfection, enlightenment, moral and spiritual elevation in knowing God's manifestations in the universe or nature and natural laws. A human being only needed to be harmoniously connected with nature in a kind of cosmic union.

Western education for Indians stimulated a consciousness of history in the Indian intellectual. The researchers from the West, call them Indologists, always treated Indian science and ancient values as 'discovered' facts. Ever since, Indian scholars have been exhorted to preserve and spread the lessons inscribed in ancient Indian, Brahmanical or Sanskrit, texts. The closed self-sufficient culture of India which is surrounded by mountains in the north and the ocean in the south from east to west has become a subject, Indology, mainly due to Western intervention. It was never ignorance that kept Indians quiet about themselves. It was an understanding of life as ephemeral.

Yoga, or meditation is now treated as an art. Suffering souls visit Yoga classes. Take the Brahmo Samaj, for instance. Take the Ramakrishna Mission. It is an assembly of all people, irrespective of caste, creed and religion. The unifying factor is their belief in the existence of one immutable Being. Peace is not just the end of war. Peace is a mental attribute.

To make peace both a means and an end, we require a federation of all the nations of the world. For the preservation of universal peace pacifists ask to diminish the expenditures of government for military purposes and avoid war. India has demonstrated peaceful means under the leadership of Mahatma Gandhi, the revered Father of the Nation who taught non-violent resistance to imperialism. Along with sovereignty for India, he also envisaged an international law and order transcending the nation-state. A World People's Assembly would be a body for promoting peace and goodwill in the world. Gandhian pacifism aims at the eradication of the seeds of war from the social and economic life of man. The book argues that for India to spread the Gandhian vision of the creation of appropriate international machinery with adequate power to establish a just and lasting peace, she should be given a permanent seat on the UN Security Council.

Viewed in this way India stands as the harbinger of peaceful coexistence. From the Buddha to the Mahatma, sons of India stand as the messengers of peace for the whole world. If we look back into our history and if we reread the Peace History of India, which this author has tried to bring across, we will be able to settle back into the most uplifting insight that our land has taught us, the essential Indian philosophy: The world is a means not an end, man mutable and without a home, the body and all life precious, but impermanent and vulnerable.

Dr. Anuradha Bhattacharyya, (author of *One Word*),
Department of English,
Postgraduate Government College, Sector-11,
Chandigarh, INDIA

Preface and Acknowledgements

This work has been a number of years in the making. The task of writing, bringing together and researching the four dominant time periods of this book has been quite a challenge. The Gupta period (320-550) would also have merited my attention, as would the life and work of the historical Gautama Buddha himself. But the four epochs here presented seemed best suited for my purpose.

Previous, shorter versions of Parts III and IV were published in academic journals, and the Part on Ashoka was originally a seminar paper that I wrote when I studied Asian history as my major subject at Kiel University under Professor Hermann Kulke, then Chair of the Department of Asian History.

I had already visited India in 1964, when I was only 20 years old, because of my teenage interest in Buddhism. I had therefore always taken an interest in India, and studied Pala Buddhism long before I officially took up studies at Kiel University in 1985. The Palas eventually became the subject of a lecture I gave at the German Asiatic Society in Tokyo in 2002. So, India had continued to occupy a central place in my mind, and I began to investigate the country's past history and its significance, including related aspects of a general philosophy of history and religion.

I found that the periodically recurring historical patterns and precedents contained clues for developing principles with the aim of implementing practical measures to shape a better future. These highlights continued to be of my prime concern. The promise of the Axial Age is yet waiting to be brought to fruition. If there were no precedents like the Ashokan Axial impact, the Nalanda heritage and the Indian Renaissance, or the Hague Peace Conferences which took place in 1899 and 1907 or Gandhi's *satyagraha*, there was little hope of ever bringing to fruition any of the promises of history. I hope that the examples from Indian history that deal with certain high points in the development of civilization may shed light on aspects that allow us to get a glimpse of what may be possible for our future and that of our children.

Since I did not begin my university studies in this field until the relatively advanced age of 41 in 1985, I have never held a special position at a University nor have I been a professor's assistant or become the Chair of a Department of a University. However, having been fortunate enough to be awarded a fine scholarship by the German-Japanese Center Berlin (GJCB) in 1992, to continue research on the Japanese pacifist diplomat Shidehara Kijuro, who had already been the subject of my MA thesis, I was able to continue research and consequently publish extensively on various issues related to Asia and peace, the United Nations, peace diplomacy, peace education and law and related topics, and stay on in Japan to complete my PhD which I eventually obtained with *magna cum laude* from Kiel University in 1996. My Dissertation on Shidehara was published in German in 1998 and an English translation in two volumes came out in 2009 (Lexington Books).

I am especially indebted to Hermann Kulke, Romila Thapar, Swapna Bhattacharya, Ramesh Chandra Tiwari, and Monica Yaman for having read and commented upon previous versions of the manuscript or parts thereof, and without whose help and encouragement this work would not have been possible. My friend Dermot McCann has helped me with the English language. For the student and researcher of oriental studies I have provided extensive material quoted in the footnotes for further reference.

PART I

Ashoka of the Axial Age, His Time and his Work—
With special reference to the theories of Max Weber

1st century BCE/CE Indian relief from Amaravathi village, Guntur district, Andhra Pradesh (India). Preserved in Guimet Museum, Paris (2005)

Sanchi Stupa in Madhya Pradesh, Northern gate, containing relics of Gautam Buddha

Ringstone from the Mauryan Empire. Northwest Pakistan. 3rd century BCE. British Museum. Source: World Imaging

Ashoka of the Axial Age—His Time and Work
With special reference to the theories of Max Weber

It has been asked: Why Max Weber? What is the relevance of Max Weber with regard to Ashoka, the famous king of the Indian Maurya dynasty? Suffice it to say: I like Max Weber, and, coming from a Protestant background myself, I like his Protestant ethic and inner-worldly asceticism. His proposed ethical principles are challenging and useful. Weber succeeds to impart insights, regarding the meaning and significance of Buddhism, which are generally relevant, and provide important points of reference that help us understand the inner-worldly asceticism and the rational mode of economic life in India, propagated by the Buddhists, and Ashoka in particular. Weber has brought Ashoka and Buddhism closer to Western readers, academic or not, and made them better understood from a socio-political point of view, through the medium of Western language. Through Max Weber's writings the road also leads us (although this was not Weber's intention) from the pacifism of the Indian emperor—rooted in what, put in modern terms, would be principles of discourse ethics—to a reasoned and justifiable train of arguments that aim at the rejection of violence, and abolishing war as an institution.

1. Entering History

The Indian king and emperor Ashoka Maurya reigned in North India from about 273/268 until around 231 BC. The capital of the Mauryan Empire was Pataliputra, today's Patna, located on the 25th latitude and the 85th longitude. Ashoka was the third great ruler of the dynasty, which held power in North India from 320 to about 185 BC.

Situated in the Gangetic plains, the metropolis was at a distance of around 400 kilometres from the holy city of Benares in the West and about 1000 kilometres from the ancient port city of Tamralipti (Tamluk) in the Southeast, on the Bay of Bengal, not far from today's Kolkata. According to a tradition Pataliputra was known as 'Kusumapura', which in Sanskrit means 'City of Flowers', which is why the city had also been labelled the 'Indian Florence'.[1] According to Megasthenes (ca. 350-290 BC), the Greek

---

1   The term 'Indian Florence' is in *A Record of Buddhistic Kingdoms: being an account by the Chinese monk Fâ-Hien of his travels in India and Ceylon, A.D. 399-414, in search of*

diplomat, historian and geographer of antiquity, who resided in Pataliputra as Ambassador to the Court of Ashoka's grandfather, Chandragupta Maurya (340-298 v. Chr.)

> the mean breadth, (of the Ganges) is 100 stadia, and its least depth 20 fathoms. At the meeting of this river and another is situated Palibothra, a city eighty stadia in length and fifteen in breadth. It is of the shape of a parallelogram, and is girded with a wooden wall, pierced with loopholes for the discharge of arrows. It has a ditch in front for defence and for receiving the sewage of the city. The people in whose country this city is situated is the most distinguished in all India, and is called the Prasii. The king, in addition to his family name, must adopt the surname of Palibothros, as Sandrakottos, for instance, did, to whom Megasthenes was sent on an embassy.[2]

Legendary feet of Chandragupta on Chandragiri, Shravanabelagola, Karnataka, India

Ashoka's grandfather Chandragupta was known to Greek historians as Sandrakottos. A Jain text by a twelfth century polymath, Acharya Hemachandra, the *Parisishtaparvan*, which had come into the possession of Colonel Colin Mackenzie, an employee of the British East India

---

the Buddhist books of discipline. Translated and annotated with a Corean recension of the Chinese text by James LEGGE, Oxford, At the Clarendon Press 1886, p. 77, note 1. (online: http://www.buddhanet.net/pdf_file/rbddh10.pdf).

2   MEGASTHENES: Description of Pataliputra (late 3rd century BCE), Book II. Fragm. Xxv. Strab. Vi. i. 35-36, p. 702.

Company, tells about Chandragupta, the founder of the Maurya Dynasty.[3] This work "threw new light" on his ascent to power "with the help of the Brahman Chanakya."[4] The text describes in detail how Chandragupta's mother, who belonged to a tribe famous for rearing royal peacocks (Skt. *mayura*), had to flee after her husband, the clan chief, had been assassinated. One day, after she had gone into hiding with her son, young Chandragupta was accidentally discovered by a Jain ascetic, the Brahmin Chanakya. Chanakya had suffered humiliation at the hands of king Nanda of Magadha, and yearned for revenge. He abducted Chandragupta, in whom he had identified the special marks of the monarch. He educated him, planning for Chandragupta to eventually defeat king Nanda and take over the rule of the kingdom. Several years earlier king Mahapadma Nanda (ruled 345-329 BC) had already moved his capital from Rajagriha (today's Rajgir) to Pataliputra, on the banks of the Ganges.

The *Parisishtaparvan* describes how Chanakya and Chandragupta eventually march toward the capital Pataliputra; however, the attack is repelled, and Chanakya retreats into the Himalayan region, where he forms a military alliance with the mountain king Parvataka. In a long-lasting campaign they conquer one area after another, until they finally take Pataliputra and force king Dhana Nanda (329-321 BC) to go into exile.[5] Having defeated the last ruler of the Nandas, Dhana Nanda, Chandragupta's

---

3   Acharya HEMACHANDRA, *The Lives of the Jain Elders*, transl. by Richard FYNES, Oxford University Press (Oxford World's Classics), 1998. On Chandragupta and Chanakya also see Charles ALLEN, *Ashoka*, London, Little, Brown 2012, p. 83.

4   Ch. ALLEN, *Ashoka*, p. 83.

5   Ch. ALLEN, *Ashoka*, p. 83: "One of the many Jain texts collected by Mackenzie was the *Parisishtaparvan*, the work of a twelfth-century polymath named Acharya Hemachandra that might be freely translated as *The Lives of the Jain Elders*. This threw new light on the founder of the Mauryan dynasty kings of Magadha, in the form of a detailed account of Chandragupta's rise to power with the help of the Brahman Chanakya. In this Jain version of events Chandragupta's mother is from a community that keeps royal peacocks, mora in Pali; *mayura* in Sanskrit. Her chieftain husband is killed and she is forced to go into hiding with the infant Chandragupta. One day the boy is seen by a Jain ascetic, who is the Brahman Chanakya in disguise. Chanakya has been humiliated by King Nanda of Magadha and has been forced to flee his wrath, and is now plotting revenge. Seeing Chandragupta lording it over other village boys, he recognises in him all the qualities of leadership required of a monarch, so he kidnaps him and educates him to take on that role. Chanakya and Chandragupta together launch an attack on Pataliputra that fails. Chanakya recognises his mistake in attacking Nanda directly and after retreating to the Himalayan regions he forms a military alliance with the mountain king Parvataka. The allies then embark on a long military campaign taking region by region until finally capturing Pataliputra and forcing King Nanda into exile."

army takes over the government and establishes the Empire of the Mauryas.

So Pataliputra came to be an important trade centre, from where cargo vessels could sail down the Ganges and out into the open sea further to the East and toward the South.[6] According to the Chinese pilgrim Faxian's account, among several holy sites, the city was noted for having "preserved the Buddha's footprint on a stone."[7]

In the Annals Ashoka is held to be the worthiest and most powerful ruler of the Maurya dynasty, said to be a *chakravartin*, i.e. a sovereign who holds the Wheel of the Law (*dharmacakra*) in his hands, being at the same time temporal and spiritual overlord.[8] The concept of the Chakravartin, however, politically speaking, probably emerged and became prevalent only some time later, though it may have originated with Ashoka.

As is well known, early in his career Ashoka renounced war as an instrument for achieving political goals. In this he disagreed with the hitherto prevailing doctrine that considered the enforcement of claims to power and conquest by taking belligerent action legitimate. Ashoka thus may lay claim to having been the most notable ruler of the ancient world, whose influence regarding peaceful policies carries through to this day. He was well ahead of his time, and as H.G. Wells writes in his book *The Outline of History*, the monarch of antiquity is "on record" to have completely "abandoned" and abolished warfare.[9] This "greatest monarch"

---

6   Edmund HARDY, *König Asoka* (King Ashoka), Mainz, Verlag von Franz Kirchheim 1902, p. 41, also refers to the Buddha's prophesy that Pataliputra would "become the capital … a trade center, for which in ancient times the position provided, in fact, a suitable image." (My translation)

7   *A record of Buddhistic kingdoms*, by James LEGGE, p. 80.

8   See Charles DREKMEIER, *Kingship and Community in Early India*, Stanford, Stanford University Press 1962, p. 157: "The chakravartin was regarded as the greatest of kings, the overlord, and not as the head of a comprehensive state controlled directly from the capital." See also Hermann KULKE, Indian Colonies, Indianisation or Cultural Convergence? Reflections on the Changing Image of India's Role in Southeast Asia, in H. SCHULTE-NORDHOLT (ed.), Onderzoek in Zuidoost-Azië (Semaian 3), Leiden 1990, p. 22, and Gerald FUSSMANN, Central and Provincial Administration in Ancient India: The Problem of the Mauryan Empire, *The Indian Historical Review*, vol. XIV, nos. 1-2 (July 1987 & Jan. 1988, publ. in 1990), pp. 45 and 70-72.

9   Herbert George WELLS, *The Outline of History. Being a Plain History of Life and Mankind*, revised and brought up to the End of the Second World War by Raymond POSTGATE, New York, Garden City 1949, p. 402.

was disgusted by what he saw of the cruelties and horrors of war ... [and] declared ... that he would no longer seek conquest by war, but by religion, and the rest of his life was devoted to the spreading of Buddhism throughout the world ... He organized a great digging of wells in India, and the planting of trees for shade. He appointed officers for the supervision of charitable works. He founded hospitals and public gardens. He had gardens made for the growing of medicinal herbs ... He created a ministry for the care of aborigines and subject races. He made provision for the education of women ... He ... set up long inscriptions rehearsing the teachings of Gautama, and it is the simple and human teaching and not the preposterous accretions.[10]

According to legend, however, Ashoka had been a shrewd and cruel leader in the beginning;[11] of course, it goes without saying that legend and historical facts must be clearly distinguished. Still, the legends, too, throw a light on what life in those days of antiquity may have been like, and therefore are a valuable source.

Although Ashoka featured prominently in the Buddhist scriptures such as the Ceylonese (Sri Lankan) Dynastic Chronicles,[12] the pre-Christian emperor and king had been forgotten over the centuries. He was rediscovered only in the beginning of the nineteenth century, when Englishmen from the East India Company found and deciphered his inscriptions. (See PART III)

2. The Buddha's Prophesy

The ancient capital of the kingdom of Magadha south of the Gangetic plain was situated in lush terrain with green forests and surrounded by rolling hills. There, in Rajagriha, the Buddha usually remained during the long rainy season to meditate in seclusion. His daily lectures on Vulture Peak, the *Griddhakuta*, were attended by his followers, among them his disciples, recluses, rich merchants and nobles as well as the king of Magadha, Bimbisara (540-490), and others, including simple folk and many who came from the nearby towns and villages.

---

10 H. G. Wells, *The Outline of History*, pp. 402-404.

11 On the Ashoka legend s. John S. STRONG, *The Legend of King Asoka, A Study and Translation of the Asokavadana*, Varanasi, Patna, Bangalore, Madras, Motilal Banarsidass 1989 (orig. Princeton 1948).

12 See Ch. ALLEN, *Ashoka*, pp. 101ff, on the Ceylonese Dynastic Chronicles.

The *Ashokavadana*, the legend of King Ashoka, a 2nd century AD Sanskrit Mahayana text, has the following story: the Buddha had once rested in the village of Kalandakavana and then walked on, followed by many monks, including his disciples Ananda, Sariputra and Subhuti. Before entering the city of Rajagriha they consulted amongst themselves. The monks then went off by different routes into the city to beg for their daily food in the habit of wandering ascetics, and the Buddha went on alone.

On his passage through the city the Buddha met two boys who were playing by the wayside, Jaya and Vijaya by name. The rainy season had brought the first rains, and out of the clay of the damp earth the two boys had formed small mud huts and carts, boats and storage for the harvest, where the clay cakes, rice grains and fruits that were transported on the ships and carts could be stored. When they saw the Buddha, Jaya respectfully offered a handful of the unformed clay as a gift to the Buddha. Vijaya respectfully folded his hands to give his assent. The Buddha was very pleased.[13] After having completed his begging rounds, the Buddha told his disciple Ananda of the incident:

> one hundred years after his Nirvana, the small Jaya would be the holy king Ashoka, reigning at Pataliputra over the whole of India and building 84,000 stupas; Vijaya would be his minister, going by the name of Rādhagupta.[14]

Jaya being reborn as King Ashoka, according to the legend, his skin is said to have been rough and unpleasant to touch, a result of the clay the

---

13   Ch. ALLEN, *Ashoka*, p. 188: "*The Legend of King Ashoka* opens with a long account of Upagupta's saintliness in a previous life before describing how Upagupta is reborn the son of a perfume seller of Mathura and ordained as a Buddhist monk. Only then does Ashoka come into the story, beginning with his previous existence as a boy who meets the Buddha, also in a previous life, on the road and makes him an offering of a handful of dirt—an action with profound karmic consequences. The Buddha accepts the offering and predicts how in consequence the boy will be reborn as Ashoka a hundred years after his own death."

14   See also Étienne LAMOTTE, *Histoire du Bouddhisme Indien. Des Origines a l'Ere Saka*. Louvain 1958, p. 261: "Venant du Kalandakavana, le Buddha penetre a Rajagrha pour y mendier sa nourriture. Son entrée dans Ia ville est marquée par plusieurs prodiges. Deux garçonnets, Jaya et Vijaya, jouaient dans Ia rue et s'amusaient avec de la terre a façonner des maisons et des greniers. Apercevant le Buddha, Jaya lui offrit respectueusement une poignée de terre; Vijaya, les mains jointes, approuvait l'acte de son compagnon. Le Bouddha prédit a Ananda que, cent ans après son Nirvana, le petit Jaya serait le saint roi Asoka, régnerait a Pataliputra sur l'Inde entière et construirait 84.000 stupa; Vijaya serait son ministre, sous le nom de Radhagupta."

boys had been playing with.[15] Young Ashoka is obstinate and needs to be disciplined.[16]

After the Buddha had spoken, he withdrew to meditate. When at the end of the rainy season he wandered northward by the side of the small village Patali on the Ganges, he prophesied that on this very spot a great city, Pataliputra, was going to arise, to become the capital of the Maurya empire. An old text, the *Katha Sarit Sagara*, describes how the city was miraculously built by the magical power of a Brahmin:

> Near Gangadvara there is a holy pond ... There lived a Brahmin from the south, given to pious repentance, with his wife, to whom three sons were born. After he and his wife had died, his sons traveled to Rajagriha, desiring to acquire knowledge of the sciences. There they learned all knowledge, and then went ... to the south, to worship Kumara. So they came to the city of Chinchini on the seacoast, and lived in the house of the Brahmin Bhojika, who gave them his three daughters to marry ... One among them became pregnant ... When the time came, she gave birth to a son, and the love of all turned to the boy [Putraka]. [Years later, after many adventures, and after he had acquired magical shoes that gave him the "power to fly" and a magic wand, he came] to a lonely dilapidated house, and saw in it an old woman. [Putraka] ... was received by her ... the old woman said to him: "I think, my son, that there is nowhere a woman out there better suited for you than the daughter of our king here, Patali; but she is guarded like a pearl up there in her rooms."[17]

> [After Putraka had married the princess secretly and against the wishes of her father, he had to flee with Patali. Finally, he conjured up] a city on the banks of Ganga ... with his [magic] wand ... became now king ... was reconciled with his father in law and ruled over the whole earth up to the sea. Thus Pataliputra, the residence of wealth and education ... was created by magic.[18]

---

15 According to legend Ashoka's skin was "rough and unpleasant to the touch." (*Ashokavadana*)

16 Ch. ALLEN, *Ashoka*, p. 188: "Ashoka grows into an unruly youth and is handed over for disciplining."

17 The creation of the city by magic is described in *Katha Sarit Sagara. Die Mährchensammlung des Sri Somadeva Bhatta aus Kaschmir* (Katha Sarit Sagara. The Fables collected by Sri Somadeva of Kashmere), First to Fifth Book, Sanskrit and German, Leipzig, F. A. Brockhaus 1839, pp. 8-10.

18 Ibid.

In the Mahavamsa, the Ceylonese chronicle, the prophecy of the Buddha is not mentioned,[19] but the compilers of the dynastic Ceylonese chronicles devoted several chapters to all the Indian monarchs who ruled over Magadha, from the time of Buddha Shakyamuni until the reign of King Darmasoca (i.e. Ashoka). The entire fifth chapter of the chronicle contains a detailed report of Darmasoca, starting with the account of his grandfather Chandragupta's rise to power with the help of the Brahmin Chanakya. The Sanskrit drama *The Minister's Signet Ring*, translated by the orientalist Sir William Jones, told, like the Mahavamsa, that Chandragupta's son Bindusara had originally intended his eldest son, Prince Sumana, to become his successor; however, one of King Bindusara's ninety-nine children was Priyadase (i.e. Ashoka).[20] Prince Priyadase was assigned as a teenager by his father to the town of Wettisa (Vidisha), where he "married the princess, called Wettisa, of the royal family called Sacca (Sakya) ... and became king of the city Udeny (Ujjain): he had one son and a daughter by this Queen Wettisa. As this king was very prosperous in everything, he was styled Asoca Prince."[21]

As successor to King Bindusara Amitraghata, son of Chandragupta, Ashoka finally (around the year 270 BC) ascended the Peacock Throne.

3. Max Weber and India

The sociologist Max Weber stated that "India was and is ... a land of trade, not only of inland trade, but also direct foreign trade, particularly with the Occident, apparently dating back to ancient Babylonian times..."[22] The main

---

19 The Mahávansi, the Rájá-ratnácari, and the Rájávali, vol. 2, by Edward UPHAM, William Buckley FOX and 5th century Mahanama, Nabu Press 2010.

20 Ch. ALLEN, *Ashoka*, p. 101: "the compilers of the *Great Dynastic Chronicle* [*Mahavamsa*] had devoted several chapters to the Indian monarchs who had ruled over Magadha from the time of Sakyamuni Buddha down to the reign of King Darmasoca. Indeed, the chronicle's fifth chapter was entirely given over to an account of Darmasoca's rule, beginning with an account of the rise to power of his grandfather Chandragupta with the help of the Brahman Chanakya very much as given in the Sanskrit verse-drama *The Minister's Signet Ring* translated by Sir William Jones. It went on to describe how Chandragupta's son Bindusara had appointed as his heir his eldest son, Prince Sumana, but that among King Bindusara's other ninety-nine children was a son called Priyadase. According to Fox's summary, this prince Priyadase had as a youth been sent away by his father to the city of Wettisa (Vidisha)."

21 Quoted in Ch. ALLEN, *Ashoka*, p. 101.

22 Max WEBER, *The Religion of India. The Sociology of Hinduism and Buddhism*, transl. by

share of the goods that eventually came to be exported were fabrics and agricultural products, tools and art objects, cotton fabrics and silk, muslin, ivory, pepper, pearls, lapis lazuli, turquoise, as well as horses and other livestock.[23] For this the Europeans paid in hard cash, as well as gold, silver and amber. With the "invasion of Alexander"[24] the Greeks, many of whom settled in Bactria, established closer contacts with the Indian continent.[25] As Max Weber rightly points out, "northwest Indian commerce was under constant perceptible Hellenic influence."[26] Subsequently a meeting of Alexander (ind. Alikasundara) with Chandragupta (gr. Sandrakottos) had taken place. Alexander's successor, Seleucus Nicator, was defeated by Chandragupta. The subsequent peace agreements included the introduction of a Greek princess into the royal harem. It is possible that Ashoka's grandmother was a Bactrian of Greek origin.

Increased trade and the emergence of new international markets both made it necessary and also served as an opportunity to develop new and more complex forms of social organization. Interestingly, this development took place not only in India, but simultaneously also in the Mediterranean and in Japan and China.

Although, according to Weber, India was "in contrast to China... a land of villages,"[27] Indian crafts and specialized industries were "highly developed."[28] Weber is right in claiming that occupational activities of Indian

---

Hans H. GERTH and Don MARTINDALE, New York, The Free Press; London, Collier Macmillan 1967, p. 3. (Orig. publ. in 1958. Hereafter referred to as GM)

23 On international trade also see Prakash Charan PRASAD, *Foreign Trade and Commerce in Ancient India*, New Delhi, Abhinav Publications 1977, pp. 196 ff., and André WINK, *Al-Hind: Early medieval India and the expansion of Islam*, vol. 1, The India Trade, Brill 1990, pp. 40 ff., and *The Trading Diasporas in the Indian Ocean*, pp. 65 ff.

24 GM, p. 72.

25 Ashoka's grandmother or mother was possibly a Bactrian Greek woman. According to Plutarch, Alex. 62,9, Alexander (ind. Alikasundara) and Chandragupta (gr. Sandrakottos) actually met. Alexander's successor, Seleucus Nicator, was defeated in battle by Chandragupta. At least the subsequent peace agreements included the introduction of a Greek princess into the royal harem. See Hermann KULKE, Ausgrenzung, Rezeption und kulturelles Sendungsbewußtsein (Exclusionism, Reception and Cultural Mission), in S.N. EISENSTADT (ed.), *Kulturen der Achsenzeit* (Cultures of the Axial Period), vol. II, Frankfurt, Suhrkamp 1992, p. 27.

26 GM, p. 3.

27 GM, p. 3.

28 GM, p. 4.

'professional castes' took place mainly in the villages, and not in the cities. "The typical Indian village craftsmen were hereditary 'tied cottagers';"[29] according to Weber these industrial activities were not rationally organized, strictly independent associations of strictly economic concerns or interests. The artisans (were) ... indeed some kind of 'cottagers', however not of serfs of individual employers but: village helots, to whom were leased, for their services, hereditary holdings ... and—as a rule the village compensated them for their services, not by payment for single services, but by a fixed share of the harvest yield or wages in kind.[30]

The merchants were generally autonomous, independent farmers and free. However, in the course of time the "old 'estates' had fallen into decay," and "the notion of free peasants (Vaiçya) had become a fiction. The sources in Buddhist times held the merchants to be the typical Vaiçya."[31] From a natural order of social ranking, there now arises an increasingly rigid and elaborate caste system. With the increase of trade, craftsmanship and art are replaced by industry, associated with a lower social status and with profit becoming an end in itself; this led to considerable changes in social stratification.

On Indian merchants' trading customs Weber states that "the acquisitiveness (Erwerbstrieb) of Indians of all strata left little to be desired and nowhere is to be found so little antichrematism and such high evaluation of wealth."[32] Strangely, however, according to Weber the "impulse to acquisition, pursuit of gain, of money—of the greatest possible amount of money—has in itself nothing to do with capitalism."[33]

Moreover, as Asia historian Hermann Kulke writes, the caste system as a whole had never been "as closed as Weber supposed, but was always

---

29 GM, p. 35. See also the "offiziellen Bericht des britischen Unterhauses über indische Fragen" (Official Report of the British House of Commons, on Indian Questions) by Karl MARX. See also GM, 37.

30 GM, pp. 56-57.

31 GM, p. 226. From a natural order of social ranking, there develops an increasingly rigid and elaborate caste system. With the increase of trade, craftsmanship and art are replaced by industry, identified with a lower social status, and with profit becoming an end in itself.

32 GM, p. 4.

33 Max WEBER, *The Protestant Ethic and the Spirit of Capitalism*, transl. by Talcott PARSONS, New York, Charles Scribner's and London, George Allen & Unwin 1950 (1930), p. 17.

open to new developments, in order to adapt to new social, economic and religious developments."[34] A system of prebends was adopted increasingly by the Brahmanical priests and—much later—Buddhist monks as well, and a depreciation of craftsmanship occurred.[35] -

In this context it may be useful to refer to the religious-social concept of the four *ashramas*, the individual's four stages in life. Max Weber describes the four Ashramas: "The *brahmacharin* (novice) was personally subordinate to the strict authority and domestic discipline of the teacher; he was enjoined to chastity and mendicancy and his life was ruled throughout by asceticism." On the level of the second *ashrama* (or 'household'), the "inner-worldly life-conduct of the classical Brahmin himself as *grihasta* (householder) was ascetically regulated." And: "The ideal way of life for the aging Brahmin ... as *vanaprastha*" consisted in "retirement to the forests." In the final (fourth) stage, "the retreat into the eternal silence of the recluse," the *sannyasin*, became the goal.[36] This is the place, where trained Brahmins and those 'caste dropouts', predestined less by a favourable rebirth than by natural disposition and inborn faculties, met on common spiritual grounds. The term "silence" here seems to be not quite adequate. Rather, it is the perfect state of being (still) 'in the world, but not (no longer) of it'. Ashoka's Buddhist ways and proclamations have to be seen against the backdrop of these social structures, which were already largely in existence.

With the progressive 'discovery' of India, merchants attained a higher social status, while internal administration, at the centres of power, was strengthened. At the height of this development "the position of the guilds

---

34 Own translation from the German. Concerning "adaptation to new social, economic and religious developments" see Hermann KULKE, Orthodoxe Restauration und hinduistische Sektenreligiosität im Werk Max Webers (Orthodox restoration and the Hindu sects' religiosity in Max Weber's work), in Wolfgang SCHLUCHTER (ed.), *Max Webers Studie über Hinduismus und Buddhismus—Interpretation und Kritik* (Max Weber's study of Hinduism and Buddhism—interpretation and criticism), Frankfurt, M., Suhrkamp 1984, pp. 300-301.

35 Foreign people poured into India from outside, who had to be integrated into the existing society, and 'absorbed' by the local strata. This led consequently and consecutively to more rigid hierarchic structures (*Verkastung*), officialdom (*Verbeamtung*) and militarization. Max WEBER does give indications to this effect. Had he known about the Indus Valley Civilization, an empire which apparently did not maintain a military and was held together without its rulers resorting to physical force, he would probably have obtained a much clearer picture of the history, and social development in ancient India.

36 GM, p. 150.

was much the same as that occupied by guilds in the cities of the medieval Occident." Yet, Weber claims that, in spite of considerable "urban development," it "did not evolve into the urban autonomy of the Occidental kind nor, after the formation of the great patrimonial states, into a social and economic organization of the territories corresponding to the 'territorial economy' of the occident." The important question Weber is asking is: why? And he finds the answer in "the Hinduistic caste system, the origins of which certainly preceded [the guilds]," which "displaced those organizations ... or crippled them."[37] Although "originally they [the castes] were undoubtedly simply status groups" or professions,[38] eventually the caste system "was entirely different from that of the merchant and craft guilds."[39] Whatever the case may be, the social fabric in India was, similar to the West, quite rigid and fixed, except that in India, in principle, anyone could escape his innate state by renouncing the world.[40]

Marine trade played a significant role. Ashoka sent "legations to foreign powers also, and above all to the great Hellenistic powers of the West, to Alexandria[41] ... and one mission with the support of the king went to Ceylon and the far East-Indian territories."[42] According to tradition, Mahendra and Sanghamitra (the children of Ashoka's first wife Devi), who were born in Ujjain, did missionary work in Ceylon and converted the country to Buddhism. Marine trade probably existed also between the capital of the Mauryas, Pataliputra, and the large seaport of Tamralipti (today's Tamluk), situated on the Bay of Bengal, and some countries in the Far East. However, neither Max Weber nor the Ashokan inscriptions yield

---

37 GM, pp. 33-34.

38 GM, p. 55.

39 GM, pp. 33-34.

40 Renouncing worldly life was apparently more difficult for women.

41 See the Great Rock Edict no. XIII, in D.C. SIRKAR, *Inscriptions of Ashoka*, Delhi 1967, pp. 58-59: "So, what is conquest through Dharma [*dharma-vijaya*] ... has been achieved by the Beloved of the Gods not only in his own dominions but also in the territories bordering on his dominions, as far away as [three thousand miles] where the Yavana [Greek] king named Antiyoka is ruling and where, beyond the kingdom of the said Antiyoka, four other kings named Turamaya, Antikini, Maka and Alikasundara are also ruling, and, towards the south, where the Cholas and Pandyas are living as far as Tamraparni [Ceylon]." English translations of the edicts understandably are more numerous. See also Jyotirmay SEN, Asoka's mission to Ceylon and some connected problems, *The Indian Historical Quarterly*, Vol. 4, Nr. 4 (1928), pp. 667-677.

42 GM, p. 241.

evidence of anything of that sort,[43] although it may seem self-evident that a connection existed. This anomaly is reflected in a similarly conspicuous absence of historical evidence concerning Ashoka in Greek and Roman sources.[44]

Interestingly, Max Weber recognizes the "inner-worldly mysticism" of Buddhism as having the highest ranking in Mahayana philosophy, stressing the "characteristic rational element in Buddhism" which is decisive. His source here is the book by Daisetsu Suzuki, *Outlines of Mahayana Buddhism*, published in 1907. It is the inner-worldly mysticism "of a world-indifferent life, which proves itself precisely within and against the world and its manipulations."[45] Thus in Buddhism, too, "besides world-fleeing mysticism there is found the inner-worldly mysticism" which Weber here characterizes as a "life in the world, which is yet indifferent to the world ... having inwardly escaped from the world and from death, [a life which] accepting birth, death, rebirth and redeath, life and its activities with all its apparent deceptive joys and sufferings, as the eternal forms of being."[46] But as is the case in other religions, one can through good deeds improve one's chances for redemption and obtain release from suffering. The Buddhist doctrine of *karma* and rebirth amplified these chances. Thus Ashoka was Jaya, who had met the Buddha, reborn. Unlike in the case of the historical Buddha, Ashoka's birth in 302 was not accompanied by miracles but took place normally.

The Hindu pantheon (which later was assimilated into Buddhism almost completely) even outside India, in its complexity represents manifestations of vital forces, distinct personified elements of nature, which are equally subject to the cycle of karma and rebirth, and which by appropriate devotion one could use to one's advantage. Here, a notable cultural variation is the "predominant faith in the migration of the soul," (Weber) which transcends time and space.

---

43 On Indian overseas trade see Vincent A. SMITH, *The Oxford History of India*, Oxford, the Clarendon Press 1961, p. 124, notes that the missions to Ceylon (and Burma) "are not mentioned; I do not know why." Even in the pre-Christian era sea-trade was pursued between India and China, but almost no records remain.

44 See Étienne LAMOTTE, *Histoire du Bouddhisme Indien—Des Origines à l'Ère Shaka*, Louvain 1958, p. 245: "Passé sous silence par les historiens gréco-romains, il est connu tant par des documents contemporains - les édits..." WEBER is silent on this point.

45 GM, p. 253.

46 Ibid.

4. Life in the Capital Pataliputra

In certain ways life in India in Ashokan times may hardly have been much different from what it was a hundred, two hundred or only fifty years from our present time. Even today, the traditional structures and lifestyles can be observed. A multi-layered society had arisen in which the caste system played a significant role, a society which distinguished itself through the supremacy of the warrior castes, referred to as the "patrimonial little kings" by Weber, and the Brahmins who supported them. In addition, traders, farmers and servants took care of the people's welfare. The caste system was also replicated in the urban areas. Each caste was, much as during the European Middle Ages, allotted a certain district of the city, which showcased its professional and social functions and matched its requirements. A "political citizenry" developed in rudimentary form, with its own "thinkers and prophets" (as was the case in Judaism and Christianity, and in ancient Greece). According to Max Weber, however, the caste system prevented the establishment of a secular 'city' in the semblance of a legally unconstrained, self-governing and sovereign unit. The reason for this was that the "interests of Asiatic intellectuality, so far as they transcended everyday life, lay primarily in directions other than the political."[47] Weber alleged that Asian political theory lacked a systematic method like that of Aristotle, and, in general, rational concepts. On the other hand, Weber does confirm that in India, too, "one finds the beginnings of a logic that is quite similar to that of Aristotle."[48] On what grounds Weber criticizes the city in Asia more than two thousand years ago for not having developed as an autonomous, unified economic power as in medieval Europe is not clear. Since it did not operate its own business independently, with a separate code of law and taxation system, Weber says it was at best a community establishment, but lacking the feature that became predominant later in Europe, i.e. to be "a special kind of fortress and a garrison."[49] What significance can we attach to these differences, when in fact in Buddha's time already, as Weber points out, "the city and the city palace with its elephant-riding king were characteristic," and the already existing "dialogue form reflect[ed] the

---

47 GM, pp. 337-338.

48 *FROM MAX WEBER: Essays in Sociology*, transl., ed. and with an intro. by Hans H. GERTH and C. Wright MILLS, New York, Oxford University Press 1946, p. 141.

49 Max WEBER, *Economy and Society: An Outline of Interpretive Sociology*, ed. Guenther ROTH, Claus WITTICH, Ephraim FISCHOFF et al., Berkeley, Los Angeles, London, University of California Press 2013 (1963), vol. I, p. 221.

advent of urban culture,"[50] in the sense of being an already highly developed form of organized society. Weber's argument is not very persuasive, and the comparison consequently misleading.

The transition effected by the axial age denotes a turning point: the newly emerging consciousness of the self as a knowing subject articulates itself and finds a clear philosophical expression. In his book *The Origin and Goal of History*, originally published in German in 1949, the philosopher Karl Jaspers argues, in the chapter "History and the Present Become Inseparable to Us:"

> While research and existence with their consciousness of Being attain consummation in mutual tension, research itself lives in the tension between the current whole and the smallest detail. Historical total consciousness, in conjunction with loving nearness to the particular, visualizes a world in which man can live as himself with his matrix. Openness into the breadth of history and self-identity with the present, perception of history as a whole, and life from present origin, these tensions make possible the man who, cast back upon his absolute historicity, has come to himself.[51]

The process is decisive: "As I see the totality of the past, so I experience the present. The deeper the foundations I acquire in the past, the more outstanding my participation in the present course of events."[52] With "axial time" (Karl Jaspers) a new system of logic and an ethical discourse on war and peace had emerged. Not altogether unlike the ancient Greek philosophers, in China Mozi (lat. Micius, ca. 470-391) taught self-restraint, self-reflection and compassionate realism, while preaching and practicing universal love, social equality and non-violence.[53] A little later the decisive impulse for the future development and spread of Buddhism in Asia came from India, advanced by Ashoka. The king, however, had the unity of the empire in mind, before as emperor and *samrat* he also engaged in missionary activities.

---

50 GM, p. 205.

51 Karl JASPERS, *The Origin and Goal of History*, London, Routledge & Kegan Paul 1953, pp. 270-271.

52 K. JASPERS, *The Origin and Goal of History*, p. 271.

53 MOZI (Mo-tse, ca. 470-391) is the Third in the 'Club' of Chinese Axial Age philosophers, besides Confucius and Laotse.

5. Taxila, Kautilya and the Arthashastra

After the kingdom was founded in or around the year 321 BC, the capital of the kingdom of Gandhara, Taxila (Takshashila), in West Punjab (now Pakistan), was conquered by King Chandragupta Maurya. Chandragupta Maurya's counsellor and prime minister was the aforementioned Chanakya Kautilya, "the crow-like," a contemporary of Aristotle. Kautilya, a professor teaching in Taxila, is supposed to have written a famous textbook, the Arthashastra, on the politics and economy of the state.[54] The text of the *Arthashastra* was only rediscovered at the beginning of the 20th century, when it was given to R. Samasastry, the librarian of the *Oriental State Library* of the city of Mysore, by an anonymous Indian pundit, and Samasastry subsequently translated the book (between 1905 and 1914).

Amartya Sen described it as the "first book ever written with anything like the title 'Economics' ('instructions on material prosperity')" as a topic. The book emphasizes, in an inclusive way, "the logistic approach to statecraft, including economic polity."[55] The title translates as something

---

54 See Thomas R. TRAUTMANN, *Kautilya and the Arthashastra, a Statistical Investigation of the Authorship and Evolution of the Text*, Leiden, E.J. Brill 1971 (with a foreword by A.L. Basham), p. 5. See also on Taxila: http://en.wikipedia.org/wiki/Taxila. A recent publication is by Michael LIEBIG, *Endogene Politisch-Kulturelle Ressourcen. Die Relevanz des Kautilya-Arthashastra für das moderne Indien* (Endogene political-cultural resources. The relevance of the Kautilya Arthashastra for modern India), 1. Edition 2014 (Series: Moderne Südasienstudien—Modern South Asian Studies), vol. 1, Nomos.

55 Ch. ALLEN, *Ashoka*, pp. 306-309: "In its surviving form the *Treatise on State Economy* was ascribed to an editor or redactor named Vishnugupta, writing in the early Gupta era, but the original work had always been credited to the Brahman Chanakya, also known as Kautilya, the 'crow-like'. This was the hero of *The Minister's Signet Ring* political drama and of the *Puranas* who in the fourth century BCE had overthrown the base-born King Nanda and placed his protégé Chandragupta on the throne. Indeed, Chanakya's authorship was confirmed within the text itself, for in its penultimate paragraph he had written that this was the work of 'one who forcibly and quickly achieved the liberation of the mother-country, of its culture and learning (and) its military power, from the grip of the Nanda kings'. The *Treatise on State Economy* had initially been passed by oral transmission by Chanakya to his disciples and they to theirs until finally committed to paper. When it resurfaced in Mysore in the early twentieth century it was quickly recognised for what it was: a highly sophisticated, practical—and in its own time, revolutionary—treatise on statecraft and government that had underpinned the administration of Chandragupta and his immediate successors. Its revolutionary aspect came from the claim by its author that the key to good government lies not in prayers, sacrifices to the gods or offerings to Brahmans but in trained leadership. The skills of kingship could be taught, but only to those who already possessed the desire and ability to learn, the capacity to retain and to draw the right inferences from what they

like "Guide to Material Wealth."[56] There is evidence to suggest that India at the time was a major economic power. The discovery of this ancient book was a surprise because of its remarkable 'this-worldliness', an aspect that

learned, and the willingness to show obedience to their teachers. Through association with learned teachers the future ruler learned self-discipline by their example, which led to increased self-possession and greater efficiency in acquiring knowledge. Only by being disciplined, learned, conscious of the welfare of all beings and devoted to just government, could a king hope to rule unopposed. 'In the happiness of his subjects lies the king's happiness', runs perhaps the most famous passage in Chanakya's *Treatise*, 'in their welfare his welfare. He shall not consider as good only that which pleases him but treat as beneficial to him whatever pleases his subjects'. These were sentiments that would be reflected in stone in the edicts of Chandragupta s grandson, who would have been steeped in the contents of the *Treatise* as part of his princely education. Kingship was the standard polity of the Aryans in India, going right back to the quasi-mythical King Prithu, imposed on anarchic humankind by the gods and infused with divinity. However, Chanakya challenged this tradition by arguing that the first king was Manu, elected by the people as the person most fit to rule, and who ruled not by divine right but by virtue of a contract between ruler and ruled. So long as he guaranteed the welfare of the people the king had the right to enforce law and order. Being of Kshatriya birth was a prerequisite, certainly, but no king was fit to rule unless he possessed the highest qualities of intellect, leadership, resolution and self-discipline. He had also to take the advice of his ministers and respect his chief minister as a son his father. That chief minister was, of course, a Brahman, and in the Treatise on State Economy he is glorified as the only person of equal standing to the king—with the right to depose him should the king became a tyrant or if he impoverished his people. As his title suggests, Chanakya laid great stress on the responsibility of the ruler to build a sound economy, since good government requires a well-ordered administration with high ethical standards that allow trade, business and agriculture to flourish. However, side by side with these high ideals, Chanakya stressed the importance of learning the cruder aspects of kingship: how to secure and hold a kingdom; what tactics to employ in invading an enemy's territory and capturing an enemy fortress; the use of spy networks; and the seven strategies for dealing with and overcoming neighbouring powers, which included appeasement, punishment, bribery, deceit, deception and dividing the opposition. It was this aspect of the Treatise that caught the public attention when it became the subject of much discussion in political and academic circles in India in the 1920s. It became fashionable to describe Chanakya as the Indian Machiavelli, a glib comparison that the future Prime Minister of India Jawaharlal Nehru rejected when writing his *Discovery of India* in a British jail. *Machiavelli, after all, was a failed theoretician, whereas Chanakya was an extremely successful one who had carried his ideas through into fruition*: Bold and scheming, proud and resourceful, never forgetting a slight, never forgetting his purpose, availing himself of every device to delude and defeat the enemy, he sat with the reins of empire in his hands and looked upon the emperor more as a loved pupil than as a master ... There was hardly anything Chanakya would have refrained from doing to achieve his purpose; he was unscrupulous enough, yet he was also wise enough to know that this very purpose might be defeated by means unsuited to the end." (Emphasis added)

56 Amartya SEN, *On Ethics and Economics*, Oxford etc., Blackwell 1987/1988, p. 5. See also M. LIEBIG, *Endogene Politisch-Kulturelle Ressourcen*, pp. 39-80.

caused Max Weber to describe it as outright 'Machiavellian': Thus, "the princes already in the epic of the Maurya epoch ... practiced as a matter of course the most naked 'Macchiavellism' without objections on ethical grounds." The author continues: "The problem of a 'political ethic' has never preoccupied Indian theory and in the absence of ethical universalism and natural right, it could hardly be otherwise. The *dharma* of the prince was to conduct war for the sake of pure power per se."[57] This opinion as held by Max Weber is no longer accepted by scholars today; it is far too general and one-sided. Weber's judgment here is based on the European experience. Indian kings were allowed by law (dharma) to fight wars only to resist evil.

However, it was this knowledge of the Arthashastra, which contributed *inter alia* to the historiography and understanding of the Mauryan Empire and the Ashoka Edicts. Although Kautilya's *Arthasastra* may have been larger than the work that has come down to us, Kautilya was not the sole author of the collection known to us today. In its preserved form the Treatise is attributed to a compiler named Vishnugupta, who edited the text, probably in the 4th century, during the early Gupta period (ca. 320-550 AD). Romila Thapar's argument is convincing: "To conclude, the *Arthasastra* was originally written by Kautilya, the minister of Chandragupta ... It was edited and commented upon by various later writers until, in about the third or fourth century AD, Vishnugupta worked over the entire text, incorporating whatever interpolations had occurred by then. The text as it is known to us today is in this later form of Vishnugupta's."[58]

Taxila, the capital and administrative centre of the north-western province, thus was an important trading post and centre of Buddhist learning as well as Hellenistic culture:

In the 6th century B.C. Taxila was the capital of the kingdom of Gandhara, and since the conquest by the Achaemenid Darius I in 516 BC of the easternmost satrapy of the Persian Empire. Already at that time apparently there were trade relations with China, because in the language of the Achaemenids there was already a word for silk. These trade routes were in later centuries to form a network of routes known as the 'Silk Road', with which Taxila was connected via the Kunjirap pass. Besides goods from western Persia and

57 GM, p. 146.

58 Romila THAPAR, *Asoka and the Decline of the Mauryas*, London, Oxford University Press 1961, p. 225. See also E. SREEDHARAN, *A Manual of Historical Research Methodology*, South Indian Studies (2007).

the Mediterranean region, from China to the East and India in the South, here also philosophies, religions and sciences from these important cultural regions met each other, whereby the city soon became a center of learning and exchange and a large university arose. Panini, an Indian scholar (5th/4th century B.C.), wrote at the University of Taxila the 'Ashtadhyayi', the most important summary of Sanskrit grammar. Kautilya (4th/3rd century BC) wrote here the 'Arthashastra' (the doctrine of material gain). [59]

When Ashoka was old enough to take responsibility in the administration of the Mauryan Empire, his father, King Bindusara Amitraghata, appointed him governor of the North-Western province, which he ruled from Taxila until the year 269 BC. Here he probably already came into contact with Buddhism and came to like the new and attractive doctrine. A little later Ashoka took over the reins of the Empire.

In the *Arthashastra*, social and political structures are projected to form a *mandala* or political diagram. The *Mandala* connects sovereign core areas, thus forming an association of small kingdoms or states, which are arranged in rings around each other.[60] According to this interpretation of the text, the "Book of Statecraft" does not represent a static system or even a super state, but must be seen as a model of a natural order of more or less autonomous political units operating as equal sovereigns in their respective spheres of influence. The federally arranged system is held together by the authority of the *Vijigisu*, the 'one desiring victory', i.e. the aspirant to regentship. However, the Vijigisu must conform to an exceptional character and meet certain conditions. In order to qualify he must possess the seven 'imperial factors', to prove the legitimacy of his claim. He must: (1) be a just ruler; (2) have the necessary ministers and civil servants; (3) have his own territory; (4) have a fixed capital; (5) have a treasury in which the revenue is collected and stored; (6) possess physical prowess; (7) have allies.[61] Historian Charles Allen describes the history of the reception of the *Arthashastra*:

---

59 Translation from the German language Wikipedia website.

60 Krishna RAO, *Studies in Kautilya*, Delhi, Munshi Ram Manohar Lal 1958, p. 135, speaks about "federal units centering around a dominating ruler." A *mandala* is a geometric diagram depicting the whole universe with Mount Meru in the middle, the order of the gods or the ground plan for a sacred building.

61 Ch. DREKMEIER, *Kingship and Community in Early India*, p. 203. See also Romila THAPAR, State Formation in Early India, *Indian Social Science Journal*, vol.XXXII, no.4 (1980), p. 10. Arthashastra, VI. 1.

Chanakya laid great stress on the responsibility of the ruler to build a sound economy, since good government requires a well-ordered administration with high ethical standards that allow trade, business and agriculture to flourish. However, side by side with these high ideals, Chanakya stressed the importance of learning the cruder aspects of kingship: how to secure and hold a kingdom; what tactics to employ in invading an enemy's territory and capturing an enemy fortress; the use of spy networks; and the seven strategies for dealing with and overcoming neighbouring powers, which included appeasement, punishment, bribery, deceit, deception and dividing the opposition. It was this aspect of the Treatise that caught the public attention when it became the subject of much discussion in political and academic circles in India in the 1920s. It became fashionable to describe Chanakya as the Indian Machiavelli, a glib comparison that the future Prime Minister of India, Jawaharlal Nehru, rejected when writing his *Discovery of India* in a British jail. Machiavelli, after all, was a failed theoretician, whereas Chanakya was an extremely successful one who had carried his ideas through into fruition: "Bold and scheming, proud and resourceful, never forgetting a slight, never forgetting his purpose, availing himself of every device to delude and defeat the enemy, he sat with the reins of empire in his hands and looked upon the emperor more as a loved pupil than as a master ... There was hardly anything Chanakya would have refrained from doing to achieve his purpose; he was unscrupulous enough, yet he was also wise enough to know that this very purpose might be defeated by means unsuited to the end."[62]

Although parts of the present account of the *Arthashastra* originated several centuries after the reign of the Maurya, the text is based on traditional listings and experiences and the insights and principles deriving from them. The kingdoms surrounding or encircling the *vijigisu* are his immediate 'neighbours', portrayed as 'natural antipodes' or potential challengers. According to this logic, the next circle, beyond (or behind) the circle of the 'natural antipodes', becomes the place of the 'natural allies'; the following circle comprises another cluster of 'natural/potential enemies', and so on. Altogether, there are seven such circles or clusters, making up a complex web of power relations. In practice, any sovereign, if he possesses the seven "imperial attributes," can attain supremacy and legitimately and properly 'neutralize' opponents of lesser virtue. In this system government policies are implemented and promoted by an 'enforcement staff' (*danda*). *Danda* literally means 'a staff' or 'scepter', and Radhakrishna Choudhuri

---

62   Ch. ALLEN, *Ashoka*, pp. 308-309.

writes that it is the "symbol of sovereignty."[63] This definition accords with Max Weber's concept: "An order will be called: ... *law*, if it is externally guaranteed by the probability that physical or psychological coercion will be applied by a *staff* of people in order to bring about compliance or avenge violation."[64]

The historian and political scientist Charles Drekmeier also refers to the moral qualifications the sovereign must possess if he wants to ascend to the rank of Chakravartin or *vijigisu*, which must be in harmony with "the principle that one should be able to rule oneself before attempting to rule others..." This was at the time "a major premise of Indian philosophy, anteceding its most famous and systematic

Rock-cut elephant above Ashoka's Edicts, Dhauli, near Bhubaneshwar, Odisha

statement in the 'Republic of Plato.'"[65] In accordance with the central doctrine of Hinduism, 'all-round victory' and conquest (*dig-vijaya*)[66] formed the core of the king's *dharma*. Even so, "[t]he victorious king was supposed to treat the defeated dynasties mildly."[67]

63 Radhakrishna CHOUDHURI, *Kautilya's Political Ideas and Institutions*, Benares (Varanasi), 1971, p. 12.

64 M. WEBER, *Economy and Society*, vol. I, p. 34.

65 Ch. DREKMEIER *Kingship and Community in Early India*, p. 203.

66 See H. KULKE and D. ROTHERMUND, *A History of India*, Calcutta, Allahabad, Bombay, Delhi, Rupa & Co. 1990, p. 86.

67 Hartmut SCHARFE, *Untersuchungen zur Staatsrechtslehre des Kautalya* (Studies on the constitutional theory of Kautalya), Wiesbaden, Otto Harassowitz 1968, p. 136.

6. The conquest of Kalinga and the subsequent pilgrimages

In one place in his text Weber points out: "Soon after the expedition of Alexander ... in the Dynasty of the Maurya," it was the "standing army and the officers, the kingly bureaucracy and its many departments and scribes, the kingly tax farmers and the kingly police ... [that] formed the ruling powers."[68] According to Max Weber, the material basis for sustaining the Maurya-kings' presumed "lust for conquest" was the flourishing urban civilization; but with Ashoka and the Kalinga campaign this changed.

It was Ashoka, who—initially still aligned with the traditional Brahmanical religion and political statecraft—was seeking to expand his kingdom to the known limits of the Indo-Himalayan continent, and who for the first time "succeeded in uniting the entire cultural territory of India into a unified empire."[69] It was the South-Eastern kingdom of Kalinga which was not yet incorporated and still outside the kingdom.

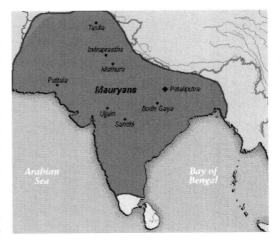

The war with Kalinga, the area that is now the state of Odisha (Orissa) in the south of Bengal (*bongo*), located on the east coast, began around 261 BC, in the eighth year of Ashoka's reign. Ashoka's grandfather, Chandragupta like his father, Bindusara who had previously tried to subjugate the state, had been unsuccessful.

But now bitter fighting took place at the Dhauli hills (*dhauligiri*) near Bhubaneswar on the banks of the river Daya (*daya* means 'mercy') not far from the coast, from which Ashoka emerged victorious. Ashoka's Dhauli inscription therefore is of particular importance. After the battle the water of the river Daya flowing past the battlefield was said to have been red

68 GM, p. 235.
69 Ibid.

with the blood of the dead; more than 150,000 Kalinga warriors and about 100,000 of Ashoka's own men were killed in the action.[70]

The hill and the open area surrounding it are large open spaces, historically significant, with some of the Great Rock Edicts of Ashoka, the Khandagiri Rock Inscription and the Dhauligiri Inscription located on the road that leads to the summit. After the battle Ashoka repented having waged war and wrote in his 13th Rock Edict:

> Beloved-of-the-Gods, King Piyadasi, conquered the Kalingas eight years after his coronation. One hundred and fifty thousand were deported, one hundred thousand were killed and many more died (from other causes). After the Kalingas had been conquered, Beloved-of-the-Gods came to feel a strong inclination towards the Dhamma, a love for the Dhamma and for instruction in Dhamma. Now Beloved-of-the-Gods feels deep remorse for having conquered the Kalingas.

> Indeed, Beloved-of-the-Gods is deeply pained by the killing, dying and deportation that take place when an unconquered country is conquered. But Beloved-of-the-Gods is pained even more by this—that Brahmans, ascetics, and householders of different religions who live in those countries, and who are respectful to superiors, to mother and father, to elders, and who behave properly and have strong loyalty towards friends, acquaintances, companions, relatives, servants and employees—that they are injured, killed or separated from their loved ones. Even those who are not affected (by all this) suffer when they see friends, acquaintances, companions and relatives affected. These misfortunes befall all (as a result of war), and this pains Beloved-of-the-Gods. There is no country, except among the Greeks, where these two groups, Brahmans and ascetics, are not found, and there is no country where people are not devoted to one or another religion. Therefore the killing, death or deportation of a hundredth, or even a thousandth part of those who died during the conquest of Kalinga now pains Beloved-of-

---

70 Charles ALLEN, *Ashoka*, London, Little, Brown 2012, p. 155: "The goodwill engendered by the return of the two stolen slabs now worked to Kittoe's advantage, for he was allowed to make a copy of the Khandagiri rock inscription, but as he did so he heard talk of a second rock inscription, said to be on a hill on the other side of Bhubaneshwar town and on the far side of the River Daya—a name that in Sanskrit means 'compassion', the significance of which would only later become apparent. However, when Kittoe tried to track down this new inscription he was again frustrated, this time by the local inhabitants, the Oriyas. Only the intervention of a passing Hindu religious mendicant from Benares enabled Kittoe to find what he was looking for."

the-Gods. Now Beloved-of-the-Gods thinks that even those who do wrong should be forgiven where forgiveness is possible. ... Now it is conquest by Dhamma that Beloved-of-the-Gods considers to be the best conquest. And it (conquest by Dhamma) has been won here, on the borders, even six hundred yojanas away, where the Greek king Antiochos rules, beyond there where the four kings named Ptolemy, Antigonos, Magas and Alexander rule,[71] likewise in the south among the Cholas, the Pandyas, and as far as Tamraparni. Here in the king's domain among the Greeks, the Kambojas, the Nabhakas, the Nabhapamkits, the Bhojas, the Pitinikas, the Andhras and the Palidas, everywhere people are following Beloved-of-the-Gods' instructions in Dhamma. Even where Beloved-of-the-Gods' envoys have not been, these people too, having heard of the practice of Dhamma and the ordinances and instructions in Dhamma given by Beloved-of-the-Gods, are following it and will continue to do so. This conquest has been won everywhere, and it gives great joy—the joy which only conquest by Dhamma can give. But even this joy is of little consequence. Beloved-of-the-Gods considers the great fruit to be experienced in the next world to be more important.[72]

This description, however, does not appear, for reasons of piety, in the Kalinga inscriptions. Instead, there are, for good reason, the two separate edicts of Dhauli and Jaugada. The remorse of the "Beloved-of-the-gods, joy-bringing" ruler (*devanampriya priyadarshi*) was so great that he undertook a pilgrimage to the holy places of Buddhism two years after the war. Ashoka wanted to be a model to his subjects and make the true meaning of the teachings of the Buddha known to them: to practice righteousness, non-violence and compassion. The first place he visited on his pilgrimage was Kushinagar, where Gautama, the Buddha, had attained his *parinirvana*. Probably the honorary designation *Devanampriya Priyadarshi*, Beloved-of-the-gods, joy bringer, originated from the population itself. Ashoka explains the purpose of his pilgrimages to the famous Buddhist sites in the 8th Rock Edict as follows:

> In the past kings used to go out on pleasure tours during which there was hunting and other entertainment. But ten years after Beloved-of-the-Gods

---

71 The kings in the text have been identified as Antiochos II Theos of Syria (261-246 B.C.), the grandson of Seleucus Nikator; Ptolemy II Philadelphos of Egypt (285-247 B.C.); Antigonos Gonatas of Macedonia (276-239 B.C.); Megas of Cyrene (300-258 B.C.); and Alexander of Corinth (252-244 B.C.) or Alexander of Epirus (272-255 B.C.).

72 The 13th Rock Edict is found in translation online: http://www.cs.colostate.edu/~malaiya/ashoka.html

had been coronated, he went on a tour to Sambodhi and thus instituted Dhamma tours. During these tours, the following things took place: visits and gifts to Brahmans and ascetics, visits and gifts of gold to the aged, visits to people in the countryside, instructing them in Dhamma, and discussing Dhamma with them as is suitable. It is this that delights Beloved-of-the-Gods, King Piyadasi, and is, as it were, another type of revenue.[73]

7. The Buddhist Dharma and Ashoka

Max Weber characterized early Buddhism as a "specific intellectuals' soteriology,"[74] a religious doctrine (*Kunstlehre*) by "a travelling, intellectually trained mendicancy."[75] Having led a cruel war to unite the nation, Ashoka "converted to Buddhism, first as a layman, then even formally as a member of the order."[76] Furthermore, through him "Buddhism received the first impulse to become an international world religion."[77] In the Deer Park at Sarnath near Varanasi (Benares), where Ashoka built a Buddhist *stupa* (relic mount) and erected one of his more than nineteen stone pillars with inscriptions, the Buddha had given his first sermon, known as the *Dharmachakra Pravartana Sutra*,[78] in which he proclaimed the Four Holy Truths; this had brought about a historical breakthrough in India's intellectual development and made an impact even beyond the borders of the Indian subcontinent. In this first sermon the Buddha is said to have turned the wheel of Dharma. Buddhism denies the existence of an *absolute* evil; instead it depicts "life as suffering."[79] This was the first of the Four Holy Truths. The Buddha's second realization was simple: suffering has a

---

73 The 8th Rock Edict is found online at http://www.cs.colostate.edu/~malaiya/ashoka.html.

74 GM, p. 205. See also GM, p. 232.

75 GM, p. 206.

76 GM, p. 235. Here WEBER seems to have been wrong; there is no evidence that Ashoka became a member of the Buddhist order.

77 GM, p. 241.

78 The *Dharmachakra Pravartana Sutra* is online: www.hdamm.de/buddha/sn56-11.php. GM, p. 235 and GAzRS II, p. 260.

79 See Shmuel N. EISENSTADT, Die Paradoxie von Zivilisationen mit außerwelt-lichen Orientierungen, Überlegungen zu Max Webers Studie über Hinduismus und Buddhismus (The paradox of civilizations with outerworldly orientations, reflections on Max Weber's study on Hinduism and Buddhism), in Wolfgang SCHLUCHTER (ed.), *Max Webers Studie über Hinduismus und Buddhismus* (Max Weber's study of Hinduism and Buddhism), Frankfurt, M., Suhrkamp 1984, p. 351 (274-297). See also GM, p. 208.

beginning. What has a beginning must of necessity find an end. The latter demonstrates the third truth, and the fourth describes the method—an action program, the Eightfold Path, for attaining this objective, the end of suffering, and conquest of death.[80]

Ashoka refers to some of those maxims from the Eightfold Path, like self-realization, right action, charity, forgiveness, tolerance and respect for all living beings. The 3rd Pillar Edict elucidates:

> Beloved-of-the-Gods, King Piyadasi, speaks thus: People see only their good deeds saying, "I have done this good deed." But they do not see their evil deeds saying, "I have done this evil deed" or "This is called evil." But this (tendency) is difficult to see. One should think like this: "It is these things that lead to evil, to violence, to cruelty, anger, pride and jealousy. Let me not ruin myself with these things." And further, one should think: "This leads to happiness in this world and the next."[81]

Buddhism from the beginning seems to have had as its aim the alleviation and removal not only of personal suffering, but the suffering of all beings,[82] by improving and developing the general conditions and inherent potential of the individual to shape his environment and achieve a better way of life. The Buddha analyzed and described the way toward a better life on the assumption that the enemy to be overcome lives deep within of every human being. One cannot agree with Weber, however, when he says, regarding external enemies, that *love of one's enemy* is "of necessity entirely foreign to Buddhism."[83] It is doubtful whether "love of one's neighbour" was "unknown" to Indians; injustice and suffering regarding other living beings was perceived and became the motivation for personal, inner-worldly positive action (karma). In fact, "nobody can be saved without

---

80 The Noble Eightfold Path (*aryaastangamarga*), s. Étienne LAMOTTE, Der Buddha, Seine Lehre und Seine Gemeinde (The Buddha, his teachings and his community), in Heinz BECHERT and Richard GOMBRICH (ed.), *Der Buddhismus—Geschichte und Gegenwart* (Buddhism—history and contemporariness), Munich, C.H. Beck 1984, pp. 53-54.

81 WEBER does not mention the Four Holy Truths. They are also not found in the inscriptions. The wheel of *dharma* likewise is not mentioned.

82 For Buddhist conceptions of an 'inner-worldly', future peaceful state of the world, an ideal type (past and future) 'Golden Age' see Emil ABEGG, *Der Messiasglaube in India and Iran* (Messianistic Faith in India and Iran), Berlin and Leipzig, Walther de Gryter & Co. 1928, pp. 145 ff.

83 GM, p. 208.

[exercising] compassion for others."[84]

Ashoka in making it his most sacred purpose to look after the general wellbeing of his subjects set up a general welfare state. The aim of Buddhism is, as the Asia historian Emanuel Sarkisyanz explains in his book *Buddhist Backgrounds of the Burmese Revolution*, to enable all people "to permit men to rise within the causality law of Dharma towards the overcoming of their suffering."[85] It should be made easy for people to adhere to the moral law. In the words of anthropologist Stanley Jeyaraja Tambiya: "It could be said that Ashokan Dharma implied that a prosperous and just society is the base upon which the pursuit of more specialized religious virtues can be raised."[86] The author quotes Sarkisyanz, who adds:

> Ashokan social emphasis was not identical with the ethos of the Buddhist order of monks striving out of the world of Impermanence toward Nirvana ... it is nevertheless Buddhist ethos: the ethos of lay Buddhism acting within the world of Impermanence, in pursuing Nirvana by creating the outward social conditions for such striving towards the overcoming of Attachment. It was this social ethos that the Ashokan tradition of historical Buddhism has transmitted, a political lay tradition within Buddhism.[87]

We shall discuss the welfare aspect in Ashoka's policy in more detail below. There existed "a political lay tradition within Buddhism," with welfare aspects that included obligations of the king toward his subjects, policies which were emulated and subsequently spread throughout Asia, and which propagated a comprehensive social ethos. Similarly, but considerably later—although most likely, within the historical context, in the Ashokan tradition—the Khmer ruler Jayavarman VII (1125-1218, governed ca. 1181-1218), who built the Buddhist monuments of Angkor, pursued in his empire a policy of public welfare for his subjects, and set up hospitals and rest houses. Hermann Kulke gives details regarding this astounding similarity to Ashokan welfare policies:

---

84 Emanuel SARKISYANZ, *Buddhist Backgrounds of the Burmese Revolution*, The Hague, Nijhoff 1965, pp. 39 and 27.

85 E. SARKISYANZ, *Buddhist Backgrounds*, p. 27.

86 S.J. TAMBIAH, *World Conqueror & World Renouncer. A Study of Buddhism and Polity in Thailand against a Historical Background*, Cambridge, London, New York, Melbourne, Cambridge University Press 1976, p. 62.

87 E. SARKISYANZ, *Buddhist Backgrounds of the Burmese Revolution*, p. 36.

In regard to Buddhist influence on Jayavarman's policy and state ideology most deserving is doubtlessly his meritorious construction of 102 hospitals and 123 rest houses for the use of pilgrims established all over the state. In an inscription Jayavarman proclaims that 'he suffered from the maladies of his subjects more than from his own; for it is the public grief which makes the grief of kings, not their own grief', a statement which reminds us of Ashoka's Dhamma ethics. A particularly fascinating aspect of his 'social policy' is the uniform foundation stelae of these hospitals and the amazingly detailed lists of their personnel and provision. The personnel housed in each hospital consisted of altogether 36 persons, beginning with 2 doctors, assisted by a man and two women, 2 store-keepers, 2 cooks, 14 hospital attendants etc. The detailed lists of food provisions which are provided thrice a year and the quantities of which are always exactly stated, reads like an account of a well flourishing grocery. The expenditure for the four large hospitals attached to Angkor exceeded the expenditure for all the hospitals in the country side. They consumed annually altogether 11,192 tons of rice produced by 838 villages with a population of 81,640 people. They were provided with 2,124 kilograms of sesame, 105 kg of cardamom 2,124 nutmegs etc.[88]

8. The Administration of the Empire

The Mauryan empire can be categorized as a "typical early state;"[89] with extensive overseas trade conducted by merchants organized in guilds, a regulated economy, professional quarters in cities, written laws and administration, the levying of taxes, and a system of education and passing on of knowledge, mainly within the precincts of religious orders or learned communities supported by the Brahmins and subsequently also by the Buddhist order. Artisan and craft skills were passed on and taught within the designated castes. As Max Weber pointed out: "Monastic schools for lay requirements in the form of primary schools had existed, presumably since the time of Ashoka."[90] Practical knowledge of the affairs of this world and instruction concerning the next were imparted in this way.[91]

---

88 Hermann KULKE, From Ashoka to Jayavarman VII: Some Reflections on the Relationship between Buddhism and the State in India and Southeast Asia, in *Buddhism Across Asia: Networks of Material, Intellectual and Cultural Exchange*, ed. Tansen SEN, Singapore, Institute of Southeast Asian Studies 2014, p. 230.

89 Sudarsan SENEVIRATNE, The Mauryan State, in Henry J.M. CLAESSEN and Peter SKALNIK (eds.), *The Early State*, The Hague, Mouton 1978, p. 382. This publication takes no notice of the Indus civilization.

90 GM, p. 256.

91 GM, p. 239: "Each good deed bears its fruit in the next world, often already in this one."

In addition, itinerant teachers and monks guaranteed the edification and information of even the lowest social strata. Role models based on historical figures, myths and epics were developed to give even the simplest mind direction and make a life based on ethical and moral principles desirable. The wandering monks and ascetics fulfilled social functions, as teachers, medicine men and therapeuticians, while portraying, by their very existence, an absolute, transcendent reality.[92] Just as in administrative matters, in education tolerance was essential.[93] Weber is right in saying that at the core of Indian otherworldly aspirations for salvation lay the realization that "virtue could be 'taught'" and "right knowledge was inevitably followed by right action."[94] Education was the basis of everything.

Buddhist rule too, according to Weber, differed considerably from Hinduistic rule. Under Ashoka the army was reduced substantially[95] as an instrument for the control or "domestication of the masses."[96] Concerning Weber's "tripartite model of political forces"[97] (which makes up patrimonial rule), Jakob Rösel states: "Military build-up necessitates increased control over fiscal resources; increased control over fiscal resources necessitates administrative supervision. There is a factual logic to this sequence."[98] This addresses the main problem "any patrimonial ruler has to solve," i.e. "to organize his own reliable means of forcible constraint, an army, to organize his own and reliable supply of natural or fiscal resources for his household, 'liturgies', and lastly to organize a system of supervision over his domain, his soldiery, and his supply, an administration."[99] In this respect Emperor

---

92 See also GERTH and MILLS, p. 269: "Buddhism was propagated by strictly contemplative, mendicant monks, who rejected the world and, having no homes, migrated."

93 GM, p. 4: "For long periods tolerance towards religious and philosophic doctrines was almost absolute; at least it was infinitely greater than anywhere in the Occident until most recent times."

94 GM, p. 331.

95 GM, p. 68.

96 GM, p. 236.

97 Jakob RÖSEL, *Die Hinduismusthese Max Webers: Folgen eines kolonialen Indienbildes in einem religionssoziologischen Gedankengang* (Max Weber's thesis on Hinduism: Consequences of an image of colonial India, reasoning from a sociology of religion), Munich, Cologne, London, Weltforum Verlag 1982, p. 144.

98 J. RÖSEL, *Die Hinduismusthese Max Webers*, p. 123.

99 J. RÖSEL, *Die Hinduismusthese Max Webers*, p. 120. See also Detlev KANTOWSKY, Recent research on Max Weber's studies of Hinduism: papers submitted to a conference held in New Delhi, 1.-3.3. 1984 (vol. 4 of the series of the International Asia Forum), p.

Ashoka found himself in a dilemma, as he could not replace army and administration simply through the institution of the *sangha*; state, law and order could not be replaced by *dharma* alone. Nevertheless, Ashoka reduced the authority of the army and appointed so-called 'Dharmamahamatras' who were to take over certain tasks as mediators, between the government on one side and the people on the other. "To begin with," as Max Weber explains, "it seems that it was their responsibility to inspect and supervise the royal and princely harems."[100]

It is doubtful, however, whether the Dharmamahamatras were primarily public 'spies' through whom the administration was able to "penetrate into the most intimate private life of the subjects".[101] The German Indologist Edmund Hardy (1852-1904) speaks of a 'spiritual supervisory authority', "whose purpose was to prevent clashes, which could scarcely be avoided between the many religious organizations in India."[102] It is to be assumed that the *Dharmamahamatras* were some kind of dedicated 'comrades', possessing certain rights and obligations, among which were the tasks of giving advice to the population on important issues of life and matters of *dharma*, and providing guidance—the monarch himself was apparently accessible to the public—was perhaps the most significant. They could travel freely throughout the country, and their tasks included implementation of "measures of public welfare and supervision."[103] This was what Ashoka was aiming at; it included elements of benevolent control as well as faithful adherence to principles of conduct avoiding extremes,

144. The quote on military armaments is also in D. KANTOWSKY, Recent research on Max Weber's studies of Hinduism, p. 123.

100 GM, p. 239.

101 GM, p. 68. It seems more likely that the official 'spies' were loyal subjects, endowed with certain rights and duties, among which the duty to be generally available to the public was paramount. Ulrich SCHNEIDER, *Die großen Felsen-Edikte Asokas, Kritische Ausgabe, Übersetzung und Analyse der Texte* (Ashoka's Great Rock Edicts, critical edition, translation and analysis of the texts), Wiesbaden, Otto Harassowitz 1978, p. 162, confirms, that it was their special task to control the giving of gifts (*danavisaga*), for a good reason: "generosity... is only tolerated, if both on the side of the giver and of the recipient (this obviously includes the religious communities) it is associated with pure intentions." Ibid. This becomes clear from Edict VII. "From all this we may deduce that one... reason for Ashoka, to establish the Dhamma-Mahamatas, was to monitor (*überwachen*) such influential persons, capable of giving gifts, persons among whom even his closest relatives were counted." U. SCHNEIDER, *Die großen Felsen-Edikte Asokas*, p. 163.

102 Edmund HARDY, *König Asoka*, p. 17.

103 U. SCHNEIDER, *Die großen Felsen-Edikte Asokas*, p. 161.

in accordance with the Buddha's middle way. The inscriptions enumerate a number of official posts, covering a variety of administrative fields, one of them being the administrative staff. The 5th Rock Edict describes the "guardians of law and morality" as follows:

> In the past there were no Dharma Mahamatras but such officers were appointed by me thirteen years after my coronation. Now they work among all religions for the establishment of Dhamma, for the promotion of Dhamma, and for the welfare and happiness of all who are devoted to Dhamma. They work among the Greeks, the Kambojas, the Gandharas, the Rastrikas, the Pitinikas and other peoples on the western borders. They work among soldiers, chiefs, Brahmans, householders, the poor, the aged and those devoted to Dhamma—for their welfare and happiness—so that they may be free from harassment. They (Dhamma Mahamatras) work for the proper treatment of prisoners, towards their unfettering, and if the Mahamatras think, "This one has a family to support," "That one has been bewitched," "This one is old," then they work for the release of such prisoners. They work here, in outlying towns, in the women's quarters belonging to my brothers and sisters, and among my other relatives. They are occupied everywhere. These Dhamma Mahamatras are occupied in my domain among people devoted to Dhamma to determine who is devoted to Dhamma, who is established in Dhamma, and who is generous.[104]

The 5th Rock Edict begins with the sentences: "Beloved-of-the-Gods, King Piyadasi, speaks thus: To do good is difficult. One who does good first does something hard to do. I have done many good deeds, and, if my sons, grandsons and their descendants up to the end of the world act in like manner, they too will do much good. But whoever amongst them neglects this, they will do evil. Truly, it is easy to do evil."[105] Even the emperor himself would receive visitors at "any time of the day," in order to have important events reported to him, "for his affairs require speed."[106] This suggests that there may have existed something like an individual's right to petition.[107] Similarly, the Dharmamahamatras and other officials in the administration would have been acting as the appellants' addressees whom

---

104 http://www.cs.colostate.edu/~malaiya/ashoka.html (online).

105 Ibid.

106 GM, p. 238.

107 In like manner, in 19th century Europe, a king would sometimes take it upon himself to answer petitions personally.

people in need could approach with their queries, or with any concerns, in order to obtain help and advice from them. It is possible that small gifts (*danavisaga*) were brought to them in return for their service. The edicts which were regularly recited to the population in many parts of India, emphasized the virtue of "generosity towards friends, relatives, Brahmins, [and] ascetics".[108] The reference can be found in a number of edicts. Ashoka is setting a good example:

> These and other principal officers are occupied with the distribution of gifts, mine as well as those of the queens. In my women's quarters, they organize various charitable activities here and in the provinces. I have also ordered my sons and the sons of other queens to distribute gifts so that noble deeds of Dhamma and the practice of Dhamma may be promoted. And noble deeds of Dhamma and the practice of Dhamma consist of having kindness, generosity, truthfulness, purity, gentleness and goodness increase among the people.[109]

The Indologist Ulrich Schneider in his book *Die großen Felsen-Edikte Asokas* confirms that it was the officers' special task to control the giving of gifts (*danavisaga*), for a good reason: "generosity ... is only tolerated, if both on the side of the giver and of the recipient (this obviously includes the religious communities) it is associated with pure intentions." (Pillar Inscription VII) On the other hand giving, "going by the heavy remarks in VII, may even be something rather low, namely when on the side of the giver or the recipient (or on both) it is associated with ulterior motives."[110]

According to Weber the Monarch makes it his sacred purpose to take care of the everyday welfare of his people, declaring that, "regardless of

---

108 GM, p. 239 (Great Rock Edict no. III). In several places Ashoka refers to this in his edicts. And he himself sets the example: "Those mentioned above and many other chief officers of mine are occupied with the delivery of the gifts of myself as well as of the queens. And, to all the members of my entire household, they are bringing, in various ways, reports regarding the worthy recipients of gifts both here and in all the quarters. And I have arranged that some of the officers shall be occupied with the delivery of gifts of my sons and of the other queen's sons, so that the noble deeds of Dharma and the practice of Dharma may be promoted." Pillar Inscription no. VII, in: D.C. SIRCAR, *Inscriptions of Asoka*, Government of India Press, Revised edition 1967, p. 75.

109 http://www.cs.colostate.edu/~malaiya/ashoka.html (online). See also D.C. SIRCAR, *Inscriptions of Asoka*, pp. 75 and 39, and pp. 49-50

110 U. SCHNEIDER, *Die großen Felsen-Edikte Asokas*, pp. 162 and 171.

their faith ... [all] are his 'children';"[111] he advises them to cultivate good deeds and to desist from evil. With a certain satisfaction Weber points to Ashoka's view, according to which mere "ceremonies and external rites are of little use;" what counts is "only the sincerity by which the practical conclusions are drawn from the teachings."[112] Quite sensational and unexpected is Ashoka's remark that he "finds it necessary to emphasize especially that not only the great,[113] but also the little men" may, "through renunciation of the world," by selfless and persistent efforts, attain freedom and happiness. Ashoka points out that it is "very difficult for the highly placed" to follow the teachings and lead a pure and sinless life, without being corrupted.[114] Great Rock Edict X declares: "This is difficult for either a humble person or a great person to do except with great effort, and by giving up other interests. In fact, it may be even more difficult for a great person to do."[115] This is reminiscent of the Christian teachings, according to which it is easier for a camel to pass through the eye of a needle than for a rich man to go to heaven.

The Ashokan inscriptions which Weber described are no doubt, "a unique evidence of international, intellectual and cultural relations," an expression of an ecumenical unity, seldom surpassed in later times.[116] This may well be the reason why Weber was attracted to Ashoka.[117]

9. Economy, Trade, Industry and Rationality

In Greece the *oikos* or 'household' was the consistent, small autonomous family unit, organized along certain principles of division of labor, authority and control, self-restraint, sharing etc. This unit developed into a larger patrimonially regulated domain as the nucleus,[118] from which the larger political dominion evolved by an extension of its sphere over

---

111 GM, p. 238 (Separate Edicts and Great Rock Edict no. IX).

112 GM, p. 238.

113 Correctly, Rupnath Edict (Little Rock Edict No. I).

114 GM, p. 240 (Great Rock Edict, No. X).

115 Ibid. Rupnath-Edikt (Little Rock Edict No. I): "not only people in a higher position like myself." D.C. SIRKAR, *Inscriptions of Ashoka*, p. 39.

116 H. KULKE, Ausgrenzung, Rezeption und kulturelles Sendungsbewußtsein (Exclusionism, Reception and Cultural Mission), p. 28.

117 Ibid.

118 See M. WEBER, *Economy and Society*, vol. II, pp. 1006-1012.

the neighbouring households. Under Ashoka this led, to a significant degree, not only to the elimination of the ancient Kshatriya-class with its countless little citadels,[119] but also to a "relative levelling of the *political* power of the distinguished status groups" (or privileged classes),[120] and in turn to a flourishing, abundant urban culture. "The patrimonialism of the great kings took the place of the ancient petty kingdoms ... inevitably the position of the aristocracy as well as that of the civil patriciate changed."[121] No longer was it exclusively "the educated nobles, but: the courtiers, the literate officials, and also the petty bourgeois and the peasants,"[122] whose families, as the smallest common denominator to guarantee and keep stable the social and political order, were at the centre of Ashoka's state.[123] Consequently, according to Ulrich Schneider, "the conclusion is perhaps not too daring that what mattered to Ashoka was primarily to strengthen and keep intact, by his Dharma-precepts, the private domain of his subjects, centred around the family."[124] We may agree, as Weber says, that "Buddhism, as well as Jainism first ascended with the support of the city nobles and, above all, the bourgeois patricians."[125]

It may well be true that the rational, purposeful discourse among a like-minded elite led to political institutions, which outlined and created the conditions for an orderly economic, commercial, political and rule-based, well regulated social life. Here, writes Max Weber, "Indian justice developed numerous forms which could have served capitalistic purposes as easily and well as corresponding institutions in our own medieval law. The autonomy of the merchant stratum in law-making was at least equivalent to that of our own medieval merchants."[126] Thus apparently already in third-century-BC India, conditions for a formal state organization and urban

---

119 GM, p. 235.

120 GM, p. 235. And p. 252: "Buddhism ... first ascended with the support of the urban nobility and, above all, the civil patriciate."

121 GM, p. 235.

122 GM, p. 236.

123 See U. SCHNEIDER, *Die großen Felsen-Edikte*, p. 159: "...then the conclusion is perhaps not too daring that what mattered to Ashoka was primarily to strengthen and keep intact, by his Dharma-precepts, the private domain of his subjects, centered around the family."

124 U. SCHNEIDER, *Die großen Felsen-Edikte*, p. 159.

125 GM, p. 234.

126 GM, p. 4.

society not unlike medieval European civilization prevailed, although it is obvious that the difference of time and space between the cultures may offset the proportions of the comparison. Asian—including Indian—urban development may be better compared to the Greek *polis*. In fact, as Weber maintains, "the conditions in India at the time of the Buddha have been … relatively similar to those in Greece during the sixth century."[127] A kind of discourse ethics prevailed in both cases.

As Günther Abramowski has shown, "city and bourgeoisie … are central issues in Max Weber's work." Max Weber wants to find out, "what constitutes the unique, the revolutionary and the present determining element (Gegenwartsbestimmende) in European history with its tendency toward rationalization," and he claims that "only in the Occident, within the realm of the medieval city … there arose a special class of citizens and a specific economic bourgeoisie." In other words, a rationally disposed "bourgeoisie as a class and together with it the industrial proletariat entered the scene."[128] The historical conditions for this particular type of development in Europe, leading to a rationally organized economic life and innerworldly-oriented (and therefore successful) ascetic "Spirit of Capitalism," claims Weber, did not exist in Asia. This hypothesis must, in its essential parts, be rejected. Max Weber himself writes:

> the characteristic of the city in the political definition was the appearance of a distinct "bourgeois" estate … It should be noted that if the above definition were to be strictly applied, even the cities of the Occidental Middle Ages would qualify only in part—and those of the eighteenth century only to the smallest part—as true "city-communes" … It is true that they all had markets and that they also were fortresses … Separate court districts for the larger trade and craft towns of these countries were also quite frequent. The seat of the administrative authorities of the large political associations was, in China, Egypt, the Near East, and in India, always in these towns—a statement which does *not* apply to precisely the most typical Occidental cities of the early Middle Ages, especially those of the North … It is true that, as a rule, town dwellers were also members of local professional associations, of guilds and crafts with a specifically urban location, and that they were members of

---

127 See M. WEBER, *Economy and Society*, vol. I, p. 444. See also vol. II, pp. 1229-1230.

128 Günter ABRAMOWSKI, *Das Geschichtsbild Max Webers. Universalgeschichte am Leitfaden des okzidentalen Rationalisierungsprozesses* (Max Weber's conception of history. World history as a guiding thread of the occidental process of rationalization), Stuttgart, Ernst Klett 1966 (Kieler Historische Schriften), p. 83.

the urban administrative districts, city wards, and blocks into which the city was divided by the local authorities—and that in these capacities they had definite duties and, at times, even certain rights. The city ward or block, as a collective entity, could in particular be made liturgically responsible for the security of persons and for other police purposes. For this reason they [e.g. the Indian cities] might be organized into communes with elected officials or hereditary elders ... In India the cities were royal seats or official centers of the royal administration as well as fortresses and market centers. We also find merchant guilds and the castes, to a large extent coterminous with the occupational associations, both of which enjoyed considerable autonomy, above all in the fields of legislation and administration of justice ... in the period of the great religions of salvation we do in fact find in India that the guilds, headed by their hereditary elders *(shreshtha)*, combine into an association in many cities; residues of this still exist at present in some cities (Ahmedabad) which are led by a common urban *shreshth* corresponding to a Western lord mayor. There also existed, in the period prior to the large bureaucratic kingdoms, some cities which were politically autonomous and were ruled by a local patriciate recruited from those families who served in the army with elephants.[129]

What constitutes rational-capitalist—and therefore successful and beneficial for world development—political ethics of typical Western provenance has not been shown here conclusively and convincingly. There were reasons for the success of the West which lay in a completely different area not considered by Weber (e.g. aspects of the Industrial Revolution) that have little to do with the development in cities that were in accord with capitalism-promoting ethics, but which, however, have been falsely represented as a success story. In fact, the success of the Industrial Revolution was based less on capitalism-promoting ethics than on systematic, organized exploitation of people and resources.

It should by now have become evident that Ashoka's rational method and appeal was 'doing and undoing' *(Tun und Lassen)*, which is to say that vices and bad actions should be avoided and banished, and good deeds accomplished and cultivated. The adherence to even such a simple rule, however, requires a constant moral effort—and this was to be attained not through external constraint, but by inner conviction and personal commitment. "The most important peculiarity in this was the

---

129 M. WEBER, *Economy and Society*, vol. II, pp. 1226, 1227 and 1229.

'tolerance' which results from the ancient Buddhistic prohibition against violence."[130] Weber acknowledges that in India "tolerance toward religious and philosophic doctrines was almost absolute," and "infinitely greater than anywhere in the Occident until the most recent times."[131] As some sort of inspired/motivational 'ethics contest' this might encourage social competition to accumulate good *karma*,[132] essentially akin to Weber's 'ideal type' of an 'inner-worldly asceticism'. In any society, national or international, such behaviour would have profound political implications.[133]

The Indian world at the time seems to have followed "the rationally most highly developed concepts—the Law of Determinism." This "strict causality in our [Western] sense"[134] apparently regulated all of the administration, with regards to taxation, grant benefits, land distribution etc. Give and take, receiving and contributing to the common cause (doing and undoing, stopping bad habits and beginning good works), seem to have been consistently propagated and pursued. Definite 'first principles' and maxims existed, served to guide one's own personal 'inner-worldly' activities, and applied to all men. Such 'laws', were not restricted to the city as a place of administration.

10. Welfare, Law and Order

Administration was essentially decentralized. In any event, Indian occupational classes living under Ashoka's rule had to pay taxes on their income. In return the king, too, had certain duties like maintaining— or, in the case of need, newly constructing—trade routes and roads for transport, sea ports, waterways and irrigation facilities, great water collecting reservoirs, fishponds, wells and tanks. A governmental department especially instituted for this purpose oversaw the construction and maintenance of irrigation systems. A good example is the Sudarshana lake, an artificial lake with dams and water supply lines situated on the

---

130 GM, p. 238.

131 GM, p. 4.

132 For example, the dismissal of certain habits and institutions, and the simultaneous acquisition of faculties, qualities and skills, procedures, adoption of supportive measures etc. In this respect, the acquisition of wealth was then at best a side-effect.

133 An international ethics of competition based on the idea of karma could be an interesting model for cooperative and development politics.

134 GM, p. 332.

peninsula Kathiawar in Gujarat on India's west coast. Road construction and planning were also the responsibility of the government.[135] A great trading nation like India had, in order to ensure the smooth transaction of business, to maintain an extensive administrational infrastructure, and it was the king who was responsible for the welfare of his subjects, to such an extent that "for the first time there appeared, within the domain of Hindu culture, the idea of the *welfare state*, of the *general good* (the advancement of which Ashoka speaks of as the duty of the king)."[136] Ashoka causes "hospitals for men and animals, as well as the required apothecaries to be established, and fruit- and shade-giving trees to be planted along the roads" (Great Rock Edict No. II). Also, "resthouses should be set up for men and animals" (Rock Edict No. VII).[137] Pillar Edict VII states: "Along roads I have had banyan trees planted so that they can give shade to animals and men, and I have had mango groves planted. At intervals of eight krosas (1 Krosa = 1,8km), I have had wells dug, rest-houses built, and in various places I have had watering-places made for the use of animals and men. But these are but minor achievements. Such things to make the people happy have been done by former kings. I have done these things for this purpose, that the people might practice the Dhamma."[138] Weber's thesis—that welfare was to be understood "to mean spiritual welfare (as the furtherance of salvation opportunities), and partially to mean charities," but *not* as a measure of rational economics[139]—is today, as Wolfgang Bechert has convincingly shown, no longer accepted.[140]

---

135 *Encyclopedia Britannica* (Mauryan Empire agriculture): "A special department of the state supervised the construction and maintenance of the irrigation system, including the dam and conduits at Sudarshana, a man-made lake on the Kathiawar Peninsula. Roads too were the government's responsibility." See also P.C. PRASAD, *Foreign Trade and Commerce in Ancient India*, e.g. pp. 31 and 111.

136 GM, p. 242.

137 GM, p. 238. Compare also Pillar Edict No. VII, cit. in D.C. SIRCAR, *Inscriptions of Asoka*, p. 76.

138 D.C. SIRCAR, *Inscriptions of Asoka*, p. 76.

139 GM, p. 242.

140 Heinz BECHERT, *Buddhismus, Staat und Gesellschaft in den Ländern des Thervada-Buddhismus* (Buddhism, state and society in the countries of Theravada Buddhism), vol.I Grundlagen (Fundamentals). Frankfurt, M. and Berlin, Alfred Metzner 1966, p. 115, giving further evidence of this "one-sidedness of [WEBER's] thesis", ibid., E. SARKISYANZ, *Rußland und der Messianismus des Orients* (Russia and the Oriental messianism), pp. 334 f. and 337 f.

Without doubt, a general welfare system cannot be maintained without fiscal levies. Weber mentions "the tremendous irrigation works of the Ceylonese kings" which, in his opinion, "like those of Northern India (already under Chandragupta)," although definitely fiscal in the sense that they are "intended to augment the number of taxpayers and the capacity to pay taxes,"[141] were nonetheless—not intended "to implement welfare politics". Weber's argument here is not persuasive.[142]

There already existed a system of land lease, which is mentioned in the inscriptions. Weber does not explicitly dwell on this issue, and his remarks are vague or appear in a different context, where he speaks of "the royal tenants." Even in India, as Weber correctly noted, the urban patricians "were used as givers of loans and commissioners of supplies and services, but they were gradually thrust into the background and the traders brought forward as bearers of liturgies and taxes in relation to the new administrative powers."[143] The question then is, properly understood: does the "Spirit of Capitalism," legitimated as it were by the "Protestant Ethic," chiefly serve to "further the chances of salvation," or should it be seen above all as a measure of "rational economics?" Weber's intention is not clear, since welfare, as we have seen, is inconceivable without fiscal levies. A system of mutual compensation, a kind of economic 'law of karma' based on performance and reward, was equally possible. In either case, according to Buddhist belief the goal was obtaining "religious merits" and not fiscal concessions.

It is probably correct to say that Ashoka built his rule on the firm material foundation of principles of justice, reciprocity and mutual rewards, yet according to Weber a concept of equality as a 'law of nature' was lacking.[144] In Asiatic countries "men were ... forever unequal ... All

---

141 GM, p. 242. See also Andreas E. BUSS, *Max Weber and Asia. Contributions to the sociology of development*, München, Weltforum 1985, p. 15, which refers to the Culavamsa XXXVII, p. 185.

142 GM, p. 242. WEBER's intention here is not quite clear, because without fiscal levies general welfare couldn't be sustained. It is more likely that there existed a custom or regulation of reciprocity, with performance and rewards, i.e. some economical 'law of karma'. According to Buddhist belief the aim was to obtain "religious merit" rather than fiscal benefits. Andreas E. BUSS, *Max Weber and Asia* (1985), p. 151, referring to the Culavamsa XXXVII, 185.

143 GM, p. 235.

144 E. LAMOTTE seems to hold the opinion, op.cit., p. 277, that Ashoka "selon les edits ...

men, however, had equal opportunities, but not in this life," and only by way of "rebirth."[145] Weber maintains: "Through rebirth they could either achieve heaven or descend to the animal kingdom or to hell."[146] Closely related to the doctrine of reincarnation, according to Weber, is the "*karma* doctrine of the universal causality of ethical compensation, which replaces the theodicy."[147] Undoubtedly, however, in Buddhism class and caste differences were devalued and levelled (transcended), as Max Weber himself admits, thus giving "the lower strata opportunities to rise."[148] Possibly, the development of the (supposedly) "totally un-Hinduistic thought of an original equality and a pacifistic golden age of men"[149] can be traced back to Ashoka; it was propagated by him, even beyond the borders of India.

We have to accept that it is not the individual as such who is evil or sinful; each "single act" has a "meaning and value" and should be evaluated in this context. Weber continues: "No single world-bound act can get lost in the course of the ethically meaningful but completely impersonal cosmic causality. One might think that an ethic based on these premises must be one of active conduct…"[150] While Max Weber doubts this, it was in fact one of active conduct, especially, when one thinks of India's erstwhile position as a great trading nation in the Asian and international context. In this respect, Andreas Buss' statement is justified in that it is likely that "welfare policies in non-modern states were based on concepts of substantive justice (*materielle Gerechtigkeit*) and not on concepts of formal justice, as in the modern Occident."[151] Heinz Bechert criticized Weber's interpretation of

---

propagea un Dharma, bien distinct de la Bonne Loi, où il se bornait à définir les grands principes de la Loi naturelle."

145 GM, p. 144. Closely related to the doctrine of reincarnation is the "karma doctrine of the universal causality of ethical compensation." (GM, pp. 206-207) Not the individual as such is 'bad' or sinful, but every "single act" carries "meaning and value," and as such is decisive (p. 207).

146 GM, p. 144.

147 GM, pp. 206-207.

148 GM, p. 235.

149 GM, p. 292. In so far, we must qualify Andreas BUSS's statement, Max Weber and Asia (1985), p. 15, that it is "likely that welfare policies in non-modern states were based on concepts of substantive justice and not on concepts of formal justice, as in the modern occident."

150 GM, p. 207.

151 A. BUSS, *Max Weber and Asia* (1985), p. 15.

Ashoka's conversion to Buddhism:

> It was in the interest of the 'patrimonialism' of the great kings of the
> Maurya Dynasty which had taken the place of the old little kingdoms, 'to
> give the lower strata opportunities to rise'. This interest was facilitated by
> 'the circumvention of status barriers by the Buddhistic salvation religion'.
> So, the decision of the Great King Asoka of the Maurya dynasty, who 'first
> succeeded in uniting the entire culture area of India into a unitary empire',
> to become a Buddhist, appears to Weber merely as a convenient political act.
> This is certainly a unique interpretation of sources; according to his own
> testimony Asoka, when he became a Buddhist layman, converted by making
> a very personal decision of conscience.[152]

Nonetheless, we must ask, to what extent and in what ways the (presumed)
"absence of a concept of natural law,[153] consisting of the existence of a
doctrine of inequality between people, may have prevented a capitalistic
economic development."[154] With Jakob Rösel we must question this
hypothesis. When Weber writes, in a Christian context: "But in this case
the lex naturæ (as distinct from positive law made by the Emperor and
the Jurists) is directly identical with divine justice,"[155] can this not apply
just the same to Hinduism or Mahayana Buddhism? The sociologist Rösel
believes, rightly it seems, that Weber has at this point not brought his thesis
to its logical conclusion. In the end we may have to accept that Weber's
thesis is somewhat mistaken.[156] Certain basic socio-political structures can
be identified even in Kautilya's *Arthashastra*, which postulates elements of
a natural law in the sense of equal rights subsumed under final, recognized
and highest ethical, 'divine' principles, according to which everyone is
responsible for and director of his or her own actions (and receives his or
her corresponding reward). In Buddhism, Bechert observes, the "doctrine

---

152 Heinz BECHERT, Max Webers Darstellung der Geschichte des Buddhismus in Süd-
und Südostasien (Max Weber's portrayal of the history of Buddhism in South and
South East Asia), in W. SCHLUCHTER (ed.), *Max Webers Studie über Hinduismus und
Buddhismus*, p. 280.

153 Max WEBER, *The Protestant Ethic and the Spirit of Capitalism*, transl. by Talcott
PARSONS, Mineola, N.Y., Dover Publications 2003, p. 215.

154 J. RÖSEL, *Die Hinduismusthese Max Webers*, p. 76. (Own translation) There is
reasonable doubt about the thesis that the existence of a doctrine of inequality can be
said to have prevented a capitalist economic development.

155 M. WEBER, *The Protestant Ethic and the Spirit of Capitalism*, p. 215.

156 See J. RÖSEL, *Die Hinduismusthese Max* Webers, p. 76.

of a universal justice [as a kind of] natural law, which in its basic outline is pre-Buddhist, became so refined that it was able to offer an explanation for all the happy and unhappy circumstances of life."[157] The legal scholar and South Asia historian Dieter Conrad writes:

> Hence if an area of specific human social coexistence is established in a common order under a (royal, i.e. human) penal power and lifted out of the sub-human and superhuman ways of existence Weber emphasized, then there is after all a common human condition ... There is on the horizon of universal obligations also a special dignity of the human, as the sentence from the Mahabharata quoted by Weber himself demonstrates: "This holy mystery I proclaim to you: nothing is more noble than humanity." However, in light of such sentence alone Weber should have questioned his statements about the lack of any basis for a common-human natural law.[158]

And he continues:

> Is it, in short, not obvious that the *Dharma* simply occupies the place where Weber fails to spot the natural law? If one does not want to see it as natural law in the strict sense, it can at least be regarded as a functional equivalent of natural law in the Hindu system of norms ... One wonders, in fact, at the mere reading of the sentences on the natural law problem in Hinduism, why an 'eternal world (order) of so many stages' cannot be understood as a 'natural order of people and things'.[159]

The Indian subcontinent is relatively protected and self-contained; so why, despite all 'initial disposition to the effect', is a 'state' "in the sense of a political association with a rational, written constitution, rationally ordained law, and an administration bound to rational rules or laws, administered by trained officials,"[160] not supposed to have developed in India? "And the

---

157 Heinz BECHERT, *Buddhismus, Staat und Gesellschaft in den Ländern des Theravada-Buddhismus*, p. 3 (my translation). Dieter CONRAD, *Zwischen den Traditionen. Probleme des Verfassungsrechts und der Rechtskultur in Indien und Pakistan*. Gesammelte Aufsätze aus den Jahren 1970-1990 (Between traditions. Problems of constitutional law and legal culture in India and Pakistan. Collected Essays from the years 1970-1990), Stuttgart, Franz Steiner 1999, p. 346, in the Chapter 'Max Webers Interpretation des Dharma und sein Begriff der Eigengesetzlichkeit' (Max Weber's interpretation of Dharma and his concept of entelechy).

158 D. CONRAD, *Zwischen den Traditionen*, p. 360.

159 Ibid.

160 Max WEBER, *The Protestant Ethic and the Spirit of Capitalism*, transl. by Talcott

Third to Fifth Rock Edict, Girnar, Junagadh District, Gujarat

same is true of the most fateful force in our modern life, capitalism," which according to Weber also only the West had produced.[161] This thesis is nowadays hardly upheld any more, and Weber, too, presumably did not mean to say that in the West mere form ranked before substance! We have sufficient evidence to show that in India a structured, rational, thoroughly organized governmental organization with social and political structures existed. Here, certainly, especially for the Buddhist rule under Ashoka, Weber's analysis is not appropriate, because a 'state' in the sense of a strictly regulated "institution," equipped with a rationally conceived "constitution," rationally organized laws, and other social structures, did in fact exist.

11. Education and Learning, Temporal and Spiritual Matters

It was the administration of common welfare which was being enhanced. Ashoka preaches "respect for life, obedience to parents (and the elderly in general)," and general restraint,[162] and provides incentives to enable laymen and non-Brahmins alike to obtain a certain degree of education. Ashoka

PARSONS, New York, Scribner 1958 (reprint 2003), pp. 15-16.

161 M. WEBER, *The Protestant Ethic and the Spirit of Capitalism*, p. 17.

162 GM, p. 239.

was presumably the founder of "[m]onastic schools for lay requirements in the form of primary schools."[163] Practical knowledge of the affairs of this world and the next was imparted in this way.[164] "Buddhism was propagated by strictly contemplative, mendicant monks who rejected the world and, having no homes, migrated."[165] As shown above, the wandering monks and ascetics fulfilled social functions, pointing by their example to an absolute, transcendent reality that surpassed their everyday life. Tolerance was essential. "For long periods tolerance towards religious and philosophic doctrines was almost absolute; at least it was infinitely greater than anywhere in the Occident until most recent times."[166] Weber is right in saying that at the core of Indian otherworldly aspirations for salvation lay the realization that "virtue could be 'taught' and that right knowledge was inevitably followed by right action."[167] Early on we see here the 'pacifist' missionary spirit of Buddhism coming to manifest itself. Ashoka wants to change and save the whole world. His world mission is expressed in the Great Rock Edict VI:

> Truly, I consider the welfare of all to be my duty, and the root of this is exertion and the prompt despatch of business. There is no better work than promoting the welfare of all the people and whatever efforts I am making is to repay the debt I owe to all beings to assure their happiness in this life, and attainment of heaven in the next.[168]

This "philosophical knowledge"[169] apparently derived from the conviction that—in contrast to Christianity—"it is not sin, but transitoriness which is evil."[170] And actually "the great root of all evil [is] *avidya* (stupidity, obtuseness or cosmic illusion)."[171] "A concept of sin based on an ethic of intentions (Gesinnungsethik) is as little congenial for Buddhism as it was

---

163 GM, p. 256.

164 GM, p. 239: "Each good deed bears its fruit in the next world, often already in this one."

165 GERTH and MILLS, p. 269.

166 GM, p. 4.

167 GM, p. 331.

168 http://www.cs.colostate.edu/~malaiya/ashoka.html. See also U. SCHNEIDER, *Die gro-ßen Felsen-Edikte*, p. 147, Großes Felsen-Edikt VI.

169 GM, p. 331.

170 GM, p. 249.

171 GM, p. 252.

for Hinduism in general."[172] Apparently what was to be taught—if possible at an early age—was an intuitive knowledge and understanding of the eternally recurring predicament of the human condition in a transient world. For this purpose the general education of subjects, most of who lived in rural areas, had to be taken care of to make sure that progress in effectively dealing with all daily affairs was to be achieved. Weber may have been misguided in his belief that "the petty bourgeois and the peasant ... could ... but think little of his yearning for *nirvana*," and "did not have the means at hand to attain these sacred objects (of salvation); for it required leisure for meditation." Weber maintains that "he had no such leisure."[173] Apparently Weber did not know that the peasant in Asia in the annual cycle of creation and recreation has ample time to indulge in leisure, meditate and put his house in order, even with two rice crops a year. A Chinese proverb says: "Qing Geng Yu Du!" (When the sun shines till the soil, when it rains continue your studies.)[174]

Weber mentions the "peculiar ... theocracy of the Buddhistic monarchs," which "first emerged under Ashoka." [175] A similar concept appears in the European Middle Ages. The emperor essentially distinguished himself, above all, by his *auctoritas*: "...he was superior," historian Robert Holtzmann explains, "to all in *auctoritas*—in *potestas* (*Amtsgewalt*) he possessed only that of his colleagues."[176] Ashoka, like Charlemagne, was able in his person to reconcile spiritual and temporal power. "With this, there emerged, for the first time in Buddhism, the beginnings of a political theory: the power of the universal monarch (*chakravarti*) must supplement the spiritual power of the Buddha, which necessarily leads away from all worldly action."[177] The historical Buddha, too, in some (probably later)

---

172 GM, p. 208.

173 GM, p. 236.

174 This is also very well known in Japan, as *seikou udoku*.

175 GM, p. 241.

176 Robert HOLTZMANN, *Der Weltherrschaftsgedanke des mittelalterlichen Kaisertums und die Souveränität der europäischen Staaten* (The idea of world rule in medieval emperorhood and the sovereignty of the European states), Tübingen, Wissenschaftliche Buchgemeinschaft 1953 (orig. lecture 1938), p. 17.

177 GM, pp. 237-238. Actually, the historical BUDDHA, too, in the scriptures is referred to as chakravartin or world-monarch, e.g. in the early Mahaparinibbana-Sutta of Digha-Nikaya (PTS), vol. III, pp. 141-142, in D.R. BHANDARKAR, *Some Aspects of Ancient Hindu Polity*, Benares, Benares Hindu University 1929, p. 95.

scriptures is referred to as *chakravartin* or world-monarch, e.g. in the early *Mahaparinibbana-Sutta* of Digha-Nikaya. While "the old Buddhism... had been simply apolitical," under Ashoka a fundamental change took place.[178] According to E. Sarkisyanz: "This 'political Ashokan Buddhism' of historical rulers is less widely known than the philosophical canon of the monastic order." [179] In this way, future developments with far-reaching consequences were anticipated.[180] Also, The Buddhist administrative system of the 'Five Mountains' (ch. *wushan*, j. *gozan*), regulating trade, revenue, and other economic affairs and land tenure, though little known, may have derived from concepts of Indian statecraft, as expounded in the *Arthashastra*. [181] It is very likely that the concept of the 'Bodhisattva-king' also originated with Ashoka.[182] Max Weber describes the spread of Ashoka's policy: "The great international expansion of Buddhism in Asia ... had its ideal beginnings at that time."[183]

One of the Emperor's prime concerns was the propagation of Dharma. The king set out sending "Ambassadors ... to foreign powers ... to make known the pure teaching to the whole world."[184] The Emperor, like the Buddha, is conceived of not merely as a "tool but a 'vessel' of the divine." The author continues: "Active asceticism operates within the world; rationally active asceticism, in mastering the world, seeks to tame what is creatural and wicked through work in a worldly 'vocation' (inner-worldly asceticism). Such asceticism contrasts radically with mysticism, if the latter draws the full conclusion of fleeing from the world (contemplative flight from the world — Weltflucht)."[185] Ashoka's inner-worldly ascetic attitude met the conditions set out in the Arthashastra that the *vijigisu*, the 'victory-aspiring', should be a true incarnation of virtue, otherwise he was to lose

---

178 GM, p. 237.

179 E. SARKISYANZ, *Buddhist Backgrounds of the Burmese Revolution*, p. 36.

180 Max WEBER here describes, GM, p. 241, the enormous impact Ashoka and his politics have had throughout Asia.

181 Erich ZÜRCHER, *The Buddhist Conquest of China—The Spread and Adaptation of Buddhism in Early Medieval China*, Leyden, E.J. Brill 1959, on the subject of the "Five Mountains."

182 See H. BECHERT, *Buddhismus, Staat und Gesellschaft in den Ländern des Theravada-Buddhismus*, p. 29, who doesn't, however, explicitly say so.

183 GM, p. 241.

184 GM, p. 241.

185 GERTH and MILLS, p. 325.

his job and be deprived of his position. Again, did Ashoka merely make use of (or misuse) religion for his own limited, if practical, purpose?[186]

Weber points out that in Buddhism "the contemplative mystic does not draw the conclusion that he should flee from the world [*Weltflucht*], but, like the inner-worldly asceticist, remain in the orders of the world (inner-worldly mysticism)."[187] Although Weber distinguishes between actively ascetic ethics, as opposed to "contemplative mystic" ethics, in both cases "*the contrast can actually disappear in practice...*"[188] Consequently, Ashoka should indeed be looked upon as an 'inner-worldly mystic' of some sort, in the Weberian sense. Max Weber here equates 'inner-worldly asceticism' with 'inner-worldly mysticism'. That which is characteristic here of the Mahayana school and of Ashoka, is precisely this 'inner-worldly mysticism'. Hermann Kulke also shows that the "category of 'inner-worldly mysticism'" contributes significantly to a "better understanding" of certain aspects of Indian "economic life." [189] Thus, through these teachings about the laws of cause and effect and their 'this-worldly' operation, i.e. "the Indian doctrine of *Karma* and *Samsara*," the "soteriologically devalued world obtained a relatively rational meaning."[190] [191] The world as Maya is the playground of both noble and unscrupulous spirits.

Weber seems to have overlooked the 'socio-political' element of

---

186 *See* H. BECHERT, Max Webers Darstellung der Geschichte des Buddhismus in Süd- und Südostasien, p. 280, who criticizes WEBER's interpretation of Ashoka's conversion to Buddhism on just this point. A. BUSS, Max Weber's Contributions, *Max Weber in Asian Studies*, p. 4.

187 GERTH and MILLS, p. 326. "That which is characteristic for the Mahayana-school," and actually also for Ashoka already, here obviously is precisely this 'inner-worldly mysticism'.

188 GERTH and MILLS, p. 326 (emphasis added).

189 H. KULKE, Orthodoxe Restauration und hinduistische Sektenreligiosität im Werk Max Webers, in W. SCHLUCHTER (ed.), *Max Webers Studie über Hinduismus und Buddhismus*, p. 318.

190 GM, p. 332.

191 See in particular Rock Edicts III sand V, Pillar Edict IV and the Kalinga Inscription I. N.A. NIKAM and Richard McKEON, *The Edicts of Asoka*, Bombay etc. New York, Asia Publishing House 1962 (University of Chicago 1959), pp. 55-59; Separate Edict XVI (Jaugada) (D.C. SIRCAR, *Inscriptions of Asoka*, p. 63) and Pillar Edict I (ibid., p. 70). G. FUSSMANN, Central and Provincial Administration in Ancient India, p. 58. See also A.L. BASHAM, *The Wonder that was India*, Calcutta etc., Rupa 1990 (1954), pp. 116-118.

justice, reconciling as it were, the spiritual and temporal realms, and connecting them. Referred to in the edicts, the idea of "justice" and its exercise or 'administration'[192] seems to have been an important principle of governance.[193] Like the emperor in the European Middle Ages, Ashoka occupied the highest judicial place and authority in all affairs brought to his attention.[194] In this way, formal agreement of the subjects to the "*idea* of subordination" under the imperial authority could be reconciled with the "complete political independence" of the subjects and political enti-ties[195] like the little kingdoms, within their fluctuating social environments. Pillar Edict I states that all people should obtain justice and treatment in accordance with the principles of the Dharma, so that they can lead a happy life in harmony with the Dharma and can claim personal protection by the rule of Dharma:

> Happiness in this world and the next is difficult to obtain without much love for the Dhamma, much self-examination, much respect, much fear (of evil), and much enthusiasm. But through my instruction this regard for Dhamma and love of Dhamma has grown day by day, and will continue to grow.[196]

The Dharmamahamatras are to support and encourage Ashoka's political subjects in this endeavour.

To achieve and guarantee observance of justice, the emperor was guided by his faith in the authority of the law, the *dharma*. "'Dharma' conveys the associated meanings of 'Law' and 'morality', with overtones of both religious piety and social obligation."[197] The king "aspires to be a 'chakkavati',

---

192 See especially Rock Edicts III, V and Pillar Edict IV and Kalinga Edict I. The Edicts of Asoka, ed. and transl. by N.A. NIKAM and Richard McKEON, pp. 55-59; Separate Edict XVI (Jaugada) (D.C. SIRCAR, *Inscriptions of Asoka*, p. 63) and Pillar Edict I (ibid., p. 70). Gerald FUSSMANN, op.cit., p. 58. See also A.L. BASHAM, *The Wonder that was India*, pp. 116-118.

193 Pillar Edict no. I. Subjects were to be treated with justice, in accordance with the principles of dharma, so that they might live a happy life in accordance with dharma, and even claim personal protection under the laws of *dharma*.

194 See for a comparison in occidental history R. HOLTZMANN *Der Weltherrschafts-gedanke des mittelalterlichen Kaisertums*, p. 21.

195 R. HOLTZMANN, *Der Weltherrschaftsgedanke*, p. 27. This seems to indicate that not the size of the 'empire' was important but, primarily, those practical, universal princi-ples which governed it, and of which the emperor was the embodiment.

196 Pillar Edict No. I. http://www.cs.colostate.edu/~malaiya/ashoka.html.

197 *The Edicts of Asoka*, edited and translated by N.A. NIKAM and Richard McKEON, p. 23, footnote.

the aim being the universality of law and order."[198] Laws (*dharma*), such as the law (Gesetzmäßigkeit) of cause and effect, were regarded as sacred, and in accordance with the higher intellectual requirements of Indian society at the time. This was the basis for all administrative acts. The "ultimately inexpressible divinity" showed a 'natural' tendency to correspond to the "*triratna* [the trinity] of ancient Buddhism," where *dharma* as a "divine potency", in Weber's understanding, even came to resemble the "Chinese 'Tao', coming to be the order and real ontological basis of the world, to equate eternal norms and eternal being."[199] This must have impressed Weber considerably, and he paid the Buddhist teachings due reverence. The striking resemblance of the notion of Trinity in both Buddhism and Christianity, consisting in the idea of the "Holy Spirit" was not lost on Weber:

> In Christianity its nature may most easily be conceived in terms of the
>
> impersonal conception of the 'Holy Ghost' which is similar.[200]

12. World Order, Peace and Justice, a Contemporary View

> There is no peace in the economic struggle for existence; only one who takes that mere semblance of peace for the truth may think that there will arise from the womb of the future for our descendants peace and enjoyment of life. We know: the economic policy is to the vulgar conception a musing over recipes for the happiness of the world, — the improvement of the "lust balance" of human existence is for them the only understandable goal of our work. Yet ... Our work is and can, if it is to retain any meaning, only wish to be: caring for the future, for our descendants ... Not how the people of the future feel, but how they will be, is the question.[201]

198 Ramila THAPAR, *From Lineage to State, Social Formations in Mid-first Millennium B.C. in the Ganga Valley*, Delhi, etc., Oxford University Press 1984, p. 151. U. SCHNEIDER, *Die großen Felsen-Edikte*, p. 147: Ashoka has "the salvation of the whole world in view..." Great Rock Edict no. VI.

199GM, p. 252: "The ultimately inexpressible divinity thereby displayed, naturally, an inclination, corresponding to the *triratna* of ancient Buddhism, in which *dharma* appeals as a divine potency to assume features of the Chinese 'Tao', namely, coming to be the order and real ontological basis of the world, to equate eternal norms and eternal being."

200 GM, p. 373, note 56.

201M. WEBER's pessimistic assessment in, *Gesammelte Politische Schriften* (Collected political writings), Tübingen, J.C. B. Mohr (Paul Siebeck) 1980 (orig. Munich 1921), p.

After the bloody conquest of Kalinga, a large kingdom on the East coast of India,[202] the emperor "declared that he regretted the unavoidable butchery and the fact that many pious people were killed, that forthwith it would not belong to the *dharma* of his descendants to conquer by the sword, but [only] by and for the power of the true faith."[203] Ashoka's conversion marked an epochal turning point that was significant from the point of view of discourse ethics; from that perspective it was also 'politically' motivated. Afterwards, among other things, he "prohibits slaughtering in the capital city of Pataliputra and festivals (*samaja*) involving meat orgies."[204] In Rock Edict I Ashoka describes how previously "in the kitchen ... hundreds of thousands of animals were killed every day to make curry ... now ... only three creatures, two peacocks and a deer are killed, and the deer not always. And in time, not even these three creatures will be killed."[205]

The social and political structures of Ashoka's empire, their underlying principles, and organization are closely linked to the problem (and idea) of universal peace. Ashoka's influence radiated far beyond the boundaries of the Indian subcontinent. Author K.J. Saunders writes:

> The missions of King Ashoka are amongst the greatest civilizing influences in the world's history ... The history of Ceylon and Burma, as of Siam, Japan, and Tibet, may be said to begin with the entrance into them of Buddhism.[206]

After the Second World War, with Indian independence and the foundation of the republic, Ashoka and his pacifism became a symbol of faith in the future of international cooperation, common welfare and a lasting peace that would be guaranteed by international law. India's national symbol, the

---

12, after the First World War. (My translation)

202 In the Great Rock Edict No. XIII there is mention of "150 thousand Men and animals," who had been "taken prisoners and displaced." "A hundred thousand were killed." D.C. SIRKAR, *Inscriptions of Ashoka*, p. 57. This text, however, does not appear in the Kalinga edicts. Instead there are the two Separate Kalinga Edicts of Dhauli and Jaugada, for a good reason.

203 GM, p. 238.

204 Ibid.

205 S. DHAMMIKA (transl.), *The Edicts of King Ashoka*, Kandy (Sri Lanka), BUDDHIST PUBLICATION SOCIETY 1993.

206 K. J. SAUNDERS, *The Story of Buddhism*, Oxford University Press, 1916, p. 76, quoted in Vincent A. SMITH, *The Oxford History of India*, Oxford, Clarendon 1961 (1958), p. 122.

capital with the three lions and the wheel (of *dharma*), is from the famous Ashokan 'pillar of truth' at Sarnath, near Benares. "The reference to the Mauryan Empire is continually present in political speeches by Indian politicians,"[207] and is of course part of the school curriculum.

We have seen that Ashoka, after having accepted the principle of non-violence as a policy, renounced all worldly, political strife and performed a "religious-pacifist turning away from the traditional king's *dharma*."[208] Disputes should henceforth be settled by peaceful discourse. Until then, in the Indian doctrine of the "Law of fishes" (*matsya-nyaya*), according to which the big fish may eat the small, was considered as an aspect of the natural order.[209]

During the centuries following the decline—or decentralization—of the Mauryan empire around 185 BC, not only Buddhist religion, but also a specific administrative type of patrimonial rule, which combined elements of spiritual and temporal power, and in which the emperor adopted the role of a *chakravartin* or (later) Bodhisattva-king, spread across Asia,[210] mixing, as it did in China, with local traditions of kingship and creed, reaching far-away Japan in the seventh century. To what extent and how in recent history the Ashokan ideal of the 'rule of law' and administrative justice has had an influence on real politics (Realpolitik) is illustrated in the case of modern Burma.

Andreas Buss has shown that modern Buddhism integrated elements of modern socialism as a movement that is

> largely rooted in traditional Buddhist ideas, in particular Ashoka's welfare state and some organizational features like the Buddhist *Sangha* (its 'democratic' constitution and the fact that all property belongs to the Sangha collectively). Buddhist socialism believes that economic injustices are among

---

207 G. FUSSMAN, Central and Provincial Administration in Ancient India, p. 44.

208 GM, p. 238.

209 H. KULKE, *Indische Geschichte bis 1750* (Indian history up to 1750), Oldenbourg Verlag 2005, p. 17.

210 Max WEBER, GM, p. 241, calls this "the peculiar theocracy of the Buddhist monarchs." See also H. KULKE, Überlegungen zur Begegnung Europas und Asiens bis ins 19. Jahrhundert (Reflections on encounters between Europe and Asia till the 19th century), *Oriens Extremus*, vol. 33, no. 1 (1990), p. 7. E. ZÜRCHER, *The Buddhist Conquest of China* (1959).

the causes of greed, hatred and delusion (*lobha, dosa, moha*) and therefore have to be abolished. This, certainly, is a complete reversal of the traditional Buddhist interpretation of history...[211]

There are aspects of the Burmese revolution after the Second World War that constitute an attempt to adopt some of the principles of Buddhist socialism. Thus in 1952 U Win, Minister for National Planning, Culture and Religion, declared in the Parliament: "At the time of the great king Ashoka ... military might was in a position of letting the world shake and perturb, and was capable of victory." King Ashoka "said, 'our victories do not give protection against Death'. In order to attain the inner victory, it is urgent to increase peace and happiness of the human multitudes ... Accordingly, he advanced the ... Buddha's Community and ... peace and happiness for the world."[212]

Whatever the case may be, the issue of *peace* as an axial age "mandate" is relevant. *Peace* is upheld by *justice* and *order*. Buddhist ideas had an effect well into modern times, with the maxim "freedom from fear" (Skt. *Abhaya dana*), also deriving from the axial age mandate, found for example in the Atlantic Charter (1941) and in the Japanese Constitution which calls for an "international peace based on justice and order." Peace and justice are preconditions for the peoples' welfare and relative happiness in the world, and not the other way round. This is not peace as mere 'contentment', as in the couplet 'happiness and satisfaction' (*Glück und Zufriedenheit*), but something far more exacting and challenging. Just as the 'administration of justice' was to guarantee material welfare and prosperity for all, so also war ("the slaughtering") was to be abolished, and the "victory (the rule) of *dharma*" to take its place.[213]

Weber recognized the rational 'inner-worldly' approach in Buddhist ethics, possibly as a method to 'enforce' peace, justice and non-violence; he nonetheless postulated irrefutable "limits to the raison d'état,"[214] before which such practical ideas as non-violence may have to stop short. In his 'Intermediate Reflection on the Economic Ethics of the World Religions' Weber maintains that "resorting to naked force as a means of coercion,

---

211 A. BUSS, *Max Weber and Asia*, p. 17. May be; but the question remains, whether cause and effect can be set apart to such extent.

212 Quoted in E. SARKISYANZ, *Buddhist Backgrounds*, pp. 204-205.

213 See also G. FUSSMANN, Central and Provincial Administration in Ancient India, pp. 51-52 and 71.

214 GM, p. 329.

directed not only outwardly but also inwardly, is basic to any political association. Moreover: it is that which in our terminology constitutes political association ... 'You shall help right to triumph by the use of force—otherwise you too may be responsible for injustice' ... Where this factor is absent, the 'state' is also absent. The 'anarchism' of the pacifist will have then come to life."[215] The use of force, however, must be legitimized by international law, not national interest; it works best in the non-military state, when war is abolished. It is this idea which will give India, "as a responsible global power, a stake in the success of the United Nations."[216]

Perhaps, if one follows Weber's argumentation, and if the individual nation-state voluntarily renounces the right of belligerency, as Ashoka did for his Empire, this may pose a problem for defining the boundaries and limits of "political association."[217] Weber describes the mental disposition on which the warrior bases his actions as a form of "organic ethical relativism." The warrior, "following his nature, would only fight just and good wars— these, however, without scruples. This theory ... represents the most far-reaching adaptation to the needs of the 'world.'"[218] So, is a state without war, not existing under the threat of "latent war," unthinkable?[219] Interestingly and quite logically, Weber states: "According to the inescapable pragmatism of all action, however, force and the threat of force unavoidably breed more force" and consequently more violence.[220] The author continues:

> War as the actualization of the threat of force, especially in modern political communities, creates a pathos and a feeling of unity, releasing thereby a devotion and unconditional sacrificial community ... as a mass

---

215 GERTH and MILLS, p. 334.

216 Shashi THAROOR, *Pax Indica. India and the World of the 21st Century*, New Delhi, Allen Lane (Penguin) 2012, p. 386.

217 See, for aspects of this question in a contemporary setting, Klaus Schlichtmann, *Japan in the World. Shidehara Kijuro, Pacifism and the Abolition of War*, Lanham, Boulder, New York, Toronto etc., Lexington Books 2009.

218 GM, p. 251.

219 The term "latent war" is from the pacifist Alfred Hermann Fried. See Klaus SCHLICHTMANN, Alfred Hermann Fried (1864–1921)—Transitioning to World Order (unpublished paper); idem, Friede als Rechtsordnung. Der Beitrag von Alfred Hermann Fried (1864–1921) zur Entwicklung des Völkerrechts (Peace as legal order. The contribution of Alfred Hermann Fried (1864-1921) for the development of international law), *Die Friedens-Warte*, vol. 87, no. 2-3 (2012), pp. 111-118.

220 GERTH and MILLS, p. 334.

phenomenon.[221]

Trapped by the laws of *karma*, we are faced with an inescapable dilemma! Responsible action can—even if it does not necessarily—include measures, which are contrary to our ethical standards and convictions; responsible action may take the risk of 'karmic' reactions and thereby lead to the perpetuation of violence.[222] Max Weber cites Ashoka: "Each good deed bears its fruit in the next world, often already in this one."[223]

Although "it is clear that Ashoka was not the naive and extreme pacifist that some historians have attempted to make him,"[224] the turning toward a world based on justice and order, motivated in the modern sense by a kind of discourse ethics, remains remarkable. Romila Thapar rightly argues that it was not Ashoka's pacifism, which led to the decline of the Mauryan empire: "Even an entire generation of complete pacifism cannot weaken an empire and lead it to fast disintegration."[225] The thesis that a nation that realizes its pacifism is fated to decline does not stand up to empirical examination.

The world model propagated and described in the *Arthashastra* appears balanced and realistic:

> This system of concentric friend-foe constellations continues up to the periphery of each mandala. This is interspersed by the 'intermediate' kings and surrounded by disinterested outsiders who in turn have their own respective 'concentric state systems' (rājamandala).[226]

---

221 Ibid., p. 335.

222 M. WEBER writes in his *Gesammelte Politische Schriften*, Tübingen, J.C. B. Mohr (Paul Siebeck), 4th ed., 1980 (orig. Munich 1921), after WWI, p. 12, pessimistically: "Even in the economic fight for existence there cannot be peace; only one who would take that appearance of peace for the truth, could believe that from the womb of the future the enjoyment of peace will arise for our successors. We know it of course: the rules of political economics are by the opinion of the vulgar a reflection on recipes for the bless-ing of the world. - The betterment of (this) 'balance-sheet pleasure' is for them the only comprehensible goal of our work. Alas: ... Our work is and can be only, if it shall have a meaning: welfare for the future, for our successors ... Not what the human being of the future would do, but how they want to be, that is the question."

223 GM, p. 239.

224 Ramila THAPAR, *Asoka and the Decline of the Mauryas*, London, Oxford University Press 1961, p. 203.

225 Ibid.

226 H. KULKE, *Indische Geschichte bis 1750*, p. 18.

The association of several or many concentric circles or regions into a kind of federation ("federal units centering around a dominating ruler") showed a tendency toward de-limitation (*Entgrenzung*) and under the already mentioned conditions—integrity of spirit, personal responsibility, tolerance, acquired virtue and so on—postulated and promoted a relative world awareness. Principles of subsidiarity and reciprocity of rewards, in a karmic way perhaps, were peace promoting. Ulrich Schneider writes:

> There is, *expressis verbis*, not any mention of a *pax mundi*, of pacifying the hither world. Nevertheless, I would like to believe that this was Ashoka's actual political aim. In any case, seen from this point of view, the mention, in this form, of the Kalinga military campaign loses [some of its] significance. The Kalinga military expedition—in Ashoka's own understanding—formed the basis for his pacifist policy, at the same time providing an admonishing and warning example not to fall back on the old methods.[227]

In the twentieth century the First World War became the paragon for the absolute futility of war; yet its lesson has evidently not yet been learnt.

The inscriptions appear to show that Ashoka had realized what conditions must be met in order to guarantee a stable and lasting peace, based on comprehensive justice and order. By establishing a stable peace and universal justice—yet apparently without losing sight of the idea of freedom and tolerance—Ashoka temporarily brings about a supra-national political system, a kind of "federation of free states" (Kant), in which both material goods and spiritual values (and their just distribution) are abundantly provided for. "The question remains, whether the term 'supranationality' is a pure legal one. It doesn't seem to be the case."[228] Sociologist Andreas Buss suggests that Weber himself might not have been against such an interpretation: "Even Utopias, based on a pure ethic of conviction, were not discounted by Weber, for he knew that purely 'value oriented actions', unconcerned about 'facts', 'realities' and consequences, can sometimes bring about social change, and that it is only by reaching beyond everyday reality that great worldly achievements come about."[229]

---

227 U. SCHNEIDER, *Die großen Felsen-Edikte*, p. 176.

228 Francis ROSENSTIEL, *Supranationalität — Eine Politik des Unpolitischen* (Supranationality—a policy of the unpolitical), Köln, Berlin, Kiepenheuer & Witsch 1964 (French orig. 1962), p. 17.

229 Andreas E. BUSS, Max Weber's Contributions to Questions of Development in Modern India, in Andreas E. BUSS (ed.), *Max Weber in Asian Studies*, Leiden, E.J. Brill 1985, p. 15.

However, Max Weber was not a pacifist,[230] not even in the sense of what his contemporary, the great authority on international law and parliamentarian during the *Weimar* Republic, Walther Schücking,[231] termed 'scientific' or 'organizational' pacifism, but he may well have sympathized with the idea, as he did with the ideas of anarchism and anarcho-syndicalism. Andreas Buss tells us that Weber sympathised with the anarchists: "... there was one type of socialism ... which Weber was prepared to take seriously, the utopian, almost anarchistic, socialism of the Russian émigrés he met in Heidelberg."[232] The question remains: why, in spite of its enormous power of diffusion (the effects of which we can still see even today in Buddhism), Ashoka's 'new order' has not been successful? Or in the end might it prove to be so?

Andreas Buss remarks that "Weber's interest in rationality ... contained," certainly, "*not* a preference for the Western style of rationalization or an ethnocentric treatment of other cultures."[233] On the contrary, Weber was very outspoken in warning of the moloch of the

> modern economic order, tied to technical and economic conditions of mechanical machinized production ... which determine with overwhelming compulsion the lifestyle of every single person who is born into this machinery–not only the unswerving economic wage earner–until the last barrel of fossil fuel has been burned away.[234]

---

230 See GERTH and MILLS, *From Max Weber: Essays in Sociology*, pp. 8-9, quoting from a letter written by Max WEBER to his mother in 1888 while participating in a military maneuver in Posen, quite typical for his stance on the issue: "I simply cannot see what moral elevation will result from placing military professionals on a footing with a gang of murderers and holding them up for public disdain." (p. 8) Max WEBERs brother, Alfred WEBER, favored a world order organized along federal principles.

231 The neo-Kantian Walther SCHÜCKING had not only been a member of the German Reichstag but also the only German who had been appointed as a judge at the Permanent Court of Justice at The Hague, where he died in 1935, banned by the Nazis. See Klaus SCHLICHTMANN, Walther Schücking (1875-1935). Völkerrechtler, Pazifist und Parlamentarier (Walther Schücking (1875-1935). International lawyer, pacifist and parliamentarian), *Historische Mitteilungen der Ranke-Gesellschaft*, no. 15 (2002), pp. 129-147.

232 A. BUSS, Max Weber's Contributions to Questions of Development in Modern India, in *Max Weber in Asian Studies*, p. 15.

233 A. BUSS, Max Weber's Contributions, *Max Weber in Asian Studies*, p. 4.

234 Talcott PARSONS (transl.), *The Protestant Ethic and the Spirit of Capitalism*, p. 181. And further, ibid., p. 182: "For the last stage of this cultural development, well and truly, it might be said: Specialists without spirit, sensualists without heart: this nullity imagines

Although the Mauryan Empire cannot easily be compared with the complexity of modern political systems, it was highly developed organizationally and in many ways more open and less rigid than the nation-state system as it evolved and became established in Europe and the world after the Peace of Westphalia. In his *Political Essays*, Weber warns of our "torpid Western civilization:"

> A lifeless machine is (nothing but) *congealed spirit. Only* by being this, is it given the power to force people into its service and to thus overwhelmingly determine their everyday working life..., as is the case in the factory. That *live machine*, too, representing bureaucratic organization and its specialization, is *congealed spirit* ... In association with the dead machine it works, producing that house of bondage of the future, to which some day men will have to resign themselves helplessly, *if for them the only and ultimate value becomes a mere technically good, i.e. rational, civil administration and supplies* [system], *which decides* [for them] *the manner of conducting their affairs.* For this purpose, bureaucracy does work incomparably better than any other rule-structure (system of domination; superimposed structure—Herrschaft).[235]

He was highly critical of the development of capitalism. The question is whether and how the development which Weber viewed very critically can be stopped and turned around. Should we use 'Beelzebub to drive out the devil'?

13. Some Conclusions

Until the 6th century AD and the Muslim invasion of India, Weber tells us, "the kings in the Punjab ... continued to live as strict vegetarians and did not mete out capital punishment ... Ashoka's empire had long since disintegrated. However, relatively pacifistic principalities prevailed in Northern India."[236]

Whatever the significance of India's central position in Eurasia, a Southern centre between East and West, with regards to the distribution and 'diffusion' of 'knowledge', it is an "extraordinary metaphysical achievement"

that it has attained a level of civilization never before achieved."

235 Max WEBER, *Gesammelte Politische Schriften*, p. 151.

236 GM, p. 246.

of Indian religiosity or *Weltanschauung* to reconcile the idea of personal salvation with an "inner-worldly vocational ethic ... [and also] with organic social ethics (and) ... with universal accessibility of salvation."[237] Thus viewed the Buddhist idea of empire under Ashoka represents a typical ideal (*idealtypisch*) form of government, combining rationality with spirituality, based on the highest form of human tolerance and virtue. As is well known, Karl Marx was quite wrong in his draconian judgment of the Asiatic mode of production and despotism. Romila Thapar notes:

> Theories such as Oriental Despotism were not, by and large, attacked directly by Indian nationalist historians, mainly because these theories were regarded as too exaggerated to even merit challenging. The nature of British imperialism, however, came in for attack ... Given all this, it's hard to believe that religion and caste were in the way of business enterprises. The documents on Indian trade and the establishment of trade centers in Central Asia and Southeast Asia, which date back to the early days, indicate a healthy striving for profit.[238]

The Orientalist William Jones (1746-1796), the 'father of Indology', was similarly disposed, arguing that in fact Indian Rajas had never been outside the rule of law: "I answer firmly that Indian princes never had, nor pretended to have an unlimited legislative authority, but were always under the control of laws believed to be divine, with which they never claimed any power of dispensing."[239] As S.N. Mukherjee relates, William Jones "shared Voltaire's enthusiasm for Asian civilization and Eastern wisdom and believed that the Asians could not have flourished if they were ruled according to the whims of their monarchs and had no experience of private property ... This was true both for the Hindus and for the Muslims."[240]

So, an inner-worldly asceticism, in Weber's understanding, was a

---

237 GERTH and MILLS, p. 359.

238 R. THAPAR, *The Past and Prejudice*, New Delhi, National Book Trust 2000 (orig. 1975), p. 12. See also R. THAPAR, *The Past Before Us*, Harvard University Press 2013, p. 28: "As a theory of explanation, Oriental Despotism was useful to the British administrator arguing for the termination of existing systems and the introduction of new institutions."

239 S.N. MUKHERJEE, *Sir William Jones. A Study in Eighteenth Century British Attitudes to India*, Cambridge Universitsy Press 1968 (Cambridge South Asian Studies No. 6), p. 126. The quote is from JONES's book *Al Sirajiyyah: or the Mohamedan Law of Inheritance; with a commentary.*

240 S.N. MUKHERJEE, *Sir William Jones*, p. 126.

component of India's fulfilling the condition of being 'in the world, yet not of it'. Everything is undertaken and accomplished for the glory of God, towards a salvation transcending the world, which can be made manifest, experienced, perceived and realized in the 'here and now'.[241] We can agree with Bechert that "in its basic points ... Weber's understanding of early Buddhism," and thus his understanding of Buddhist rule under Ashoka was correct.[242] However, Weber's assessment of the political environment and (Buddhist) idea of government can be applied only in a restricted way. His view that the Maurya Empire was ruled by a strictly centralized authority is untenable. I have tried to show that on the contrary federative principles and a conception of decentralization furthering autonomy and self-determination were equally effective. Weber himself was a federalist. Hans Norbert Fügen states: "Concerning the question of the degree of centralization of the state, Weber strictly maintained federative principles."[243]

Max Weber made it clear that it cannot be our aim to "replace a one-sided 'materialist' with an equally one-sided 'spiritualist' causal account of culture and history. *Both* are *equally possible*."[244] However, Weber says, as a "conclusion, of an investigation, [this] accomplishes ... little in the interest of historical truth."[245] Reinhard Bendix, referring to the historian Otto Hintze,[246] supports this fundamental and important premise in Weber's conception: "this double aspect ... was the leading idea of the works on the Religion of Sociology."[247] Although in fact the two are complementary, Bendix continues, "in none of his [Max Weber's] works... is this view

---

241 The conception of 'God' is here used in the sense of the "ultimately unspeakable divine." GM, p. 252.

242 H. BECHERT, Max Webers Darstellung der Geschichte des Buddhismus in Süd- und Südostasien, p. 218.

243 Hans Norbert FÜGEN, *Max Weber*, Reinbek bei Hamburg, Rowohlt 1985, p. 107 (own translation).

244 GERTH and MILLS, pp. 267-268.

245 Ibid.

246 Reinhard BENDIX, *Max Weber—Das Werk, Darstellung, Analyse, Ergebnisse* (Max Weber, his works, portrayal, analysis, results), München, R. Piper & Co. 1964 (engl. orig. 1960), p. 43. Otto HINTZE, Kalvinismus und Staatsraison in Brandenburg zu Beginn des 17ten Jahrhunderts (Calvinism and reason of state in Brandenburg at the beginning of the 17th century), *Historische Zeitschrift*, no. 144 (1931), p. 232.

247 Reinhard BENDIX, *Max Weber—Das Werk*, p. 44. Compare this with the medieval distinction between *temporalia* and *spiritualia*, viz. spiritual and worldly rule.

about the mutual relationship between ideas and economic interests fully expressed." And moreover: "All human activities, both in political and religious life, stem from a common source. The real interests everywhere— political and economic ...—as a rule provide the first impulse for man's social activities. The idealistic interests, however, inspire them, spiritualize them, serve as their justification. Man does not live by bread alone."[248] According to Romila Thapar the "domain need not be restricted to the political for in the Buddhist concept the spiritual domain is also open to the cakkavatti."[249] The concept is similar to that of the *Reich* and the role of the European emperor in the Middle Ages. However, where the central, ordering political element tends too much to one side—either the ideal or the material—the equilibrium is upset.

As an alternative to the bipolar, dialectic worldview, we perhaps should consider not *two*, but *three* principles, 'ideas' or 'material interests': the *economical*, the *political* and the *spiritual*.[250] In this setting the political, which Weber says is missing in Indian philosophy, is central.[251] Weber's assumption in this regard is questionable; here Weber was wrong: "The problem of a 'political ethics' has never preoccupied Indian theory, and in the absence of a universal ethics and (concept of) natural law, it could hardly be otherwise."[252] Andreas Buss appears to agree: "Since Ashoka's time, Buddhists believe, nevertheless, that for the spiritual growth of man, a healthy material, social and political environment is necessary."[253]

If we look at the political as the proper social, ordering element, in which material and spiritual values are brought into equilibrium (being two sides of the same coin), then we may realize in the Mauryan empire under Ashoka an 'ideal type'—in the Weberian sense—of a traditional, political government or regime, which can "rest ... upon *personal authority*. Such personal authority can, in turn, be founded upon the sacredness of

---

248 R. BENDIX, *Max Weber—Das Werk*, p. 43.

249 R. THAPAR, *From Lineage to State* (1984), p. 161.

250 See A. BUSS, *Max Weber and Asia* (1985), p. 23: "Since Ashoka's time, Buddhists believe, nevertheless, that for spiritual growth of man, a healthy material, social and political environment is necessary." Instead of 'political', here and in the following we might better also say 'socio-political'.

251 GM, p. 146.

252 GM, p. 146.

253 A. BUSS, *Max Weber and Asia*, p. 23.

tradition."[254]

In applying his political principles, Ashoka could draw on the tradition of Buddhism. The concept of a universal monarch (later the 'Bodhisattva-king'), combining spiritual and temporal powers in one single individual, was apparently not new. D.R. Bhandarkar maintains there is "nothing to prevent us from supposing that universal monarchs were known to India prior even to the time of Chandragupta."[255]

How can the prophecy of the axial time with its promise of a peaceful future be fulfilled in our time? Modern India was founded on the idea of Ashoka's pacifist order, albeit a political system somewhat akin to a rational, inner-worldly organization of the world, which Weber commended. If the reception of Weber's essays, including the 'Sociology of Hinduism and Buddhism' in India has not been favourable, it is presumably because Weber could not appreciate and acknowledge the possibility of another world.[256] However, the obsessive idea (or progressive delusion, *Zwangsvorstellung*) of a "specifically occidental form of world adaptation and domination," the idea of the 'iron cage', has fascinated Indians and been even quite popular.[257] In all likelihood, hidden behind this disposition is the (unspoken) assumption that ultimately the Indian cause and realization of a 'perfect' state can be successful and endure *against* this predicament *only*, paradoxically, if it first identifies and equips itself with the same means and instruments that were used to subdue India, which it would reject if it was true to its original purpose. Should not the approach tried at the Hague Peace Conferences to replace the institution of war by a legally binding order or institution, in these times be an example and serve as a model for the future? Had the Conferences in 1899 and 1907 been successful, then Weber's views would have been different.[258] It is interesting, though idle, to speculate what influence on Max Weber's

---

254 M. WEBER, *Economy and Society*, p. 954.

255 D.R. BHANDARKAR, *Some Aspects of Ancient Hindu Polity*, p. 97.

256 See Detlef KANTOWSKY, Die Fehlrezeption von Max Webers Studie über 'Hinduismus und Buddhismus' in Indien: Ursachen und Folgen (The failed reception of Max Weber's study on 'Hinduism and Buddhism' in India: causes and consequences), *Zeitschrift für Soziologie*, vol. 14, no. 6 (December 1985), pp. 466-474.

257 D. KANTOWSKY, Die Fehlrezeption von Max Webers Studie, p. 471.

258 See Klaus SCHLICHTMANN, Japan, Germany and the Idea of the two Hague Peace Conferences, *JOURNAL OF PEACE RESEARCH*, vol. 40, no. 4 (2003), pp. 377-394.

conception the conferences would have had if the institution of war had been replaced by an international legal system to guarantee peace and justice. With the failure of the twentieth century to organize human society according to rational principles, the concept of overall 'progress' has been discredited, and the works of Max Weber in the end remain unsatisfactory. Max Weber himself has not done much to add to our understanding of an international peace based on justice and order. However, he has provided important information and knowledge about Buddhism and India as well as shown a rational approach to understanding so-called *reality*, including that of the Indian Emperor, and creating a vocabulary to differentiate between innerworldly and transcendental asceticism.

PART II

The Palas in India and Abroad

Ganesha Statue in Borobudur, Source: http://www.vanamaliashram.org/bganesh. jpg

Uma-Maheshwar, North-eastern India (Bihar) Pala dynasty, 10th/11th century, Basalt © Renzo Freschi

Nalanda University site. Source: Incredible India

Dharmapala, Gold dinar, c. 775-810 CE, King on horseback left, brandishing spear at animal at left, Brahmi legend: sriman dharmapalah kailavo. Lakshmi seated facing on lotus in padmasana, holding lotus in each hand, Brahmi sri at top left, Pala Empire, Weight: 7.59 gm., Diam: 21 mm. This coin is the first and only known coin of the great Pala king Dharmapala. Source: http://coinindia.com/Dharmapala. See also the paper by Pankaj Tandon, A Gold Coin of the Pāla king Dharmapāla, online at http://people. bu.edu/ptandon/Dharmapala.pdf

The Palas in India and abroad: Indianization, Brahmanization, Sanskritization. Culture and Trade in Southeast Asia—with special reference to the Borobudur

Focus and aim of this narrative is the message and prominence of Pala-culture seen from the point of view of peace history. It is also an attempt to shed some light on a "'dark period' of Indian history" (Brajadulal Chattopadhyaya) and discover what influence this culture had outside India. The predominantly Buddhist dynasty continued for almost four centuries (750-1120 AD) and exhibited at its peak a unique period of cultural advancement, peace, prosperity as well as cultural activities overseas and beyond the borders of the kingdom, in particular in Southeast Asia.

1. Backdrop

Much water had flowed down the holy river Ganges from the Himalayas, when in Bengal, in the year 750, South Asia's first democratic elections took place. The elected king, Gopala I, was beginning his twenty-year long rule by ending anarchy, the 'Law of the Fishes' (*matsyanyaya*), according to which the bigger fish eats the smaller. Historian Swapna Bhattacharya writes:

> The rise of the Pala dynasty is related to the well-known tradition of a political anarchy (*matsyanyaya*) that prevailed in Bengal in the 8th century. According to the evidence of the inscriptions and literary sources Gopala was the first king of the Pala dynasty. The account of the Khalimpur inscription asserts that he was elected to be king by the people (*prakrti*), in order to deal with the anarchy.[1]

Gopala's successors Dharmapala (781-821) and Devapala (821-861) expanded the empire, like Ashoka Maurya before them, over much of the South Asian continent. At this time not only the immediate history of "pre-Islamic Bengal," as Swapna Bhattacharya writes, but the history of almost the entire Indian sub-continent was "in large part the story of the Pala

---

1 Swapna BHATTACHARYA, *Landschenkungen und Staatliche Entwicklung im frühmittelalterlichen Bengalen (5. bis 13. Jh. n. Chr.)* (Land grants and development of the state in early medieval Bengal, 5th to 13th century AD), Wiesbaden, Franz Steiner 1985, p. 20. All translations from the German are my own.

dynasty."[2] Devapala's kingdom extended over Assam and Utkala in the east, Kamboja (modern Afghanistan) in the Northwest and the Deccan in the South.

The Pala era is notable for its intellectual and artistic achievements. Supported and financially sponsored by the Palas, the universities of *Vikramashila* and *Nalanda* near Rajagriha, the capital of Magadha, broke new ground, harbouring students from all over Asia, from China, from Persia, Turkey and Greece. Both universities were located in what is now the Indian state of Bihar— the name 'Bihar' has its origin in the Sanskrit word *vihara*, meaning a monastery. The University of Nalanda possessed

Somapur Monastery, Paharpur, Bangladesh. Source: http://www.thetigertrail.com/old.html

an extensive library, possibly the largest in Asia,[3] and attached to the university was "one of the world's biggest and richest monasteries."[4] The aforementioned Dharmapala built the Somapura Temple Complex (Mahavihara), the largest Buddhist establishment (Vihara) on the Indian subcontinent in what is now Bangladesh. (See the elephants engraved in

---

2   S. BHATTACHARYA, *Landschenkungen*, p. 119.

3   Charles ALLEN, *Ashoka*, London, Little, Brown 2012, pp. 3-4 describes the Nalanda library: "For centuries Nalanda had been the most important seat of learning in Asia. It contained the most extensive repository of Buddhist knowledge in the world, housed in three multi-storeyed libraries: the *Ratnasagara*, or 'Sea of Jewels'; the *Ratnadadhi*, or 'Ocean of Jewels'; and the *Ratnaranjaka*, or Jewels of Delight. Generation upon generation of the Buddhist world's most gifted scholars had come here to study and teach the sacred texts of the Buddhist canon."

4   John VILLIERS, *Südostasien vor der Kolonialzeit* (Southeast Asia before the colonial era), Frankfurt, Fischer Weltgeschichte 1990 (orig. 1965), vol. 18, p. 45. [Original English Allan (John) VILLIERS, *The Indian Ocean*, London, Museum Press 1952 or *Monsoon seas; the story of the Indian Ocean*, New York, McGraw-Hill 1952?]

stone!)

The university was founded in the fifth century, at the time of the Gupta dynasty (ca. 320-550). It was said to have been burned and completely destroyed around 1193 by the Muslim invaders under General Muhammad Bakhtiar Kilji,[5] a thesis that has been challenged by Delhi

---

5   Ch. ALLEN, *Ashoka*, pp. 3-5 describes how the library was destroyed: "It was at this point, with the upper Gangetic plains secured for Islam, that Muhammad Bakhtiyar was given permission to push on with his small band of mujahideen. Hardened by years of campaigning, inspired by the belief that they were engaged in jihad, he and they gave no thought to their own comfort. We may imagine them whipping their ponies on, intent on covering the 160 miles to their goal as fast as humanly possible. They earned little other than swords, spears and shields, knowing that God would provide. Their immediate goal was Bihar, which was both the name of the plains country they rode through and the seat of the last of the Pala dynasty of kings. The riders were probably unaware that the very name of Bihar was derived from the numerous Buddhist *viharas*, or monastic centres, scattered across the countryside. They may not even have known that an hour's ride west of Bihar fort was a second seat of power; one without ramparts or garrison but presenting a direct challenge to their belief in the oneness of God. This was the *Mahavihara*, or 'Great Monastery', of Nalanda, known throughout the Buddhist world as the *Dharmaganja*, or 'Treasury of the Moral Law' … Nalanda's glory days had long gone but the great library still drew students from a dozen countries— none of whom could have been unaware that a new and terrifying military power had descended on the Indian plains from the north, had scattered to the winds every army sent against it and was ever now working its way down the Ganges crushing all before it. Surprise and terror were the twin pillars of Muhammad Bakhtiyar's success as a military commander. He took the fortress of Bihar before most of its occupants even knew they were under attack. He then turned his attentions on Nalanda but not before sending a messenger to enquire if its libraries contained a copy of the *Quran*. On learning that they did not, he ordered the destruction of the Great Monastery and all it contained. What followed was chronicled by Minhaj-ud-din, a judge of Ghor who had accompanied Muhammad of Ghor's invading army into India: 'The greater number of the inhabitants of that place were Brahmans … and they were all slain. There were a great number of books there; and when all these books came under the observation of the Musalmans they summoned a number of Hindus that they might give them information respecing the import of these books; but the whole of the Hindus had been killed … When that victory was effected, Muhammad-i-Bakhtyar returned with great booty, and came to the presence of the beneficent Sultan Kutb-ud-Din Ibak, and received great honour and distinction.' But Minhaj-ud-din was wrong in thinking that Nalanda's inhabitants were Hindus. They were, of course, Buddhist monks, whose numbers included many Indians of the Brahman caste. Nor did Minhaj-ud-din trouble to mention that the raiders put the entire site, extending over many acres, to the torch or that the task of burning the library took them several months, during which time 'smoke from burning manuscripts hung for days like a dark pall over the low hills'. There were at this time three major centres of Buddhist learning in Bihar and two more in Bengal. Nalanda was the first to go up in flames, quickly followed by the nearby monastery of Odantapuri, then the larger site at Vikramashila, on the north bank of the Ganges. A decade later Muhammad Bakhtiyar completed the work begun in Bihar by staging another of his lightning strikes

University Professor D.N. Jha.[6]

The transmission of Indian religious practices, Indian writing and literature, art and music to Southeast Asia reached a climax during the reign of the Palas, and this enhanced the local culture. A general introduction to the history of the cultural, linguistic and religious penetration of Southeast Asia will provide the setting for this period, which is also referred to as 'colonization' or 'Indianization'.[7] The colonization or Indianization of Southeast Asia[8] went down peacefully, as many authors have consistently noted.[9] Thus, this chapter of Indian history fits well in the context of the peace history presented in this book.[10]

on the capital of the Sena kings of Bengal at Nuddia. Here, too, he applied fire and sword to the last two remaining Buddhist Great Monasteries at Somapura and Jagadalala on the banks of the lower Ganges, and to as many lesser monastic sites as he could find. Muhammad Bakhtiyar was afterwards assassinated in his bed, but he lived to see Muslim dominion extended over Bihar and Bengal. The destruction he wrought at Nalanda and the other great Buddhist libraries has a superficial parallel in the burning of the great royal library at Alexandria—but there is a crucial difference in that what was lost at Alexandria occurred by stages over many centuries. What Muhammad Bakhtiyar did at Nalanda and the other Great Monasteries in Bihar and Bengal was once and for all. For Buddhism in northern India it was the final *coup de grace* and its consequences were catastrophic: the virtual obliteration of every page of a thousand years of Buddhist history on the subcontinent. Thus India's Buddhist past was all but lost—and very soon forgotten."

6   See D.N. JHA, former Chair, Department of History, University of Delhi, who argues that the Nalanda library was not burned and destroyed by the invaders but by Hindus, at http://kafila.org/2014/07/09/how-history-was-unmade-at-nalanda-d-n-jha. I thank Romila THAPAR for having drawn my attention to this source.

7   On Indianization see Helmut LUKAS, THEORIES OF INDIANIZATION. Exemplified by Selected Case Studies from Indonesia, Insular Southeast Asia, online: http://www.oeaw.ac.at/sozant/files/working_papers/suedostasien/soa001.pdf. This is a slightly revised version of the paper, which was published in *Proceedings of Papers. Sanskrit in Southeast Asia: The Harmonizing Factor of Cultures*, International Sanskrit Conference, May 21-23, 2001. Sanskrit Studies Centre and Department of Oriental Languages, Silpakorn University (Mahachulalongkornrajavidyalaya Press), Bangkok 2003, pp. 82-107.

8   See also Georges COEDÈS, *The Indianized States of Southeast Asia*, Honolulu, Kuala Lumpur, Singapore etc., University of Malaya Press 1968 (French orig.: *Histoire ancienne des états hindouisés d'Extrême-Orient*, Hanoi 1944) and Nicolaas Johannes KROM, *Hindoe-Javaansche geschiedenis*, 's-Gravenhage 1931.

9   It is commonly supposed that the spread of Buddhism, unlike that of Christianity and Islam, was consistently peaceful..

10 The eighth to twelfth centuries are a striking example of a pre-modern axial age as defined by Shmuel EISENSTADT, not only for India and Southeast Asia, but also for the Spanish Umayyad period (755-1092), and the Tang Dynasty (618-907) in China and in Japan the Heian period (794-1192).

2. Geopolitics and Prehistory[11]

The Ganges-Brahmaputra delta, extending over approximately 56,700 square kilometres, is the largest river delta in the world. The 2,600 km long Ganges River is navigable for about 1,500 km upstream,[12] and the 2,900 km long Brahmaputra (*Tsangpo* in Tibetan) in Bangladesh for approximately 1,290 km, as far north as Assam in India. On an average approximately 29,692 cubic metres of water per second disgorge into the Bay of Bengal throughout the year, an area of about 2,171,000 square kilometres. From north to south the Gulf measures about 2,090 km, forming with the eastern coast of India and the west coast of mainland Southeast Asia a kind of an isosceles triangle the bottom width measuring about 1,610 km. Sri Lanka to the west, and southern Thailand as well as the northern tip of Sumatra in the east—the latter two separated by the Straits of Malacca—lie at the base of the isosceles triangle at opposite ends: Sumatra and southern Thailand lie on the right (eastern) side and Sri Lanka in the left (western) south angle. To the South the triangle is open toward the Indian Ocean. At the top of this triangular configuration as well as north of the delta of these great Indian trade and commerce dominating waterways, the Ganges and the Brahmaputra,[13] lies the heartland of the Pala Territory. Tibet in the North and Burma (Myanmar) to the East border directly or indirectly on Bengal.[14] Via adjoining Myanmar (Burma) and nearby Tibet, there exists an ancient overland trade route to the Nanzhao Kingdom located in Southwestern China, in today's province of Yunnan.[15] The independent Nanzhao state

---

11 On the Indian trade routes in pre-Christian times see Nayanjot LAHIRI, *The Archaeology of Indian Trade Routes upto c. 200 BC*, Oxford India Paperbacks 1999, especially pp. 391 ff.

12 I.e. up to Benares (Varanasi) and beyond.

13 The river Meghana, which flows near the capital Dhaka into the Brahmaputra, coming from the northeast, must also be mentioned.

14 Lhasa can be reached by the Nathu La Pass via the Indian state of Sikkim bordering on North Bengal, about 1,100 km distance from Kolkata.

15 See for example Sachindra Kumar MAITY, *Cultural Heritage of Ancient India*, Abhinav 1983, p. 120: "One trade route passed through the Brahmaputra valley in Assam, Burma and Yunnan and the other ran through Nepal and Tibet. There was an indirect contact between India and China by way of Assam before the second century B.C. Indian domestic fowl along with some other articles first appeared in China in the late Shang period. But these trade routes by their very nature were difficult and discouraging to the travellers. Unhealthy condition of the countries through which they passed, scarcity of food and drink, insecurity of roads due to barbarian inroads very much discouraged the travellers to take those routes. However, the Assam-Burma route to China started from Pataliputra (Patna), passed through Champa (Bhagalpur), Kajangal (Rajmahal),

with its capital Dali on Erhai Lake existed from about 737/750 to 902 during the Tang Dynasty. The country had large gold deposits.

After the Palas in Magadha (South Bihar) and Pundravardhana (North Bengal) had come to power at the end of the 8th century, they became "the most important transregional power" in Eastern India,[16] which at times also included parts of central India.

From Bengal—as from Varanasi (Benares), Pataliputra (Patna) and Champa (Bhagalpur) situated further in the Northwest—ships could sail down anywhere along the east coast of the Bay of Bengal or along the west coast to the southern tip of India and to Sri Lanka. Thus the Palas were connected not only with the Indian kingdoms in the South and with Sri Lanka (Ceylon), but equally with its Southeast Asian neighbours also. From their position they could survey the whole area both down the western flank and the eastern side of the Bay of Bengal and—at least theoretically—geostrategically control both. As historian Susan Huntington notes, however, from the traditional sources it is difficult to determine the exact "degree of control which the Pala kings actually had over these valuable sea lanes of Bengal.[17] The probable reason is that the Palas apparently had no ambitions to exert political or military control.[18]

Evidence that the Palas were active at sea and also successful as entrepreneurs, may perhaps be found in a verse in the historical Sanskrit poem from the early 12th century, the *Ramacarita* by Sandhyakaranandin, which describes king Dharmapala as a pioneer and trailblazer preceding the ocean-cruising sailors whose "fleet of stone-boats appears splendidly when they plow the sea as bitter Gourds, (and) whose impeccable reputation shines even after crossing the lake [in splendour]."[19] Doubtless, as historian

---

Pundravardhana (North Bengal), Kamrupa (Gauhati), Burma and finally reached Yuunan-fu (Kun-ming) in South West China."

16 That the Palas at the end of the 8th century were the most important inter-regional power shows S. BHATTACHARYA, *Landschenkungen*, p. 119.

17 Susan L. HUNTINGTON, Introduction to Southeast Asia and Southern China, in Susan L. HUNTINGTON and John C. HUNTINGTON, *Leaves from the Bodhi Tree: The Art of Pala India (8th-12th centuries) and Its International Legacy*, Seattle and London, The Dayton Art Institute and University of Washington Press 1990, p. 197.

18 Ibid.

19 See S. L. HUNTINGTON, Introduction to Southeast Asia and Southern China, p. 197: "At the apex of this roughly triangular configuration is the Bengal region, the eastern flank of the Pala territories and the delta of India's major trade artery—the Ganges

Roderich Ptak has shown, the two kings Dharmapala and Devapala engaged in a foreign policy in a bustling international environment, committing themselves as trading partners and promoters of trade and cultural relations.[20] Swapna Bhattacharya states:

> Due to their long rule and military expansion [in India] the Palas occupied a prominent position among the dynasties … The importance of the Pala Dynasty lies equally in the regional expansion of their empire … in the widely ramified administrative apparatus, which required the establishment of numerous offices, the coexistence of Buddhism and Hinduism, and not least in its cultural relations with South East Asia.[21]

Relations with South-East Asia had already started a thousand or more years before the founding of the Pala dynasty.[22] Indians had long had a fairly precise idea of the whole of Southeast Asia, according to historian R.C. Majumdar:

> The ancient Hindus designated the country described above, *viz.* Indo-China, and the Malay Archipelago, by the general name of Suvarnabhumi or Land of Gold. They, however, also used the name Suvarnadvipa or Island of Gold to denote particularly the islands, including the Malay Peninsula. Particular regions in Indo-China (such as Burma and Siam) and the Malay Archipelago were also called respectively Suvarnabhumi and Suvarnadvipa.

River. From Bengal, ships could sail along both the eastern and western coastlines of the Bay of Bengal. This position linked Bengal not only with its Southeast Asian neighbours, but with the kingdoms further south along India's eastern coast as well. The extent to which the Pala kings actually controlled the valuable sea routes beyond Bengal is unknown. A verse in the Ramacarita describes the second Pala king, Dharmapala, as the 'light of (Samudra's [Ocean's]) race, whose fleet of stone-boats appeared splendid, when it crossed the sea (floating) like bitter gourds, (and) whose pure fame also became resplendent after having crossed the sea'. However, the political ambitions of the Palas and other dynasties ruling portions of Bengal do not seem to have included control of the sea routes." The fleet of stone-boats probably transported stones, which is why the ships as floating pumpkins lay low in the water. See also Haraprasad SASTRI (ed.), *Ramacaritam of Sandhyakaranandin,* Memoirs of the Asiatic Society of Bengal, vol.3, no.1 (1910); revised with English translation by Radhagovinda BASAK, Calcutta, The Asiatic Society 1969, p. 3.

20 Roderich PTAK, *Die maritime Seidenstraße* (The maritime silk road), Munich, C.H. Beck 2007, p. 134.

21 S. BHATTACHARYA, *Landschenkungen,* p. 1.

22 For India's relations to Southeast Asia having begun already a thousand years earlier see George COÈDES, *The Indianized States of Southeast Asia,* Honolulu, University of Hawaii Press, 1971 (1968).

The names indicate that the Hindus, like the Arabs, believed that this region produced gold in large quantities, or was rich in precious commodities.[23]

There are, in addition to the copper plate inscriptions, many Chinese and Arab sources, which give an account of the Indian settlements.

The following traditions[24] should not be dismissed, as they, too, are likely to contain a kernel of truth and hence can give testimony to the charisma of India and the northern Indian Gangetic civilization. Thus the Bengali Prince Vijaya, who in the Ceylonese tradition is quoted as the country's first king, is supposed to have colonized Sri Lanka in the 5th century BC.[25] Likewise Emperor Ashoka's descendants are said to have colonized and sent missions to parts of East and Southeast Asia. The establishment of Ligor (today's Nakhon Sri Thammarat, 610 km south of Bangkok) on the east coast in the north of the Malay Peninsula[26] is attributed to one of these pioneers, Prince Dantakumara.[27] A Javanese

---

23 Ramesh Chandra MAJUMDAR, *Hindu Colonies in the Far East*, Calcutta, K.L. Mukhopadhyay 1944, p. 4 (1944 edition).

24 See R.C. MAJUMDAR, *Hindu Colonies in the Far East*, p. 12 [2nd expanded edition, 1963, p. 13]: "To mention briefly only a few [more] of the many traditions, there is first the story of a Bengali Prince Vijaya, colonizing the island of Ceylon. Secondly, the foundation of Ligor is ascribed by tradition to a descendent of Ashoka who fled from Magadha, embarked a vessel at Datapura and was wrecked on the coast of the Malay Peninsula. There is also the story preserved in the chronicles of Java that the Hindus from Kalinga coast colonized the island. Similar traditions of colonists from Kling and Kalinga are preserved in many other islands ... Lastly, there is the story preserved in the chronicles of Java that the island was first colonized by a Gujrati prince who landed there in 75 A.D." The port, from which ships from Kalinga (now Orissa) could sail, is Gopalpur near today's Berhampur.

25 The Ceylonese chronicles *Dipawamsa* and *Mahavamsa*, written down by Buddhist monks, describe in detail how Prince Vijaya reached the island of Sri Lanka "in 483 B.C, on the Buddha's death-day." Douglas FERNANDO, *Tsunami in Sri Lanka*, Tenea Verlag, 2005, p. 123. See also Max DEEG, *Das Gaoseng-Faxian-Zhuan als religionsgeschichtliche Quelle. Der älteste Bericht eines chinesischen buddhistischen Pilgermönchs über seine Reise nach Indien mit Übersetzung des Textes* (The Gaoseng-Faxian-Zhuan as a religious-historical source. The oldest report of a Chinese Buddhist pilgrim monk about his trip to India with text translation), Wiesbaden, Harrassowitz 2005, p. 159.

26 See Keat GIN OOI, *Southeast Asia: A Historical Encyclopedia, from Angkor Wat to East Timor*, Band 1, ABC-CLIO, 2004, pp. 787f. J. VILLIERS, *Südostasien vor der Kolonialzeit*, p. 61: In the 8th century then "the northern part of the Malay Peninsula came to be under the influence of the Pala Empire, which, as we have seen, played an important role in the spread of Mahayana Buddhism." (My own translation)

27 See K. R. SUBRAMANIAN, *Buddhist Remains in Āndhra and the History of Āndhra between 224 & 610 A. D.*, Diocesan press, Vepery, 1932, p. 138. See also p. 141.

tradition tells of Hindus from Kalinga, now Orissa, as well as of settlers from Gujarat, who are said to have settled and colonized the island at the same time, about 75 AD.[28] We will have occasion to revisit the narrative a little later.

Also well known is the following story of the king of 'Gujerat' who around 603 AD sent his son to Java "with five thousand settlers, including skilled craftsmen, agriculturists, doctors and officers, on six vessels."[29] It is remarkable that ships sailed toward Southeast Asia from ports geographically opposite to each other on the Indian continent, i.e. from the port of Bharuch (Broach) at the mouth of the Narmada river, north of present Mumbai, in Gujarat on the west coast, and the Bengali port of Tamralipti (Tamluk) on the east coast; or even from the inland ports of Champa not far from the

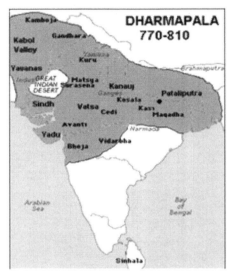

ancient Buddhist university of Vikramashila, located on the Ganges in Bihar (Bhagalpur), and of course Pataliputra and Varanasi. Under Dharmapala northern India appears to have been unified from the east coast to the west; between the ports of both coasts there existed an overland route and there were periods of close economic cooperation.[30]

---

28 See Radha Kumud MOOKHERJI, *Indian Shipping. A History of the Sea-Borne Trade and Maritime Activity of the Indians from the Earliest Times*, New Delhi 1999 (orig. 1912), p. 148 mentions: "As far back as the 75th year of the Christian era a band of Hindu navigators sailed from Kalinga, and, instead of plying within the usual limits of the Bay of Bengal, boldly ventured out into the open limitless expanse of the Indian Ocean and arrived at the island of Java. There the adventurous navigators planted a colony, built towns and cities, and developed a trade with the mother country which existed for several centuries."

29 J. VILLIERS, *Südostasien vor der Kolonialzeit*, p. 62. See also R.K. MOOKHERJI, *Indian Shipping*, p. 45.

30 *Journal of the Oriental Institute*, vol. 38, Oriental Institute, Maharaja Sayajirao University 1988, p. 239: "Starting about the 4th century BCE, trade routes began to run all through the territory south of the Yamuna. A major route ran from Pataliputra through Varanasi,

The importance of the monsoon winds for maritime transports is well known, but the principles operating the system had not been understood for a long time. Previously, for western seafarers the Greek merchant Hippalus was supposed to have been the first to describe the benefits of the winds that, depending on the season, would blow starting from the Himalayas in the northern hemisphere, cyclically moving significantly in more or less opposite directions in accordance with the season prevailing at any one time. More recently the name 'Hippalus' has been associated not with a person but the wind *hypalos* that "carried the sailors from the coast of Arabia to India."[31] In this day and age it is asserted that their benefits had been recognized much earlier. For navigation in the seas east of India this was certainly not different. At least from Bengal the ships could easily sail eastwards along the coast even without having to cross vast oceans.[32] On the west coast, in winter, from October to May, ships could use the north wind and sail southwards or, as the case may be, toward Southeast Asia. From Bengal ships could sail along the east coast southwards in winter using the south wind, and then between June and September return north.

Trade routes had been forged for many generations; numerous markets and galleries had been set up along the commercial routes, crucibles for goods from India, Southeast Asia, China, Persia and Africa. The Indianization or Sanskritization (also Brahmanization) of Southeast Asia that began after the Axial Period[33] had advanced considerably by the

---

Kausambi, Vidisha, and Ujjain and eventually reached the sea at Bharuch."

31 See Kostas BURASELIS, Mary STEFANOU and Dorothy J. THOMPSON, *The Ptolemies, the Sea and the Nile: Studies in Waterborne Power*, Cambridge University Press 2013, p. 205. I am grateful to Romila THAPAR for having pointed this out to me.

32 N. LAHIRI, *The Archaeology of Indian Trade*, p. 394, who points to the importance of the monsoon winds, however, primarily regarding the westward trade: "Much importance used to be attached to Hippalus discovery of the monsoon in the first century AD, before which, it was argued, a direct sea route was unlikely. Presently, it is being increasingly recognized that knowledge of the monsoon winds was known well before its formal discovery and therefore, direct maritime commerce between India and countries across the Arabian sea was likely. In this regard, the large number of references to sea voyages by traders and travellers in the Jataka tales are exceedingly important—that they are known to have carried birds that were meant to guide ships towards the land also implies that ships were often sailing through the oceans and not along routes from where lands could be seen shimmering in the distance." Of course, this was true also for the overseas trade and the shipping lanes directed to East Asia.

33 See Karl JASPERS, *The Origin and Goal of History*, London, Routledge & Kegan Paul 1953.

mid-8th century, and the peoples of Southeast Asia had long adopted and internalized both Buddhism and Hinduism and adapted it to their own ways of thinking and traditions. The kingdoms were in full bloom, established and constituted following Indian legal principles and statecraft.[34] The South Indian Pallavas, who had assumed the northern Sanskrit culture, were also seen as 'colonizers'.[35] The Pallavas were an ancient Indian tribe, existing since about the middle of the 3rd century. They were mostly followers of Sivaism and possibly descendants of a North Indian dynasty. The Pallavas created significant artworks in its heyday between 575 and 897.

Historian John Villiers describes the process of Indianization:

> The mathematical, astronomical and astrological knowledge of Southeast Asia and much of its science and medicine were derived almost without change from India. The Indian moon-sun year was taken over and with it Indian chronology, especially the Saka era [which began in the year 78 AD] ... throughout Indochina and the island world can be seen the strong Indian impact on music, dance and drama. Many of the musical instruments

---

34 See Susan L. HUNTINGTON, Introduction to Southeast Asia and Southern China, p. 197: "Contacts between the Indic world and Southeast Asia had been going on for nearly a millennium by the time the Pala dynasty rose to power in the eastern Gangetic region."

35 Hermann KULKE, *Indische Geschichte bis 1750* (Indian history up to 1750), Oldenbourg Verlag 2005, pp. 53-54: "The prosperity of the Pallava kingdom can be effectively traced to an intensification of agriculture ('agrarian extension') due to rural irrigation systems and the expansion of rice cultivation areas. Also of great importance was the participation in the flourishing maritime trade in the Bay of Bengal, which since the middle of the 1st millennium AD connected East India's coast more and more also with the 'indianised' states in Southeast Asia. The two great South Indian merchant guilds Ayyavole and Manigraman made their appearance during the Pallava era. An inscription in Takuapa on the Isthmus of Siam from the reign of King Nandivarman III. (ca. 844-866) for example tells of a fortified settlement of South Indian merchants. For the strong presence of South Indian merchants and Brahmins in Southeast Asia also speaks the fact that the oldest inscriptions in Indonesia and the Malay Peninsula are written in the Pallava Grantha alphabet." (My translation.) While in their inscriptions the Pallava used Prakrit, they also promoted Sanskrit, and later Tamil. Via its seaport Kadal Mallai (aka Mamallaparam) the economic and cultural influence of the Pallava extended up to Malaya, Java and Cambodia. See also https://en.wikipedia.org/wiki/ Pallava_dynasty: "K. A. Nilakanta Sastri postulated that Pallavas were descendants of a North Indian dynasty of Indian origin who moved southwards, adopted local traditions to their own use, and named themselves as Tondaiyar after the land called Tondai. K. P. Jayaswal also proposed a North Indian origin ... Pallavas were followers of Hinduism and made gifts of land to gods and Brahmins ... The Chinese monk Xuanzang who visited Kanchipuram during the reign of Narasimhavarman I reported that there were 100 Buddhist monasteries, and 80 temples in Kanchipuram."

depicted on bas-reliefs are apparently of Indian origin ... The old Indian myths and epics were added and blended with indigenous themes.[36]

The author also discusses the unique characteristics of Buddhism in Bengal and its influence in Southeast Asia:

> Two top peculiarities of Mahayana Buddhism as practised in Southeast Asia deserve to be mentioned here. One was its propensity for Tantric mysticism which was widespread in Bengal under the Pala dynasty, and the other was its remarkable tendency toward syncretism with the existing Hindu cults and even with the autochthonous pre-Hindu faiths.[37]

The Palas therefore did not come to Southeast Asia with their culture as pioneers, but found themselves in an already functioning international environment, in which some major powers had been engaged for some time. Besides the Colas and Pallavas of South India there were the great Southeast Asian kingdoms of Funan (in today's Kamboja), Pagan (in Myanmar) and Srivijaya (on Sumatra). Primary among these powers were the Chinese, whose sea power during the Tang Dynasty (618-906) reached a climax. Increasingly, starting from the 7th century, the Arabs also gained influence.[38]

The ethnic communities of Southeast Asia had developed "to a large extent already before the occurrence of the Indian influence. They possessed intricate political organizations—though usually only at the village level—and they knew the application of advanced techniques in irrigation and

---

36 J. VILLIERS, *Südostasien vor der Kolonialzeit*, pp. 91-92. See also p. 44: "The Indianization basically occurred gradually, peacefully and without political implications; in the various regions it varied considerably in intensity and duration. Nowhere did it destroy the indigenous cultures ... but enriched it in most areas." (My translation.)

37 J. VILLIERS, *Südostasien vor der Kolonialzeit*, p. 49.

38 See Susan L. HUNTINGTON, Introduction to Southeast Asia and Southern China, p. 197: "Thus Pala culture did not arrive in Southeast Asia as a pioneer, but rather as a participant in an already active international arena in which several other major powers played principal roles. The story of Pala cultural impact on Southeast Asia is inextricably linked to the destinies of these other major participants — including other Indic dynasties, primarily die Colas of south India; major Southeast Asian kingdoms of the day, most notably Pagan and Srivijaya: the Chinese, particularly during the Tang dynasty (618-906), when Chinese maritime power was at an apogee; and the Arabs, who became a major force m die complex pattern of maritime trade during the Pala ascendancy." See also André WINK, *Al-Hind: Early medieval India and the expansion of Islam*, vol. 1, The Kingdom of Dharma (Palas of Bengal), Brill 1990, pp. 254 ff.

agriculture, and their craftsmanship was highly developed."[39] John Villiers speculates that the "process of Indianization of Southeast Asia" may be compared to the process "with which the Aryans first made themselves masters of the indigenous peoples of India."[40] Brahman priests exercised a dominant influence and acquired "a role not to be underestimated as culture carriers and colonizers."[41]

> The Indians really engaged in commercial enterprise could never have spread all the complicated religious ideas and rituals, the scholarly language, the highly developed art forms and the social and political systems to which the earliest inscriptions and other facts give testimony. Such things could have been communicated only by the Brahmins.[42]

Since the Southeast Asian tribes and kingdoms had themselves already reached a rather civilized state, they welcomed the Indian thrust, which they felt was an enrichment of their own culture.[43] "The *dharmasastras* and in particular the laws of Manu gave the Southeast Asian nations' customary law a codified framework, in much the same way Roman law did with regard to the laws of the European peoples, without ever replacing them."[44] Whether one puts the case for a diffusionism (Robert Heine-Geldern),

---

39 J. VILLIERS, *Südostasien vor der Kolonialzeit*, p. 76. Already in the pre-Christian centuries bronze casting had been introduced to Indonesia by the expanding Dong Son culture which was native to North Vietnam. Jaques DUMARÇAY, *Borobudur*, Oxford in Asia Paperbacks, 1978, p. 16: "Several centuries before the Christian era, the so-called Dong-son civilization spread as far as Indonesia, bringing Bronze-casting techniques."

40 Did the Aryans make themselves masters of India? J. VILLIERS, *Südostasien vor der Kolonialzeit*, p. 76. According to a theory, Aryans are the 'Enlightened Ones' who evolved migrating around the Great Himalayan mountain complex, which appears like a merry-go-round, i.e. those beings knowledgeable of geography, language, arts, esoteric and exoteric matters and so on.

41 S. BHATTACHARYA, *Landschenkungen*, p. 1.

42 J. VILLIERS, *Südostasien vor der Kolonialzeit*, pp. 76-77. See also p. 82: "In the literature, the great epics of the Hindus, the Ramayana, Mahabharata, Harivamsa and the Puranas became an important source of inspiration for the national languages of Southeast Asia and up to the present day provide the themes for the dramas and dances of Indochina, Malaya, Java and Bali. The oldest Javanese version of the Mahabharata was published in 996."

43 In this way, according to the founder of Southeast Asian Studies, Robert HEINE-GELDERN, based on its own "synchretist synthesis" an independent civilization originated. Quoted from Helmut LUKAS, THEORIES OF INDIANIZATION, online at http://www.oeaw.ac.at/sozant/files/working_papers/suedostasien/soa001.pdf.

44 J. VILLIERS, *Südostasien vor der Kolonialzeit*, p. 82.

according to which cultural achievements and innovations are unusual phenomena which are adopted by other cultures without them doing anything creative and innovate themselves, or whether one believes in the "miracle" (K. Jaspers) of a simultaneous evolutionary development that, even if it uses a stimulus, substantially proceeds in a parallel fashion (as in the case of Jaspers' "threefold manifestation of the Axial Period"[45]); the result is the same, and in the end any progress results from the interaction of numerous peoples and factors, rather than one single influence.[46]

From Bengal it was easy, as already stated, to sail along the coast to the south. Besides Burma (Myanmar), which was within the Indian sphere of influence anyway, the south of Indonesia and especially the fertile Mekong Delta were the areas in Southeast Asia that were indianized early on. The first known indianized kingdom, Funan, had arisen here. Funan, so the Chinese name (writes John Villiers),

> extended its power between the 2nd and 6th centuries over almost all of the southern parts of present-day Cambodia and South Vietnam. It probably also controlled parts of Siam, Malaya, Java and Burma. It was situated strategically on the overland trade route, which led along the Burmese and Siamese coast, and two major sea routes, one of which crossed the Bay of Bengal, ran across the Kra Isthmus and through the Gulf of Siam, the other down the coast of Sumatra, proceeding between Sumatra and Java through the Sunda Strait.[47]

Around the 4th century Buddhism is found in Indonesia.[48] In China, there had already been Buddhist settlements in the first century AD. The first

---

45 Karl JASPERS, *The Origin and Goal of History*, p. 18.

46 It is doubtful whether, as British historian John VILLIERS states, "the term Southeast Asia is a purely geographical term for an area … lacking any real coherence," from the point of view of the religious and cultural history this can be upheld. J. VILLIERS, *Südostasien vor der Kolonialzeit*, p. 11. And ibid.: "the use of the term Southeast Asia for an area that includes the present states of Burma, Vietnam, Cambodia, Malaysia, Indonesia and the Philippines is relatively new. For the first time it was circulated in 1943, when the Southeast Asian High Command was formed, which had to lead the campaign of the Japanese in these areas."

47 J. VILLIERS, *Südostasien vor der Kolonialzeit*, p. 64.

48 J. VILLIERS, *Südostasien vor der Kolonialzeit*, p. 49: "According to archaeological and epigraphic evidence Buddhism had reached the Indonesian archipelago around the 4th century." See also, ibid., p. 61: "Some of the earliest Indian settlements to which Chinese accounts refer, lay on the peninsula, which for most of the Indian ships crossing the Bay of Bengal was the first landmark after a long voyage."

Buddhist monks had reached China under the Han Emperor Wu (Wudi) around 120 BC via the Silk Road; their religion, however, was officially recognized only in the year 65 AD. The "first allusion to a Buddhist community" in China dates from this year[49] and the community is found on the coast of the Yellow Sea, in northern Jiangsu in the commercial centre Pengcheng (Xuzhou/ Sukhov). It is possible that the new religion also reached Pengcheng by sea. Tradition has it that there was an Ashoka Monastery nearby.[50] The first Buddhist temple was built in Luoyang, the capital of the Han Empire, far inside the country on the Luo River in 68 AD.[51] Travellers from the West usually arrived by sea through the Gulf of Tonkin to continue travelling to China's interior via Jiaozhi[52] on the Red River (Song Hong). However, it was just as easy to travel further by ship via Canton to Shandong to reach a location near the coast and visit the monastery dedicated to Emperor Ashoka near the Ashoka Mountain (Ayuwang-shan) in Ningbo, near Shanghai.

For a time the Ceylonese Hinayana Buddhism of the old school still competed in Southeast Asia with the emerging Mahayana Buddhism.[53] Around the year 395 the king of Sri Lanka, a territory which had been converted to Buddhism by Ashoka's son Mahinda, had even sent a learned Buddhist monk to the court of the Chinese Emperor.[54] But only a few

---

49 Jacques GERNET, *A History of Chinese Civilization*, Cambridge University Press (2nd edition) 1996, p. 213.

50 Erik ZÜRCHER, *The Buddhist Conquest of China—The Spread and Adaptation of Buddhism in Early Medieval China*, Leyden, E.J. Brill 1959, pp. 277 f., "there had been an 'Ashoka-monastery' at P'eng-ch'eng, the capital of the kingdom of Ch'u and one of the earliest Buddhist centres in China in the middle of the first century A.D." A short distance from Ningbo, not far from Shanghai, lies the vast complex of the Ashoka Monastery with the Ashoka Mountain, still much frequented and inhabited by numerous monks.

51 Interestingly, in the year 166 AD for the first time an emissary sent by the Roman Emperor Marcus Aurelius reached Luoyang after he had traveled there by sea via Vietnam (Jiaozhi).

52 The region on the Song Hong River was called Jiaozhi. Occasionally only a part of Vietnam or even Vietnam as a whole was named as Jiaozhi by the Chinese sources. See also Rinan (Nhat Nam), also in Vietnam.

53 Susan L. HUNTINGTON, Introduction to Southeast Asia and Southern China, p. 197: "Sri Lankan Buddhism became Pala Buddhism's most powerful rival in Southeast Asia."

54 E. ZÜRCHER, *The Buddhist Conquest of China*, p. 152: "...the fame of emperor Hsiao-wu as a dharmaraja [Dharmaking, K.S.] had already reached what was to the Chinese the very limits of the known world. In or shortly after 395 the king of Ceylon ... dispatched the sramana T'an-mo-I ... to the Chinese court with a valuable Buddha-statue of jade, four feet and two inches high ... For unknown reasons the journey lasted more than ten

centuries later, in the eighth century, "Mahayana Buddhism, the spread of which coincided with the rise of the Pala dynasty in Bengal and Magadha, superseded Hinayana Buddhism in Indonesia and Indochina."[55]

The development of writing in Southeast Asia should also be briefly discussed in the context of Indianization. Most Southeast Asian scripts newly introduced from India into these countries were based on the Indian (*Brahmi* and *Devanagari* and derivations) alphabet. These include the *Cham* alphabet that had been introduced in Vietnam and Cambodia around 200 AD, and in which both Hindu and Buddhist texts were written. After this came *Tocharian*, as evidenced in West China by approximately 500 AD; the *Assamese* script (6th century.); the *Khmer* script (by about 600 AD, into Cambodia); the *Tibetan* script (by about 650 AD into Tibet); the *Mon* script (by about 700 AD into Burma); the *Burmese* alphabet (to about 1050 AD into Burma); the *Old-Kawi* (about 775 AD into Indonesia), the South Indian *Pallava* script (4th century); *Kawi* (10th century); the *Javanese* script (by about 900 AD into Indonesia); the *Balinese* alphabet (about 1000 AD into Indonesia) and the *Thai* writing system, which was introduced into Thailand around 1283.

3. The Pala Influence in Burma (Myanmar)

Bengal was through its extensive river system interconnected, as we have seen, both with the central regions of northern India—the cities Pataliputra (Patna) and Benares (Kashi)—as well as in the Indian Northeast with Assam. Assam was the stopover en route to Tibet, Burma (Myanmar) and China; previously emperor Ashoka is said to have sent missions to Burma (see PART I).[56] The Bengal region was of central importance not only for overseas trade, but also for overland transport—probably as important as the access road to the northwest (via Bactria/Afghanistan)—connecting India with the Silk Road, by which invaders frequently entered the subcontinent to raid and rob the country of its treasures.

---

years ... This mission marks ... the beginning of Sino-Singhalese relations." See also the very prolific and informative 'Notes', ibid., III, p. 378.

55 J. VILLIERS, *Südostasien vor der Kolonialzeit*, p. 49. Astounding: In "717 the monk Vajra-Bodhi from Ceylon arrived to preach a tantric form of Mahayana Buddhism in Sumatra."

56 Already before the Second World War author Nihar-Ranjan RAY, *Sanskrit Buddhism in Burma*, Orchid Press, 2002 (Amsterdam–H.J. Paris, 1936), p. 3, wrote that "evidence is daily accumulating in favour of an early introduction of Buddhism in Burma."

Via the Assam link India was connected by land with the mainland states of Southeast Asia and China. Myanmar especially was under the influence of the culture of the Palas and in turn took a key position from where their influence could spread further.[57] Huntington writes:

> The Pala cultural impact was only a single element in the complex story of Southeast Asian history. In some places, most notably Myanmar and Java, the influence of Pala culture was felt strongly, and the Pala-derived artistic styles that flourished in these regions comprise an important chapter in the story of India's cultural influence abroad.[58]

This profound cultural penetration is most remarkable: architecture; literature—notably both Buddhist scriptures and Hindu Dharma Shastras and Artha-Shastras among others—music and musical instruments; writing; religious art and sculpture etc., have become permanently established in South-East Asia and China, and all the way up to Japan.[59] The Mon migrating into Burma from the northwest of China acquisitioned Buddhism and the Pali script.

When exactly Buddhism entered into these regions is difficult to make out. Burmese traditions tell of a disciple of Buddha, Gavampati,[60] and two

---

57 HUNTINGTON, Introduction to Southeast Asia and Southern China, p. 198: "The Bengal region was also connected to the Southeast Asian mainland by overland routes, particularly through Assam. Most strongly affected by this land contact was Myanmar (Burma). Not only did the art and culture of Myanmar profoundly experience the impact of Pala culture, but Myanmar served as a center from which Pala influence was distributed to other regions of the mainland."

58 Ibid.: "However, much of Pala influence in Southeast Asia was limited to the elite members of society, where its Sanskritic traditions served largely as a court culture. Because it did not achieve the broad, popular base that it enjoyed in India [or because of the Muslim impact?], Pala culture may have been doomed to extinction m Southeast Asia."

59 And further, ibid., p. 199: "It is likely that Mahayana and perhaps Tantric Buddhism had spread to northern Myanmar from the Pala lands during the early Pala period ... The most visible effect of Pala culture on Myanmar survives from the Pagan period (1044-1287), the rise and florescence of which coincided with the late Pala period. During the Pagan period, the kings of Pagan not only dominated virtually all of the Myanmar region but ranked among the most important kings in Asia. During its heyday, the capital of this powerful kingdom, the city of Pagan, is estimated to have had some three thousand Buddhist monuments."

60 Edmund HARDY, *Der Buddhismus nach älteren Pali-Werken* (Buddhism according to older Pali texts), Münster i.W., Aschendorffsche Buchhandlung 1926, p. 52, tells the old story of the sixty-one disciples of the historical Gautama Buddha. Buddha, after

missionaries who are supposed to have been active in Burma, namely Sona and Uttara, are known from the Pali canon to have been sent by Emperor Ashoka. Around 800 the Mon people, a tribe related to the Khmer, migrated to Burma from the northeast. The Mon kingdom of Dvaravati, which existed from the 6th to the 11th century and extended over parts of Burma and Thailand, was an important gateway for the transmission and establishment of Indian tradition. It is likely that relations with the Pala Empire were particularly strong, at least as extensive as those with Ceylonese Buddhism.

> Dvaravati was historically important as a transmitter of Indian culture. Having had early commercial and cultural contact with India, the Mon assumed the role of disseminators of the main features of Indian culture.[61]

There possibly existed a loose confederation with the Mon Empire of Thaton and Haripunjaya in northwest Thailand.

The actual Burmese themselves only immigrated to the central plains of the Irrawaddy in the course of the eighth and ninth century. The capital of the Mon kingdom, the port city of Thaton, was conquered in 1057 by the Burmese, who were advancing southward; the kingdom, however, continued to exist. The Burmese Kingdom of Pagan which was subsequently founded was noted for its competition—or perhaps syncretistic relationship—between Mahayana and Theravada Buddhism. The question is, as art historian and Buddhologist Nihar-Ranjan Ray writes in his book *Sanskrit Buddhism in Burma*:

---

his first sermon in the Deer Park at Benares, sends them in all directions to spread the teachings (dharma) in the world. The "sixty" were to participate in establishing the "empire of the law" (dharmarajya). The Buddha instructs the monks: "Go forth for the gain of the many, for the welfare of many, out of compassion for the world, for the good, the benefit, and for the salvation of gods and men! No two must go on the same path! Preach the doctrine which is glorious in the beginning, glorious in the middle and glorious at the end, according to the Spirit (attha) and following the letter (vyancana)! Proclaim a perfect and pure life (brahmachariya)! There are beings whose spiritual eyes are barely covered with dust; if however the doctrine is not preached to them, they cannot reach salvation. They will understand the teachings..." (My own translation from the German.)

61 On Dvaravati see the *Encyclopaedia Britannica*, online http://global.britannica.com/ EBchecked/topic/174783/ Dvaravati.

The question now will naturally be asked: When did Thaton receive the faith of Theravada Buddhism, or more correctly speaking, the Hinayana form of Buddhism? Are we to accept the tradition, so insistent in Burmese records, of the Ashoka mission of Sona and Uttara to Suvannabhumi? Shall we also believe the later tradition, equally vocal in Burmese chronicles, of Buddhaghosa's [5th century] crossing over to Burma and preaching there the religion of the Master?[62]

While a few decades ago little was known concerning the early reception of Buddhism in Burma, the picture has become much clearer today.[63] Obviously the Mon were the main carriers and agents who were open to the Indian influences and had internalized them, had taken over Buddhism and the (Pali) script, and even after the demise of their kingdoms continued to operate as the original teachers and mediators.[64] Thus culturally the kingdom of Pagan was little more than a continuation of the Buddhist culture of the Mon. Not only that, the connection to the Palas persisted. "Pala influence is visible everywhere, from the smallest clay plaques to the grandest architectural structures."[65]

The first Great King of the kingdom of Pagan was Aniruddha (Anawrahta, ca. 1044-1077), who united the country, establishing almost everything that constitutes Myanmar today. His successor Kyanzittha (Jnancitta?), who had led the army as Aniruddha's general and thus

---

62 Nihar-Ranjan RAY, *Sanskrit Buddhism in Burma*, p. 3. Buddhaghosa had spent a long time in the first Buddhist monastery in Sri Lanka, the Mahavihara in Anuradhapura, which king Devanampiya Tissa (307-247 BC) had donated.

63 And ibid.: "Available evidence is so meagre that none of these questions can be answered satisfactorily. Recent criticism has thrown doubt on both traditions, referred to above, though evidence is daily accumulating in favour of an early introduction of Buddhism in Burma."

64 The Mon continued to perform as agents of Buddhist culture. This is reminiscent of the Greeks who, after Rome had taken over administrative control, still acted as their masters' teachers.

65 See *Encyclopedia Britannica* (1998), p. 305: "Dvaravati was historically important as a transmitter of Indian culture. Having had early commercial and cultural contact with India, the Mon assumed the role of disseminators of the main features of Indian culture. They were the most receptive of Southeast Asian peoples..." HUNTINGTON, Introduction to Southeast Asia and Southern China, p. 200: "Aniruddha apparently was also a follower of Mahayana, which further suggests the strength and continuity of Pala culture in Myanmar. It is believed that Aniruddha had religious, cultural, and possibly matrimonial contacts with Bengal: he is even believed to have travelled and 'planted magical images' there."

completed the establishment of the Pagan Empire,[66] stood out in particular because of his intense relations with India, where he had sent an embassy, as the temple inscription of the Shwehsandaw Stupa relates.[67] In the same inscription Kyanzittha is compared to King Ashoka Maurya.[68]

Built in 1105 by Kyanzittha in Bagan (Pagan), the Ananda Temple also testifies to the continuity and propinquity of Pala influence.[69] Kyanzitthas first wife was a Bengali (from Pattikera in Southeast Bengal/Samatata?); it was she who had inspired him to build the Abeyadana temple, and he named the temple after her.

That Pala related Buddhism that was flourishing at Kyanzittha's court is demonstrated nowhere more clearly than at the Abeyadana temple, which was built by [for?] Kyanzittha's chief queen, Abeyadana, around 1090. The iconographic program of the temple is a virtual compendium of Mahayana and Tantric Buddhist deities, executed in a purely Pala style.[70]

---

66 On the founding of Pagan see HUNTINGTON, Introduction to Southeast Asia and Southern China, pp. 199-200: "The builders of Pagan's city walls had settled on the Irrawaddy River basin by about the ninth century, but the city did not grow in power until the eleventh century under king Aniruddha ... Today, Pagan is an archaeological treasure house, with its hundreds of temples, images, murals, and other artistic works attesting to its former glories." See also Thomas William RHYS DAVIDS and Caroline Augusta Foley RHYS DAVIDS, *Buddhist Birth Stories (Jataka Tales)*: the commentarial introduction entitled Nidāna-kathā, The story of the lineage, London, Routledge 1925, p. 106.

67 HUNTINGTON, Introduction to Southeast Asia and Southern China, p. 201: "Indeed, contact between Myanmar and Pala India during Kyanzittha's reign is documented by an inscription at the Shwehsandaw Stupa at Prome in Myanmar, which reveals that Kyanzittha sent a Mission to die Mahabodhi Temple at Bodh Gaya. The mission is believed to have taken place around 1098." See also G.E. HARVEY. *History of Burma*. London, Longmans, Green and Co. 1925, p. 30, who relates that King Aniruddha had—possibly together with his general, Kyanzittha—also visited Bengal after a victorious campaign to Arrakan, i.e. "probably Chittagong" (in today's Bangladesh).

68 HUNTINGTON, Introduction to Southeast Asia and Southern China, p. 201: "In the Shwehsandaw Stupa inscription Kyanzittha is compared to Ashoka of the Maurya dynasty."

69 See HUNTINGTON, Introduction to Southeast Asia and Southern China, p. 201: "The ties between the Ananda Temple and the Pala artistic traditions suggest an ongoing, contemporary knowledge of the Pala idioms rather than a holdover from an earlier period of contact."

70 HUNTINGTON, Introduction to Southeast Asia and Southern China, p. 202. See also Swapna BHATTACHARYA, The Ari Cult of Myanmar, in Uta GARTNER and Jens LORENZ, *Tradition and modernity in Myanmar: proceedings*, LIT Verlag Münster, 1994, pp. 264 f.

Curiously, the impact of the Palas, though it had significantly declined and practically ceased to exist, indirectly became prominent once again when the art of the Mahayana Buddhism of Tibet and China, which had been under strong Pala influence, gained a foothold in Burma.[71] On the other hand in Thailand, relatively little can be traced of the influence of the art of the Pala period.[72] In the end it was Sri Lanka, which for the Thai and the Burmese—as opposed to the Tibetans and Chinese—became the source of the pure Buddhist faith; the tradition of Mahayana Buddhism and Tantrism did not continue or develop there anymore.[73]

4. Pala and Suvarnadvipa (Sumatra: Sri Vijaya)

As early as 671 the Chinese monk Yijing (I-ching, 635-713 AD.), enroute from Canton to India, visited Shrivijaya, where he studied Sanskrit grammar for six months.[74] The Chinese name for Shrivijaya was Foshi (*Fo-shih*), while among Indians the name Suvarnadvipa, literally Island (*dvipa*) of gold (*suvarna*), was common. From the capital Palembang in the South of Sumatra, Srivijaya was able to control maritime trade in the Strait of Malacca.[75] The city's slightly inland location on the river Musi was suitable

---

71 See HUNTINGTON, Introduction to Southeast Asia and Southern China, p. 204: "In light of the ultimate rejection of Pala Buddhism, it is interesting that Myanmar Buddhist art eventually experienced the impact of Sino-Tibetan art, which was in turn deeply indebted to the Pala tradition."

72 HUNTINGTON, Introduction to Southeast Asia and Southern China, p. 205: "On the whole the general flavor of Pala art is absent in the artistic traditions of Thailand. However, during two discrete phases associated with two separate regions of the country, Pala stylistic and iconographic influences were felt. In addition to these two primary manifestations, minor elements from the Pala artistic tradition appear occasionally in other schools of Thai art."

73 HUNTINGTON, Introduction to Southeast Asia and Southern China, p. 199: "In contrast to the Tibetans, for example, who saw the Indic Buddhism flourishing in the Pala lands as authentic and worthy of faithful emulation, the Myanmaris and the Thais looked to Sri Lanka as the source of die genuine Buddhist tradition and ultimately eradicated die Pala-based Mahayana and Tantric Buddhism from their kingdoms."

74 R. C. MAJUMDAR, *Hindu Colonies in the Far East*, p. 30: "On his way to India, the pilgrim [Yijing, I-tsing] halted in Sri-Vijaya for six months, and learnt the Sabdavidya (Sanskrit Grammar). During his return journey also he stopped at Sri-Vijaya, and after a short stay in China, he again returned to the same place. Here he was engaged in copying and translating the voluminous Buddhist texts which he had brought with him from India."

75 J. VILLIERS, *Südostasien vor der Kolonialzeit*, p. 93: "Some experts believe that Djambi was of greater importance than Palembang, which, as they claim, was called at only by ships operating between the Straits of Malacca and Java, whereas Djambi was facing the

for trade, among other things, because of an offshore island with a bay and the Selat Bangka Strait (April to October steady southeast wind). Djambi (Jambi), located a little further northwest, also was an important seaport for Srivijaya. It was a time of intense international relations that reached as far east as China and Japan and in the west to Persia, Europe and East Africa.[76] Curiously, the actual "origins of Sri Vijaya are ... very dark," remarks Villiers. It is believed, however, that "a powerful maritime state of that name" had at the end of the 7th century taken over supremacy over the Malacca Straits and "replaced" the ancient Funan Empire in the region.[77] Nonetheless, "The great mercantile empire of Srivijaya remains one of the most enigmatic yet fascinating subjects of Southeast Asian history," writes Huntington.[78]

Through its political and cultural superiority vis-à-vis Sumatra, Java, Borneo and the Malay Peninsula, Srivijaya's Kings were able to exercise control over some of the most lucrative maritime trade routes of Asia which linked China, Southeast Asia, India, the Middle East and East Africa with each other. When the maritime Malay kingdom of Srivijaya is referred to as a coherent sovereign territory with extensive maritime trade relations, the question arises regarding its relationship with India, which traditionally held a prominent position as a maritime trading nation in South and Southeast Asia. The kingdom of Srivijaya was at its peak[79] at about the same time the Palas ruled—around the 8th to 13th centuries. The fact that

---

open sea and therefore formed a perfect seaport."

76 HUNTINGTON, Introduction to Southeast Asia and Southern China, p. 212: "...the maritime empire of Srivijaya played a crucial role in the cross-pollination of Asian culture during a period of intense international activity." See also J. VILLIERS, *Südostasien vor der Kolonialzeit,* p. 95: "The power of Sri Vijaya was based on its international trade relations. The armed forces, the army as well as the Navy, were needed to maintain this power, obtain tributary vassals and subjugate independent rivals." However, it is likely that the "armed forces" were more of a decorative accessory, while trade and cultural exchange were the main components that afforded the key institutions keeping and furthering peace.

77 J. VILLIERS, *Südostasien vor der Kolonialzeit,* p. 93.

78 HUNTINGTON, Introduction to Southeast Asia and Southern China, p. 210.

79 And ibid.: "Holding political and cultural sway over Sumatra, Java, Borneo, and the Malay Peninsula ... the kings of Srivijaya controlled some of the most lucrative maritime routes of Asia, linking China, Southeast Asia, India, the Middle East, and eastern Africa. Although the empire is known as early as the seventh century, its period of greatest power was from the eighth through the thirteenth centuries."

Pala culture at the time, represented by its typical religious figurines and other manifestations, was conveyed by "brave pilgrims, intrepid monks and brave merchants with their riches,"[80] who crossed the sea on numerous Pala merchant ships, is beyond doubt. Historian Villiers resumes:

> It appears that the ships belonged to the rulers, the aristocracy provided the forces and trade was kept going by a large number of merchants from many countries. Rulers and nobility came to wealth and fortune carrying on trade on their own accounts, collecting taxes and duties from the intermediate trade and the trading stations, and from time to time by warfare and buccaneering ... Among the gifts given to the Emperor of China by Sri Vijaya in the 10th century were ivory, incense, rose water, dates, canned peaches, white sugar, bracelets made of rock crystal, glass bottles, mineral oils, coral, cotton fabrics, rhinoceros horns and perfumes; all of which reveal the pattern of the import and transit trade of Sri Vijaya defined by its luxury, rarity and the variety of the countries of origin.[81]

Trade made the kings of Srivijaya rich, not least because of their trade relations with China, India and beyond that Persia, Arabia and Africa.[82] Moreover, they invested their wealth in the maintenance of numerous Buddhist temples and monasteries, the construction and maintenance of which they generously supported, and their capital became a well-known and much frequented palladium of Buddhist learning in the world at the time.[83] Chinese Buddhist scholars and monks, among others, stayed in and near Palembang, in their travels to India, to study in one of the flourishing

---

80 See HUNTINGTON, Introduction to Southeast Asia and Southern China, p. 212: "Carried along on the many ships that traversed the seas were the instruments of the spread of Pala culture—the intrepid pilgrims, monks, and merchants and the treasures they brought with them." See also J. VILLIERS, *Südostasien vor der Kolonialzeit,* p. 95.

81 J. VILLIERS, *Südostasien vor der Kolonialzeit,* p. 95. See also Richard M. EATON, *The Rise of Islam and the Bengal Frontier, 1204-1760,* University of California Press, 1996, pp. 11-12, and A. WINK, *Al-Hind,* vol. 1, The India Trade, Brill 1990, pp. 40 ff., and The Trading Diasporas in the Indian Ocean, pp. 65 ff

82 HUNTINGTON, Introduction to Southeast Asia and Southern China, p. 211: "Because of the flourishing trade within their kingdom and the handsome duties they collected from those who traversed their waters, the kings of Srivijaya became immensely wealthy."

83 HUNTINGTON, Introduction to Southeast Asia and Southern China, p. 211: "Their lavish patronage of Buddhist monasteries is well known from historical sources, and their capital became a center of Buddhist scholarship that was famous throughout the Buddhist world."

monasteries, while they were making preparations for their onward journey to India.

The main Indian port at which the Chinese pilgrims went ashore to take up studies at the universities of Nalanda and Vikramashila, or conversely, from which they returned (via Srivijaya) to China, was Tamralipti (Tamluk) in Bengal. This was the main port of the Palas, with—as Yijing reported—many Buddhist temples and monasteries where thousands of monks resided.[84] Maintenance of the monastery of Nalanda was "provided by an endowment of one hundred villages," the financial support affording "thousands of students" their studies.[85]

Nalanda University ruins, Source: Creative Commons

---

84 Ronald M. DAVIDSON, *Indian Esoteric Buddhism: A Social History of the Tantric Movement*, Colombia University Press, New York, 2002, p. 109, cites the Chinese travellers Hsuan-tsang (Xuanzang, ca. 602-664), and I-Ching (Yijing, 635-713 AD.), who identified several thousand monks who studied in Nalanda. The author continues: "How realistic are these estimates? The surviving site has eight large monasteries … and two smaller ones; these latter are most probably the oldest monasteries built."

85 Romila THAPAR, *The Past and Prejudice*, New Delhi, National Book Trust 2000 (orig. 1975), p. 41: "The income for the monastery at Nalanda was provided by an endowment of one hundred villages, which in part explains how it could accommodate so many thousands of students free of cost."

Yijing (I-ching), having himself spent some time in Srivijaya, therefore advised the studious Chinese monks to interrupt their journey from China to India for one or two years in order to prepare themselves in one of the local monasteries for the study of Sanskrit and Buddhism.[86] Thus the kingdom became a meeting place and centre of activities not only for the Chinese monks, but also for numerous important Indian Buddhists who were drawn there. As early as the seventh century, a certain Dharmapala from Kanchi, who was a professor at the University of Nalanda, had visited Suvarnadvipa. And in the early eighth century Vajrabodhi, a South Indian monk, interrupted his journey from Ceylon to China in Srivijaya, where he remained for five months. Vajrabodhi and his disciple Amoghavajra were both masters of Tantric Buddhism, and are said to have been the first to introduce this important Buddhist school to China and make it known there.[87]

Vajrabodhi was the son of a teacher at the court of the King (*rajaguru*) of Kanchipuram in today's South Indian state of Tamil Nadu. Around the year 720 AD he set out on a voyage to China, carrying with him a major Tantric text in his luggage. The story is that twenty days before he reached Canton on the Chinese coast, the entire fleet of thirty Persian ships sank in a raging tropical storm. Only the boat in which Vajrabodhi was sailing was spared, the monk saving himself and his ship simply by reciting a Buddhist text.[88] Perhaps even more famous, three hundred years after Vajrabodhi,

---

86 HUNTINGTON, Introduction to Southeast Asia and Southern China, p. 211: "After having visited Srivijaya, Yijing (I-tsing) … recommended that all pilgrims from China spend a year or two there [in Srivijaya] before proceeding to India." S. also R. C. MAJUMDAR, *Hindu Colonies in the Far East*, p. 30: "[H]e recommended that 'If a Chinese priest wishes to go to the West in order to hear (lectures) and read (the original), he had better stay here one or two years and practice the proper rules and then proceed to India.'"

87 R. C. MAJUMDAR, *Hindu Colonies in the Far East*, p. 30: "Several eminent Indian Buddhists visited this region [Suvarnadvipa] … For the seventh century A.D. we have a distinguished example in Dharmapala, an inhabitant of Kanchi, and a professor at Nalanda, who visited Suvarnadvipa. Early in the eighth century A.D., Vajrabodhi, a South Indian monk, went from Ceylon to China, stopping for five months at Sri-Vijaya. He and his disciple Amoghavajra, who accompanied him, were teachers of Tantrik cult, and are credited with its introduction in China."

88 Lokesh CHANDRA, Borobudur, *Kebar Seberang*, 1986, No. 18 (Center for Southeast Asian Studies, James Cook University of North Queensland, 1987), p. 34: "[Frederik David Kan] Bosch has proved the close affinity of Indonesian Buddhist iconography with the Shingon iconography of Japan. It is but natural that the two traditions should agree as they represent the same yoga-tantra school of Buddhism. The basic tantra of

Atisa, a Bengali Pandit and reformer of Tibet, and one of the most famous Tantric teachers, spent a full twelve years, from 1013 to 1025, in Srivijaya.[89]

Tantric manifestations of Mahayana Buddhism, Vajrayana and Kalachakra, and "other syncretistic variations" reached Indonesia at a very early date. Villiers lists among others an "old Malay inscription from Sri Vijaya dating from the year 684," according to which "the Vajrayana sect ... was known in Sumatra" and Borobudur was likely to have been "a center of the Vajrayana school" and, not long after, the above-mentioned Vajrabodhi taught the Buddhist Tantra there.[90]

Although our historical knowledge of the kingdom of Srivijaya is extensive and sources are abundant, there are few remaining examples of its art and architecture. "One of the reasons that Sri Vijaya has left so few monuments," says Villiers, "may be found in the fact that as a seafaring and trading nation it simply did not have enough manpower to bother with such grand construction projects as were carried out by the agrarian inland states of Java with their highly complex and static social structure."[91] Even if significant art works and architecture existed, no relevant remains have been excavated because of the use of perishable materials.[92] Nevertheless it

this school was carried to China by Vajrabodhi who arrived in Canton in 720 by the sea route on board a Persian ship. He was the son of the Royal Preceptor (*rajaguru*) of Kanchi. En route they encountered a storm just twenty days before they reached Canton. All the thirty ships were lost, except that which carried Vajrabodhi, who saved it by his recitation of Mahapratisara-dharani."

89 See HUNTINGTON, Introduction to Southeast Asia and Southern China, p. 211: "Atisa, a famous Bengali pandita whose teachings were of profound importance to Tibetan Buddhism, spent twelve years in Srivijaya, from around 1013 to 1025." S. also J. VILLIERS, *Südostasien vor der Kolonialzeit*, p. 56.

90 J. VILLIERS, *Südostasien vor der Kolonialzeit*, p. 56.

91 J. VILLIERS, *Südostasien vor der Kolonialzeit*, p. 95. See also HUNTINGTON, Introduction to Southeast Asia and Southern China, pp. 210-211. "Major commodities in this intercontinental trade included Chinese ceramics, which were highly prized by the Persians; Persian luxury goods, which were eagerly sought by the Chinese; and products from India and Southeast Asia, such as spices, silks, aromatic woods and even elephants."

92 HUNTINGTON, Introduction to Southeast Asia and Southern China, p. 211: "One very likely reason for the lack of surviving Srivijayan monuments is that the architects and artists may have used perishable materials, such as wood, in the creation of their works, rather than more durable materials like stone. Thus the buildings and images they fabricated would have deteriorated over the centuries and ultimately vanished. It should be recalled that virtually no architecture survives from the Pala period, when brick and presumably wood were the most important construction materials."

is surprising in the light of the monumental buildings of the Sailendra on Java, especially the splendiferous Borobudur.[93]

5. The History of Java before the Pala Era—Hinduism and Buddhism

According to historian R.C. Majumdar, Java was first colonized by Indian Hindus in the first century AD.[94] Among other references he cites a Javanese tradition according to which around 56 AD a prince from Gujarat named Aji Saka established the first Hindu state and introduced the Indian calendar. The mention of Java as "Java Dion" (Javadvipa = Java Island) by Claudius Ptolemy (c. 100-170 AD) shows that the Indian name was already well-known; around 132 AD, a Javanese king by the Indian name Devavarnam is supposed to have sent an embassy to China.[95] Majumdar states:

> Another report, this time from A.D. 132, and again a Chinese source, reveals more interesting information. It says that a king of 'Ye-tiao' sent an embassy to the emperor of China to offer tribute. We must not attach too much importance to the expression 'to offer tribute', for the Chinese were accustomed to regard every present sent to His Celestial Majesty as a token of submission. The name 'Ye-tiao' has been explained as a Chinese transcription

93 And ibid.: "Although a great deal is known about Srivijaya from historical and epigraphic sources, virtually nothing is known about its artistic traditions. Scholars have long puzzled over the lack of correspondence between the historical information and the archeological record, for it is certain that the kingdom's prosperity would have fostered generous patronage of religious establishments not only by the royal family but also by the laity. It has been hypothesized that the Srivijayans were more' concerned with commercial ventures than artistic ones ... The absence of evidence of major architectural and artistic achievements in Sumatra is especially puzzling in light of the legacy of extraordinary artistic accomplishments of the Sailendras in Java. One need only think of Barabudur, a Sailendra production that is rightfully considered to be one of the most impressive architectural monuments in the world."

94 A detailed description of the colonization of Java can be found in R. C. MAJUMDAR, *Ancient Indian Colonies in the Far East*, vol. ii, Suvarnadvipa, Dacca 1937, pp. 94-104.

95 And ibid., pp. 21-22 (pp. 18-19 in the 1944 edition): "A tradition preserved in Java, in a late period, seems to refer the foundation of the Hindu State to A.D. 56. The Javanese era, commencing from Aji Saka, starts from 78 A.D., the epoch of the Saka era in India." In the expanded 1963 edition, there are also the following sentences: "Ptolemy in the second century A.D. refers to the island as Javadion (Javadvipa) which shows that the Indian name of the island was much earlier. But in any case the Hindus must have established their authority in Java by the beginning of the second century A.D., for in 132 A.D., king Devavarman of Java sent an embassy to China."

of 'Yavadvipa', and the name of its king, given in the Chinese text as 'Tiao-pien', as a transcription of the Sanskrit name 'Devavarman'. The latter seems rather dubious, but the first transcription is generally accepted.—This name gives us a clue to further information on the early history of the Indies. 'Yavadvipa' is a Sanskrit name which means 'Millet Island' and is found in the Hindu epic of the *Ramayana*. The epic mentions 'Yavadvipa', 'adorned by seven kingdoms, the Gold and Silver Island, rich in gold mines', as one of the most remote parts of the earth.[96]

According to another source, residents of Kalinga (now Orissa) also colonized Java, when a prince from Kling (Kalinga) sent twenty thousand families to Java, where they settled and increased in number. However, the living conditions seemed difficult for a time, because only in the year 289 of the Saka era, when another prince, by the name of Kano, appeared were they able to accomplish their life's work and find fulfilment.[97] About this Kano, however, nothing more is known.

A few centuries later thousands of settlers from Gujarat in Northwest India are said to have settled in Java. Sir Stamford Raffles, discoverer of Borobudur and British Lieutenant Governor of Java from 1811 to 1814, describes the 'Exodus' of the Gujaratis as follows:

> In the year 525 (Saka era = 603 A.D.), it being foretold to a king of Gujarat that his country would decay and go to ruin, he resolved to send his son to Java. He embarked with about 5000 followers in 6 large and about 100 small vessels, and after a voyage of four months reached an island they supposed to be Java; but finding themselves mistaken, re-embarked, and finally settled at Matarem, in the center of the island they were seeking. ... The prince now found that men alone were wanting to make a great and flourishing state. He accordingly applied to Gujarat for assistance, when his father, delighted

---

96 R. C. MAJUMDAR, *Hindu Colonies in the Far East,* p. 37.

97 Donald Maclaine CAMPBELL, *Java: past & present: a description of the most beautiful country in the world, its ancient history, people, antiquities, and product,* W. Heinemann 1915, pp. 31-32: "[T]wenty thousand families were sent to Java by the prince of Kling [Kalinga]. These people prospered and multiplied. They continued, however, in an uncivilized state till the year 289 (of Javanese era i.e. Saka era) when the almighty blessed them with a prince, named Kano." R. C. MAJUMDAR, *Hindu Colonies in the Far East,* p. 18. (1944 edition, 1963 edition: p. 21) "The Hindu colonization of Java is by far the most outstanding event in the early history of that island. Many legends associate the original colonists and their leader Aji Saka with the heroes of the heroes of the Mahabharata ruling at Astina, i.e. Hastinapura, as their capital."

at his success, sent him a reinforcement of 2000 people ... From this period Java was known and celebrated as a kingdom; an extensive commerce was carried on with Gujarat and other countries, and the bay of Matarem was filled with adventurers from all parts.[98]

The Buddhist Jatakas are also a valuable historical resource. Some stories tell of voyages between India and Suvarnabhumi that apparently took place in pre-Christian times. One of the Jatakas tells of the King of Videha the capital of which was Mithila. After he was defeated in a war with hostile neighbours and killed in action, the widowed queen fled with her belongings to Champa (Bhagalpur). When their son became of age he made the proposal to his mother: "Give half your treasure to me and I will go to Suvarnabhumi, get great riches there and then seize back my paternal kingdom." He was able to secure a place on a merchant ship as a passenger, and reaching Suvarnabhumi was successful in his business and after some time recaptured Mithila.[99]

The following Jataka story tells of a conclave of carpenters near the city of Benares, who had received news about the island located beyond the sea. The whole clan decided now to construct a large ship and sail down the Ganges and across the open sea to the island. "In that island grew wild all manner of plants and fruit trees, rice, sugar-cane, banana, mango, rose-apple, jack [fruit], coconut and other fruits." There they founded a settlement.[100]

Another story tells of the son of a shipmaster from the aforementioned seaport Bharukachchha (Bharuch, or Broach, in Gujarat), who had learned the art of seafaring at an early age. When his father died, he became

---

98 Sir Stamford RAFFLES, *History of Java*, London, Black, Parbury, and Allen 1817, pp. 87 ff., quoted in *The Periplus of the Eritraean Sea*, p. 245.

99 R. C. MAJUMDAR, *Hindu Colonies in the Far East*, pp. 9-10: "Several Buddhist Jataka stories which were probably current long before the Christian era refer to voyages between India and Suvarna-bhumi ... : — (1) A king of Videha being defeated and killed in battle, the widowed queen fled in disguise to Champa (Bhagalpur) with her treasures ... [Eventually he went on] board a ship with some merchants bound for Suvarnabhumi. ... [and finally] regained the kingdom of Mithila."

100 R. C. MAJUMDAR, *Hindu Colonies in the Far East*, p. 10: "Near the city of Benares was a great town of carpenters, containing a thousand families who decided to go to a foreign land. The carpenters cut down trees from forest, built a mighty ship and launched her in the river. Having put their families on board the ship, they proceeded in due course to the ocean."

commander and chief of the local sailors' union. Under his leadership, the ventures on the open sea were successful and travellers always survived the dangers they encountered without coming to harm. Unfortunately, the shipmaster went blind as a result of the frequent exposure of his eyes to the salt water. Yet, when a freshly equipped merchant ship set sail to go to sea, he was the one to be hired, because he was still the best pilot to undertake the passage. The blind skipper was able to lead numerous merchants across the sea, and always escort them back safely to the home port with their abundant treasure of gold, diamonds, silver, emeralds and coral.[101]

Similar tales of travels to distant Java are told in other scriptures, such as the *Brihatkatha* collection of writings that originated in pre-Christian days. This hoard of ancient Indian stories tells, among other things, of an adventurer named Sanudasa whose famous story was told and retold in the world at the time. They give us a glimpse of what life may have been like in those days.[102]

It was only later that Buddhists reached the country. According to Chinese sources, at the start of the 5th century AD Buddhism was practically non-existent in Java. However, there were already many Brahmins living there, and so in the beginning it was Brahmanism that was politically and culturally dominant.[103] It did not take long, however, and Hinduism and Buddhism existed side by side or in mixed form in Java and elsewhere in Southeast Asia. In any case, as Dutch historian Johannes Nicolaas Krom has pointed out, all this was most likely primarily a matter for elites, whose

101 R. C. MAJUMDAR, *Hindu Colonies in the Far East*, p. 10: "There was a sea-port town named Bharukachchha (Broach in Gujarat). The son of the master-mariner in that city gained at an early age a complete mastery over the art of seamanship. Afterwards when his father died he became the head of the mariners and plied the mariner's calling. He was wise, and with him on board, no ship ever came to harm. Unfortunately it so happened that injured by the salt water both his eyes lost their sight. But still when some merchants had got ready a ship and were looking out for a skipper they selected the blind mariner. Passing through many seas and braving many perils the merchants were brought back with a rich cargo of diamonds, gold, silver, emeralds and coral."

102 R. C. MAJUMDAR, *Hindu Colonies in the Far East*, p. 10: "Similar stories of mercantile voyages to Suvarnadvipa are told in the Brihatkatha, another treasure-house of old Indian stories, dating from a period before the Christian era. The most interesting of all is, however, the adventurous story of Sanudasa..."

103 See N.-R. RAY, *Sanskrit Buddhism in Burma*, p. 8: "When Fa-hien visited Java (from Ceylon) in about 412 A.D., there were many Brahmins in the island, and Buddhism was practically of no importance. In fact, Java was mostly given up to Brahmanism till it came under the political and cultural domination of the Sumatran empire of Srivijaya."

dispositions and preferences were subject to constant change.

Finally, the Chinese sources also give evidence of a Kashmiri prince named Gunavarman who is said to have introduced Buddhism in Java. R.C. Majumdar likewise reports, that "Buddhism soon made its influence felt in Java," as shown by the story of Gunavarman, "preserved in 'Kao seng tchouan' or 'biography of famous monks' [a Chinese work], compiled in A.D. 519."[104] The Prince (ch. Ki-pin) from Kashmir had from childhood taken an interest in religious matters. When the king of Kashmir died without heir, Gunavarman was offered the throne but, having just turned thirty years old, declined the offer, first travelling to Ceylon and then a little later on to Java, where he succeeded in converting the Queen Mother, and subsequently also the King to Buddhism. When Java was attacked by enemy forces, the king asked Gunavarnam if it would be contrary to the Buddhist law (Dharma) to enter into the war and fight back against the attackers. Gunavarman replied that it was a human duty to punish the thieves, and so the King took up the fight and won a great victory. Little by little Buddhism spread all over the land.[105] Majumadar continues:

> The king now wished to take to the life of a monk, but was dissuaded from this course by his ministers, on the express condition, that henceforth no living creatures should be killed through the length and breadth of the kingdom ... The name and fame of Gunavarman had now spread in all directions. In A.D. 424 the Chinese monks requested their emperor to invite Gunavarman to China. Accordingly the Chinese emperor sent messengers to Gunavarman and the king of Java. Gunavarman embarked on a vessel, owned by the Hindu merchant Nandin, and reached Nankin in A.D. 431. A few months later he died at the age of sixty-five ... The story of Gunavarman shows how Buddhism was introduced and then gradually took root in Java in the fifth century A.D. The accounts left by I-ching [Yijing, 635-713] leave

---

104 R. C. MAJUMDAR, *Hindu Colonies in the Far East*, p. 29.

105 R. C. MAJUMDAR, *Hindu Colonies in the Far East*, p. 29: "Gunavarman, a prince of Kashmir (Ki-pin), was of a religious mood from his boyhood. When he was thirty years old, the king of Kashmir died without issue and the throne was offered to him. But he rejected the offer and went to Ceylon. Later he proceeded to Java and converted the queen-mother to Buddhism. Gradually the king, too, was persuaded by his mother to adopt the same faith. At this time Java was attacked by hostile troops and the king asked Gunavarman whether it would be contrary to the Buddhist law if he fought against his enemy. Gunavarman replied that it was the duty of everybody to punish the robbers. The king then went to fight and obtained a great victory. Gradually the Buddhist religion was spread throughout the country."

no doubt that towards the close of the seventh century A.D. Buddhism had spread over other regions.[106]

With the arrival of the Pala Dynasty relations with India became stronger.

> It is possible that the association with Bengal arose naturally as a byproduct of Indonesian interactions with the Pala lands. Ships from the islands of Indonesia are likely to have travelled to ports of Bengal, and passengers on such ships, such as those destined for Nalanda, would have had to travel through Bengal to reach Bihar. Thus, the Bengal region is likely to have played a crucial role in the interactions between the Pala world and Indonesia. An eighth century image from Java shows unmistakable affiliations to the eastern Bengal tradition.[107]

A Kelurak inscription in Central Java from the year 782 AD commends the Pandit Kumaraghosa from Bengal (*Gaudidvipa* or *Gaudavisaya*), who was supposed to have been responsible for the consecration of a statue in the temple of Manjusri Candi Sewu, located not far from Jogjakarta.[108] An undated inscription in the Candi Plaosan temple dating from the first half of the 9th century informs that the temple consecrated to the Buddha was built to accommodate the continuing flow of pilgrims from the country Gurjara (*satata-gurjara-desa-samagata*).[109] Gurjaradesa could either again

---

106 Ibid., p. 29.

107 HUNTINGTON, Introduction to Southeast Asia and Southern China, p. 209.

108 See Karl-Heinz GOLZIO, *Die Ausbreitung des Buddhismus in Süd- und Südostasien: Eine quantitative Untersuchung auf der Basis epigraphischer Quellen* (The spread of Buddhism in South and Southeast Asia: A quantitative investigation on the basis of epigraphic sources), Peter Lang, 2010, p. 96.

109 Dr. Caesar VOÛTE, the residing UNESCO/UNDP Coordinator for the Borobudur Reconstruction Project from 1971 bis 1975, writes in a publication, *Travelling the Silk Road*, 2005: "Equally important for a better understanding of Borobudur is that other question, dealing with the extent to which the design and construction of the many ancient Hindu and Buddhist sanctuaries and monuments of Central Java are largely the exclusive work of the Javanese themselves. A number of other archaeologists and art historians, however, have expressed an opposite assumption, suggesting that more or less important sources of religious and artistic inspiration and architectural traditions and knowledge, including even some construction techniques, were imported from abroad, in particular from India, from where according to some authors the Shailendra dynasty also originated. Candi Kalasan is an often cited example, since the Kalasan inscription mentions a guru (religious teacher and learned man) who introduced in the Shailendra kingdom the worship of the Buddhist goddess Tara to which the temple of Kalasan is dedicated. This guru was most probably the same one as the guru Kumaraghosa mentioned in the Kelurak inscription as being involved in the foundation of Candi

be referring to Gujarat or the Kingdom of the Gurjara Pratiharas in central Northern India.[110]

How far-reaching the overseas connections and how interconnected the numerous Buddhist centres were becomes clear when one considers that in 752 the Daibutsu Mahavairocana in Nara was consecrated by an Indian monk, Baramon Sojo, whose exact origin, however, is unknown. A biography was compiled by his student Shuei and recorded in a stone monument for Baramon Sojo from India (*Nan Tenjiku Baramon Sojo Hi*) as well as at the Daian-ji Temple in an unofficial record of Todai-ji temple (*Todaiji Yoroku*) in Nara, in the *Daianji Bodai Denraiki* (introduction to enlightenment—bodhi).[111]

6. The Shailendra and the Palas

The Buddhist Shailendra came into power in Java at roughly the same time the Buddhist Sri Vijaya dynasty in Sumatra ruled, and was flourishing through its extensive trade with various commodities, mainly fabrics, jewels, raw silver, ivory, elephants, exotic woods, spices, amber and camphor.[112] The kingdom in Central Java, which was dominated by the

Sewu. That guru came from Gaudidvipa (or Gauda or Gudavisaya), the state of Bengal (Vangala) ruled by Pala kings who especially venerated the goddess Tara. One of her temples, also an important pilgrimage site, was at Nalanda, with which the Shailendra kings maintained close relations." (Roy JORDAAN, 1997 and Lokesh CHANDRA 1995). See also Vadime ELISSEEFF, *The Silk Roads: Highways of Culture and Commerce*, Berghahn 1998, p. 62. See also H. KULKE, Indian Colonies, Indianization, or Cultural Convergence?, p. 31.

110 According to Pauline C. M. Lunsingh SCHEURLEER und Marijke J. KLOKKE, *Ancient Indonesian Bronzes: A Catalogue of the Exhibition in the Rijksmuseum Amsterdam with a General Introduction*, Brill Archive, 1988, p. 6, the Candi Plaosan Temple is "said to be visited by people who were continuously arriving from Gurjaradesa, which might refer to Gujarat in western India or to the kingdom of the *Gurjara* Pratiharas in central North India."

111 "His biography was recorded in 'NanTenjiku Baramon Sojo Hi' (Stone Monument for Baramon Sojo [high Buddhist priest Barahman] from India) compiled by his disciple Shuei, and in 'Daianji Bodai Denraiki' (Introduction of bodhi at Daian-ji Temple) of 'Todaiji Yoroku' (the Digest Record of Todai-ji Temple)." Online: http://ejje.weblio.jp/con tent/%E5%A9%86%E7%BE%85%E9%96%80%E5%A4%A9.

112 See J. VILLIERS, *Südostasien vor der Kolonialzeit*, p. 96: "Around the time when Sri Vijaya was nearing the apex of its power and prosperity, a Buddhist dynasty that came to be known as the Sailendra dynasty, ruled in Central Java over a kingdom called Mataram. It seems that it came to power between 732, when a sivaistic ruler, Sanjaya, ruled and 778, when 'Chandi Kalasan' was built, where the name Sailendra appears for

Shailendras, was known as the Kingdom of Mataram or Medang. The question of the origin of the Shailendra is still unsolved.[113] The dynasty was established between 732 and 778 AD during the reign of the Shaivite 'Pirate King' Sanjaya (732-750). The name "Shailendra" actually means "king of the mountain," perhaps not entirely coincidentally also an epithet of the Hindu god Shiva.

The concept of a "Sacred Mountain," which is well known in the Mediterranean region, too, also plays an equally prominent role in Asia, in China and Japan.

> The merging of Indian religious concepts into the indigenous beliefs, which took place all over Southeast Asia, is made very clear through the development of the idea of the 'Sacred Mountain'. In all of Southeast Asia the 'Sacred Mountain' emerges, revered as the resting place of the souls of the departed, and especially as a residence of the oldest ancestors.[114]

Villiers suggests that the Buddhist Sailendra were "descendants of the lords of Funan."[115] Because the Sailendra on Java, just like the rulers of Funan before them, also referred to themselves as as 'Kings of the Mountains',

> It was not very difficult to identify these sacred mountains with the Hindu *Mahameru* or 'mountain of the heavens in the center of the universe', on which the gods themselves were thought to be residing. Java and Cambodia bear witness to this relationship in detail. The Javanese and Khmer temples were both built as very accurate reproductions of Mahameru. They were subjected

---

the first time."

113 On the origin of the Sailendra see Roy E. JORDAAN, Why the Sailendras were not a Javanese Dynasty, *Indonesia and the Malay World*, vol. 34, no. 98 (March 2006), p. 3: "But the unsolved question preying on the minds of scholars for many decades now is the origins of this dynasty."

114 J. VILLIERS, *Südostasien vor der Kolonialzeit*, p. 50. See also ibid., pp. 50-51: "In Bali at first Gunung Panulisan was the sacred Mountain, later ... the Gunung Agung; the Burmese revered Mount Popa, and in Northern Borneo the mountain Kinabaluu, Southeast Asia's highest mountain, was regarded as the Holy Mountain."

115 J. VILLIERS, *Südostasien vor der Kolonialzeit*, p. 96: "Before the appearance of the Sailendra king Indra in the late 8th century nine rulers [are likely to] have existed ... they had bridged the period between the fall of Funan and the year 752, when the first known Sailendra king [Bhanu] appeared." See however also pp. 100-101: "R.C. Majumdar, the well-known Indian historian, took the view that the Sailendra did not descend from the rulers of Funan, but from the Saila- and Ganga dynasties of Kalinga and Orissa in India, they conquered Sri Vijaya, and then, after 775, also Java."

to strict laws of symmetry, geometry and earth-related divination.[116]

Evidently the coexistence and even synthesis of Shaivism and Buddhism was a typical feature of the culture of Southeast Asia. Thus the Shaivite phallus, the *Linga*, also symbolizes the mountain of the gods, *Mahameru*, which is also important in Mahayana Buddhism and frequently found in Khmer buildings and temples such as the Chandi Singosari (Candi Singhasari) on Java. "Both represent the axle of the cosmos, both being sources of the elixir of immortality."[117]

In addition to the Javanese inscriptions, which mention the Shailendra—the earliest from Batang in Central Java dates back to 725—it is worth taking into account extra-Javanese inscriptions such as the early inscription from Ligor (775 AD) on the Malay Peninsula, written in Sanskrit;[118] or an Indian inscription from the University of Nalanda, dating from 860, which mentions the Shailendra. The Chandi Kalasan Temple, erected in the second half of the eighth century AD, and located near the Borobudur, is dedicated to the goddess Tara, especially venerated in Bengal. The famous Kalasan inscription has been written by the Shailendras themselves, bearing impressive witness to their Buddhist beliefs.[119] The inscription states that "the Maharajah Pananikarana,[120] the 'adornment of the Sailendra' [and presumably initially a vassal prince of Sanjaya], at the

---

116 J. VILLIERS, *Südostasien vor der Kolonialzeit,* p. 51.

117 J. VILLIERS, *Südostasien vor der Kolonialzeit,* p. 52.

118 N.-R. RAY, *Sanskrit Buddhism in Burma,* p. 11: "The earliest dated Sailendra record from the Malay Peninsula hails from Ligor. It is written in Sanskrit, and records the erection of three brick temples dedicated by a Sailendra king to the Sakyamuni and his two associates, Padmapani and Vajrapani. The inscription is dated in the Saka year 697 which corresponds to 775 A.D."

119 N.-R. RAY, *Sanskrit Buddhism in Burma,* p. 11: "The earliest dated Sailendra inscription from Java is also a Mahayana document. It is the celebrated Kalasan inscription, dated in the Saka year 700 (= 778 A.D.), which records the erection of a temple dedicated to the goddess Tara, at the instance of the Sailendra king of Srivijaya. The temple of Kalasan which stands to this day not very far from the magnificent Barabudur, it is certainly that temple of Tara referred to in the inscription."

120 "The association of Śailēndra with Mahayana Buddhism began after the conversion of Panaraban or Panangkaran to Buddhism. This theory is based on the *Carita Parahyangan,* which tells of the ailing King Sanjaya ordering his son, Rakai Panaraban or Panangkaran, to convert to Buddhism ... The conversion of Panangkaran to Buddhism also corresponds to the Raja Sankhara inscription, which tells of a king named Sankhara (identified as Panangkaran) converting to Buddhism because his Shaiva faith was feared by the people." (Wikipedia, Sailendra)

request of his spiritual masters, donated a sanctuary to the Buddhist deity Tara."[121]

It was then especially the Shailendra King Indra (782-812) who presumably was not only pursuing "an aggressive foreign policy" (with a similar approach to trade), but also initiated the construction of numerous Buddhist temples such as the Chandi Mendut, Pawon, Borobudur and other Buddhist buildings of Central Java.[122] The construction of the Borobudur was completed under the reign of Indra's son Samaratunga (812-833).

> The appearance of the [Sailendra][123] ... is an event of great importance for the origin of Borobudur since it is this dynasty which established Mahayana Buddhism and caused Hindu worshippers who had constructed the Dieng temples to move eastward.[124]

The Shailendra developed quickly to become the largest naval commercial power in Southeast Asia, entering into close relationship not only with the cultural and commercial centres of India (especially the Ganges area) but also with more distant neighbours to the east, Tang dynasty China in particular, and the west (the Middle East) with the Abassid Caliphate. In the years 860 and 873, the Chinese emperor sent a diplomatic mission to

---

121 J. VILLIERS, *Südostasien vor der Kolonialzeit,* p. 96, gives part of the inscription about the foundation dedicated to the goddess Tara.

122 S. also Roy E. JORDAAN, Tara and Nyai Lara Kidul: images of the divine feminine in Java, *Asian Folklore Studies,* Vol. 56, No. 2 (Oct. 1997), p. 287 (285-312): "The Sailendras are connected with the building of many Buddhist shrines—of which Borobudur is the best known—in Central Java during the late-eighth and the first half of the ninth centuries. Very little is known of this period of nearly a hundred years (known in the literature as the 'Sailendra Interregnum') other than the remains of temples and a few inscriptions. Thus the origin of the Sailendras is still a great mystery..." S. also R. C. MAJUMDAR, *Hindu Colonies in the Far East,* p. 33: "Suvarnadvipa, or the greater part of it, achieved a political unity as integral parts of an empire, and we shall see later, how this empire rose to a height of glory and splendor unknown before. But the Sailendras did more than this. They introduced a new type of culture. The new vigor of the Mahayana form of Buddhism, and the highly developed art which produced such splendid monuments as Chandi Kalasan and Barabudur in Java, may be mainly attributed to their patronage."

123 Was the appearance of the Buddhist Sailendra the cause for the exodus of the Hindu population? J. VILLIERS, *Südostasien vor der Kolonialzeit,* pp. 97-98: "It might have been the seizure of power by the Sailendra, which drove the conservative Hindu population, whose presence on the Dieng Plateau in Central Java is testified by the oldest temples, to the east of the island."

124 J. DUMARÇAY, *Borobudur,* p. 3.

Java.[125]

> The emergence of the Sailendras as the leading naval power in Indonesia constituted an international event of outstanding importance. The Arab merchant Sulayman narrates a romantic story of the conquest of Kambuja [Cambodia] by the Sailendra king and concludes by saying that 'this incident raised the king (of Zabag)[126] in the estimation of the rulers of India and China'.[127]

That the clan of the Shailendra could achieve such dominance so quickly had probably to do primarily with their access to the Indian Buddhist sources and masters and their continued cultural (and economic) influence. The last ruler of the Javanese interregnum of the Shailendra, Balaputra (832-860),[128] in particular had a close relationship to the University of Nalanda in the Ganges region. Being the most famous such establishment of that time Nalanda produced some of the greatest thinkers of the era, and

---

125 J. DUMARÇAY, *Borobudur,* p. 3: "An echo of this visit can be found in the *New History of the T'ang* which says that the Javanese 'make fortifications of wood, and even the big houses are covered in palm thatch. They have ivory beds and matting made of the bark of bamboo. The country produces tortoise shell, gold, silver, rhinoceros horns and ivory. ... They have an alphabet and have a knowledge of astronomy.'"

126 Zabag could be a collective term for Java and Sumatra or the region around the Strait of Malacca, perhaps also Javaka or Savaka. R. C. MAJUMDAR, *Hindu Colonies in the Far East,* p. 34: "The Sailendra empire is referred to by various Arab writers, who designate it as Zabag, Zabaj, or the empire of the Maharaja, and describe its wealth and grandeur in glowing terms. It is quite clear from these accounts that the authority of the king of Zabag extended over nearly the whole of Suvarnadvipa, and possibly also, for some time, over die two mighty Hindu kingdoms of Suvarnabhumi, viz., Kambuja (Cambodia) and Champa (Annam)." And pp. 35-36: "the most detailed account of Zabag is furnished by Abu Zayd Hasan who published, about A.D. 916, the account originally written by Sulayman in 851 A.D., with additional remarks of his own. He applied the name Zabag both to the kingdom and its capital city." MAJUMDAR states further: "The distance between Zabag and China is one month's journey by sea-route. It may even be less if the winds are favorable ... The town of Kalah [not Keddah?] is the most important commercial center for trade in aloe, camphor, sandalwood, ivory, tin, ebony, spices, and various other articles. There was a regular maritime intercourse between this port and Oman."

127 R. C. MAJUMDAR, *Hindu Colonies in the Far East,* p. 34.

128 "According to the portrayal in an inscription from Nalanda (India) Samaragraira (aka Samaratunga) married Princess Tara of Srivijaya, apparently the daughter of king Dharmasetsu (reigned around 775). From the union issued his youngest son Balaputra. Balaputra was expelled from Java and about 850 took over the government in Srivijaya, because his mother was from there." (German Wikipedia, Sailendra, my translation)

perhaps of all time.[129]

It was this Balaputra, the son of Samaratunga and his Sri Vijaya-born wife Tara, who, according to a copper plate inscription from Nalanda, probably left or had to leave Java well before the year 851 in order to take over dominion in Sri Vijaya.

This inscription tells of Balaputra's generous grant of "revenues from five villages for the comfort of the monks and for the upkeep of a monastery."[130] However, close contact must already have been established, facilitated by the commercial and cultural activities of the Palas, even before relations with India intensified. Beyond doubt India remained in many ways at the heart of the international order at that time.

> Balaputra's choice of Nalanda as the recipient of his gift was probably not random or unprecedented. Javanese metal images of the Sailendra period, that is, the eighth and ninth centuries, prior to Balaputra's departure for Sumatra, already show close affiliation with metal images from Nalanda, and *Balaputra's gift to Nalanda probably reflected an already established relationship between his family and this renowned Buddhist institution. Further, since the vast majority of metal images from Indonesia have been found on Java, not Sumatra, it must be assumed that Javanese ties to Nalanda were strong prior to his departure and continued to be so even after he left.*[131]

In spite of the close relationship between the Shailendras and Sri Vijaya due to Samaragravira's (Samaratunga) marriage with the Shrivijayan Princess Tara resulting in the birth of their son Balaputra—who was eventually to become king of Sri Vijaya—no Javanese artefacts reflecting the culture and

---

129 HUNTINGTON, Introduction to Southeast Asia and Southern China, p. 209.

130 HUNTINGTON, Introduction to Southeast Asia and Southern China, pp. 208-209: "It is likely that Balaputra had left Java a few years earlier, for by about 851 he was already king of Srivijaya, as may be inferred from an inscription on a copperplate grant found at Nalanda monastery in the Pala lands. This inscription records a grant of the revenues from five villages for the comfort of the monks and for the upkeep of a monastery at Nalanda by King Balaputradeva of Suvarnadvipa, whose father and grandfather are identified as Sailendra kings of Java. The inscription is dated in the thirty-ninth regal year of King Devapala (ca. 851), who sanctioned the gift. Since Balaputra is called a king in that inscription, it is apparent that he had left Java even before 851. The term Suvarnadvipa is well known from Sanskrit sources to refer to Sumatra."

131 HUNTINGTON, Introduction to Southeast Asia and Southern China, p. 209. (Emphasis added)

architecture of the Shailendra are to be found in present-day Sumatra.[132]

> The decline of the power of the Sailendra in Central Java in the late 9th
> century was accompanied by a resurgence of Hindu cults in this area [Java],
> confirmed by the huge complex of the 190 temples of Lara Djonggrang (in
> Prambanan) ... Samaratunga, son of Indra, was the last Sailendra who ruled
> in Java.[133]

Perhaps already,

> towards 820 the Hindus who had migrated to the east regained power by
> reuniting central and east Java ... Hindu renaissance showed itself in the
> construction of the whole ensemble of Prambanan, the consecration date
> of which is 856. In spite of the return of Hinduism, *which must have been
> accompanied by a new cultural wave from India,* Buddhism continued to
> flourish.[134]

The Prambanan temple complex, built in the second half of the 9th
century, located 16 kilometers north-east of Yogyakarta and situated in
the Prambanan Valley (dedicated to the Hindu trinity Brahma, Vishnu
and Shiva) was home not only of Hindu, but also Buddhist temples.[135]

---

132 HUNTINGTON, Introduction to Southeast Asia and Southern China, p. 211: "Although
the histories of the Sailendras in Java and the kings of Srivijaya are inextricably linked
through Balaputra, prince of the Sailendras and subsequently king of Srivijaya, it is
difficult to trace the Sailendra legacy in Sumatra. If indeed Balaputra and his successors
in Sumatra built monuments based on the Sailendra tradition, apparently none were
comparably enduring. Major Srivijayan architectural achievements also have not been
found elsewhere in the Srivijayan empire, such as the Malay Peninsula ... However,
historical records document construction of religious buildings by Srivijayans. For
example, although not built within his kingdom, King Balaputra's gift to Nalanda
signifies that the king patronized Buddhist establishments and suggests that he is likely
to have made gifts at home as well." See also R. C. MAJUMDAR, *Hindu Colonies in the
Far East,* pp. 34-35: "By the middle of the ninth century A.D., their [the Sailendras]
supremacy was successfully challenged by the two great neighboring states of Kambuja
and Java. The Kambuja king Jayavarman II (802-850 A.D.) threw off the yoke of the
Sailendras, and there is no evidence that the latter had any pretensions of supremacy
over the kingdom after Jayavarman's time. About the same time, the Sailendras lost their
hold on Java. Unfortunately we know almost nothing of the circumstances which led to
the loss of the kingdom some time before 879 A.D."

133 J. VILLIERS, *Südostasien vor der Kolonialzeit,* p. 98.

134 J. DUMARÇAY, Borobudur, p. 3.

135 Hans BRÄKER, *Indonesien* (Indonesia), Freiburg i.Br., Walter-Verlag Olten 1987,
pp. 181 and 193: "In 1549 the Prambanan ... was completely destroyed by a massive
earthquake. Once this temple compound is restored, it will be a lot larger than the

Prambanan Temple, Java, Indonesia. Source: http://viralscape.com/
airplane-views

Alongside the Hindu temple complex Chandi Kalasan and Chandi Sari stands the Chandi Sevu complex, apart from Borobudur Java's largest Buddhist sanctuary.[136] The main temple in the center of the sacred area of the Prambanan Valley was surrounded by smaller temples that were arranged in several rows around the center.[137]

Buddhist Borobudur sanctuary. The temples, arranged in two rows, are dedicated to the Hindu Trinity, Shiva, Vishnu and Brahma. The Shiva temple is the most important of the three temples on the west side. ... With a height of 47 meters, it towers above all the others temples significantly. ... Opposite the three major temples on the east side of the compound, stand three smaller religious buildings for the vehicles of the gods, the Nandi bull (Shiva), the Garuda bird (Vishnu) and the Hansa-Swan (Brahma)." See also R. C. MAJUMDAR, *Hindu Colonies in the Far East,* pp. 104-105: "A famous group of Buddhist temples lies in Prambanan valley which forms a rich treasure-house of the products of the art of Central Java. The region stands on the border of the modern districts of Jogyakerta and Surakerta. It was a seat of one or more cities or capitals, and not merely a city of temples like Dieng."

136 R. C. MAJUMDAR, *Hindu Colonies in the Far East,* p. 105: "The most notable temples in this region are Chandi Kalasan, Chandi Sari and Chandi Sevu. Chandi Sevu is the biggest Buddhist sanctuary except Barabudur. A rectangular paved courtyard, measuring about 200 yds. by 180 yds., is surrounded on each side by two rows of temples, altogether 168 in number."

137 R. C. MAJUMDAR, *Suvarnadvīpa: Cultural history,* Gian Publishing House 1986, p. 185, describes the temple complex: "The main temple [im Prambanan-Tal] which occupies the center of the courtyard is ... surrounded by two rows of temples in the form of squares, with 12 and 8 respectively on each side, thus making a total of 72. The main temple is thus surrounded by 240 temples, and there are traces of five more between

Towards the end of the tenth century the Cholas became very powerful in the South Indian state of today's Tamil Nadu and even conquered some parts of Bengal.[138] Although the Cholas first maintained friendly relations with Sri Vijaya,[139] in the year 992 the fleet of the Cholas launched an attack on Sri Vijaya, possibly provoked by a trade dispute, and in 1006 "King Chula (or his son Malavijayottungavarman) invaded East Java, sacked the capital, destroyed the royal palace, and took the rulers prisoner."[140] The fact that an Indian dynasty, the Cholas, launched such an aggressive military operation is unusual given that the cultural penetration of Southeast Asia throughout proceeded for by-far the most part non-violently.

---

the first two and the last two rows. The group thus formed had, again, one anterior temple on each side, at a distance of about 330 yds. There were thus altogether 250 temples including the main temple (Pl. II).—The main temple, situated on an elevated plane, formed the worthy center of this vast complex of sanctuaries, each successive row of which was on a lower plane than the others. The sloping roofs of the vestibules of the first and last rows of temples accentuated the gradual slope and gave a pyramidal appearance to the whole which was probably constructed in the ninth century A.D." The text can also be found in the 1963 edition of R.C. Majumdar, *Hindu Colonies in the Far East*, p. 105. However, I have not been able yet to actually trace this description.

138 R.C. MAJUMDAR, *India and South East Asia,* B.R. Pub. Corp., 1979, p. 63: "The Cholas were also a great naval power and this naturally brought them into contact with Indonesia. At first there existed friendly relations between the Chola kings and the Sailendra rulers. We learn from a Chola inscription that the Sailendra king, Chudamonivarman, commenced the construction of a Buddhist *Vihara* at Nagapattana, modern Negapatam, in or shortly before the 21st year of Rajaraja, when a village was granted by the Chola king for its upkeep." The text is found also in the 1963 edition of *Hindu Colonies in the Far East*, p. 37.

139 See Alaka CHATTOPADHYAYA, *Attisa and Tibet: life and works of Dīpamkara Śrījñāna in relation to the history and religion of Tibet with Tibetan sources transl.under Professor Lama Chimpa,* Delhi, Motilal Banarsidass 1999 (orig. 1967), p. 90.

140 J. VILLIERS, *Südostasien vor der Kolonialzeit,* p. 103. See also R. C. MAJUMDAR, *Hindu Colonies in the Far East,* p. 38: "In any case, hostilities broke out, and Rajendra Chola sent a naval expedition against his mighty adversary beyond the sea. The details preserved in the Chola records leave no doubt that the expedition was crowned with brilliant success, and various parts of the empire of the Sailendras were reduced by the mighty Chola emperor. – It appears that the chief stronghold of the Sailendra power at this time was Kataha or Kadara (Kedda in Malay Peninsula), and they also exercised suzerainty over Sri-Vijaya and other smaller States in Sumatra, Malay Peninsula and the neighboring islands. Rajendra Chola defeated the Sailendra king, conquered ten or eleven of these States specifically named in the records, and concluded the campaign by taking Kadara itself." On p. 39 MAJUMDAR gives the reasons for attack of the Cholas!

7. The Predominance of the Pala Culture in Jambudvipa (Java)

The educational institutions of the Palas with their workshops and institutions of academic activity, research and Buddhist epistemology are of central importance, and to all intents and purposes responsible for the spread of Mahayana Buddhism and its reception in Southeast Asia and beyond. The five monasteries in Bengal and Magadha—Nalanda, Vikramashila, Somapura, Odantapurā, and Jaggadala—formed a cooperative network.[141] These Buddhist educational institutions were nationally administered under the Palas and formed a well organized, coordinated system within which the various centres communicated with each other and probably an exchange of curricula, instructors and artefacts took place.[142]

Evidently such exchanges, though probably mainly originating from India, took place not only among the five universities, but also extended to areas that were outside India, like the Mataram kingdom of the Shailendra. The artistic influence of Bengal is particularly evident in the famous Pala bronze statuettes. A variety of bronzes from Bengali workshops, or more specifically bronzes derived from the Pala tradition, are therefore also found on Java.[143] As far as can be determined, the majority of the bronze statues derived from that tradition were made in Java itself.[144] More generally,

---

141 "A number of monasteries grew up during the Pāla period in ancient Bengal and Magadha. According to Tibetan sources, five great Mahaviharas stood out: Vikramashila, the premier university of the era; Nalanda, past its prime but still illustrious, Somapura, Odantapurā, and Jaggadala." (Wikipedia, Nalanda)

142 See also Sukumar DUTT, *Buddhist Monks And Monasteries Of India: Their History And Contribution To Indian Culture*, George Allen and Unwin Ltd, London, 1962, pp. 352–353: "it seems from the evidence that the different seats of Buddhist learning that functioned in eastern India under the Pāla were regarded together as forming a network, an interlinked group of institutions."

143 HUNTINGTON, Introduction to Southeast Asia and Southern China, p. 208: "The strength of the Pala impact may be seen in the stunning corpus of surviving Javanese metal images. Displaying extraordinary iconographic richness, stylistic sophistication, and technical virtuosity, Javanese metal images are often exquisitely rendered with jewellike precision. Most of the surviving images are fairly small; like Pala images, the majority are under twelve inches in height, though a few are larger (cat. No.72), and many are tiny miniatures (cat.no.81)."

144 And ibid.: "In contrast to Myanmar, where Pala influence was felt strongly in every medium of art and architecture, Indonesia displays Pala influence mainly in the medium of metal sculpture. As far as can be determined, most of the surviving metal images were products of workshops on the island of Java, although some also may have been created elsewhere, such as Sumatra. The main period of florescence occurred approximately contemporaneously with the early Pala period, around the eighth through the tenth

the influence of the workshops of the Palas was strong in several distant countries as well, and though relatively short (725-851), the tradition can be traced to places as far away as China (particularly in the statues of the Tang Dynasty and later),[145] and Japan.

However, the temple *architecture* of Java has no Pala-models or affiliation to a Bengali 'Bauhaus'. Similarly, examples or remnants of paintings are also lacking, so, in this respect, too, a connection cannot be recognized, although the development of Tibetan religious paintings shows some influences.[146]

With the repeated relocation of Java's capital from Central Java eastward and the increasing abundance of Hindu elements in the architecture and other cultural works, the Buddhist influence of the Palas starts to recede.[147]

or eleventh centuries, during what are usually called the Central and Eastern Javanese periods. Some Pala-related images also date from the twelfth century, but these are fewer in number and suggest that Javanese contact with the Pala world had waned by that time ... Like their Pala counterparts, the majority are made of copper alloys, although quite a few in silver have been preserved (cat.no.81 and *85)* and a few precious survivals in gold (cat. no.82) are also known. As in the Pala tradition, many of the images must have been parts of groups, as eloquently illustrated by the famous sculptural *mandala* that was found at Nganjuk (cat. No.83)."

145 HUNTINGTON, Introduction to Southeast Asia and Southern China, p. 70: "In some cases, Pala models were copied so closely that art historians disagree vehemently about whether a given piece is in fact a Pala creation or a work inspired by the Pala style but produced elsewhere ... For example, in Nepal and Tibet traces of the Pala idiom are visible in art produced during the twentieth century. Other areas experienced late resurgences of the Pala style, as in the case of the Pala revival that occurred in China under the patronage of the Qianlong Emperor (1736-1796). In other regions, such as Indonesia, the essence of Pala art was quickly transformed and even abandoned as new cultural directions emerged."

146 HUNTINGTON, Introduction to Southeast Asia and Southern China, p. 208: "It is curious that the stylistic impact of Pala art is visible primarily in a single medium, for at the same time that these strongly Pala-influenced metal images were being produced, the kings of Java were commissioning extraordinary architectural monuments richly embellished with exquisite stone carvings in a different style. Instead of resembling works of the Pala artistic tradition, these structures and their decoration probably ultimately derived from Gupta period sources, enriched by associations with other Indic styles. In addition, the temple and stone sculpture traditions of Java were already marked by a distinctive local character that testifies to the existence of strongly developed indigenous ateliers. Examples of Central and Eastern Javanese period painting have not been identified, and therefore it is unknown whether the Javanese painting tradition was related to the Pala idiom."

147 And ibid., note 50, for p. 208 (on p. 214): "The Javanese capital shifted from the central region to the east in the early tenth century, followed by a brief period of transition until

Since the Javanese bronze sculptures bore little resemblance to comparable stone statues of the Palas (a comparison with the lack of similarity in architecture suggests itself), it is assumed that patterns and templates of the bronzes were probably imported from Bengal, and served as model prototypes. Javanese are likely to have had little opportunity to attend workshops in Bengal, while, conversely, Bengali and Indian masters visited Java and taught there.[148] The main influence seems to have come from Nalanda and Vikramashila.[149]

As stated above, in addition to the images of gods cast in bronze, the Buddhist teachings in general were also based on the Bengali tradition

about 928, during which a number of kings seem to have ruled Central and Eastern Java simultaneously. At least four phases can be identified in the eastern Javanese period: from the early tenth century to about 1049, when the center was in the region south of Surabaya; from about 1049 to 1222, when the center was in Kadin in present Kediri; from 1222 to 1292, when the center was in Sighasari near Malang; and from 1292 to the early sixteenth century, when the center was in Majaphit, which has been identified as Trowulan near Mojokerto ... The stylistic association with Pala imagery is seen mainly in the Central Javanese phase and the earliest phase of the Eastern Javanese period."

148 And further, ibid., p. 208: "in general the Javanese images have little in common with Pala stone sculptures. This suggests that one means of transfer of the style was through the importation into Java of metal images that might then have served as inspiration for others of the same medium. One Pala image ... (cat. No.45), is likely to have come to Java in this way. ... Examples of Javanese metal images bearing dates are unknown, and therefore only a relative dating sequence can be established for the images; they are generally dated on a stylistic basis based in part on parallel developments in Pala art. The styles of the Central and Eastern Javanese periods are distinctive, and thus the images fall into two general groups, Central Javanese (ca. eighth and ninth centuries) and Eastern Javanese (ca. tenth and eleventh centuries), with some transition between the two..."

149 HUNTINGTON, Introduction to Southeast Asia and Southern China, p. 209: "The relationship between the Nalanda and Indonesian (mainly Javanese) metal image traditions are undeniable. In some cases, it is the configuration of an image, although not necessarily the stylistic details, that recalls works from Nalanda. (cat. No.72). In other cases, the Nalanda model is so apparent that it is difficult to judge whether a work is in fact from India or Indonesia (cat. No. 73)." And ibid., p. 209: "In spite of the fact that both inscriptional and artistic ties verify that Nalanda was an important source of artistic information for the Javanese, Nalanda was not the exclusive Pala source for Indonesian metal imagery, for other schools of Pala art also had a profound impact on the art of Indonesia. This fact has become more apparent as recent studies of Pala art have defined the various subschools of the Pala idiom itself. The most obvious source for Javanese metal images, aside from Nalanda, is the eastern Bengal region, where a metal image tradition was founded at least as early as that at Nalanda and which developed its own distinctive characteristics at an early date. Although the influence of eastern Bengal may have arisen by direct associations, inscriptional evidence, such as Balaputra's grant to Nalanda, has not been discovered to substantiate it."

and within that tradition especially the school of Nalanda. Accordingly the historical Buddha, Shakyamuni, was never or rarely depicted; instead the 'sun god' Vairochana or Mahavairochana, who also plays a dominant role in Japan (as Dainichi Nyourai), was the focus of the iconographic representations.[150]

> In Javanese Buddhism, the emphasis on Mahavairocana was probably inextricably associated with notions of kingship, for Mahavairocana—the supreme Mahayana divinity and the center of the Buddhist universe—would have been a fitting model for the Javanese Buddhist king presiding over his domains. Like Mahavairocana, the Javanese Buddhist king dwelled at the heart of his kingdom, surrounded by the princes, guardians, and subjects of his realm.[151]

Evidently Javanese Buddhists had contact with the Buddhists of Sri Vijaya and through middlemen or Indian Masters also to the University of Nalanda and other Buddhist sites, enabling them to be informed of the latest developments in Buddhist epistemology, and also craft secrets and methods for manufacturing devotional objects, extending also to the fields of music and theatre.

The following thesis presents itself as a descriptive heuristic model: in both Hinduism and Buddhism the master-disciple relationship associated with an initiation ceremony into the teachings (and often a craft) is of prime consequence. Traditionally, twelve years of apprenticeship—which is also

---

150 HUNTINGTON, Introduction to Southeast Asia and Southern China, pp. 209-210: "In addition to the unmistakably stylistic and technical debt of Javanese metal images to Pala works, there is a strong iconographic association. Interestingly, the Javanese idiom appears to be the only Pala-dependent tradition that did not emphasize Sakyamuni Buddha, the events of his life, or the places where they occurred ... Rather, the Javanese emphasized the forms of Buddhism that were practiced at sites like Nalanda, in which Mahavairocana (cat. nos.82 and 84), the Jina Buddhas (cat. no.78), various Bodhisattvas (cat. nos. 73, 81, and 86), Tara, Prajnaparamita, and other Mahayana and Tantric divinities predominated (cat. no.87). Most important of these deities was Mahavairocana, the Buddha in whom the totality of the universe is personified and who resides at the center of the Buddhist universe."

151 HUNTINGTON, Introduction to Southeast Asia and Southern China, p. 210. And ibid.: "One can only wonder if the famous sculpted *mandala* found at Nganjuk (cat. no. 83), with Mahavairocana at its center, was intended as a model of the kingdom of the monarch who reigned at the time it was made." The Indian influence is repeatedly emphasized.

the time for learning Sanskrit—are usually anticipated.[152] Atisa therefore studied 12 years in Java under his teacher, Dharmakirti. A substantial number of initiations must thus have been carried out in a relatively short time, in various subjects, corresponding to the curriculum of the Buddhist University, with all the teachers likely to have come from India or be second-generation Indians who had settled in Sumatra. *Indianization in Southeast Asia—this is the thesis—proceeded through rites of passage. It was 'Colonization by Initiation'.*

Late 10th Century Pala bronze, Kurkihar style, Bihar. Source: http://www.metmuseum.org/toah/works-of-art/1993.311ab

As noted earlier, Mahayana Buddhism and Hinduism generally coexisted, and the impact of Pala Shaivism and Tantrism on Java is significant.[153] In addition, not only were Shiva and Ganesha, the elephant

---

152 Twelve years of apprenticeship are standard both in the arts and crafts, as in academic studies.

153 HUNTINGTON, Introduction to Southeast Asia and Southern China, p. 210: "Both Buddhism and Hinduism had penetrated Java at an early date, and by the time the Palas had risen to power in Bihar and Bengal, both religious traditions were not only already well established in Java, but were flourishing side-by-side. Although there are fewer Hindu than Buddhist images, a number of Hindu examples are known, many of which may have been produced under the aegis of the Hindu Sanjaya dynasty of Central Java." "Images of Ganesa, the elephant-headed god, seem to have been especially popular in Java (cat. no.76), along with depictions of Siva (cat. no. 77), Vishnu and the other gods. The mechanism by which the Javanese patrons of Hindu art maintained contact with

god (who appears as a Buddhist icon), widespread, but traditional Javanese elements such as ancestor worship were also incorporated.[154] This tendency is a distinctive feature of the process of Indianization and the reception in Southeast and East Asia, which again allows us to conclude that initiation rites must have preceded dogmatic considerations. Majumdar:

> The close association between Siva and Buddha was a characteristic feature of Javanese religion. The two deities have been identified in such books as *Kunjarakarna* and *Sutasoma*. In modern Balinese theology Buddha is regarded as a younger brother of Siva, and there is a close affinity between the two doctrines. A similar Siva-Buddha cult existed in Java. Further, Siva, Vishnu and Buddha were all regarded as identical and so were their Saktis.[155]

But it was in Java and Sumatra that Tantrism or Tantrayana took on greater significance. During this period Mahayana Buddhism, Vajrayana (yana = vehicle; Vajra = diamond) and the cult of Siva inspired each other and merged, providing a context in which the *Sang Hyang Kamahayanikan*, a text written in Sanskrit, stands out. The text consists of two parts, written in verse and containing an old Javanese commentary. Sir Charles Eliot (*Hinduism and Buddhism, An Historical Sketch*, 2 vols. 1921) points to the parallels with Nepalese Tantric literature which, as we know, was also based on the teachings of the Buddhist monks of Magadha and Bengal during the Pala period. According to that school, Brahma, Vishnu and Shiva are emanations of the Dhyani-Buddha Vairocana. The *panca makara* used in the Tantra practice (that five "m": *madya* = wine; *mansa* = meat; *matsya* = fish; *mudra* = grains; and *maithuna* = sexual union[156]) are also mentioned in this remarkable work. The *Kawi* text,[157] which tells the story

---

the Pala sources are unknown; it is possible that they did not have extensive ties with Pala Hinduism, but rather that the Pala-related Hindu art styles developed as a by-product of the intense interaction between Buddhists of Java and the Pala kingdom."

154 HUNTINGTON, Introduction to Southeast Asia and Southern China, p. 210: "Although the model of Sanskritik Indic kingship was grafted onto the hierarchical Javanese system, an indigenous cult involving the veneration of deceased ancestral chieftains imbued Javanese culture with its distinctive character."

155 R. C. MAJUMDAR, *Hindu Colonies in the Far East*, p. 99.

156 An interesting question is to what extent Tantric sexual practices could be conducive to peace, e.g. in the sense of "Make Love Not War!" The magic of reciting mantras and prayers also are meant to create an inner peace, the radiance of which is said to be conducive to external peace.

157 "Aksara Kawi (from Sanskrit *kavi*, 'poet') is the name given to the writing system originating in Java and used across much of Maritime Southeast Asia from the 8th

of Kunjarakarna,[158] praises Vairocana as Shiva and Buddha manifesting one and the same being.[159]

Cultural activities and trade went hand in hand. The goddess Tara, venerated by the Palas, was also a patroness of the sailors and traders and apparently inscribed as an emblem on the banner of Dharmapala in his undertakings and on those of the merchant ships sailing from Bengal. The Bengali historian D.C. Sirkar writes that the goddess

> Tara of Dharmapala's standard or banner [was] very probably the dynastic emblem of the Palas for their standard or banner just as the Dharmacakra was for their seals. The official records of the Palas speak of their seal as the Dharmachakra-Mudra ... As in the case of several other ruling families of early medieval India, the Palas thus appear to have had two different emblems, viz. the Dharmacakra for their seal and the goddess Tara for their standard or banner.[160]

The same author mentions the Khadiravani-Tara, also known as Syama-Tara for her green color, and probably the form of the goddess worshiped in Candradvipa, being "one of the most celebrated deities in Bengal during the Pala epoch." Sircar considers this representation not only the most

century to around 1500 AD. It is a direct derivation of the Pallava script brought by traders from the ancient Tamil Kingdom of Pallava in India, primarily used for writing Sanskrit and Old Javanese language. Kawi is the ancestor of traditional Indonesian scripts, such as Javanese and Balinese, as well as traditional Philippine scripts such as Baybayin." (http://en.wikipedia.org/wiki/Kawi_script)

158 Mpu DUSUN, A. TEEUW, Stuart O. ROBSON, *KUNJARAKARNA DHARMAKATHANA*: liberation through the law of the Buddha: an Old Javanese poem, vol. 21 of *Bibliotheca Indonesica,* M. Nijhoff, 1981.

159 Nihar-Ranjan RAY, *Sanskrit Buddhism in Burma*, Bangkok 2002, pp. 15-16: "But it was in Java and Sumatra that Tantrayana seems to have attained greater importance. The Mahayana Buddhism and the cult of Siva, both deeply imbued with Tantric influence, are to be seen often blending with one another during this period. The *Sang hyang Kamahayanikan*, consisting of Sanskrit verses explained by an old Javanese commentary, professes to teach the Mahayana and the Mantrayana. Sir Charles Eliot thinks that it offers many parallels to Nepalese Tantric literature, which, as we know, consists of the teachings of the Buddhist monks of Magadha and Bengal during the Pala period. According to this treatise, Brahma, Visnu and Siva are emanations of the Dhyani-Buddha Vairocana. The *panca makaras* are also referred to in this strange work. Another Kawi text, which gives the story of Kunjarakarna, extols Vairocana as being Siva and Buddha in one."

160 D.C. SIRCAR, The Tara of Candradvipa, in D. C. SIRCAR (ed.), *The Sakti cult and Tara*, Calcutta 1967 (University of Calcutta), pp. 131-132.

common, but also points out that the famous green Syama is "one of the earliest forms of Tara, and Syama the name of the mother deity still very popular in Bengal."[161]

8. The Palas and Tibet (Atisa)

According to the legend, the god Brahma fashioned five heads for himself, in order never to lose sight of the beloved consort he had created for himself. According to tradition, each of these five heads incessantly recites one of the five Vedas. Four of these are the Rig, Yajur, Sama and Atharva, but the title of the fifth Veda is unknown, and iconographic images always depict Brahma with only four heads. How Brahma lost his fifth head, is brought to light in the following story, which happens to take place in the world of the gods: at one time Brahma and Vishnu quarrelled over who was the highest-ranking deity. So, they were looking for evidence in the scriptures and finally found that the god Shiva was considered the most powerful. Accordingly the four heads, looking in all directions, sang the praise of Shiva. Only the fifth head, with its face looking up, insulted him, which prompted Lord Shiva to strike it off with a mighty blow.[162] However, since it is a punishable offence to 'behead' a Brahmin—let alone Brahma himself— Siva thenceforth had to roam the world with the skull of the fifth head of Brahma as his begging bowl, asking for alms like a wandering monk. The fifth Veda, which the fifth head had recited, containing the secret tantric teachings, subsequently 'landed' in Tibet.[163]

---

161 And ibid., pp. 128-130: This Tara was "one of the most celebrated deities in Bengal during the age of the Palas ... it also appears that Syama of the green variety is one of the earliest forms of Tara, Syama as the name of the Mother-goddess being still very popular in Bengal."

162 Romila THAPAR, *The Past Before Us: Historical Traditions of Early North India*, Bangalore, New Delhi Kolkata etc.. Orient Blackswan 2013, pp. 56, 100, 146, 151, 158, 172, and 271-272 has nothing of the sort. Instead she offers several scriptures as having possibly been the fifth Veda, i.e. the *itihasa-purana*: "It is described as the fifth *Veda*, which makes it an important but separate branch of knowledge, although the term included the more esoteric kinds of knowledge, such as *sarpavidya* (serpent lore), and *asuravidya* (demonology). Promotion to the status of a fifth *Veda* was sometimes given to texts whose subject matter was initially outside the interests of Vedic Brahmanism but which had a specific importance of their own." (p. 56)

163 Elisabeth-Chalier VISUVALINGAM, Bhairava's Royal Brahmanicide: The Problem of the Mahabrahmana, in Alf HILTEBEITEL (ed.), *Criminal Gods and Demon Devotees: Essays on the Guardians of Popular Hinduism*, SUNY Press 1989, pp. 157 ff. According to the *Niruttara Tantra* the Tantra is the fifth Veda.

History is full of secrets. Heaven and earth are intertwined with each other in the ethereal regions of the high Himalayas. Electromagnetic or electro-chemical reactions take place constantly at those heights.[164] Since Buddhism and the Tibetan script were introduced only between the seventh and eighth centuries in Tibet, one might assume that previously there had existed at best a primitive animism. Perhaps this does not coincide with the idea of the Himalayan region as the spiritual centre of Asia, around which everything revolves. However, this need not necessarily have been the case.[165] The shamanist Bon religion (Bon-Po) that prevailed in Tibet before the introduction of Buddhism can lay claim to a tradition several thousand years-old, and in important aspects its teachings correspond to the Buddhist teachings. Bon followers, however, do not recognize the exclusive spiritual authority of the Buddha. The meaning of the word "Bon" or "Bön" is controversial, probably meaning "conjure up" and "conjurer," which some authors (Walter Simon, Uray) interpret as "ask" or "invite;" another possible meaning is "seed."[166]

India and Tibet are historically, culturally, religiously—and ecologically—closely intertwined.[167] The Himalayan mountains along with Tibet are not only the seat of the gods; everything revolves around this axis. The people of the Silk Road as well as the winds, (see the simple graphic on the next page!); nomadic peoples of the north such as the Kalmyks migrating across the vast steppes of Siberia from east to west and from west to east and perhaps, like the Mongols, occasionally invading the south, when conditions like lack of food etc., created a necessity.

The Tibetan alphabet, like the scripts of Southeast Asia, is essentially

---

164 As to the pressures and movements in the ethereal heights of the Himalayas: The *Prajapati* (also meaning "butterfly" in the Bengali language) is an early manifestation of Brahma which possibly refers to the Himalayan airstream system, with its two wings covering all of Asia to the east and the west like a giant butterfly.

165 In fact, if the story of the gods and early Buddhas as personified forces of nature have not only sprung from human imagination, but have a reality corresponding to a 'material' background, then an all-encompassing unity of an essential primeval world religion may be assumed.

166 Walter SIMON, A Note on Tibet, *Asia Major*, new series vol. 5 (1955-1956), pp. 5-8. David L. SNELLGROVE, *The Nine Ways of Bon*, Oxford University Press 1967 (reprint 1980), p. 1, note 1: "The discussion would leave us with at least two homonyms *bon*, (i) meaning 'invoke' and 'invoker' of which Simon (followed by Uray) understands the original meaning to be 'entreat' or 'invite', and (ii) meaning 'seed." Bon could also point to Brahma, who is called Bon-ten in Japan.

167 Narendra Kumar DASH (ed.), *Indo-Tibetan Culture*, Kolkata, Visva-Bharati 2003.

based on the Indian alphabet. The records deal with the introduction of the Tibetan writing system in the religious historical documents of Bu-ston (1290-1364). According to these records King Songtsen Gampo (Sron-btsan sgam-po, 617/627-ca. 650) sent a certain Thon-mi Anai-bu[168] with sixteen companions to India with the mandate to find out and study a suitable script. They studied under a Pandit called Lha-rig pai Senge, and eventually Thon-mi Anai-bu created an alphabet that was based on the Kashmiri prototype; he wrote a total of eight works on language and grammar.[169]

High- and Low-Pressure Areas in January

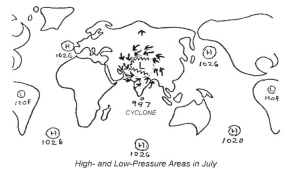

High- and Low-Pressure Areas in July

168 A. CHATTOPADHYAYA, *Attisa and Tibet*, p. 198. See also ibid., pp. 209-210: "Thon-mi also played a significant role in the contemporary politics of Tibet. He was an important minister of Sron-btsan-sgam-po ... there is no doubt that the work of Thon-mi Sambhota gave the first great impetus to Tibetan literary activity." See also Sam van SCHAIK, A New Look at the Invention of the Tibetan Script, *Old Tibetan Documents Monograph Series*, vol. III, edited by Yoshiro IMAEDA, Matthew KAPSTEIN and Tsuguhito TAKEUCHI, Tokyo, Tokyo University of Foreign Studies 2011, p. 45 (45–96) who, though acknowledging Tönmi Sambhota (Thon-mi Sambhota) as the likely inventor of the Tibetan script, states that the "exact source is uncertain."

169 Stephan V. BEYER, *The Classical Tibetan Language*, Albany, State University of New York Press 1992, p. 40: "The traditional account of the invention of the Tibetan writing system is set forth in the ecclesiastical history of Bu-ston (1290-1364). There we are told that Thon-mi Anui-bu (Thon-mi Sambhota?) was sent to India by king Sron-btsan sgam-po (who ruled from about 627 to 650) along with sixteen companions in order to study writing; he studied with a pandita named Lha-rig pa'i sen-ge, created the Tibetan alphabet based on a Kashmiri prototype, and composed eight works on writing and grammar." Sam van SCHAIK, A New Look at the Tibetan Invention of Writing, online at https://earlytibet.files.wordpress.com/2007/06/vanschaik_2011a.pdf.

Songtsen Gampo not only officially introduced writing into Tibet. In addition, he is said to have built up to 900 monasteries, surrounded himself with learned monks from India, Nepal and China, and had a palace built in Lhasa, which he called the Potala. The period from 750 to 850 AD was a golden age of Buddhism. Under Trhisong Detsen (Khri-srong Ide-btsan, reigned 755-797/804), a successor to Songtsen Gampo, Buddhism became the state religion. It was Trhisong who invited the famous teacher and abbot of Nalanda University, Shantarakshita (725-788), to Tibet and then appointed him the High Priest.[170] Equally famous, if not more so, was Padmasambhava, who was born in the district of Swat in Kashmir, in what is now Pakistan; he also taught at Nalanda and likewise was invited in 747 to Tibet. Another famous teacher in Tibet is Shankarakshita's disciple Kamalashila (713-763), who was trained in Nalanda and then called to Tibet to 'defeat' the opponents of Mahayana Buddhism. The dispute was settled in the famous debate that was held in the Samye Monastery co-founded by Padmasambhava and Shankarakshita.

There followed a period of decline, and the persecution of Buddhism under King Langdarma (Glang Dar Ma, likely reigned 838-841/846), who adhered to the Bon religion. After the assassination of Langdarma by a Buddhist hermit the empire fell apart. Civil war and a war of succession between Langdarma's two sons Yumtän (Yum-brtan) and Ösung ('Od-srung) divided the empire into two parts. In the late 10th century finally Nyima Gon (sKyid-Ide Nyima-gon) was able to conquer western Tibet and initiate a second wave of Buddhization.

Once more it was Bengali teachers among others, monks teaching in Nalanda and Vikramashila who promoted the spread of Buddhism and Buddhist literature in Tibet and definitively established the Buddhist doctrine as the state religion, this time irrevocably. Above all it was the monk Atisa (982-1054), who (after a long period of study in Sumatra) taught at the Buddhist University of Vikramashila in Bhagalpur in Bihar, and who then was called to Guge in Tibet in 1042 at the invitation of the Tibetan king.

Atisa was born into a royal family as Chandragarbha, one of three brothers in Vikramapur in today's Bangladesh. Similar to the historical Buddha, who as Prince Siddhartha renounced the material world and

---

170 Shailendra Nath SEN, *Ancient Indian History and Civilization*, Second Edition, New Delhi 1999 (orig. 1988), p. 515.

family life, Chandragarbha renounced his heritage and became a monk. The twenty-nine year-old was initiated by Shilarakshita, the Chancellor of the monastic school of Odantapuri in Magadha, in what is now the Indian state of Bihar, and was named Dipankara Srijnana.

Before Atisa Dipamkara Srijnana arrived in Tibet, he spent twelve years (from 1012/1013 to 1025) in Shri Vijaya (Sumatra), where he studied under the Acharya Dharmakirti (Dharmarakshita) and gained an extensive knowledge of Mahayana Buddhism.[171] The next 15 years Atisa spent in India, initially in Bodhgaya (c. 1025-1027), where he revealed the Buddhist teachings and established Mahayana Buddhism in Magadha. When some years later Magadha was invaded by the king of Karnya (Kanauj)—the Bengali king Nayapala (reigned 1038-1053 according to Majumdar, and 1027-1043 according to Sircar) had just appointed Atisa as abbot of the monastery school of Vikramashila—it was he who mediated in the armed conflict and finally participated in the drafting of a peace treaty.

Atisa was well versed in nearly all the schools of Buddhism and published and edited a total of more than two hundred books, incorporating translations and songs, as well as 79 separate works which were translated into the Tibetan language and are preserved in the Tibetan Tengyur collection (bstan-sgyur). His three students, Ku-tön Tsön-dru, Ngo Leg-pe Sherab and Dromtönpa (Drom-tön Gyal-we Jungne, 1005-1054) were also famous. Dromtönpa was the chief disciple of Atisa; he established the practice of Lodjong (Mind Training), which is still practiced to achieve compassion and wisdom.

9. Description of Borobudur

The Kedu Plain is situated almost exactly between the Prambanan Valley in the southeast and the Dieng Plateau in the northwest. Here are found some of the greatest religious Indo-Javanese monuments, including the most important, the Barabudur.[172] The Barabudur or Borobudur was the

---

171 HUNTINGTON, Introduction to Southeast Asia and Southern China, p. 211: "There he studied with the acarya Dharmakirti, whose erudition was known throughout the Buddhist world. Atisa is believed to have acquired his great knowledge of Mahayana under Dharmakirti's tutelage."

172 R. C. MAJUMDAR, *Hindu Colonies in the Far East*, p. 104: "On Dieng Plateau, 6,500 ft. high and surrounded by hills on almost all sides, are a number of temples called after the heroes and heroines of the Mahabharata. They are generally regarded as the oldest in Java and probably belong to the eighth century A.D. Although they are

"last great monument of Mahayana Buddhism" built in Java.[173]

Tradition has it that the *stupa* of the Borobudur sprang from the imagination of the poet, thinker and architect Gunadharma. Gunadharma's facial features are supposed to be recognizable in the contours of the Menoreh Mountain range located nearby.[174] According to Professor Lokesh Chandra Borobudur is a Tantric *mandala*, a so-called *Vajradhatu Mandala*, mandala of the indestructible, completely unshakable (spiritual) region. It is not surprising that this period of the eighth century is considered the Golden Age of the Yoga Tantra and of the Vajrayana, the 'Diamond vehicle' of Buddhism.[175] J. Dumarçay states:

> Borobudur consists of a foundation with a base, followed by the four superimposed galleries in the middle part and the circular terrace on the upper platform. A square with protrusions on all sides is the foundation of the building. The length from one corner to the other is 113 meters ... The base follows the exact specifications of the foundation ... and it reaches a height of nearly 4 meters. The walls were left smooth and have, except for a cornice of 1.5 meters height and 3 meters width, no ornaments.[176]

comparatively small in dimensions, their simple and clear outline, and restrained but well-conceived decorations endow them with a special importance. The sculptures are also characterized by a simplicity and vigour worthy of the temples which they adorned. ... The images found in the plateau Dieng belong exclusively to the Brahmanical pantheon. We have images of Siva, Durga, Brahma and Vishnu ... mainly of Saivite character." See also J. VILLIERS, *Südostasien vor der Kolonialzeit*, p. 62. See also HUNTINGTON, Introduction to Southeast Asia and Southern China, p. 210: "Keeping apace with the most advanced religious developments of Pala Buddhism, the Javanese Buddhists apparently were in constant contact with the Pala kingdom or other Buddhist strongholds, such as Srivijaya, that were renowned as centers of contemporary esoteric Buddhist practices." R. C. MAJUMDAR, *Hindu Colonies in the Far East*, p. 105, describes the Javanese monuments: "About midway between the Dieng Plateau in the northwest and the Prambanan valley in the south-east stands the Kedu plain which contained some of the noblest monuments of Indo-Javanese architecture ... There are the ruins of numerous fine temples, both Brahmanical and Buddhist, and two of them, Chandi Mendut and Chandi Pavan, which are fairly preserved, are beautiful specimens of Indo-Javanese art. But all these have been cast into shade by the famous Barabudur."

173 J. VILLIERS, *Südostasien vor der Kolonialzeit*, p. 56.

174 L. CHANDRA, Borobudur, p. 1: The stupa of Borobudur was "conceived and concretized by a poet, thinker and architect, named Gunadharma ... architect Gunadharma is integrated into the mountain range of Menoreh where you can see the silhouette of his chin, mouth and nose."

175 See also L. CHANDRA, Borobudur, pp. 5 and 19.

176 J. DUMARÇAY, *Borobudur*, pp. 4-5.

The full name of Borobudur is probably—this name is mentioned in an inscription—*Bhumi Sambhara Bhudhara*, which means something like the 'mountain of the accumulation of virtue on the ten stages of the Bodhisattva'. The name supposedly also points to Tantric practices.[177]

The construction of the entire complex lasted about 75 years,[178] and is usually divided into five phases of construction: around 780 the excavation and the foundation of the first stage; around 792 the beginning of the second and third stages with the execution of the entire structure; and finally around 824 the fourth and then around 833 the fifth construction period.[179]

The monument was much frequented and an important sanctuary for the whole of East Asia—pottery and other artefacts from the Tang Dynasty of China, among others, were found nearby. Until well into the 10th century and in some cases even until the 14th century Borobudur was revered as a place of pilgrimage and of worship.[180]

The hidden foot of the monument, from the final phase of the first period of the initial construction stage, is decorated by an ornately sculpted cornice, whose base plate is decorated by 160 bas-reliefs with illustrations from the *Kannaivibhangga*. The *Kannaivibhangga* is a text that contains a detailed description of the doctrine of causation and the effects of good and evil deeds. About forty of these reliefs in the upper part are equipped with inscriptions which, written in Old Javanese—however, with Sanskrit letters—contain brief descriptions of the various images.[181]

---

177 Vgl. L. CHANDRA, Borobudur, p. 47. Presumably, this refers to the Sri Kahulunnan inscription of the Saka era year 764.

178 J. DUMARÇAY, *Borobudur*, p. 28: "The construction, with those numerous stops and starts, lasted a period of about seventy-five years."

179 And ibid., p. 4: "In sum, the approximate dates in the construction of Borobudur can be fixed as follows: ± 780: The pegging out of the first monument and the first period of construction; ± 792: Second and third periods of construction, and the complete reconstruction of the monument; ± 824: Fourth period; ± 833: Fifth period."

180 J. DUMARÇAY, *Borobudur*, pp. 4-5: "After this last date, the monument continued to be used until the tenth century; T'ang period potteries have been found on the site. Some activities doubtless continued to the fourteenth century..."

181 J. DUMARÇAY, *Borobudur*, p. 32: "A richly carved cornice decorates the hidden foot [from the end of first period of construction], the plinth of which is decorated with 160 reliefs illustrating the *Kannaivibhangga*. This text describes the doctrine of the causes and effects of good and evil. About forty of these reliefs (the exact number is not known

The lowest loft or gallery is reached by (originally four?) door walks, of which only the remains are preserved at the eastern entrance and in the south. The gallery itself consists of the retaining wall of the second gallery and the balustrade blocking the view to the outside. The retaining wall is decorated on two levels with 120 panels. The level or platform situated higher up shows Illustrations from the *Lalitavistara*, an autobiographical collection illustrating the whole story of the Buddha's life from his birth to his first sermon in the Deer Park at Benares. The lower level or platform shows sections from the five episodes in the past lives of the historical Buddha as recorded in the *Jatakamala*, written in the fourth century, and especially also preserved in Tibet.[182] On the inside of the balustrade there are also two platforms with bas-reliefs, depicting more episodes from the Buddha's previous lives. On the higher platform, completely in the northeast, there are panels that have as their content the lives of many Bodhisattvas; these Bodhisattva stories are told in the "One hundred stories of the Awadana" ("Awada" or *Awadanasataka*).[183]

The subsequent upper galleries follow the same pattern, with a shielding, retaining wall to the next platform and a balustrade. The retaining wall, which forms the foundation of the three upper galleries, is decorated by a single row of bas-reliefs, consisting of illustrations of the second and third gallery, which are taken from the *Gandawyuha*. The *Gandawyuha* is

---

because of the damage caused by the building of the added foot) are topped with a brief description in Old Javanese but written in Sanskrit letters."

182 Once the Buddha Was a Monkey. Arya Sura's 'Jatakamala', transl. by Peter KHOROCHE, University of Chicago Press 1989/2006.

183 See Theodor ZACHARIAE, Zur Geschichte vom weisen Haikar (On the history of the wise Haikar), *Zeitschrift des Vereins für Volkskunde*, vol. 17 (1907), pp. 190-191: "Avadanaśataka, a collection of 100 Buddhist legends that Léon Teer has made known in a French translation (Annales du Musée Guimet 18. Paris 1891). The creation of the work Speyer has set around the year 100 of our era. A Chinese translation of the Avadanasataka was written between 223-253 BC." See also the description in J. DUMARÇAY, *Borobudur*, p. 33: "The first gallery is reached by gateways which have now almost completely disappeared, though a few fragments remain to the east and the south. ... The gallery itself is composed of the retaining wall of the second gallery and the balustrade stopping the view to the outside. The retaining wall is decorated at two levels with 120 panels each. The upper level illustrates the *Lalitavistara*, the story of the life of the Buddha from his birth to the sermon at Benares ... The lower level illustrates five episodes in the former lives of the historic Buddha; these tales, the *Jatakamala*, were collected in the fourth century. On the inside face of the balustrade can be seen also two levels of reliefs likewise illustrating previous lives of the Buddha but in the north-east corner the panels of the upper level illustrate another text, the *Awada*. This collection of tales relates not to the previous lives of the historic Buddha, but to Bodhisattvas."

considered one of the finest Buddhist texts and tells of Sudhana, the son of a merchant, who encounters numerous Bodhisattvas in his quest for wisdom, some of whom, such as the future Buddha Maitreya, are depicted in the reliefs on the third gallery. Obviously the builders assigned great importance to the *Gandawyuha*, because they devoted to it over 488 panels, whereas, as we have seen, the illustrations for the *Lalitavistara* comprised only 120 panels.[184]

The main wall of the fourth gallery is decorated by 72 panels— depicting stories that are taken from another text, the *Bhadratjari*. The *Bhadratjari* is a summary of the *Gandawyuha* and tells mainly about Sudhana's vow to emulate the example of the Bodhisattva Samantabhadra. There are in the first gallery 104 Buddha statues, in the second also 104, in the third 88, and the fourth 72 Buddhas, altogether 368.[185]

> The upper platform is surrounded by a fifth balustrade, plain on the inside and similar to the three previous balustrades on the outside. However, the sixty-four niches decorating this balustrade contain Buddhas in the same position on all sides, unlike the other balustrades where the position of the Buddhas is different on each side. The right hand of the Buddha is raised like those of the northern side, but the first finger touches the thumb in a gesture symbolizing reasoning. This series brings the number of Buddhas to 432.[186]

Furthermore, there are three circular terraces in the upper portion. The first terrace has 32, the second twenty-four, and the third terrace sixteen smaller *stupas*, thus making altogether 72; each of the 72 *stupas* contains a

---

184 J. DUMARÇAY, *Borobudur*, pp. 34-35: "The upper galleries comprise the same elements, the retaining wall of the next level and a balustrade. The retaining wall which forms the base of these three galleries is decorated with a single level of reliefs illustrating, on the second and third galleries, the *Gandawyuha*, considered to be one of the most important Buddhist texts. It describes the search for wisdom by Sudhana, the son of a merchant who wishes to acquire great knowledge and to do so meets a large number of Bodhisattvas among whom can be noted, on the reliefs on the third gallery, the Maitreya, the next Buddha … the supervisors in charge of the monument attached much importance to this text; they gave over 488 panels to it, whereas, as has been seen, 120 were enough to illustrate the *Lalitavistara*."

185 And further, J. DUMARÇAY, *Borobudur*, p. 35: "The main wall of the fourth gallery however is decorated with seventy-two panels illustrating another text, the *Bhadratjari*, a kind of long conclusion to the *Gandawyuha*, illustrating the pledge of Sudhana to follow the example of Bodhisattva Samantabhadra."

186 J. DUMARÇAY, *Borobudur*, p. 35.

Buddha statue. All in all, we come to 504 Buddha statues.[187] A golden statue of the Buddha is said to have stood in the central *stupa* at the top.

10. The Meaning of Borobudur

It was the Briton Thomas Stamford Raffles who, after the victory of the English over the Netherlands in 1811 ("after a brief Napoleonic interlude") was appointed Lieutenant-Governor of Java and first realized the importance of the Borobudur and ordered an investigation. (See also PART III) In May 1815 Raffles himself visited Borobudur and subsequently wrote in his diary:

> the ruins of two great places, Brambana and Boro Bodo, are admirable as majestic works of art, the extent of the masses of buildings covered, in some parts, with the luxuriant vegetation of the climate, the beauty and delicate execution of the separate portions, the symmetry and regularity of the whole, the great number and interesting character of the statues and the bas-reliefs, with which they are ornamented, excite our wonder that they were not earlier examined, sketched and described.[188]

Borobudur is clearly the largest and most impressive Buddhist monument outside India. It is, as Villiers states, an extremely complicated Stupa, whose symbolic meaning is adequately reflected in its external appearance. It depicts the three "spheres of being" referred to in the Buddhist teachings regarding our universe. "The highest is completely abstract and amorphous (*Arupadhatu*), the second is the realm of forms (*Rupadhatu*) and the third is the unique world where people reside and live (*Kamadhatu*)." In the Mahayana, the Buddha reveals himself in these three regions always in a different form, "in the *Arupadhatu* (he is) purely abstract in nature (*Dharmakaya*), in the *Rupadhatu* his appearance consist of many Buddhas and Bodhisattvas (*Sambhogakaya*), while it manifests itself in the Kamadhatu as Nirmanakaya, which includes all the human Buddhas (*Manushibuddhas*), and among those the historical founder of

---

187 Ibid.

188 J. DUMARÇAY, *Borobudur*, p. 58: "After a brief Napoleonic interlude, the British took over the administration of Java. In 1811 Thomas Stamford Raffles was created Lieutenant-Governor of Java by the Governor-General of India. It was Raffles who was the first to understand the importance of Borobudur. In 1814 he ordered Cornelius, a surveyor at Semarang, to inspect the monument."

Buddhism."[189]

> The floor plan of the temple is designed so that it allows the pilgrims from the earthly, materialistic world, symbolized by the square terraces, to rise to the round terrace that embodies the spiritual world, in order finally to reach the absolute tranquility, nothingness and dissolution of the summit. At the same time, the Buddha manifests himself on the passage down from the Dharmakaya to the Manushibuddha ... In Borobudur's middle dagob [Dagob(a) = Pagoda or Stupa] originally there was a statue of Buddha.[190]

Hence Borobudur and the neighbouring temples of Pawon and Mendut were representative and symbolic evidence of the path of the Mahayana Buddhist to Nirvana. It is believed that the construction also, besides its religious significance, was a symbol of the rulers of the Shailendra and thus at the same time a sanctuary for the departed Shailendra kings. Borobudur's nine stories were, according to this tradition, supposed to correspond to the nine stages of Mount Meru or Sumeru.[191]

Villiers speculates that the (missing) statue of Buddha in the upper central stupa could just as well have been "a statue of a deified ruler ... such as were erected by the Khmer rulers."[192]

If we follow Lokesh Chandra's interpretation that Borobudur is a Tantric *mandala*, i.e. a *Vajradhatu Mandala*, then this was undoubtedly dedicated to the Buddha Vairocana. Vairocana's abode on top of Sumeru is described in the *Nispanna-yogavali* in the chapter on the Vajradhatu Mandala, where he "sits in the Vajraparyanka position in the middle of the Kutagara on Sumeru." Similarly, in the Japanese tradition of the

---

189 J. VILLIERS, *Südostasien vor der Kolonialzeit*, pp. 52-53. A description of the three spheres can be found, ibid., p. 53: "In the centermost Dagob or Stupa of Borobudur the *Dharmakaya* of the Buddha and the *Arupadhatu* are shown. The transition to the *Rupadhatu* is represented by the barred Dagobas on the upper circular terraces, and the *Rupadhatu* itself is made visible through the square terraces where the Buddha in his various manifestations, described by the different hand positions, is shown. Finally, the Buddha appears arranged all around on the lower balustrade in the *Kamadhatu* in his manifestation as *Manushibuddha*."

190 J. VILLIERS, *Südostasien vor der Kolonialzeit*, p. 53.

191 According to J. VILLIERS, *Südostasien vor der Kolonialzeit*, p. 53, temple mounts like the Borobudur, "just like the temple mounts of the Khmer, were symbolic representations of the cosmos and at the same mausoleums of the rulers of Angkor."

192 Did the missing statue of Buddha is in the middle stupa really represent the deified ruler? J. VILLIERS, *Südostasien vor der Kolonialzeit*, p. 53.

Kongochokyo, Vairocana ascends to Mount Sumeru to reveal the *mandala* to the creatures."[193]

It is therefore assumed that in the central *stupa* there stood a golden Buddha statue of the Vairocana. Lokesh Chandra points out a remarkably similar parallel case, where the "central image of the Buddhist vihara at Nagapattinam was made of solid gold." And in Sidorejo in Central Java, a bronze statue of Vairocana has been found, which was coated "with hammered gold leaf."[194] Today, instead of the golden Vairocana statue, an unfinished stone Buddha has been placed in the central *stupa*, filling the gap and used as a substitute for the missing statue.[195]

According to an inscription in the year 824 from Karangtengah (or Central Karang), a district of present Tangerang City in Banten, Central Java, a monastery (vihara) was also part of the Borobudur. Indeed, archaeologists have excavated remains in the northwest of the Stupa (Borobudur) that support this assertion,[196] consisting of ground plans and remains of several monastic buildings, which place the Borobudur at the centre of an extensive sacral region.[197]

---

193 L. CHANDRA, Borobudur, p. 53: "[T]he Borobudur is a mandala dedicated to Vairocana of the Vajradhatu. The abode of Vairocana is atop Sumeru as it is clearly pointed out in the Nispanna-yogavali in the chapter on the Vajradhatu-mandala that Lord Vairocana is seated in the vajraparyanka posture in the center of the kutagara situated on Sumeru ... In the Japanese tradition of Kongochokyo (STTS) Vairocana ascends Mount Sumeru to reveal the Mandala to sentient beings."

194 L. CHANDRA, Borobudur, pp. 61-62. And ibid.: "A bronze statue of Vairocana, covered with hammered gold leaf, has been found from Sidorejo (Central Java). [9th century AD]."

195 And ibid., p. 61 : "The central image of the Borobudur enshrined in the final stupa has not been found, and its absence has engendered a continued controversy. The intrusion of the unfinished image has complicated the issue. Its solutions have varied according to the interpretation of the type of Buddhism represented by the Borobudur: ... We agree with Kempers that the unfinished statue was secretly introduced in the cella to compensate the disappearance of the golden image of Mahavairocana enshrined therein."

196 A.J. Bernet KEMPERS, *Ancient Indonesian Art*, Harvard University Press 1959, p. 45.

197 Compare also L. CHANDRA, Borobudur, p. 51: "The Borobudur was a vihara: it is attested by the Inscription of Karangtenah of A.D. 824 (line 15: *dstam vuharah*, Casparis 1950: 40). The presence of the vihara has been proved by archaeological excavations. Its remains were found to the NW. of the monument (KEMPERS 1959: 45). It had a number of structures of which the monument now famous as *the* Borobudur was one, most probably in the center of the ordering of the entire sanctified space."

Lokesh Chandra also sees in the number of Buddha statues, totalling one thousand, a sign that the shrine was dedicated to Vairocana.

In the Brahmajala-sutra (Jap. Bonmokyo, Chin. Fan-wang-ching, Nj. 1087 = T. 1484) translated by Kumarajiva in A.D. 406 it is said: 'I am called Vairocana (Jap. Roshana) and live in the ocean of the lotus-world ... I incarnate myself into one thousand Buddhas' (T. 24.997c quoted by Matsunaga 1969: 163). The thousand Buddhas were, thus, an integral aspect of Mahavairocana as early as the fourth century.[198]

The Borobudur. Source and Copyright: Taman Visata Chandi

Another text that we have already referred to plays a role in connection with the Borobudur, i.e. the *Sang Hyang Kamahayanikan*. The oldest passages of this text date back well to the first half of the tenth century, and it is believed that the descriptions in this text correspond to the form of Buddhism practiced in the Borobudur.[199]

The mythology of Tantric Buddhist coinage lists five Dhyani Buddhas or wisdom manifestations. They are Vairochana, the Radiant; Akshobhya,

---

198 L. CHANDRA, Borobudur, p. 54.

199 According to J. DUMARÇAY, *Borobudur*, p. 11, "the oldest parts were written in the first half of the tenth century. It is usually agreed that the Buddhism described in this text must be close to the form practiced in Borobudur."

the Unyielding; Ratnasambhava, the Shining Jewel; Amitabha, the Infinite Light; and Amoghasiddhi, of Incessant, Lasting Progress. These major mythological archetypes do not represent ordinary Buddhas that have migrated through numerous reincarnations, they exist, quite on the contrary, in perpetuity as Buddhas, have never been anything else, and represent the entire universe. Each of them has a consort and is incarnated in a celestial bodhisattva and in an earthly Buddha and rules over an entire region, which is inhabited by relatively lower celestial beings which constitute his family.[200]

There is another text, the *Mahavairocana Sutra*, which had already been translated into Chinese and commented upon (by Yijing?) in the first half of the 8th century. The Chinese monks Yijing (I-ching) and the lesser-known Wu-hsing met in Nalanda in 685; both visited Srivijaya at different times, where Yijing himself stayed in 672 and again from 685 to 695 translating numerous Buddhist texts. Wu-hsing also visited Srivijaya several times between 650 and 680. As we saw, there was lively traffic in East Asia in the latter half of the seventh and the first half of the eighth century, when Indonesia was an important center of the Vajrayana.[201]

As is known, Tantrism also had a "highly erotic nature" and was "connected to primitive fertility rites." However, it is questionable whether

---

200 See J. DUMARÇAY, *Borobudur*, p. 9: "Tantric Buddhism stresses an important mythology which rests on the five Jinas (which are also called the Dhyani Buddhas): Vairocana, the illumined of the brilliant one, Aksobhya, the imperturbable one, Ratnasambhava, issued from a jewel, Amitabha, infinite light, and Amoghasida, eternal success. These five Buddhas are not ordinary Buddhas who have reached their state through numerous rebirths; they are Buddhas of all eternity, having never been anything else, and comprise the body of the universe. Each one is mirrored in a celestial Bodhisattva and in a terrestrial Buddha and rules over a whole family of lesser celestial beings."

201 L. CHANDRA, Borobudur, p. 66: "Mahavairocana-sutra was translated into Chinese by Subha-karasimha and I-hsing [Yixing, 683-727, Gernet: 197] in A.D. 724-725. The explanations offered by Subhakarasimha during the translation were noted down by I-hsing who wrote his own commentary on the Mahavairocana-sutra wherein he also transliterated some Sanskrit verses of the sutra in Chinese characters (Jong 1974: 478). The Chinese tradition is that the Sanskrit manuscript translated by Subhakara and commented upon by I-hsing was the one obtained by Wu-hsing [?]. It is highly significant that some times between 650-680 Wu-hsing was in Srivijaya. In A.D. 685 I-tsing met Wu-hsing at Nalanda. I-tsing himself was in Srivijaya in 672 and again from 685 to 695 where he translated many texts. Thus during the late seventh century, Indonesia was an important center of Vajrayana."

the sexual practices of Tantra actually had anything to do with fertility rites.[202] Most likely, it is more a question of harnessing the creative energy of man for the purpose of enlightenment. Therefore, John Villiers assessment of the later development of Tantra is perhaps too conservative and somewhat inaccurate:

> In Southeast Asia Buddhism soon lost its prophetic and contemplative character that distinguished it from its Indian origins, and came to be just as other-worldly, rigid and hierarchical as the strictest Brahmanism. It was also at an early stage influenced by Tantra, a Buddhist doctrine, which favoured magical practices, many of which were of an erotic nature.[203]

Tantrism is very old, it had already entered Southeast Asia in the 7th century and was certainly not only or "especially predominant in the Java and Sumatra of the 13th and 14th centuries."[204] The remarkable parallels in the Buddhist iconographic images of Indonesia and Japan, where the Shingon School also plays a prominent role, are surprising. "[Frederik David Kan] Bosch has proved the close affinity of Indonesian Buddhist iconography with the Shingon iconography of Japan. It is but natural that the two traditions should agree, as they represent the same yoga-tantra school of Buddhism. The basic Tantra of this school was carried to China by Vajrabodhi who arrived in Canton in 720 by the sea route on board a Persian ship. He was the son of the Royal Preceptor (*rajaguru*) of Kanchi. As we have seen, *en route* they encountered a storm just twenty days before they reached Canton. All the thirty ships were lost, except that which carried Vajrabodhi, who saved it by his recitation of Mahapratisara-dharani." [205]

---

202 See J. VILLIERS, *Südostasien vor der Kolonialzeit*, p. 56.

203 VILLIERS, ibid.

204 Ibid.

205 J. VILLIERS, *Südostasien vor der Kolonialzeit*, p. 56. For the iconography in Indonesia and Japan see again L. CHANDRA, Borobudur, p. 34.

Padma Sambhava

PART III

A Little Axial Age around 1800

Sir William Jones, the Father of Indolology

British East India Company employee with servants. Source: http://www.pandosnco.co.uk/ a_pando_passage_to_india.html

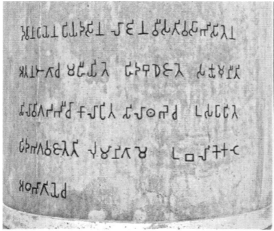 

Ashokan Pillar inscription deciphered and translated by James Prinsep, Lumbini, Nepal. Source: http://www.nepalibuddha.com/ashoka-pillar

Ashokan Pillar capitel. Source: http://www.cs.colostate.edu/~malaiya/bullcap.gif

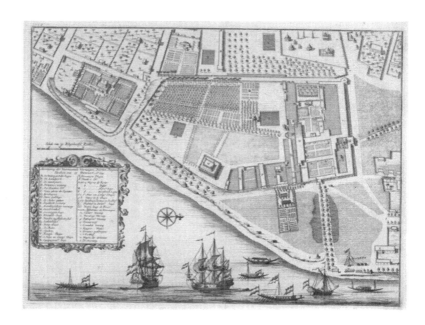

Chinsura, Dutch settlement, at Kolkata. Source: http://www.columbia.edu/itc/mealac/ pritchett/ 00routesdata/1600_1699/calcutta/chinsura/plan1721.jpg

A Little Axial Age around 1800
The Age of Enlightenment, Asia and the West

A Critical Inquiry into the History of the Organization of the World around 1800 –with emphasis on the so-called Bengal Renaissance

"This is the problem of the present age. The East, for its own sake and for the sake of the world, must not remain unrevealed. The deepest source of all calamities in history is misunderstanding. For where we do not understand, we can never be just." (Rabindranath Tagore, *Creative Unity*)

"We have now good reasons to think that the problems of the world will never be solved so long as they are considered only from a European point of view. It is necessary to see Europe from the outside, to see European history, and European failure no less than European achievement, through the eyes of that larger part of humanity, the peoples of Asia (and indeed also of Africa) ... European-American values are offered, as it were, at the point of a Bren gun, with the atomic mushroom looming in the background. Christian civilization shows no better Christian humility today than it did at the time of the Crusades..."[1]

1. Prelude to a Global Renaissance of Peace

Karl Jaspers described "the threefold manifestation of the Axial Period", when between 800 and 200 BC certain events occurred that were similar, encompassing the major civilizations of India, China and the Mediterranean world as being "in the nature of a miracle,"[2] as if happening in some magical synchronized time. As Joseph Needham recounts, even in earliest times "the almost simultaneous appearance of ideas and techniques at both ends of the world" was striking.[3] Despite astonishingly similar developmental features, no direct link appears to have existed between the three Axial civilizations at the time which Karl Jaspers talked about. As sociologist S.N.

---

1   Joseph NEEDHAM, *Within the Four Seas, The Dialogue of East and West*, London etc., George Allen & Unwin 1979 (1969), pp. 11 and 12.

2   Karl JASPERS, *The Origin and Goal of History*, London, Routledge & Kegan Paul 1953 (*Vom Ursprung und Ziel der Geschichte*, 1949), p. 21.

3   Joseph NEEDHAM, *Science and Civilisation in China*, vol.1, Introductory Orientations, Cambridge etc., Cambridge University Press 1975 (1956), p. 161; Fernand BRAUDEL, *A History of Civilisations*, New York etc., Penguin 1995 (orig. French 1963).

Eisenstadt noted, these "particularly surprising and baffling (similarities),"
in "cases predating the modern period, in which there was no contact
between the West and Japan,"[4] are not easy to explain. Karl Jasper's Axial
Age paradigm opened up an entirely new field of research. In the Pala era
(see PART II) on the other hand international trade and cultural exchange
and interaction had advanced significantly and diffusion was at an
unprecedented height. This narrative argues that the period around 1800
was similar in nature.[5] Subrata Dasgupta sees "what historians and literary
scholars have uneasily called the 'Bengal Renaissance'" as "resulting [in a]
shared cognitive identity" that "represent a genuine *cognitive revolution.*"[6]
The age of 'discoveries', in the fifteenth, sixteenth and seventeenth
centuries, when international relations expanded, reached its apex in
the eighteenth century. During this period communication between the
European Enlightenment, the Indian 'Renaissance' and the Japanese late
Edo period attained new meaning and depth. The events around 1800 are
a late milestone in this overall history, a 'little Axial Period'.

The period I have called a little Axial Period saw a pacifist impulse,
which radiated worldwide and in retrospect appears, among other things,
like the groundwork, an underpinning preparing for the Hague Peace
Conferences convened a hundred years later, and at which for the first time
in the outgoing nineteenth and the beginning of the twentieth century,
transcending Europe, an international legal community constituted itself.
The International Union of the Hague Conferences[7] became the forerunner

---

4   S.N. EISENSTADT, *Japanese Civilisation, A Comparative View*, Chicago and London
    University of Chicago Press 1996, p. 16. Japan can in so far be considered as an Axial
    Age culture, as wet-rice cultivation began several centuries before the Christian era
    which changed the organizational structure of society decisively.

5   Jürgen OSTERHAMMEL, *Die Entzauberung Asiens. Europa und die asiatischen Reiche
    im 18. Jahrhundert* (Demystifying Asia. Europe and the Asian empires in the 18th
    century), Munich, C.H. Beck 1998, p. 11, speaks of "the decisive 'bridge time' (Sattelzeit)
    around 1800 ... [which] it would be premature to maintain that it had been completely
    overcome" even today.

6   Subrata DASGUPTA, *THE BENGAL RENAISSANCE. Identity and Creativity from
    Rammohun Roy to Rabindranath Tagore*, Bangalore, New Delhi etc., Orient Blackswan
    2007, p. 2 (italics in the original). The "framework" the author draws for himself
    regarding the Bengal Renaissance is "unequivocally humanistic." (p. 3)

7   See Walther SCHÜCKING, *The International Union of the Hague Peace Conferences*,
    Oxford, At the Clarendon Press (London, Edinburgh, New York, Toronto, Melbourne
    and Bombay, Humphrey Milford) 1918. Online at https://ia800804.us.archive.org/16/
    items/cihm_991657/cihm_991657.pdf.

of the League of Nations and the United Nations Organisation.[8] In this narrative India plays a vital part.

2. The Historical Setting

Specific aspects of a policy and historiography of peace as a particular strand of world historic significance and merit have so far not been considered in the Orientalism discourse. The author of *The Oriental Renaissance*, Raymond Schwab, had pointed out that historically, throughout the entire ancient world Europe and Asia had been "trustees-in-common" of a large area which they jointly managed and for which they carried responsibility, an area "representing two scarcely divergent branches of a common immemorial tradition,"[9] which by now had fallen into oblivion. Now again, with India being rediscovered, a "whole world that had been entirely lost became, within a few years, completely known." Up to now India had "remained behind its wall," a wall of ignorance and mysteriousness. With India's history recovered, the new insights "in a single wave ... poured forth" into humanity.[10] Schwab's assumption that "after 1771 ... the world

---

8 Klaus SCHLICHTMANN, Japan, Germany and the Idea of the two Hague Peace Conferences, *JOURNAL OF PEACE RESEARCH*, vol. 40, no. 4 (2003), pp. 377-394.

9 Raimond SCHWAB, *The Oriental Renaissance. Europe's Rediscovery of India and the East, 1680-1880*, New York, Columbia University Press 1984 (Paris 1950), p. 3: "No one believes any longer that such communication is of recent date. The relative regularity of sailings and caravans has been proved by the significance attached to the discovery of the monsoon and of the silk and amber roads. The great navigators of the fifteenth century did not have to undertake their Asian voyages entirely uninformed. The reality and extent of the Hindu debt to Europe and of the Western debt to India were frequently discussed, especially in the nineteenth century. The preconception of India as 'schoolmistress of the human race' was replaced for a time by one of India as an insular civilization and was, in turn, refuted by the facts. Later historians acknowledge, with Grousset, that analogous problems received quasi-universal solutions, and with Masson-Oursel, that throughout antiquity Europe and Asia were trustees-in-common of a shared estate, their explanations of the world representing two scarcely divergent branches of a common immemorial tradition, probably Sumerian in origin. For his part, Foucher, who unveiled Greco-Buddhist art, concluded that aesthetic problems had posed themselves in similar terms across a diversity of climates and epochs."

10 R. SCHWAB, *The Oriental Renaissance*, p. 7: "A whole world that had been entirely lost became, within a few years, completely known. For the first time the image of India regally entered the configuration of the universe. Except perhaps in those times drowned in legend, when more rumor than information would have reached him, a 'cultivated' man would not necessarily have included India in his considerations of the cosmos. Judea would have been included because of biblical tradition; Persia because of wars and its traditions of magic; Arabia because of its conquests and physicians, the Crusades and the schoolmen; and, for the last two hundred years, China, seemingly

[became] truly round,"[11] is revealing and persuasive, pointing in the right direction. Indeed, the era of Orientalism in India covered the years from around 1772 to 1830 (David Kopf).

The historian Jadunath Sarkar has compared the Bengal Enlightenment with the epoch of the Greek cultural state under Pericles.[12] With the discovery of the Indo-Himalayan continent and the exploration of its culture and religion, the world-view which had until then been defined by the Mediterranean culture cradle, was enriched and expanded by a vital element. Oriental studies had, in the years after 1600, largely ceased to be a mere subdivision of Christian theology.[13] Orient and Occident began, following the rediscovery of Aristotle in the 13th and 14th century, to take a common stance, as the literary historian Edward Said has noted: "The vision [was] that... of an integral humanism."[14] Until then "merely Mediterranean," now, owing among other things to the recent discovery and analysis of numerous old scriptures, "humanism began to be global."[15] This does not suggest a 'branch' of European humanism, but the general humanism rooted in all cultures. And just as there developed a new humanism, a new universalism also emerged.

As Carol A. Breckenridge and Peter van der Veer have pointed out:

because of the missions. The Indic world alone remained behind its wall. And then, in a single wave, it poured forth. One came to know more and more what to think about it, and subsequently one no longer knew what to think about it." David KOPF, *British Orientalism and the Bengal Renaissance. The Dynamics of Indian Modernisation, 1773-1835*, Berkeley, University of California Press 1969, p. 2.

11 R. SCHWAB, *The Oriental Renaissance*, p. 16.

12 Jadunath SARKAR quoted in R.C. MAJUMDAR, *Glimpses of Bengal in the Nineteenth Century*, Calcutta, Firma K. L. Mukhopadhyay 1960, p. 3: "If Periclean Athens was the school of Hellas, the eye of Greece, mother of arts and eloquence, that was Bengal to the rest of India under British rule..." D. KOPF, *British Orientalism*, p. 3, cites Raja Rammohun ROY, who compared the developments occurring in Bengal around 1800 with the European Renaissance.

13 S. N. MUKHERJEE, *Sir William Jones. A Study in Eighteenth Century British Attitudes to India*, Cambridge University Press 1968 (Cambridge South Asian Studies No. 6), p. 16: "Oriental studies had ceased to be a branch of theology in the seventeenth century."

14 Edward W. SAID, Foreword, in R. SCHWAB, *The Oriental Renaissance*, p. VIII. (From André ROUSSEAUX, Raymond Schwab et l'humanisme integrale, *Mercure de France*, Décembre 1956, no. 1120, pp. 663-671.)

15 R. SCHWAB, *The Oriental Renaissance*, pp. 4-5. "For so long merely Mediterranean, humanism began to be global when the scientific reading of Avestan and Sanskrit scripts unlocked innumerable unsuspected scriptures."

"Early Orientalism developed alongside European Enlightenment."[16] Not only that, it was itself very much "constitutive ... of the Occident" as well.[17] The philosopher Arthur Schopenhauer, having partaken of the "benefit conferred by the Vedas," expressed himself to the effect that the impact of Sanskrit literature "will penetrate no less deeply" upon European intellectual life than "the revival of Greek literature" in the fifteenth century.[18] To what extent and in what ways the newly revealed contents of the ancient literature influenced events and developments in Europe and especially in Germany is an interesting chapter in historiography.

The humanistic idea of Man and the "Great Peace"[19] is found in virtually all cultures, and developed especially since the Axial Age of which Karl Jaspers spoke. The idea of peace is closely linked with the idea of law, order, universal justice and equality; they complement each other. Peace for the colonizers meant primarily the maintenance of "law and order." The peace of the Pax Britannica in the British colonial empire was, as the Pax Romana before, "an armed peace, both internally and externally, not a self-reproducing permanent condition."[20] For the subjugated peoples the same idiom revealed a counter-face, pointing at the opposite, an aspect that entailed a rightful claim, in which the demand for equality and justice, liberation and independence stood first and was articulated accordingly.

---

16 Carol A. BRECKENRIDGE and Peter van der VEER, Orientalism and the Postcolonial Predicament, in C.A. BRECKENRIDGE and P. van der VEER (eds.), *Orientalism and the Postcolonial Predicament*, Philadelphia, University of Pennsylvania Press 1993, p. 7. I owe Professor Hermann KULKE thanks for having recommended this title to me.

17 C.A. BRECKENRIDGE and P. van der VEER, Orientalism and the Postcolonial Predicament, p. 5.

18 Arthur SCHOPENHAUER, *The World As Will And Idea*, vol. I, Preface To The First Edition, transl. by R.B. HALDANE and J. KEMP, London, Kegan Paul, Trench, Trübner & Co. 1909, pp. xii-xiii: "And if, indeed, in addition to this [having "lingered in the school of the divine Plato" and having been thoroughly acquainted with the philosophy of KANT] he [the reader] is a partaker of the benefit conferred by the Vedas, the access to which, opened to us through the Upanishads, is in my eyes the greatest advantage which this still young century enjoys over previous ones, because I believe that the influence of the Sanscrit literature will penetrate not less deeply than did the revival of Greek literature in the fifteenth." See also R. SCHWAB, *The Oriental Renaissance*, p. 13: "Sanskrit literature will be no less influential for our time than Greek literature was in the fifteenth century for the Renaissance."

19 "Taiping" (the Great Peace) in the Chinese tradition bears witness to this.

20 See Ekkehart KRIPPENDORFF, *Staat und Krieg. Die historische Logik politischer Unvernunft* (The State and War. The historical logic of political unreason), Frankfurt, edition suhrkamp 1985, p. 388.

From this point of view nationalism and the struggle for freedom in the colonies were not disturbing the peace, but ultimately served as an instrument of peaceful change.[21]

3. India's Central Place, a Gangetic Hub

What about the assertion that Indian culture (e.g. Buddhism) and science spread (mainly) to the East and Chinese culture and science to the West? According to sinologist and science historian Joseph Needham, it is possible to show "throughout the whole Christian era ... a slow but massive advance of technical inventions of the East into the West."[22] This applies to a certain extent even for food and vegetation in Mediterranean Europe, which in ancient times had no cypresses, no oranges, lemon or peach trees, no eggplants and no fig trees etc.[23] Generously, R.C. Majumdar claims the predominance and influence of Indian culture, religion, philosophy, music, mathematics and Indian law "upon the countries lying to her west, north, east and south."[24] Indian science has, as Indologist Arthur L. Basham noted, burgeoned westward: "The debt of the Western world to India in this respect cannot be overestimated. Most of the great discoveries and inventions of which Europe is so proud would have been impossible without a developed system of mathematics, and this in turn would have been impossible if Europe had been shackled by the unwieldy system of

---

21 On the concept of peaceful change see Norbert ROPERS, *Annäherung, Abgrenzung und friedlicher Wandel in Europa* (Rapprochement, delimitation and peaceful change in Europe), Bonn-Bad Godesberg, DGFK-Hefte 8 (1975), Gerda ZELLENTIN (ed.), *Annäherung, Abgrenzung und friedlicher Wandel in Europa*, Boppard am Rhein, Harald Boldt 1976. For a more recent evaluation after the end of the Cold War see Janie LEATHERMAN, *From Cold War to Democratic Peace: Third Parties, Peaceful Change, and the OSCE*, Syracuse University Press 2003.

22 Joseph NEEDHAM, *Wissenschaftlicher Universalismus, Über Bedeutung und Besonderheit der chinesischen Wissenschaft* (Scientific universalism, on the significance and peculiarity of Chinese science), ed., introd. and transl. by Tilman SPENGLER, Frankfurt, M., Suhrkamp 1979, p. 91. (My translation from the German)

23 Fernand BRAUDEL (ed.), La Méditerranée. L'espace de l'histoire, les hommes et l'héritage, Paris, Flammerion 1985, pp. 9-10.

24 R.C. MAJUMDAR, Indian Culture as a factor in the World Civilization, in *Sir William Jones*, Bicentenary of his Birth. Commemoration Volume, 1746-1946, Kolkata, The Asiatic Society (published by Professor Dilip Coomer Ghose) 1948 (reprint 2002), p. 98. See also p. 97: "The debt which European civilization owes to Greece and Rome is a familiar story. But it is seldom realized that India played a similar part in respect to a large part of Asia and even beyond its limits."

Roman numerals."[25] Amartya Sen expresses regret that a "similar history of India's science and technology [such as Joseph Needham had provided for China] has not yet been attempted."[26] Joseph Needham recognized clearly that "to suppose that pure and applied science sprang fully formed from the body of the European Renaissance is entirely false; there had been a long preparation of centuries which had seen the absorption by all Europe of Arabic learning, Indian thought, and Chinese technology."[27]

However, it has been discussed in detail in historiography if indigenous developments took place in parallel, independent of each other, or if cultures exposed to foreign influences merely imitated foreign products, innovations and ideas.[28] Although, obviously, some of the most spectacular modern inventions, "the magnet, the printing press, and gunpowder" were "without exception Chinese inventions," much of Western science supposedly developed without the benefit of these contributions.[29]

Bengal had over long periods been one of the richest provinces of India.[30] The immense wealth of the Muslim rulers of Bengal is well known.

25 A.L. BASHAM, *The Wonder that was India*, Calcutta etc., Rupa & Co. 1990 (orig. 1967), p. 498.

26 Amartya SEN, *On Interpreting India's Past*, Calcutta, The Asiatic Society of Japan 1996, p. 32, note 37.

27 Joseph NEEDHAM, *Within the Four Seas, The Dialogue of East and West*, London etc., George Allen & Unwin 1979 (1969), p. 16.

28 On the diffusion theory see: "In cultural anthropology and cultural geography, cultural diffusion, as first conceptualized by Leo Frobenius in his 1897/98 publication *Der westafrikanische Kulturkreis*, is the spread of cultural items—such as ideas, styles, religions, technologies, languages etc.—between individuals, whether within a single culture or from one culture to another." (https://en.wikipedia.org/wiki/Trans-cultural_diffusion)

29 H. Floris COHEN, The Emergence of Early Modern Science in Europe; with remarks on Needham's 'Grand Question', including the Issue of the cross-cultural Transfer of Scientific Ideas, *Journal of the Japan-Netherlands Institute* (Papers of the First Conference on the Transfer of Science and Technology between Europe and Asia since Vasco da Gama (1498-1998), Amsterdam & Leiden, June 5-7, 1991), vol. III (1991), p. 19 (9-31).

30 See Thomas BOWREY, *A Geographical Account of Countries Round the Bay of Bengal, 1669 to 1679*, New Delhi, Munshiram Manoharlal 1997 (Facsimile reprint of the original edition of 1905), p. 132, note 3, quoting Jean-Baptiste TAVERNIER. Jean-Baptiste TAVERNIER, *Travels in India*, 2 vols., ed. William Crooke, Oxford University Press 1925. See also an early English edition, *Collection of Travels &c.. being the Travels of Monsieur Tavernier, Bernier and other great men*, 2 vols., London, 1684, vol. ii, pp. 140f. (quoted by Thomas BOWREY, p. 132, note 3). A third English edition, *Travels in*

According to François Bernier, the French traveller who had landed in India in 1656 and spent thirteen years there,[31] Bengal in 1600 was "by far the richest ... part of India."[32] The Ganges was an ancient trade route, which connected Bengal with the hinterland, Benaras (Varanasi), Patna and Champa to the north and northwest, and there were road links with the ancient cities Kausambi, Vidisha (Sanchi) and Ujjain with its old port town Bharukacha (now Bharuch) at the mouth of the river Narmada on the west coast, north of the present-day Mumbai.[33] For centuries, perhaps millennia, Indian merchant families had traded with East Asia. Before the arrival of the Portuguese in 1518 foreign trading communities on the Hoogly River included the Malays, the Chinese, and the Arabs.[34] After the Dutch established a factory at Chinsura around 1632, and the British at Hoogly in 1651, Job Carnock, an Englishman, founded Calcutta in 1690. This quickly resulted in Greeks, Armenians and Prussians also settling there to engage in the region's profitable trade. Turkish ships also came to Calcutta, and "the Jews began to settle in the city around 1791."[35]

The Chinese pilgrim monk Fuxian (born 339; traveled from 399-413) reported that this wealthy region, with its bustling port city, Tamralipti, maintained extensive trade relations. Under the Turkish Ilyas Shahi dynasty (1342-1414) Bengal was an independent sultanate, maintaining diplomatic relations even with the 'Dragon Throne' in Nanjing. When the great 'treasure fleet' of Chinese Emperor Zhu Di on its fourth expedition in 1414 called on Bengal, the Bengali king (Nawab) Saif-ud-Din (ca. 1396-1405) is said to have accompanied the Chinese on their way back as an emissary, and gifted an African giraffe to the Chinese imperial court as a present.[36]

India, MacMillan 1889 is available for download on the internet.

31 S. N. MUKHERJEE, *Sir William Jones*, p. 11.

32 Quote in Fernand BRAUDEL, *A History of Civilisations*, New York etc., Penguin 1995 (orig. French 1963), p. 163. The old trade routes formed a network that practically covered the whole subcontinent. A.L. BASHAM, *The Wonder that was India*, p. 225; Hermann KULKE und Dietmar ROTHERMUND, *A History of India*, Calcutta, Allahabad, Bombay, Delhi, Rupa & Co. 1990, pp. 68-69.

33 Until about the 15th century the Hugli was the main arm and the main estuary of the Ganges, until, wandering further and further east, it eventually entered the Brahmaputra, with which it now disgorges into the Bay of Bengal.

34 Samaren ROY, *Calcutta, Society and Change 1690-1990*, Calcutta etc., Rupa 1991, p. 15.

35 S. ROY, *Calcutta*, pp. 16 and 5.

36 Louise LEVATHES, *When China Ruled the Seas. The Treasure Fleet of the Dragon*

After the death of the Grand Mogul of India, Aurangzeb, in 1707, the reign of the Mughals, who still ruled from Delhi, quickly declined. But Persian still remained the official language and was only abolished in 1837. However, when in 1757 the British won the Battle of Plassey (in West Bengal), this had a huge impact on the course of history.[37] It was the definitive turning-point towards the superiority of the 'West' vis-à-vis the 'East'. Until then, India and China had been economically, culturally, technologically and in its sciences superior to the West in many respects.[38]

4. The East India Company

The officers of the East India Company took pains to study the language and culture of the Hindus and Muslims and establish archives, collecting numerous scriptures which they made accessible to the general public in translations. In 1750 they had adopted a resolution for this purpose—although obviously this was also a measure intended to consolidate British rule in India. Needless to say the history of exploitation and financial bleeding of India (by taxation, expropriation, etc.)

Warren Hastings, Governor General of Bengal. Source: http://www.columbia.edu/itc/mealac/pritchett/00routesdata/1700_1799/companyrule/hastings/hastings.jpg

Throne, 1405-1433, New York und Oxford, Oxford University Press 1994, p. 140.

37 Brooks ADAMS, *The Law of Civilization and Decay*, New York, Vintage 1955 (orig. 1896), pp. 255-261; K. M. PANIKKAR, *Asia and Western Dominance. A Survey of the Vasco Da Gama Epoch of Asian History 1498-1945*, London, George Allen & Unwin 1961, p. 79.

38 'Imperialist' orientalists eventually tried to deny their subject peoples the cultural and civilizational equal rank and legal parity. See Martin BRANDTNER, Koloniale Archäologie: Monopolisierte Vergangenheitsdeutung und Herrschaftslegitimation in Britisch-Indien (Colonial archeology: monopolizing interpreting the past and legitimizing rule in British India), in Stephan CONERMANN (ed.), *Mythen, Geschichte(n), Identitäten: Der Kampf um die Vergangenheit* (Myths, histories, identities: contesting the past), Hamburg, E.B.-Verlag (Beiträge des Zentrums für Asiatische und Afrikanische Studien (ZAAS) der Christian-Albrechts-Universität zu Kiel) 1999, pp. 303-366.

demonstrably led to the repression and impoverishment of large segments of the population. The employees of the East India Company, who like William Jones emerged as promoters of Asian culture, history and literature[39] were, indeed, paid for out of the taxpayers' money, which was collected from the Indians primarily on agricultural products. However, their service to humanity in opening up and imparting precious cultural commodities and scientific knowledge can hardly be overestimated.

In Kolkata, a *madrasa* was founded to cultivate Urdu, and Benares was selected for the conservation and development of Sanskrit.[40] The young officers in Bengal developed a lasting interest in Asian studies. Warren Hastings, who governed Bengal from 1772, "encouraged the young officers who were thus pioneering the field of Indology."[41] Hastings had come to India at a young age, and his long residence had "made him an admirer of Indian manners and customs." He knew the Persian language, "gathered Indian paintings and manuscripts, and in his letters to his wife he used to quote from the [Bhagavad] Gita."[42]

In 1786 the Frenchman Abraham Hyacinthe Anquetil Duperron,[43]

---

39 See S.N. MUKHERJEE, *Sir William Jones*, und Dilip Coomer GHOSE, *Sir William Jones*, Bicentenary of his Birth. Commemoration Volume, 1746-1946, Kolkata, The Asiatic Society 1948 (reprint 2002).

40 Somewhat apologetically Wikipedia: "To establish their rule in India, the officers of the East India Company thought it necessary to preserve the knowledge of Hindus and Muslims. In the year 1750 they passed a resolution for that purpose. To preserve Urdu, they established a madrasa at Calcutta, whereas for protection and development of Sanskrit, they chose Benares." http://en.wikipedia.org/wiki/Government_Sanskrit_College,_Varanasi.

41 S. N. MUKHERJEE, *Sir William Jones*, p. 77: "During this time there was in Bengal a group of young officers who were keenly interested in Asiatic studies." And p. 79: "The only man to encourage the young officers who were thus pioneering the field of Indology was Warren Hastings, who had been ruler of Bengal since 1772."

42 S. N. MUKHERJEE, *Sir William Jones*, p. 79: Hastings "came to India at an early age and a long stay in this country had made him an admirer of Indian manners and customs. He mastered the Persian language, gathered Indian paintings and manuscripts, and in his letters to his wife he used to quote from the Gita, which he found a source of inspiration. It was only natural that he should patronize Oriental learning. He encouraged most of the pioneer Indologists in their work, fought for them in the Supreme Council and held long discussions with them on their subjects. They acknowledged their debt to this man. In 1781 Wilkins dedicated his first work to Hastings."

43 Edward W. SAID, *The World, the Text, and the Critic*, Harvard University Press 1983, p. 254, describes Abraham Hyacinthe DUPERRON as "the French scholar, theoretician of egalitarianism, and ecumenist of beliefs..."

who had come to India in 1754, translated the Vedic Upanishads from Persian into Latin, making a lasting impression not only on Arthur Schopenhauer but on European intellectuals in general. Anquetil Duperron had already translated the Persian *Zend Avesta* in 1759; this was published in German in 1776[44] and exerted a great influence on Voltaire, Kant and the Orientalist William Jones.[45] However, the publication of the philosophical treatise caused a controversy in which the church protested the book, because in crucial passages it questioned prevailing orthodoxy. Christian Europe had formerly, at least until the end of the 17th century, believed that the world had been created in the year 4004 BC., and that the earth was the centre of the universe, and the Mediterranean the only (relevant) civilization.[46] This belief was now being shattered, permanently, with far-reaching consequences.

The Indians had apparently fallen behind culturally. Nathaniel Halhed, one of the Orientalists of the East India Company, who had been assured that the literary tradition of Bengal was rich in treasures, after his own investigation found that there existed "no more than a half-dozen old Bengali works," asserting mistakenly that there was not even any "clear cut division between colloquial and literary Bengali."[47] Was this merely a preliminary and in addition subjective view? After all, there had been a strong religious-mystical Bhakti movement[48] in Bengal in the 16th century, which made its appearance also in works of literature. Thus Chaitanya (1486-1533), giving fresh relevance to Hinduism and Vaishnavism, had

---

44 Johann Friedrich KLEUKER, *Zend-Avesta, Zoroasters lebendiges Wort*, Riga 1776.

45 Raymond SCHWAB, *Vie d'Anquetil-Duperron suivie des Usages Civils et religieux des Parses par Anquetil-Duperron*, Paris, E., Leroux 1934, S. 6, quoted in Edward. W. SAID, Foreword, in R. SCHWAB, *The Oriental Renaissance*, p. xiii: Anquetil "had dug a channel between the hemispheres of human genius, freeing the old humanism from the Mediterranean basis."

46 As regards the alleged precedence of Europe see the definition of civilization and Europe's role in Samuel P. HUNTINGTON, *The Clash of Civilizations and the Remaking of the World Order*, London etc., Touchstone 1998, pp. 40ff., esp. pp. 45f.

47 D. KOPF, *Orientalism and the Bengal Renaissance*, p. 58: "He [Nathaniel Halhed] found 'no clear cut division between colloquial and literary Bengali'. Furthermore, he had been assured that Bengal's literary tradition was rich, but upon investigation he could discover 'no more than a half-dozen old Bengali works.'"

48 On the origins of the Bhakti ideology see also Brajadulal CHATTOPADHYAYA, Political Processes and the Structure of Polity in Early Medieval India, in Hermann KULKE (ed.), *The State in India, 1000-1700*, New Delhi, Oxford India Paperbacks 1997, pp. 209-210.

established the Gaudiya Vaishnava school, in which the worship of the divine couple Radha and Krishna had an important function, and which enjoyed a large following among the people. Nevertheless, the British studies and reports initially showed that Bengal was "suffering from literary and academic sterility," and only "primitive forms of religion" were observed. The surveys conducted in the early years of the 19th century showed staggering results, conveying a negative image of the indigenous institutions. Even in Nabadvip, a stronghold of Vaishnavism, and allegedly an "illustrious center of Bengali language and literature," there were "no more than 40 separate works, all in manuscript," representing at that time "the whole literature of 30,000,000 people."[49] A cultural Renaissance was heralded. Or were the Indians just being secretive?

Eventually however, a treasure trove of literature and artefacts revealed itself. Although the philologist William Jones (1746-1796), the 'father of Indology' and discoverer of the Indo-European family of languages, was with Voltaire of the opinion that "the multitude of the Hindus were superstitious," there were two aspects that impressed him "most" in Hinduism, firstly "the non-duality of God and the human soul as explained by Sankara in his commentary on Vedanta," and secondly the "transmigration

Sir William Jones as a young man. Source: http://asi.nic.in/images/history/Sir_William_Jones.jpg

49 D. KOPF, *Orientalism and the Bengal Renaissance*, p. 58: "Several British surveys and reports of the first decade of the nineteenth century portray Bengal as suffering from literary and academic sterility, primitive forms of religion, and progressive stiffening of social attitudes and practices. The Wellesley-sponsored survey of the Twenty-four Pargannas, Hooghly, and Midnapore in 1801, and Francis Buchanan's survey of most of the other districts of Bengal in 1807, 1808, and 1809, were depressingly negative in their depiction of the prevailing state of indigenous institutions. Individual reports such as Carey's on his mission to Nabadvip in 1801 on behalf of the College of Fort William were also extremely unfavorable. Interestingly enough, Carey had gone to Nabadvip to enlist support for the college from 'the illustrious center of Bengali language and literature' but discovered that there existed 'no more than 40 separate works, all in manuscript, as the whole literature of 30,000,000 of people up to that time.'"

of the soul." In this regard Jones found that Hinduism was "superior to Christianity." He did not believe in the Christian doctrine of punishment and eternal torment in hell. He found that the Hindu notion of the transmigration of souls was far more 'rational' than the Christian idea of a "future state."[50] Jones confessed:

> I am no Hindu but I hold the doctrine of the Hindus concerning a future state to be incomparably more rational, more pious and more likely to deter men from vice than the horrid opinions inculcated by the Christians on punishment without end.[51]

Jones was able to show that "India had excelled in arithmetic, geometry and logic. He thought that it was possible that Aristotle based his system of logic on Brahmanic syllogisms." Similarly, the Hindus could "boast of three discoveries, the decimal scale, the game of chess and the science of grammar."[52] It was David Kopf's opinion, Subrata Dasgupta relates, that Jones's work "enhanced our understanding of human knowledge."[53] Jones quickly became familiar with the language and legal terminology of the Hindus and Muslims; he even learnt to see through their occasional tricks and deceptions. After he was appointed judge to the Supreme Court of Bengal on March 4, 1783, he wrote:

> I have the delight of knowing that my studies go hand in hand with my duty, since I now read both Sanscrit and Arabick with so much ease that the native lawyers can never impose upon court in which I sit. I converse fluently in Arabick with Maulavis and in Sanscrit with Pundits and in Persian with nobles of the country.[54]

---

50 S. N. MUKHERJEE, *Sir William Jones*, pp. 117-118: "The two aspects of Hinduism which attracted Jones most were the conception of the non-duality of God and the human soul as explained by Sankara in his commentary on the Vedanta and the transmigration of the soul ... He agreed with Voltaire that the multitude of the Hindus were superstitious." And on p. 119: "In one respect Jones thought Hinduism was superior to Christianity. He could not believe in the Christian doctrine of punishment and eternity of pain. He found that the Hindu idea of transmigration of soul [was] 'more rational' than the Christian idea of the future state." See William JONES, On the Hindus, *Asiatick Researches*, vol. 1, p. 429, quoted in S.N. MUKHERJEE, *Sir William Jones*, p. 119.

51 Ibid.

52 S. N. MUKHERJEE, *Sir William Jones*, p. 119: "He showed that India had excelled in arithmetic, geometry and logic. He thought that it is possible that Aristotle based his system of logic on Brahmanic syllogisms."

53 S. DASGUPTA, *THE BENGAL RENAISSANCE*, p. 22.

54 S. N. MUKHERJEE, *Sir William Jones*, p. 129.

The translation works and text collections of the officials of the British East India Company in Kolkata (Calcutta) are evidence of a cross-cultural exchange similar in nature to events in Japan, where at about the same time Japanese studies were inaugurated by the Dutch on Dejima near Nagasaki and much of Western scientific literature was translated into Japanese.[55] In 1783 the *Bhagavat Gita* (Song of God), one of the most important and perhaps the most famous scripture of Hinduism, was translated into English by the Orientalist Charles Wilkins. The text had already been translated into Persian in 1600, but had remained unknown in Europe. Then in 1787, Wilkins and Nathaniel Halhed, a friend of Jones since 1768, made the first Bengali printing press in order to publish the translated texts in the Bengali language. Furthermore, one year after Wilkins' translation of the *Bhagavat Gita*, William Jones established the *Royal Asiatic Society of Bengal of Calcutta*. This was a big step and membership increased from 30 to 110 between 1784 and 1792,[56] including a number of European scholars as well.

5. Cosmopolitan Kolkata's (Calcutta) 'Cognitive Revolution'

After Warren Hastings had become Governor General of Bengal in 1772/1773, Kolkata became the main base of the East India Company, and finally, in 1877, also the capital of British India. No doubt: the disposition of the British elite in 1800 was "cosmopolitan" rather than "nationalist."[57]

Hastings had his own ideas on how India should be managed. Yet he was just as

> ready to assert British sovereignty. The so-called 'dual government' was to go, and the Company was to take the management of the whole of Bengal into its own hands. But this did not mean the introduction of English laws and English ways in India. His idea was to rule the conquered in their own way. This was how the Romans maintained their empire, this was how he

---

55 See Amartya SEN, *Identity and Violence. The Illusion of Destiny*, New York and London, W.W. Norton 2006, p. 111: "By 1913 ... Japan ... had become one of the largest producers of books in the world, publishing more books than Britain and indeed more than twice as many as the United States."

56 S. N. MUKHERJEE, *Sir William Jones*, p. 84. And p. 91: "The beginnings of Indology are generally associated with the birth of the Asiatick Society and Jones is often described as 'the Father of Indology.'"

57 D. KOPF, *British Orientalism and the Bengal Renaissance*, p. 22.

could elevate 'the British name'. [58]

Hastings wanted to reconcile British rule with the Indian institutions.

In 1789 William Jones put out the first issue of the *Asiatick Researches*. This magazine, which could well compare with any of the European scientific journals at the time, published

> numerous original papers which would readily appeal to the readers of *Archaeologia* or *Philosophical Transactions*. The contents were carefully chosen to satisfy men with varied tastes; there were articles on ancient land grants, a Sikh college in Patna, a journey to Tibet, on the manners, religion and languages of the Hindus, on Indian literature, trial by ordeal, and a number of other articles on natural sciences.[59]

For the first time works of Indian scholars were published as well. The magazine aroused such a stir in the European literary world that in London pirated copies were printed and circulated. Translations of entire volumes were made in several European languages. A German periodical, *Asiatisches Magazin*, was launched in Germany in 1802 by Heinrich Julius Klaproth (1783-1835).

The missionary and founder of the Baptist Missionary Society of the Danish settlement working in Serampore in Kolkata, William Carey (1761-1834), was the first to write prose in Bengali. His translation of the Bible into Bengali appeared in 1793.[60]

William Carey had come to Bengal as late as November 1793, and hired a certain Ramram Basu as his Bengali and Sanskrit teacher.

---

58 S. N. MUKHERJEE, *Sir William Jones*, p. 79: "Hastings's encouragement of Oriental Studies had a practical side. He had his own ideas of how India should be ruled. He was ready to assert British sovereignty. The so-called 'dual government' was to go, and the Company was to take the management of the whole of Bengal into its own hands. But this did not mean the introduction of English laws and English ways in India. His idea was to rule the conquered in their own way. This was how the Romans maintained their empire, this was how he could elevate 'the British name'. He founded the Calcutta Madrasa and provided money for it to 'soften the prejudices' which he said were 'excited by the rapid growth of the British dominion'. Thus he wanted to reconcile British rule with Indian institutions. This meant a further investigation into the manners and customs of the country, and more studies in the literature and the laws of the Indians. The Gentoo Laws of Halhed was one realization of his schemes."

59 S. N. MUKHERJEE, *Sir William Jones*, p. 88.

60 D. KOPF, *British Orientalism*, p. 3.

Fort William, reproduction of an engraving by I. Van Ryne, 1754

In 1801 Basu became a *Munshi* (teacher/writer) in the college of Fort William. Translations like the *Bhagavad Gita, Sakuntala*, and Mrityunjay Vidyalankar's *Rajaboli* (a history of the kings), or Ramram Basu's *Pratapaditya* (a historical essay on Raja Pratapaditya), were the norm and well received. Regrettably, however, Buddhist India, the history of the Greek Bactrians, the India of the Guptas or Mauryas, or Tibet initially received but little attention.

It should be noted that William Jones not only convincingly refuted the thesis of "oriental despotism," he was particularly sensitive on this point, abhorred any form of slavery and did not hesitate in this respect to agree with progressive Americans,[61] whom he supported "in their struggle for independence." Obviously, "the chief reason was that they held similar ideas on freedom and the slave system," maintaining in common with Jones that slavery was a violation "against the primary law of nature."[62] He maintained

---

61 S. N. MUKHERJEE, *Sir William Jones*, p. 169, note 3, tells of another progressive American: "It is interesting to note that it was Alexander Hamilton [the cousin of the American Alexander Hamilton, who was born in India], a member of the Asiatick Society, who taught [Friedrich] Schlegel Sanskrit in Paris, when he was there as a prisoner of war."

62 S. N. MUKHERJEE, *Sir William Jones*, pp. 133-134: "To Jones this is against the natural law. A man cannot claim a property in rational beings, 'since our creator had given our species a dominion to be moderately exercised over the beasts of the field and the fowls of the air but not to man over man' ... So slavery must be condemned not only because it violates 'the primary law of nature' but also because the system is economically unsound

that

> our creator had given our species a dominion to be moderately exercised over the beasts of the field and the fowls of the air but not to man over man.[63]

Slavery and the slave trade had to be condemned, not only because they violated natural law, "but also because the system is economically unsound."[64]

6. The Works

As time went by, not only major Indian and Ceylonese, but also Tibetan texts[65] were translated and published in European languages. Vedic and Buddhist literature was systematically collected and translated—not only into English but also into Indian vernaculars such as Bengali. The drama of the poet Kalidasa, the Sanskrit poem *Sakuntala*, and Jayadeva's *Gita Govinda* were published in 1802 in German translation in the *Asiatisches Magazin*.[66]

William Jones, who had also translated the *Gitagovinda*, translated *Shakuntala* into English. Johann Gottfried Herder, Friedrich Schlegel, Chateaubriand, Victor Hugo and Johann Wolfgang von Goethe simply loved the drama, and in 1819 Goethe praised Jones' achievements, contributing to the fame and dissemination of his works. Schopenhauer "throughout his life ... celebrated the blessings that he ceaselessly derived" from the Vedanta.[67] The European reception proceeded according to a set pattern:

... There were many reasons why he supported the Americans in their struggle for independence but perhaps the chief reason was that they held similar ideas on freedom and the slave system."

63 S. N. MUKHERJEE, *Sir William Jones*, p. 133.

64 Ibid., p. 133.

65 S. N. MUKHERJEE, *Sir William Jones*, p. 85: "On April 1784 the Governor General [Hastings] sent Samuel Turner's description of Tibet to be read by the Society."

66 See Vinoy DHARWARKAR, Orientalism and the Study of Indian Literatures, in C.A. BRECKENRIDGE und P. van der VEER, *Orientalism and the Postcolonial Predicament*, p. 178. See also S. N. MUKHERJEE, *Sir William Jones*, p. 121: "His publication of *Sakuntala* and the *Gita Govinda* put Indian literature on the world map." See also R. SCHWAB, *The Oriental Renaissance*, p. 53: "Jones's *Shakuntala* had five editions and gained him an international reputation. 'The merits of this man are universally known and have been emphasized and detailed on numerous occasions', Goethe wrote in 1819, and forty years later Goethe recalled how the orientalist Eichorn had given him Jones's Works."

67 R. SCHWAB, *The Oriental Renaissance*, p. 427: "... throughout his life he celebrated the blessings that he ceaselessly derived from it."

"Calcutta provided, London distributed, Paris filtered and generalized."[68] The German reception became the basis for promoting and inventing a tradition of its own, which led to a particular cultural identification that occasioned racist-ideological theories. Schopenhauer proclaimed that from now on a philosophy that was not consistent with the teachings of Vedanta was no longer acceptable.[69] Raymond Schwab writes that "while England was the native land of Indic studies, the native land of the Indic Renaissance was Germany, first at Jena, Weimar, and Heidelberg, then at Bonn, Berlin, and Tübingen."[70] In the 1790s the impact of the works of the Indian Renaissance had hit the German intelligentsia "like a rapid-fire series of explosions."[71] In the end Germany was even awarded the title "the India of the Occident. This was not, in [Victor] Hugo's frame of reference, a very good mark for Germany."[72] David Kopf pointed out a certain "bias of the German scholars" who "increasingly viewed the *Vedanta* as a unique manifestation of the 'Aryan genius.'"[73] The "comparison of Germany with India was widespread; Germany itself took pride in it."[74] Sheldon Pollock saw Orientalism in Germany as leading to and endorsing a special "complex of 'knowledge as power'," that tended to "construct the concept of a historic German character and [thus] to define Germany's place in the destiny of Europe,"[75] whatever that was supposed to mean. The general tenor at the time, however, was, as the Orientalist Henry Thomas Colebrooke (1765-

---

68 Edward W. SAID, Foreword, in R. SCHWAB, *The Oriental Renaissance*, p. ix.

69 R. SCHWAB, *The Oriental Renaissance*, p. 427: "On being introduced to the *Oupnek'hat* [Upanishad] by [Friedrich] Maier at the age of twenty-five, Schopenhauer immediately announced that no philosophy would be acceptable unless it was in agreement with Vedantic doctrine." However, the author criticizes the philosopher, ibid., p. 445: "Schopenhauer failed to recognize the true esotericism of the Upanishads."

70 R. SCHWAB, *The Oriental Renaissance*, p. 53.

71 Ibid., p. 53: "During the 1790s the impact of oriental studies in Germany was like a rapid-fire series of explosions."

72 R. SCHWAB, *The Oriental Renaissance*, p. 366: "In the end, Germany would be called 'the India of the Occident.'"

73 D. KOPF, *British Orientalism*, p. 38.

74 R. SCHWAB, *The Oriental Renaissance*, p. 366.

75 Sheldon POLLOCK, Deep Orientalism? Notes on Sanskrit and Power Beyond the Raj, in C.A. BRECKENRIDGE und P. van der VEER, *Orientalism and the Postcolonial Predicament*, p. 7. By contrast, R. SCHWAB, *The Oriental Renaissance*, p. 217, believes it should have been Germany's historical mission to present for a modern Europe "a fusion of the mythological traditions of all humanity." Apparently, Germany has not done justice to this task.

1837) acknowledged in 1837 before the Asiatic Society, that "civilization had its origin in Asia" and the West "owed a debt of gratitude" to the Asian cultures.[76] Like Colebrooke, the German Indologist Richard Garbe (1857-1927) came to the conclusion that even the ancient Greek world of thought itself had clearly been influenced by India.[77] The Russian reception, since it probably influenced Tsar Alexander I. and promoted concepts of peace there, deserves a special mention.[78]

In Ceylon and in Odisha (Orissa, on the Indian east coast) Orientalists contributed valuable translation work that threw new light on Ashoka. In 1837, Lieutenant Markham Kittoe, James Prinsep's man in Odisha, discovered the Dhauli rock inscription. The text in Magadhi Prakrit, the language in which the historical Buddha is said to have preached, was written in the Brahmi script. Dhauli in Cuttack (Odisha) was home to eleven of the fourteen new edicts of Girnar, and "Prinsep saw immediately ... the great historical significance of these ... inscriptions originating on the eastern side of India."[79] "[Lieutenant Markham] Kittoe was allowed to make a copy of the Khandagiri rock inscription, but at the same time as he did so he heard talk of a second rock inscription, said to be on a hill on the other side of Bhubaneshwar town and on the far side of the River Daya—a name that in Sanskrit means 'compassion', the significance of which would only later become apparent."[80] There were also two special edicts.

Henry Thomas Colebrooke participated in the translation of the *Kalpa Sutra* of the Jainas,[81] which was finally published in 1848 by John Stevenson. Buddhist literature was brought by George Nadoris (de Silva) from Siam (Thailand) to Ceylon. The Orientalist George Turnour (1799-

---

76 Henry Thomas COLEBROOKE, Discourse at the Royal Asiatic Society of Great Britain and Ireland, *Miscellaneous Essays*, London, William H. Allen 1837, quoted in D. KOPF, *British Orientalism*, p. 39. See also Charles ALLEN, *Ashoka*, p. 113.

77 Richard von GARBE is mentioned by R.C. MAJUMDAR, Indian Culture as a factor in the World Civilization, p. 99.

78 R. SCHWAB, *The Oriental Renaissance*, pp. 449 ff.

79 Ernst WINDISCH, *Geschichte der Sanskrit-Philologie und indischen Altertumskunde, 1., 2. Teil sowie nachgelassene Kapitel des 3. Teils* (History of Sanskrit Philology and Indian Archaeology), Berlin, New York, de Gruyter 1992 (orig. 1917, Karl J. Trübner), p. 108. (My own translation.)

80 Charles ALLEN, *Ashoka*, p. 155.

81 John STEVENSON D.D., *The Kalpa Sutra, and Nava Tatva: Two Works illustrative of the Jain Religion and Philosophy* (1848).

1843), an official in the British administration which had been operating in Ceylon from 1933, edited the Pali text of the *Mahāvamsa*, with English translation, which was published in 1837.[82] A certain Edward Upham had allegedly also been involved in the translation, having assumed the work on behalf of Sir Alexander Johnston, the Chief Justice of Ceylon, and in 1833 he published the *Mahāvamsa* along with two chronicles, the *Raja-Ratnakara* and *Rajavali*, in three volumes.[83] The English translation of the *Mahāvamsa* also contained a masterful historical introduction; it was the first longer Pali text ever printed at the time, and among other things contained useful details about the Mauryan Emperor Ashoka.

Numerous are the names of those that contributed to the 'rediscovery of India'. A Scottish officer in the British East India Company, Colonel Colin Mackenzie (1754-1821), was a collector of antiques and an Orientalist. One of the many Jain texts he had collected was the *Parisishtaparvan* (*Lives of the Jain Elders*), the work of a polymath named Acharya Hemachandra of the 12th century. It threw new light on the Maurya dynasty of Magadha. As the first surveyor of India he surveyed southern India by using local interpreters and scientists to orally study the religion, the handed down histories, inscriptions and other testimonies, initially out of personal interest, and later as a surveyor. Having been commissioned, shortly after the British victory over Tipu Sultan in 1799, to survey the Mysore region, he produced the first maps of the region, including pictures of landscapes and references to archaeological sites. His collections of thousands of manuscripts, inscriptions, translations, coins and paintings were acquired after his death by the library of the India Office and are an important source for the study of Indian history.[84]

---

82 See G. P. MALALASEKARA, *The Pali Literature of Ceylon*, Colombo, M. D. Gunasena 1928/1958, pp. 5-6: "In 1833 Edward Upham made at the request of Sir Alexander Johnston, Chief Justice of Ceylon, translations of the Mahavamsa, together with two chronicles in Sinhalese (the Raja-ratnakara and the Rajavali) and published them in three volumes under the title *The Sacred and Historical Books of Ceylon*."

83 However, UPHAM's translation included only 88 of the total of one hundred chapters of the Mahavamsa. Edward UPHAM (ed.), *The Mahavansi, the Raja-ratnacari, and the Raja-vali: forming the sacred and historical books of Ceylon; also, a collection of tracts illustrative of the doctrines and literature of Buddhism: translated from the Singhalese.* London, Parbury, Allen, and Co. 1833 (3 vols.).

84 http://en.wikipedia.org/wiki/Colin_Mackenzie

7. A 'Golden Age'?

"'Western universalism' no less than 'Oriental exceptionalism' can be shown to be only a particular form of a richer, more diverse, and differentiated conceptualization of a new universal idea." (Partha Chatterjee)

In 1800 the College of Fort William was founded south of Kolkata, in which not only British, but also Indian students could enrol. The "dream of a University of the East" had become a reality.[85] A 'Sanskrit College' had already been founded in Benares in 1791.[86] The College of Fort William had an Asian faculty, in which the main Indian languages and Sanskrit were taught, and a European faculty. Warren Hastings' policy was "designed to encourage Orientalists and Bengalis to work together for common goals."[87] Jawaharlal Nehru had to admit that India owed the Orientalists, especially the employees of the East India Company like Hastings and William Jones, who had devoted themselves to the study of Indian history and literature, "a deep debt of gratitude for the rediscovery of her past literature."[88] A year or two later, the first regular library of oriental books and manuscripts was set up in the College of Fort William.[89]

Despite initial difficulties in motivating the Bengali Pandits to cooperate, a good and fruitful cooperation developed by and by. Surprisingly, however, some fantastically rich men like Radhakant Deb, "son of the fabulously wealthy Naba Krishna Deb," completely shunned

---

85 D. KOPF, *British Orientalism*, p. 62.

86 "To establish their rule in India, the officers of the East India Company thought in necessary to preserve the knowledge of Hindus and Muslims ... In 1791 ... Jonathan Duncan, the representative of the East India Company, proposed the establishment of a Sanskrit college for development and preservation of the Sanskrit Vangmaya and to show that the English people were in favour of the development of the Indian culture. This was sanctioned by Governor General Lord Cornwallis. Kashi Naresh Mahip Narayan Singh donated a huge tract of land in the southern part of Benares for construction of the college. The first teacher of this Institution was Pandit Kashinath. The Governor General initially sanctioned a budget of Rs. 20,000 per annum." http://en.wikipedia.org/wiki/Government_Sanskrit_College,_Varanasi.

87 D. KOPF, *British Orientalism*, p. 178.

88 J. NEHRU, *The Discovery of India*, New Delhi, Jawaharlal Nehru Memorial Fund and Oxford University Press 1990 (orig. Calcutta, Signet Press 1946), p. 317.

89 D. KOPF, *British Orientalism*, p. 118: "The first institutional library of Oriental books and manuscripts in India was founded at the College of Fort William in 1801-02."

"professional or commercial contact with Englishmen."[90]

The intensive cooperation and cultural exchanges meant that in Bengal a whole new educated intellectual class was formed. [91] In 1813 the British Parliament made available a sum of 100,000 rupees a year "for the promotion of native education, *both* 'oriental' and 'Western'."[92] Much as in the 19th century the Japanese had done, Indian scholars travelled to the West for studies. For example, Mirza Abu Taleb Khan (1752-1806), a scholar who had on various occasions provided useful services to the East India Company, visited England and other European countries in 1799, and returned back to Bengal in 1803 with his newly discovered data. He lamented the backwardness of the Indians, wished to introduce Utilitarianism and brought with him valuable information on the advancement and achievements of the West.[93] He considered it had become an utter necessity to meet the challenges of the modern age and follow the Western example, modernize and bring Asian and Western civilization to an equitable level that could be mutually profitable. This was no doubt a challenging task, but just "as Europe liberated itself by reviving its classical literature, so might Hindu India do the same."[94]

---

90 D. KOPF, *British Orientalism*, p. 108.

91 D. KOPF, *British Orientalism*, p. 213: "The class that he [Bhabinicharan Bannerji] described and to which he himself belonged was, therefore, a distinctively new social grouping in India. It was composed of an elite and an intelligentsia. The class was urban, not rural; it was literate and sophisticated; its status was founded more on wealth than on caste; it was a professional, not a literati, group; it was receptive to new knowledge, ideas, and values; it absorbed new attitudes and its intellectuals created a syncretic cultural tradition; and perhaps most important, it mentally transcended kin and caste and thought in broader social terms."

92 Benedict ANDERSON, *Imagined Communities. Reflections on the Origin and Spread of Nationalism* (revised ed.), London and New York, Verso 1996 (1983), p. 90.

93 Abu Taleb KHAN, *The Travels of Mirza Abu Taleb Khan in Asia, Africa, and Europe during the Years 1799, 1800, 1801, 1802, and 1803*, transl. by Charles STEWART, London, Longman, Hurst, Rees, and Orme, 1810. According to Samaren ROY, *Calcutta, Society and Change 1690-1990*, p. 72, Taleb's book, *The Travels of Mirza Abu Taleb Khan*, "written in Persian in 1803 on his return from Europe, was circulated in Calcutta in manuscript copied from the original." See also Amrit SEN, 'The Persian Prince in London': Autoethnography and Positionality in Travels of Mirza Abu Taleb Khan, *Asiatic*, vol. 2, No. 1 (June 2008), pp. 58-68. A new edition of the book was published in 2005 in Oxford under the title *Westwardbound: Travels of Mirza Abu Talib*. The text is online: https://archive.org/details/travelsmizraabu01khgoog.

94 D. KOPF, *British Orientalism*, p. 102.

The connection between the "enlightened few in Calcutta and the few enlightened from England"[95] contributed to promoting modernization and progress, facilitated liberal development in India, and encouraged a synthesis of Christian and Hindu values[96] through common ideas of social reform.[97] Considering these ideas and weighing the prospects, it was hoped that "the perfectibility of mankind could be achieved" if social reforms and the idea of rational religion were reconciled.[98]

As David Kopf has shown, in the "golden age of British Orientalism in India" between 1813 and 1823 Kolkata became, "as a result of unprecedented experiments in cultural fusion" of the various cultural traditions, and facilitated by the labours of the Orientalists, "the earliest of Asian cities to develop the qualities necessary for what Daniel Lerner has described as the transformation of a traditional to a modern society."[99] It is not too far-fetched to compare these developments to the events in Japan: in both places a socio-intellectual revolution was taking place. Kolkata may then have been, together with Edo (Tokyo),[100] one of the largest cities outside the western world.[101]

---

95 David KOPF, *The Brahmo Samaj and the Shaping of the Modern Indian Mind*, Princeton, Princeton University Press 1979, p. 3.

96 D. KOPF, *The Brahmo Samaj*, p. 3: "The first was liberal religion, or the substitution of rational faith for the prevailing popular religions of the world..."

97 D. KOPF, *The Brahmo Samaj*, p. 3: "The second was the idea of social reform, or emancipation in which all known penalised classes and groupings such as workers, peasants, and women were to be elevated through education and the extension of civil rights to participate fully in the benefits of modern civilisation."

98 D. KOPF, *The Brahmo Samaj*, p. 3: "Three simple though radical ideas for the time (1815 to 1835) provided the link between the enlightened few in Calcutta and the enlightened few in England and the United States. The first was liberal religion, or the substitution of a rational faith for the prevailing popular religions of the world ... The second was the idea of social reform ... to participate fully in the benefits of modern civilisation. Finally ... the notion that the perfectibility of mankind could be achieved by joining social reform to rational religion."

99 Daniel LERNER, *The Passing of Traditional Society*, New York, Glencoe Free Press 1964, p. 62, quoted in D. Kopf, *British Orientalism*, p. 178.

100 W.G. BEASLEY, *The Rise of Modern Japan*, Tokyo, Tuttle 1991, p. 10 has it that "Edo itself had a population of a million persons (half a million being Samurai) in the early eighteenth century."

101 D. KOPF, *British Orientalism*, p. 178, note 1: "In 1801-1802, Wellesley ... found that there were 600,000 people in Calcutta and 2,225,000 living within a 25-mile radius of the city. Through 1830, most estimates of the metropolitan population ranged between 1,000,000 and 2,000,000."

8. Rammohun Roy

A personality of paramount importance and stature was the scholar Rammohun Roy (1772-1833), "a new type combining in himself the old learning and the new,"[102] and a polymath (S. Dasgupta) who established links between East and West by forging a synthesis of Vedic traditions with Christianity. Rammohun came from a Brahmin family located in a small village near Calcutta, and had received his "first education from the Sufis."[103] In 1804 he published his first book, *Tuhfat-ul-Muwahiddin* (A Gift to Monotheists), in Persian. Rammohun had not only studied Persian, Sanskrit and Arabic, but also took to learning English, Latin, Greek and Hebrew.[104] He vigorously sought the dialogue with the Christian missionaries of the Baptist Mission at Serampore. According to Basham he was "the first Indian to learn enough from the West to be able to hold his own with the best minds of Europe, and yet still to love and respect his own culture."[105] Monier-Williams, the famous Orientalist, considered him "perhaps the first earnest-minded investigator of the science of Comparative Religion that the world has produced."[106] As Raymond Schwab writes, he "boldly sought to reconcile Vedism with the Gospels."[107] R.C. Majumdar considered him "worthy to rank by the side of [Francis] Bacon and [Martin] Luther."[108]

---

102 J. NEHRU, *The Discovery of India*, p. 315.

103 R. SCHWAB, *The Oriental Renaissance*, p. 246.

104 For a critical evaluation of the role of the Bengali intelligentsia and of Rammohun ROY's intellectual background in particular *see* R.C. MAJUMDAR, *Glimpses of Bengal in the Nineteenth Century*, Calcutta, Firma K.L. Mukhopadhyay 1960, p. 22 (on Rammohun): "As a matter of fact very little is known of [his] early life ... There are, for example, no grounds to believe that [he] studied Persian and Arabic at Patna or Sanskrit at Benares, for a long period..."

105 "... the friend of Jeremy Bentham. Ram Mohun Roy ... advocated the frank acceptance of all of value that Europe had to teach ... From the days of Ram Mohun Roy young Indians, at first very few but soon in great numbers, began to come to England for education." (p. 27) A.L. BASHAM, *The Wonder that was India*, Calcutta etc., Rupa & Co. 1990 (1967), pp. 23 and 27.

106 J. NEHRU, *The Discovery of India*, p. 315.

107 R. SCHWAB, *The Oriental Renaissance*, p. 245.

108 R.C. MAJUMDAR, *Glimpses of Bengal in the Nineteenth Century*, p. 53: "The standard of revolt he thus raised against the medieval tyranny of dogma unleashed forces which created what may be called Modern India and makes him worthy to rank by the side of Bacon and Luther."

In 1823, Rammohun, together with the social reformer and entrepreneur Dwaraknath Tagore, and a young Baptist by the name of William Adam, founded the *Calcutta Unitarian Committee*. Out of this came a great intellectual movement, the *Brahmo Samaj*, established in 1828. This was an entirely new and revolutionary concept. "The precepts of Brahmoism were meant to replace some of the beliefs and practices of orthodox Hinduism," though "not obliterate the Hindu religion ... both Hinduism and Brahmoism (as invented by Rammohun Roy) take the Vedanta and the Upanishads as their scriptural sources."[109] On his visit to England in 1830, officially as "an emissary of the Great Mughal who was still the nominal sovereign of India,"[110] Rammohun was received by the aged Jeremy Bentham with whom he had become friends.[111] By then Rammohun

---

109 S. DASGUPTA, *THE BENGAL* RENAISSANCE, p. 44. (Italics in the original.) However: "Even Rammohun Roy allowed that ordinary people needed their many deities and their physical representations." (p. 48)

110 H. KULKE and D. ROTHERMUND, *A History of India*, Rupa 1991, p. 252.

111 Rammohun Roy's correspondence with Jeremy Bentham:
"Intensely admired and dearly beloved collaborator in the service of Mankind!
Your character is made known to me by our excellent friends, Colonel Young, Colonel Stanhope, and Mr Buckingham. Your works, by a book in which I read, a style which, but for the name of an Hindoo, I should have ascribed to the pen of a superiorly well-educated and instructed Englishman. A just-now-published work of mine, which I send by favour of Mrs Young, exhibits my view of the foundations of human belief, specially applied to the practice of this country in matters of law.
Now at the brink of the grave, (for I want but a month or two of fourscore,) among the most delightful of my reflections, is the hope, I am notwithstanding feeding myself with, of rendering my labours of some considerable use to the hundred millions, or thereabouts, of whom I understand that part of your population which is under English governance or influence is composed.
With Mr Mill's work on British India you can scarcely fail to be more or less acquainted. For these three or four-and-twenty years he has numbered himself among my disciples; for upwards of twenty years he has been receiving my instructions; for about the half of each of five years, he and his family have been my guests. If not adequately known already, his situation in the East India Company's service can be explained to you by Colonel Young. My papers on *Evidence*,—those papers which you now see in print— were in his hands, and read through by him, while occupied in his above-noticed great work; a work from which more practically applicable information on the subject of government and policy may be derived (I think I can venture to say) than from any other as yet extant; though, as to style, I wish I could, with truth and sincerity, pronounce it equal to yours.
For these many years a grand object of his ambition has been to provide for British India, in the room of the abominable existing system, a good system of judicial procedure, with a judicial establishment adequate to the administration of it; and for the composition of it his reliance has all along been, and continues to be, on me. What I have written on these subjects wants little of being complete; so little that, were I to die

to-morrow, there are those that would be able to put it in order and carry it through the press.

What he aims at above all things is,—the giving stability and security to landed property in the hands of the greatest number throughout British India; and, for this purpose, to ascertain by judicial inquiry, the state of the *customs* of the people in that respect. For this same purpose, a great *increase* in the number of *judicatories,* together with the *oral examination* of all parties concerned, and *recordation* of the result will be absolutely necessary: the mode of proceeding as simple as possible, unexpensive and prompt, forming in these respects as complete a contrast as possible with the abominable system of the great Calcutta Judicatory: nations of unmixed blood and half-caste, both of whom could serve on moderate salaries, being, on my system, as much employed as possible. Though but very lately known to your new Governor-general, Mr Mill is in high favour with him; and (I have reason to believe) will have a good deal of influence, which, in that case, he will employ for the purpose above-mentioned. ...

"For I know not how many years—a dozen or fifteen, perhaps—I have never paid a single visit to anybody, except during about three months, when a complaint I was troubled with forced me to bathing places, and at length to Paris. Thus it is that Lord William and I have never come together; and now there is not time enough. Half jest, half earnest, Mr Mill promised him a meeting with me on his return from India; for, old as I am, I am in good health and spirits, and have as yet lost but little of the very little strength I had in my youth. Though the *influence* of my writings is said to be something, of anything that can be called *power* I have not had any the least atom. I have some reason for expecting that, ere long, more or less use will be made of my work on Judicial Procedure by government here. But, from the influence possessed by Mr Mill, and the intense anxiety he has been manifesting for some years past for the completion of it, my hopes have in relation to your country been rather sanguine. Of the characters of it I cannot find time to say anything, except that, by the regard shown in it to the interests of the subject many, and by its simplicity, which I have endeavoured to maximize, I have little fear of its not recommending itself to your affections.

What regards the Judiciary Establishment will form about half of the second of two volumes, a copy of the first of which (with the exception of six introductory parts) being already in print, is designed to form part of the contents of this packet.

While writing, it has occurred to me to add a copy of a work called Panopticon; the rather because, at the desire of Mr Mill, it is in the hands of your new Governor-general, Lord William Bentinck, to whom Mr Mill has been recommending, and, as he flatters himself, not altogether without success, the erection of a place of confinement, upon the principles therein displayed. More than thirty years ago, but for a personal pique taken against me by the late king, George the Third, all the prisoners in the kingdom, and all the paupers, would, under my care, have been provided for by me upon the same principle. To the Prime Minister of the time, (from 1792 to 1802,) with his colleagues, it was an object of enthusiastic and persevering admiration; and not only was an act of the Legislature, which (you know) could not have been enacted without the king's consent, obtained for the purpose, but so much as related to the experimental prison carried into effect as the purchase of a large spot of ground for the purpose, and the greatest part put into my possession; but when the last step came to be taken, George the Third could not be prevailed upon to take it; and so the affair ended. ...

Farewell, illustrious friend! You may imagine from what is above, with what pleasure I should hear from you. Information from you might perhaps be made of use with reference to the above objects. But you should, in that case, send me two letters—one

had become famous and when he visited Paris in 1832, he "attracted a great deal of attention."[112] Raymond Schwab reports that "according to Romain Rolland, Roy's 'journals were enthusiastic' about the revolutionary cause in various European countries, particularly 'in revolutionary France in the days of July 1830.'"[113] He deeply sympathized with the aims and objectives of the French and their liberal-democratic revolution.

Rammohun published several journals during his lifetime, and many historians regard him as "one of the founders of the Indian press."[114] With Ganga Kishore Bhattacharya he published the first Bengali weekly, the *Bengal Gazette*, early in 1818, and in April a Bengali magazine entitled *Dig Darshan* appeared. In the same year the first commercial newspaper, the *Samachar Darpan*, was published in Bengali. Both were printed in Serampore. Not surprisingly, Rammohun is also regarded as one of the "father[s] of modern India."[115] Brajendra Nath Seal (1924) described Rammohun Roy as a "Universal Man," "one of the 'heroes of synthesis and conciliation', a 'prophet of humanity' who envisioned an 'enlightened India'

---

confidential, another ostensible. If I live seven days longer, I shall be fourscore. To make provision for the event of my death, you should do by your letters to me, as Colonel Young has done by his: send it open, enclosed in one to Bowring.

We have high hopes of Lord William's good intentions: so much better than from so high an aristocratical family as his could have been expected.

I have been asking our common friends here, over and over again, for their assurance that there is some chance of your paying a visit to this strange country. I can get little better from them, than a shake of the head.

P.S. Panopticon. Should this plan, and the reasoning, meet your approbation, you will see that none of the business as to which it is applicable, could be carried on well otherwise than by contract. What say you to the making singly, or in conjunction with other enlightened philanthropists, an offer to Government for that purpose? Professors of all religions might join in the contract; and appropriate classification and separation for the persons under management: provision correspondent to their several religions, and their respective castes; or other allocations under their respective religions. How it would delight me to see you and Colonel Young engaged in a partnership for a purpose of that sort!" Unabriged text online: http://oll.libertyfund.org/titles/bentham-the-works-of-jeremy-bentham-vol-10-memoirs-part-i-and-correspondence.

112 R. SCHWAB, *The Oriental Renaissance*, p. 245.

113 Ibid., p. 245. See also R.C. MAJUMDAR, *Glimpses of Bengal*, p. 40.

114 J. NEHRU, *The Discovery of India*, p. 315.

115 Or the "inaugurator of the modern age in India." N.S. BOSE, *The Indian Awakening and Bengal*, Calcutta, K.L. Mukhopadhyay 1960, p. 10, quoted in KOPF, *British Orientalism*, p. 196.

as a 'golden link' between East and West."[116] Rammohun died in 1833 in Bristol, England, at the age of 61.

According to Adrienne Moore who wrote perhaps "the first American graduate thesis on Rammohun Roy," published in 1942, Rammohun was in his time "almost a household word" in New England, and the Americans' first "important contact" with the subcontinent, whose writings had been received even by such lumeries as Ralph Waldo Emerson.[117] Obviously, although Roy's "creative encounters" with the Americans, since he never visited the United States, were "conducted from a distance,"[118] he had made a notable impression in the New World.

9. Modern Science takes Roots and Buddhism once more becomes a World Religion

Another educational institution established in 1830 by Horace Wilson was the Calcutta Sanskrit College, which included in its curriculum not only "the traditional Sanskritic studies of rhetoric, sacred literature, law, and grammar," but also sciences such as "mechanics, hydrostatics, optics, astronomy, chemistry, mathematics, anatomy, and medicine."[119] In 1828 a certain Dr. John Tyler, an anatomy professor at the Sanskrit College, introduced "anatomical dissection to his class." It was noted that "Hindu students trained in the traditional manner had no difficulty in responding to Western course-work."[120] Subrata Dasgupta relates how "Western doubt over whether Indian medical students could do a proper anatomy course"[121] was finally dispelled, when in the 1830s several students passed the scientific medical examinations of the Calcutta Medical College, founded in 1835; and in October 1836 Madhusudan Gupta became the first known Indian to perform a human dissection.[122]

116 Quoted in S. DASGUPTA, *THE BENGAL* RENAISSANCE, p. 54.

117 Quoted in S. DASGUPTA, *THE BENGAL* RENAISSANCE, pp. 75-76, who has more of this on the following pages.

118 S. DASGUPTA, *THE BENGAL* RENAISSANCE, p. 75.

119 D. KOPF, *British Orientalism*, p. 183.

120 See also D. KOPF, *British Orientalism*, pp. 183-184: "In 1828, Dr. Tyler, the anatomy professor, introduced anatomical dissection to his class, and before the end of the year, 'the students not only handled the bones of the human skeleton without reluctance, but in some instances themselves performed the dissection of the softer parts of animals.'"

121 S. DASGUPTA, *THE BENGAL* RENAISSANCE, p. 136.

122 See S. DASGUPTA, *THE BENGAL* RENAISSANCE, pp. 135 ff. for further details.

With the creation of the Supreme Court in Kolkata in 1774 the interest in the indigenous legal traditions led to an improved system of legal justice developed in practice. Hastings had commissioned the translation of the Code of Manu, the most effective compendium of Brahmanic social teachings.[123] Apparently, according to Joseph Needham, the "development of Indian law had followed a course somewhat parallel to that of China."[124] Indian and Chinese law was an administrative and equity law, based essentially on principles of natural law. Basic criteria of justice and generally accepted moral and ethical standards and social norms were central. Scriptures like the Buddhist 'law' (Dharma) aimed at individual perfection, enlightenment, moral and spiritual elevation in knowing God and His manifestations, the universe or nature and its laws, to which one wanted to be harmoniously connected in 'cosmic union'. There was a connection.

So, in Kolkata in this fertile period of British Orientalism—David Kopf spoke of the "golden age of British Orientalism"[125]—having become the first Asian city, as we have seen, in which a cultural fusion took place, universally applicable values and new perspectives emerged that determined what the future should hold. The comparison of Kolkata, with a population of between 1-2 million people, with Edo, today's Tokyo, around 1800, probably the largest and most populous cities in Asia, is very intriguing.

Perhaps the most spectacular discovery of the British orientalists were the inscriptions of the 'pacifist' Emperor Ashoka Maurya (see PART I), chiselled in rock and stone pillars. In 1837 the Orientalist James Prinsep, Wilson's successor at Sanskrit College, who also translated the edicts,[126] "unravelled the mystery of the Brahmi script."[127] To many, Ashoka stands out in the history of the world for having renounced war as an

---

123 H. KULKE und D. ROTHERMUND, *A History of India*, p. 97.

124 J. NEEDHAM, *Science and Civilisation in China*, 1975 (1956), vol. 2, *History and Scientific Thought*, p. 529.

125 D. KOPF, *British Orientalism*, p. 178: "There seems little doubt that the era of Marquess Hastings was the golden age of British Orientalism in India."

126 The discovery of the Ashokan inscriptions could be seen as a precedent to later developments and modern pacifist trends. See Klaus SCHLICHTMANN, *Japan in the World. Shidehara Kijûrô, Pacifism and the Abolition of War*, Lexington, pp. 22ff. (Chapter I. 1. Buddhism and Peace).

127 D. KOPF, *British Orientalism*, p. 266.

Ashokan Lion Pillar, Sarnath.

instrument of politics, replacing it by the spread of Dharma, an ethics of conduct based on discourse rather than imposing force. Sensational as this was, however, initially it was not known from whom the inscriptions originated; the Ashokan pillars, it was believed, had been erected by Alexander the Great to commemorate his victory over Porus.[128]

"The rediscovery of Buddhist India was the last great achievement of the British orientalists."[129] It was the findings of William Jones and the Asiatic Society he had launched that showed Indic civilization as an equal to the other major cultures in the ancient world. The findings gave India and the Indians a new dignity, at the same time becoming a "factor in the growth of Indian nationalism." It is no wonder that after the Second World War the Ashokan "pillar of truth" (Gita Mehta) with the lion capital became the symbol and national emblem of modern, independent India. Moreover, with the *Sakuntala* of Kalidasa William Jones had given the Indians their own Shakespeare. When Raja Rammohun Roy spoke of the "unitarian concept of God in the Vedanta," this was a projection of the ideas of William Jones, and when Vivekananda spoke of the Vedanta as the "fountain source of all religions," his argument was similar to that which Jones had used "a hundred years earlier." Jones gave the Indians "a weapon with which to hit back whenever the European administrator scholars had attempted to belittle the Indian civilization."[130]

---

128 S. N. MUKHERJEE, *Sir William Jones*, p. 8: "The Ashokan pillars and other such columns were explained as posts erected by Alexander commemorating his victory over Porus."

129 D. KOPF, *British Orientalism*, p. 266. *See also* R. SCHWAB, *The Oriental Renaissance*, p. 111: "The figure of Buddha was growing larger in the world."

130 S. N. MUKHERJEE, *Sir William Jones*, pp. 140-141: "It was Jones and his Society which he founded who discovered that India had produced a civilization equal to any other in the ancient world. The dignity and pride this discovery gave to the Indians is an undeniable factor m the growth of Indian nationalism. Jones's Sakuntala gave them a Shakespeare in Kalidasa and other works inspired them. When Raja Rammohan Roy

10. Backlash

Quite a "different reconstruction of early Indian history" (R. Thapar) was put forward by James Mill in his *The History of British India*, which "critiqued earlier British Orientalist views sympathetic to Indian civilization," especially "those associated with the Asiatic Society at Calcutta." Historian Romila Thapar explains

> Mill saw Jones' view of the Orient as the product of undisciplined imagination, dangerous on epistemological and political grounds. Mill's History was an attempt at defining a new idiom for the empire. His project was different from that of the Orientalists, who were seeking parallels in India to European ideas of the past and insisting on understanding the indigenous law and the social articulation of India. Mill's notion of empire was, of course, modelled on the Roman. But because the British empire required a particular kind of economic link with its colonies, his emphasis, and that of those who thought like him, was gradually less on campaigns to acquire land and revenue and more on restructuring the colonial economy to enhance the wealth of the colonial power. Mill also realized that Support for what was viewed as indigenous law could result in the endorsement of a position far more conservative in India than was practised all the time. Mill rejected Jones' contention that historical material could be the epics and other Indian sources. The Orientalists were accused of legitimizing themselves by deploying indigenous idioms."[131]

To the enlightened Indians this must have seemed like a lot of gibberish. Nevertheless, it should be pointed out that there were two different, though complementary trends of political thought that became manifest in this period of Orientalism in India: "The various strands of neo-Hinduism showed different tendencies—some aimed at a universalism embracing all nations and religions of the world; others were eagerly reconstructing a national tradition so as to achieve a solidarity based on a glorious past."[132]

spoke of the unitarian concept of God in the Vedanta, he was enlarging upon Jones's ideas and, when Vivekananda talked about the Vedanta as the 'fountain source of all religions', he was using a similar argument used by Jones a hundred years earlier. In fact, Jones gave India a weapon with which to hit back whenever the European administrator scholars had attempted to belittle the Indian civilization."

131 Romila THAPAR, *The Past Before Us: Historical Traditions of Early North India*, Bangalore, New Delhi, Kolkata etc., Orient Blackswan 2013, p. 25.

132 H. KULKE und D. ROTHERMUND, *A History of India*, pp. 267-277. Regarding

In any event, both Hinduism and Buddhism traditionally held, each in its own way, inherently universalistic views. According to the American political scientist D. Mackenzie Brown the two tendencies comprized "on the one hand, the reaffirmation of the ancient Dharma principles and, on the other, an emphasis on reform and universal ideals. In this spirit," the author continues, Rabindranath Tagore who subsequently received the Nobel Prize for literature "acclaims India's ancient virtues and at the same time pleads for internationalism."[133]

The high time of Orientalism in India ended—around the year 1830. With the taking over of the highest judicial office in Calcutta by Lord Macaulay in 1835, social Darwinist tendencies were brought to the fore. Of course, the "world of scholarship and the world of administration" had never been quite "complementary to each other", and were often "worlds apart". While the Orientalists were "rarely extended patronage by the administration", in spite of the fact that "most of them were in the civil service",[134] they had nevertheless been instrumental in establishing a permanent bridge and furthering understanding between East and West.[135]

This new development, however, also resulted in "dividing the loyalties of the Bengali intelligentsia into two opposite camps," one which was driven by the new 'Macaulayism' toward Indian nationalism,[136] and the other

---

universalistic tendencies and equality of religions see as one of many examples the sentence from the two and a half millennia old Upanishads, here the *Chandogya-Upanishad*, 8.7.1: "He who, after knowing the self realizes it, attains all the world and all the desires."

133 D. Mackenzie BROWN, *The White Umbrella. Indian Political Thought from Manu to Gandhi*, Berkeley and Los Angeles, University of California Press 1958, p. 84. See also Amartya SEN, *On Interpreting India's Past*, p. 3.

134 O.P. KEJARIWAL, *The Asiatic Society of Bengal and the Discovery of India's Past 1784-1838*, Delhi etc., Oxford University Press 1988, p. 227. And ibid.: "Nor is there any evidence that the administration directed in any manner their scholarly efforts. The administration did encourage the compilation of Indian laws by Halhed, Jones and Colebrooke but this work was only an insignificant part of their overall scholarship." See also R.C. MAJUMDAR, *Glimpses of Bengal*, e.g. pp. 23 and 28. One should not underestimate the role of business in furthering Asian studies, including Bengali entrepreneurs.

135 R.C. MAJUMDAR, *Glimpses of Bengal*, p. 23, states in clear terms that "English education was introduced in this country, not by the British Government, but in spite of them."

136 D. KOPF, *British Orientalism*, p. 272: "It seems evident, therefore, that the process of polarization represented by Macaulayism had the immediate impact of dividing the

which was still inclined towards enlightenment and universalism.[137] Romila Thapar recounts how the impact of the colonial legacy with its divisionist "views on Indian history and society"—exemplified by the "trilogy of Mill-Macaulay-Mueller as the authors of a colonial construction of the Indian past"—"encouraged the emergence of religious nationalism," which is still agonizingly felt and experienced today.[138] As Partha Chatterjee relates, the colonial hangover of the West having "thought out on our behalf not only the script of colonial enlightenment and exploitation, but also that of our anticolonial resistance and postcolonial misery," implies the distasteful notion that our nations' "imaginations must remain forever colonized."[139] Notwithstanding this colonial inheritance, the Orientalists had "served as avenues linking the regional elite with the dynamic civilization of contemporary Europe ... a major intellectual revolution had taken place in Kolkata between 1772 and 1828."[140]

> loyalties of the Bengali intelligentsia into two opposite camps. The Calcutta cultural mediator who for decades had responded favorably to the culture of the European (who was himself favorably impressed with Indian culture) now faced the different view that all patterns of reform were an integral part of western civilization and that all Asian civilizations were almost by definition static and decadent. The intelligentsia in Calcutta were compelled to confront a crisis in identity. The Derozians temporarily set themselves adrift in a cultural limbo between their own heritage, which they rejected, and the Utopia across the seas, which they understood only imperfectly and to which they could never belong. Most of the intelligentsia, however, responded to the crisis by identifying with the orientalist-reconstructed view of Hinduism, which they romanticized as apologists."

137 D. KOPF, *British Orientalism*, p. 280: "When Modernization took on the guise of Macaulayism, the older response pattern collapsed and cultural barricades of nationalism were rapidly erected." See also Ch. ALLEN, *Ashoka*, p. 154: "In Britain the year 1837 is best remembered for the start of the Victorian era. To political historians of India, 1837 represents the black year in which the Orientalist movement, led by Professor H. H. Wilson in Oxford and James Prinsep's elder brother Henry Thoby Prinsep in Calcutta, was finally defeated by the Anglicists and the evangelicals under Thomas Macaulay and Lord Bentinck; a defeat that led to the imposition of English as the chief medium of instruction and the ending of government funding for the printing of works in the vernacular."

138 Romila THAPAR with Sundar SARUKKAI, Dhruv RAINA, Peter Ronald DESOUZA, Neeladri BHATTACHARYA, and Jawed NAQWI, The Public Intellectual in India, ed. by Chandra CHARI and Uma IYANGER, New Delhi, Aleph Book Company 2015, pp. xix and xxii. This is not to discount Max MÜLLER's otherwise great achievements in the field of Indology. See Bankim Chandra CHATTERJEE, Buddhism and the Sankhya Philosophy, in idem., *Essays & Letters*, New Delhi, Rupa & Co. 2010, pp. 65-84.

139 Partha CHATTERJEE, *The Nation and its Fragments. Colonial and Postcolonial Histories*, Princeton, Princeton University Press 1993, p. 5.

140 D. KOPF, *British Orientalism*, pp. 275 and 285.

As portrayed in this book, the Orientalists bear little resemblance to the dismal image that has been theirs since the Victorian era. ..... They contributed to the formation of a new Indian middle class and assisted in the professionalization of the Bengali intelligentsia. They started schools, systematized languages, brought printing and publishing to India, and encouraged the proliferation of books, journals, newspapers, and other media of communication. Their impact was urban and secular. They built the first modem scientific laboratories in India, and taught European medicine. They were neither static classicists nor averse to the idea of progress; and they both historicized the Indian past and stimulated a consciousness of history in the Indian intellectual. It was they who transmitted a new sense of identity to Bengalis that enlarged what Robert Bellah has called 'the capacity for rational goal setting', an instrumental process in the development of a modern outlook.[141]

Through the Indological studies and Orientalist revelations Europe as a whole had also received a decisive intellectual boost which entailed further research and developments.

11. Japan (and China) at the Other End of the World

The Confucian political philosophy in China and Japan was based on the principle of the "unity of ethical and cosmic order."[142] This included maxims like: "The way is the goal!" and "Within the four seas all men are brothers." Apparently these were universalist principles that were "never subsequently forgotten."[143] Humaneness (ch. *ren*, j. *jin*) was a Confucian virtue.[144] Although the 'Middle Kingdom' demanded tribute from the

141 D. KOPF, *British Orientalism*, pp. 275-276. However, ibid.: "The fact that British Orientalists were modernizers of Indian culture despite their opposition to Westernization should suggest that these two processes are not necessarily synonymous. Guy Metraux, in the preface of a UNESCO book of studies by various authors entitled *New Asia* seems to have diagnosed correctly the confusion which results from the proposition that Westernization equals modernization."

142 J. NEEDHAM, *Science and Civilisation in China*, vol. 2, p. 526.

143 J. NEEDHAM, *Within the Four Seas*, p. 27 Needham continues: "In India, Kabir was only one of many poets and prophets of human solidarity." It is better to travel well than to reach.

144 William Theodore De BARY, *Sources of Japanese Tradition*, vol. 2, 1600 to 2000, New York , Columbia University Press 2005, p. 107. See also Heiner ROETZ, *Die chinesische Ethik der Achsenzeit* (Chinese ethics of the Axial Period), Frankfurt, Suhrkamp 1992, pp. 195-241; Gregor PAUL, *Philosophie in Japan. Von den Anfängen bis zur Heian-Zeit*,

surrounding Asian countries, yet within this order dominated by China there was a fair degree of equality, and peace was regarded as the highest good with a circumspect statecraft as the goal. Joseph Needham noted: "In other civilizations the 'power of the sword' constitutes the all-domineering authority ... it is the Chinese belief that though the sword can win, only the *logos* was able to preserve the power."[145]

The Japanese had largely adopted China's "immense and remarkable legal tradition," which was "based on principles quite different from those ... in Europe,"[146] but quite similar to those of India, namely principles of justice and equity. In medieval Japanese criminal law, however, punishments were milder than in China, and ritual 'cleansing' stood in the forefront. Although positive law was not unknown in China and Japan, it was feared that "for each new law a new way of circumventing it will arise," a thesis that is historically and psychologically very perceptive,[147] and which has been applied in legal issues. From one of the five Confucian classics, the *Shu Ching* (jap. *Shu Jing*), the following statement is derived: "Virtue has no invariable rule but fixes on that which is good as its law. And goodness itself has no constant resting-place, but accords only with perfect sincerity."[148] Such an attitude undoubtedly presupposes a high degree of understanding human nature.

Where there is a society there has to be law. Yet, in the Chinese tradition, stress was laid on preventive measures, to avert crimes and disorder, through education and character training to follow universal 'laws' and moral norms. "[C]rimes, or even disputes ... were felt to be disturbances of the Order of Nature."[149] If human nature tended toward always trying to

Eine kritische Untersuchung (Philosophy in Japan. From the beginnings to the Heian period, a critical inquiry), Munich, iudicium 1993, p. 244.

145 Joseph NEEDHAM, *Wissenschaftlicher Universalismus*, p. 68. (My translation from the German.)

146 J. NEEDHAM, *Within the Four Seas, The Dialogue of East and West*, p. 23. See also Percy R. LUNEY, Jr., Traditions and Foreign Influences: Systems of Law in China and Japan, *Law and Contemporary Problems*, vol. 52, no. 2 (1989), p. 129: "Japan imported several early Chinese legal codes in the seventh and eighth centuries and adapted this law to existing Japanese social and economic conditions. The Chinese Confucian philosophy and system of ethics was introduced to Japan in the fourteenth century."

147 J. NEEDHAM, *Within the Four Seas,* vol. 2, p. 522.

148 Ibid., p. 522.

149 J. NEEDHAM, *Within the Four Seas,* vol.2, p. 526.

circumvent positive law, it was not wise to indulge in making too many laws. Indeed, when there is corruption, it exists no matter how elaborate the law. Studying the 'law' therefore meant studying the scriptures. The Japanese word for 'law' was (and is) the same as that for the Buddhist teaching (skt. *Dharma*). Moreover, as in India, it was an administrative law.

In Japan since the 15th and 16th century the Confucian school of Zhu Xi (1130-1200; jap. *Shushigaku*) had become the official ideology supported by the state. Fujiwara Seika (1561-1619), a Buddhist priest, advisor to Tokugawa Ieasu and teacher of the famous Hayashi Razan (1583-1657), contributed greatly to the spreading of the teachings of Zhu Xi.[150] More clearly than in China, Japanese syncretist energies were able to merge Buddhism with Confucianism. Shushigaku and the works of Laozi (Lao-tzu) and Mozi (Mo Tzu), together with other traditional subjects (perhaps not unlike in the ancient universities of India), were taught in the 'sacred halls' (*Yushima Seidô*) of Edo University, founded in 1630 by Hayashi Razan in the Ueno district, under the patronage of the third Shogun, Tokugawa Iemitsu. The institution, which was equipped with a library, moved in 1691 to Kanda district and was named 'Shoheiko' (short for: *Shoheizaka Gakumonsho*) after the birthplace of Confucius, Chang-ping (jap. *Shohei*) in Shantung Province. In this institution, the principal state university of Edo, the Confucian scholars of the 200 domains[151] were trained. In 1765 a medical faculty was added.

Following the Genroku period (1688-1704), when Osaka had been the "center of townsmen culture",[152] towards the end of the eighteenth century, Edo became the cultural and political center. There existed in the eighteenth century already in "the main cities ... lucrative publishing businesses. Publishing houses acquired stables of writers and illustrators..." In the 'Bunka-Bunsei period' (1804-1829) Edo became the center of a refined urban culture,[153] which may well have resembled certain features of

---

150 Hermann OOMS, Neo-Confucianism and the Formation of Early Tokugawa Ideology, Contours of a Problem, in Peter NOSCO (ed.), *Confucianism and Tokugawa Culture*, Princeton, N.J., Princeton University Press 1975, p. IX, talks about a 'Tokugawa-ideology', promoted by Fujiwara Seika and Hayashi Razan, the two 'founding fathers' of this ideology. Fujiwara seems to have studied Mohism intensively.

151 J.W. HALL, *Japan. From Prehistory to Modern Times*, Tokyo, Charles Tuttle 1971, pp. 218-219.

152 Edwin O. REISCHAUER and Albert M. CRAIG, *Japan, Tradition & Transformation*, Tokyo, Charles E. Tuttle 1978, p. 105.

153 John Whitney HALL, *Japan. From Prehistory to Modern Times*, pp. 228-229.

urban life in Kolkata.

The first modern Japanese, who cultivated 'Western learning' (Yôyaku), were the astronomer and geographer Nishikawa Joken (1648-1724) and the Confucian scholar Arai Hakuseki (1657-1725).[154] The eighth Shogun, Tokugawa Yoshimune (1684-1751; ruled 1716-1745), was a promoter of Western science. In 1720 he ended the ban on foreign books, and even ordered scholars to learn Dutch. Under Tanuma Okitsugu (1719-1788), a Daimyô, who had risen to power by conducting affairs of state under Shogun Ieshige (ruled 1745-1760), and Ieharu (1760-1786), the trend continued and there was a lively exchange of information and fancy items with the employees of the Dutch trading station in Dejima. "Daimyo collected clocks and field glasses, drank out of glass goblets and even watched experiments with electricity."[155] Tanuma Okitsugu developed agriculture, "encouraged an increase of the Nagasaki trade ... and ... stimulated the production of copper for export."[156] Being "an energetic and liberal-minded administrator", he adopted policies which "had ... constructive and lasting effects," such as the "extensive program of colonization and development in Hokkaido," which he pursued.[157] This was an idea formulated by the scholar Kudo Heisuke who had learned the Dutch language and had a special interest in foreign countries.[158]

Japanese scholars published numerous books on Western science. The Japanese Studies of the Dutch on the island of Dejima, an artificial island off the coast of Nagasaki, in turn also began to bear fruit. The German

---

154 ARAI Hakuseki published two books about the West, the *Seiyô Kibun* (*A Strange Story about the West*, 1715) and the *Sairan Igen* (Various opinions on the geography of the world, 1713, rev. 1725). The latter work, comprising 5 volumes, had been commissioned by Tokugawa Ienobu, and was based on the work of the Italian Jesuit missionary Mateo RICCI. In English translation there is Arai HAKUSEKI, *Told Round a Brushwood Fire. The Autobiography of Arai Hakuseki*, trans. and intro. by Joyse ACKROYD. Tokyo, University of Tokyo Press 1980.

155 John Whitney HALL, *Japan. From Prehistory to Modern Times*, p. 224.

156 George SANSOM, *A History of Japan, 1615-1867*, Stanford, Stanford University Press 1978 (1963), pp. 176-177.

157 Edwin O. REISCHAUER and John K. FAIRBANK, *East Asia—The Great Tradition*, Boston, Houghton Mifflin 1958 and 1960, p. 624. And ibid.: "He added new monopolies, particularly in items imported from abroad, such as alum, camphor, and the supposedly medicinal root, ginseng. He even attempted to establish monopolies in lime and lamp oil."

158 G. SANSOM, *A History of Japan*, p. 182.

physician Engelbert Kaempfer (1651-1716) who had been employed by the Dutch on Dejima between 1690 and 1692, published his *The History of Japan*.[159] Most Japanese probably experienced the era of seclusion as a time of peace.

12. Chinsura and Dejima

The Dutch scholar Isaac Titsingh (1745-1812) was the Head (Opperhoofd) of the trading post on Dejima (between 1779 and 1796, three times), and under him a lively cultural exchange with Japanese scholars took place. Titsingh and the Swedish physician Carl Peter Thunberg (1743-1828), who also was at the time in the Dutch service, "imparted a great deal of first-hand scientific information to the Japanese who flocked to their quarters."[160] For twenty years Titsingh kept up a lively correspondence with the eminent Edo scholars of his time. In 1822 he published his book, *Illustrations of Japan*, in London.[161] Titsingh maintained an extensive and exquisite collection of Japanese art treasures and literature,[162] of which a large part is in museums in Paris and London.[163] He had also been the *Opperhoofd* in the Dutch trading post in Chinsura in Kolkata, knew the British Orientalists there—among others he maintained a close friendship with British Orientalist William Jones,[164]—and had himself been one of the

159 Engelbert KAEMPFER, *The History of Japan, Together with a Description of the Kingdom of Siam, 1609-1692*, 2 vols., London 1727-1728 (Glasgow 1906).

160 J.W. HALL, *Japan. From Prehistory to Modern Times*, p. 224.

161 Frank LEQUIN, *The Private Correspondence of Isaac Titsingh*, vol. I (1785-1811), intr. and ed. Frank LEQUIN, Amsterdam, J.C. Gieben 1990 and idem, *Het personeel van de Verenigde Oost-Indische Compagnie in Azie in de achttiende eeuw, meer in het bijzonder in de vestiging Bengalen*, Diss. Leiden, 1982. On TITSINGH see also C.R. BOXER, *The Mandarin at Chinsura*, Amsterdam, Koninklijke Vereeniging Indisch Instituut 1949 (Mededeling No. LXXXIV, Afdeling Volkenkunde No. 32), and Gertrude C. SCHWE-BELL, *Die Geburt des modernen Japan in Augenzeugenberichten* (The birth of modern Japan in eyewitness accounts), München, dtv 1981 (Düsseldorf 1970), p. 50.

162 C.R. BOXER, *Jan Compagnie in Japan: an essay on the cultural, artistic and scientific influence exercised by the Hollanders in Japan from the seventeenth to the nineteenth centuries*, The Hague, Martinus Nijhoff 1950, second revised ed. (orig. The Hague, 1936), p. 149: TITSINGH had "brought with him From Batavia to Bengal a vast collection of Japanese books, manuscripts, and coins," which he sought to make full use of during his stay there.

163 C.R. BOXER, *The Mandarin at Chinsura*, p. 8, tells Titsingh "provided the French Bibliothèque du Roi at Paris (today's Bibliothèque Nationale) with a complete set—243 volumes—of the 'monumental history of Japan', the *Dai Nihon-shi*."

164 C.R. BOXER, The Mandarin at Chinsura, p. 7 f. See also Frank LEQUIN, *The Private*

cofounders of the 'Royal Asiatic Society of Bengal'. Jones came to consider the 'imperial island' of Japan as a country of "pre-eminence among eastern Kingdoms analogous to that of Britain among the natives of the West."[165]

Isaac Titsingh. Source: http://science-2ch.net/wp-content/uploads/2013/12/ dvPEG3V7.jpg

Titsingh had succeeded in revitalizing the Dutch settlement in Bengal, which before 1883, due to "Holland's disastrous participation in the American Revolutionary War ... [had] temporarily extinguished Dutch maritime trade in Asia." But, as Titsingh narrates, the Hollanders "had regained all their most profitable possessions after the Peace of Paris ... [and] yearly sales averaging 15.7 million florins between 1784 and 1795" once more prevailed.[166] Trade and intelligence gathering went side by side. Deshima was "Japan's ear to the outside world",[167] and with many of the native interpreters speaking and writing Dutch "fluently ... the Tokugawa bureaucracy displayed a keen interest in being kept informed of the political situation in Europe" and surely in the European colonies as well.[168] Again, because of the political situation in Europe following the spread of the French Revolution, no Dutch ships reached Deshima from 1809 to 1818,[169] except when Britain occupied Java in 1813-14, and Thomas

---

Correspondence of Isaac Titsingh. See also for a more extensive biography of Issac Titsingh C.R. BOXER, *Jan Compagnie*, pp. 134-164. TITSINGH died in Paris.

165 Quoted in C.R. BOXER, *The Mandarin at Chinsura*, p. 8.

166 C.R. BOXER, *The Mandarin at Chinsura*, p. 11.

167 Hermann KULKE, Überlegungen zur Begegnung Europas und Asiens bis ins 19. Jahrhundert (Reflections on the encounter between Europe and Asia until the 19th century), *Oriens Extremus*, vol.33, no.1 (1990), p. 11.

168 C.R. BOXER, *The Mandarin at Chinsura*, p. 4. See also J. OSTERHAMMEL, *Die Entzauberung Asiens*, p. 376, who points out that in all of Asia "only in Japan ... systematic European studies" were being pursued.

169 J. Feenstra KUIPER, Some Notes on the Foreign Relations of Japan in the Early Napoleonic Period, *Transactions of the Asiatic Society of Japan*, vol. I (1923, 1924), pp. 80-81 (55-82). Already in 1808 a British frigate, with orders to capture Dutch trading ships, had entered the port of Nagasaki.

Stamford Raffles, an admirer of Japan, as temporary governor "tried to initiate... trade with Nagasaki under the Dutch flag", and to bring Deshima under British control.[170] Eventually, in 1825, Chinsura was ceded to Britain, in exchange for Bencoleen in Sumatra.[171]

Thus, increasingly, knowledge about Japan also reached Europe. Perhaps because of the Dutch connection to India—the trading post of the Dutch East India Company in Bengal—Indian cooks may occasionally have came to Dejima, and it is possible that the liking of the Japanese for curry dishes has its origin there.

Japan was not as closed as it seemed to the Europeans. Even during their self-imposed seclusion,[172] the Japanese had, through the Dutch at Dejima and the Chinese traders in Nagasaki, contacts reaching as far as Kolkata.[173] In 1811, the Tokugawa Bakufu "recognized the need to keep abreast of developments in the West by establishing a body of official translators of Western books (*Bansho wage goyoukata*) within the shogunal astronomical observatory."[174] Japan was preparing thoroughly for the new age. By 1869 several thousand Japanese had studied Western science, mainly in Dutch, and besides English, French, German and Chinese books, 670 works were translated from the Dutch into Japanese[175]—a necessary prerequisite to cooperate peacefully in an increasingly interdependent world. The result of the Dutch-studies movement (*rangaku*), according to Donald Keene, was that the Japanese from around 1800 were "better acquainted with European civilization than the people of any other non-

---

170 William G. BEASLEY, *The Rise of Modern Japan*, Tokyo, Charles E. Tuttle 1990, p. 23. See also J. OSTERHAMMEL *Die Entzauberung Asiens*, p. 98, who mentions that the British had brought an elephant along on their ship, "the fourth animal of its kind," which the Japanese had seen.

171 *See* Michel VATIN, *Calcutta*, Singapore, APA 1991, p. 209.

172 Trade relations continued to exist with Korea, Siam (Thailand) and China. In 1630 TENJIKU Tokubei (1612-ca.1692), a trader from Kyoto, sailed to India and acquired riches there. https://en.wikipedia.org/wiki/Tenjiku_Tokubei.

173 *See* J.P. LOSTY, *Calcutta, City of Palaces. A Survey of the City in the Days of the East India Company 1690-1858*, London, The British Library, New Delhi, Arnold Publishers 1990, pp. 11-13, 21, 54 and 59-60 on the Dutch settlement at Chinsura.

174 J.W. HALL, *Japan. From Prehistory to Modern Times*, p. 225.

175 Masato FUJII, *Die Wahrheit über Japan* (The truth about Japan), Tokyo, Japanisch-Deutsche Gesellschaft 1982, p. 19, containing a list also. According to the author, among the 670 texts, 130 were books on medicine, 70 on military science, 50 on chemistry and physics, 40 on astronomy, and 30 on politics.

Western country,"[176] except for the Calcuttans, perhaps.

13. The Bengal Plunder—an Excursus

"All profound changes in consciousness, by their very nature, bring with them characteristic amnesias." (Benedict Anderson)

Already at the close of the seventeenth century, knowledge about the 'trans-oceanic world' had become "available in sufficient quantity to exercise a marked influence on European ways and thought."[177] The Oriental Renaissance resulted in the globalization of the ideals of humanism and universalism, which previously (for Westerners) had been confined to the limits of the Mediterranean world. Those responsible for and engaged in the making of modern Europe were shaped by the new discoveries.

Before Plassey, the Europeans had been "poor compared to Asia before 1800."[178] Also, the Enlightenment shook their belief that the earth was the centre of the universe, and Europe the only notable civilization on the planet. Until then it had been believed, as already pointed out earlier, that the creation of the world took place some six thousand years ago, "around 4004 B.C."[179] The church had "assumed the wickedness of man" and persecuted disbelievers,[180] however, the Enlightenment "rejected the idea of religious persecution,"[181] and promoted the belief that all humans were equal. Looking for inspiration, Montesquieu "roamed mentally over

---

176 Donald KEENE, quoted in Paul A. COHEN, Europe goes East. The first impact of the West on China and Japan, in Arnold TOYNBEE (ed.), *Half the World. The History and Culture of China and Japan*, New York, Chicago, San Francisco, Holt, Rinehart and Winston (Thames and Hudson) 1973, p. 292.

177 Norman HAMPSON, *The Enlightenment*, Penguin, The Pelican History of European Thought, vol.4, 1968, p. 19.

178 Andre Gunder FRANK, ReOrient or Not, That IS the Question (response to Peer VRIES, Should we really ReORIENT?), *Itinerario*, vol.22, no.4 (1998), p. 20. Also, "[a]s late as the early nineteenth century" the Chinese for example "wanted practically nothing of what Europe produced, and Europe was sending missions of investigation down to the middle of the century to search out the secrets of traditional Chinese industries (ceramics, textiles, dyeing, tea, lacquer, etc.)." J. NEEDHAM, *Within the Four Seas*, p. 19.

179 HAMPSON, *The Enlightenment*, p. 20.

180 Ibid., p. 17. I.e. although the secular Greek and Roman scriptures had already been employed as "a useful corrective." Ibid.

181 Ibid., p. 252.

the whole world, including India ... to provide illustrations for his *Esprit des lois*," while Voltaire "looked to China and India ... to demonstrate the debasement of Europe and Christianity."[182] Perhaps the Europeans were debased — but soon the picture changed. Humanism,[183] having already fed on the reception of Greek (hedonist) classic literature through Arab transmission, received a boost with the new reception of classical extra-European literature and the study of alien civilizations.

The thesis that universalism and humanism have always been valued as common goods of humankind is confirmed by the great monotheistic religions, and in the numerous works of the Buddhists, Hindus, Confucians, Taoists and Mohists.[184] It is perhaps a coincidence that the Europeans—and not the Chinese—first conquered and then dominated the world in the last five centuries.[185] To distinguish between humanism and universalism, it might be said that *humanism* primarily and perhaps decisively comprises 'humaneness', 'justice' and 'equality', while *universalism* especially aims at 'peace', 'order' and 'community'. A fine example is the reformer Kang Youwei (1858-1927), who advocated a peaceful human community of nations in his book, the *Ta T'ung Shu. The One-World Philosophy*.[186] Although different

182 O.P. KAJARIWAL, *The Asiatic Society of Bengal and the Discovery of India's Past 1784-1838*, Delhi etc., Oxford University Press 1988, p. 26-7.

183 According to Fernand BRAUDEL, *On History*, p. 275, modern humanism was "a relative neologism ... a learned expression, coined by German historians in the nineteenth century (and, to be precise, in 1808)."

184 Taoists and Mohists: Mohism, which was received already early on in Japan, was a rational, pacifistic and religious movement, which harks back to the third great Chinese of the Axial period, namely Mozi/Moti (Mo-tzu, ca. 480-390). Mohism inspired Confucianism with its logic and philosophy of love and compassion.

185 Would the Chinese, if they had become the world's dominant power, also have been so cruel?

186 KANG Youwei (K'ang Yu-wei) is the author of the *Ta T'ung Shu. The One-World Philosophy of K'ang Yu-Wei*, transl. and intr. by Laurence G. THOMPSON, London, George Allen & Unwin London 1958. The German sinologist Wolfgang BAUER called KANG "one of the most fascinating and influential figures on the borderline between the old and the new China," who produced "the most comprehensive plan for an ideal social system ever to have been produced in China," a plan of global proportions and comparable to the best plans Europe ever produced for an ideal universal order. The reformer Kang also reverted to the teachings of the Chinese pacifist MOZI: "It was no mere accident that these had been rediscovered during the second half of the Manchu Dynasty [1644–1912], for they had always been closely associated with socialist trends." Wolfgang BAUER, *China and the Search for Happiness: Recurring Themes in Four Thousand Years of Chinese Cultural History*, New York, Seabury Press 1976, p. 306. See also J. NEEDHAM, *Wissenschaftlicher Universalismus*, pp. 224-225.

concepts, universalism and humanism are two sides of the same coin; both sides are relative to each other and closely interlinked. These new shared, 'global values', in the period studied here, brought about increased cooperation and cultural interaction in international relations, so that the idea of peace, and the necessity and desire for peaceful cooperation were increasingly being recognized. Thus the basic conditions for the emergence of a genuine, common international order of humanity had been stated.

It would have been a miracle if the Japanese did not have a perception of and interest in British imperial policy and trade. The British victory at Plassey (1757) and the subsequent "plunder of Bengal" had ramifications that certainly did not go unnoticed in Japan. It was the decisive step from informal to formal empire under British rule in India, and the end of the Mughal Empire in India. Certainly, this—as also the "striking growth of the [British] China trade after 1784"[187]—must have been observed by the Japanese leadership. Brooks Adams in his book *The Law of Civilization and Decay*, first published in 1896, revealed the facts surrounding the 'Plunder of Bengal', following the British victory at Plassey. Adams claimed in his book that the loot had had far-reaching consequences: it triggered the Industrial Revolution. He writes: "Very soon after Plassey the Bengal plunder began to arrive in London, and the effect appears to have been instantaneous, for all authorities agree that the Industrial Revolution, the event that has divided the 19th century from all antecedent time, began with the year 1760 ... probably nothing has ever equalled the rapidity of the change which followed ... In themselves inventions are passive, many of the most important having laid dormant for centuries, waiting for a sufficient store of force to have accumulated to have set them working. That store must always take the shape of money, and money not hoarded, but in motion ... Before the influx of the Indian treasure, and the expansion of credit, which followed, no force sufficient for this purpose existed ... The factory system was the child of the 'industrial revolution', and until capital had accumulated in masses, capable of giving solidity to large bodies of labour, manufactures were carried on by scattered individuals ... Possibly since the world began, no investment has ever yielded the profit reaped from the Indian plunder, because for nearly fifty years Great Britain stood

---

187 Om PRAKASH, From Hostility to Collaboration: European Corporate Enterprise, pp. 255, and 252-253: "[T]he commercial revolution ... completed by the 1780s, consisted in the first place of a clear domination in the Indian Ocean and the South China Sea by private English shipping based in Calcutta and Bombay."

without a competitor."[188] There must have been, if one believes Max Weber, other reasons, too. China had never seen such massive 'economic incentive' and therefore could not boast of a comparative development; it "failed to reach the decisive stage."[189]

Numerous authors confirm Brooks Adams' report. Here are some quotes. British author Geoffrey Moorhouse gives the numbers: "Within a month, a hundred boats were sent downstream to the British city, laden with 7,500.000 silver rupees; six weeks later another four million rupees went coasting into the Calcutta treasury, to be received with flags flying and bands blaring. This was the compensation money."[190] And the British

---

188 Brooks ADAMS, *The Law of Civilization and Decay*, New York: Vintage, 1955 (orig. 1896), pp. 255-259. Geoffrey MOORHOUSE, *Calcutta—The City Revealed*, Penguin (India) 1994, pp. 45f, gives figures. On p. 46 he quotes Sir Percival Spear: "the financial bleeding of Bengal had begun." J.P. LOSTY, *Calcutta, City of Palaces*, p. 33: "Never before did the English Nation at one time obtain such a prize in solid money..." Alfred Comyn LYALL, *History of India*, vol. VIII (9 vols., ed. By A.V. WILLIAMS JACKSON), vol. VIII, New Delhi, Asian Education Services 1987, pp. 177-178: "All authorities agree that in the eighteenth century the richest province of all India, in agriculture and manufactures, was Bengal. Colonel James Mill, in his memoir ... points out that it has vast wealth and is indefensible toward the sea." Karl Marx is quite wrong, The Future Results of British Rule in India, [New-York Daily Tribune, No. 3840, August 8, 1853]: "The Arabs, Turks, Tartars, Moguls, who overran India in succession were quickly hinduized, because according to an immutable law of history the barbaric conquerors are always themselves conquered by the higher civilization of the peoples, which they subjugated. The British were the first conquerors, who were at a higher stage of development and therefore for the Hindu civilization inaccessible. They destroyed it by smashing the local communities, uprooted the local industry and everything was great and leveled everything that was sublime in the native society. The history of British rule in India shows hardly anything that goes beyond this work of destruction. Traces of a renewal are barely noticeable under the rubble. Nevertheless, it has already begun." Apparently Marx knew nothing of the Orientalists' work. (Text translated from the German)

189 F. BRAUDEL, *A History of Civilizations*, p. 372. And ibid: "Much earlier than the West, China possessed the rudiments of science, in an elegant and advanced form. But she failed to reach the decisive stage." This argument and the argument that generally "Bengal was being 'ravaged' and was undergoing an 'annual plunder'" after 1757 must be seen apart. Nevertheless, although industrial activities and output as well as indigenous trade in and from Bengal did not diminish, after 1757 "direct competition within such trades between an Indian merchant and the East India Company or a British private trader was not likely to be advantageous for the Indian merchant." Also, although British trade "probably offered increased employment" in various fields, it was "on terms which left little scope for bargaining for improved living standards." P.J MARSHALL, *East Indian Fortunes, The British in Bengal in the Eighteenth Century*, Oxford, Clarandon Press 1976, pp. 261, 265 and 270 respectively.

190 G. MOORHOUSE, *Calcutta. The City Revealed*, New Delhi usw., Penguin 1994 (1971), p. 46. See also Nick ROBINS, *The Corporation that Changed the World. How the East*

historian Percival Spear, who lived and taught in India, writes: "The financial bleeding of Bengal had begun."[191] The Indian historian J. P. Losty states: "Never before did the English nation at one time obtain such a prize in solid money; for it amounted (in the mint) to 800,000 pounds sterling."[192] Alfred Comyn Lyall reports similarly: "All authorities agree that in the eighteenth century the richest province of all India, in agriculture and manufactures, was Bengal."[193] Lyall further refers to James Mill who in his memoirs also "points out that it has vast wealth and is indefensible toward the sea."[194] Fernand Braudel, with regard to China, writes: China "failed to reach the decisive stage, because she never experienced the

India Company Shaped the Modern Multinational, Hyderabad, Orient Longman 2006 (orig. London, Pluto Press), p. 3: "Clive had defeated the Nawab of Bengal at Plassey (Palashi), 90 miles north of its trading base of Calcutta (Kolkata). The Company quickly installed Mir Jafar—a general who had betrayed the defeated Nawab—as the first of a series of puppet rulers of Bengal. More of a commercial transaction than a real battle, Plassey was followed by the systematic looting of Bengal's treasury. In a powerful symbol of the transfer of wealth that had begun, the Company loaded the treasury's gold and silver onto a fleet of over a hundred boats and sent them downriver to Calcutta. In one stroke, Clive had netted £2.5 million for the Company and £234,000 for himself. Today this would be equivalent to a £232 million corporate windfall and a cool £22 million success fee for Clive. Historical convention views Plassey as the first step in the creation of the British Empire in India. It is perhaps better understood as the East India Company's most successful business deal ... the wealth of the East began to pour into England. This represented an extraordinary turnaround. Before Plassey, the 'balance of trade was against all nations in favour of Bengal', wrote Alexander Dow in his 1773 History of Hindostan. Bengal had been 'the sink where gold and silver disappeared without the least prospect of return'. Now that flow was reversed."

191 Cited in G. MOORHOUSE, *Calcutta*, p. 46. N. ROBINS, *The Corporation that Changed the World*, p. 178, writes that "the estimates of modern academics do not differ greatly from the annual £1.2 million that Burke calculated in 1783. In the 1960s Professor N.K. Sinha derived a somewhat higher figure of £1.6 million averaged between 1757 and 1780, while Rajat Datta more recently cut the amount drained to £1 million in the years between Plassey and 1794. These are likely to be significant underestimates as they fail to account for the significant value the Company's monopoly position gave it in extracting below-market rates for commodities such as textiles and opium, and the resulting subsidy this provided to the China trade. The drain, of course, changed its character radically in the nineteenth century, when the Company ceased trading. For Montgomery Martin, writing in 1838, the average transfer of the previous 30 years had amounted to some £3 million, which he calculated as equivalent to £723,997,917 at a 12 per cent compound rate of interest. In terms of twenty-first-century purchasing power, this represents a tribute of well over £40 billion."

192 J.P. LOSTY, *Calcutta, City of Palaces*, p. 33.

193 A. C. LYALL, *History of India*, vol. VIII, pp. 177-178.

194 Ibid., p. 178.

economic impetus that spurred Europe on—that 'capitalist' tension which at the end of the race, or during it, enabled Europeans to cross the decisive threshold." And furthermore: "The key years 1780-1820 raised a final problem: crossing the threshold that led to truly modern science."[195]

14. The Economic Downturn

Author Nick Robins discounts the role of the Orientalists working in Kolkata, stressing the more negative side when he points out, for example, that Warren Hastings saw his primary role not in promoting Indian culture, but in increasing the profits of the East India Company and its shareholders; it was he who used the salt and opium monopoly of the company and first ordered and organized the opium smuggling to China.[196] The author compares the aims of the British in exploiting India with the corporate abuses and the financial and banking crises that have made headlines in recent years. He rightly points to the significant defects of today's globalization, which already started to manifest itself at that time, and which carries significantly more weight today, as the extent of the exploitation of our planet has attained an much higher and dangerous level:

> Today, the globalization of markets has still not been matched by an
> equivalent globalization of justice. Compared with the immense political

---

195 F. BRAUDEL, *A History of Civilizations*, pp. 372 und 370.

196 Nick ROBINS, *The Corporation that Changed the World*, p. 17: "Yet, these cultural interventions were always secondary to Hastings's primary role of generating wealth for the Company and its shareholders. This was the man who monopolised Bengal's salt and opium production for corporate benefit, and ordered the first mission to smuggle opium into China..." Furthermore the author states, p. 178: "Contemporaries were clear. 'We may date the commencement of the decline', wrote Alexander Dow in 1772, 'from the day on which Bengal fell under the domination of the foreigners'. Turning to Britain, controversy rages over the links between the Company's conquest of India in the financing of the Industrial Revolution. For Brooks Adams, writing at the end of the nineteenth century, the coincidence of the influx of Bengal plunder with the deployment of new industrial technologies was compelling. Without the resources provided by the Indian drain, Adams argued that the spinning jenny, Crompton's mule and Watts's steam engine would have lain dormant ... Adams's conclusions were deployed extensively by Indian nationalists in the struggle for independence. But modern Indian historians have been more cautious, arguing, for example, that 'it is highly unlikely that these private fortunes constituted an element of any importance in the financing of the Industrial Revolution'. " Concerning this last point see Om PRAKASH, *European Commercial Enterprise in Pre-Colonial India*, New Delhi, Cambridge University Press 2000, p. 349.

capital that has been expended in recent decades to liberalize international trade, precious little has been done to ensure that common human rights are respected and enforced.[197]

True, although industrial activities and output as well as indigenous trade in and from Bengal did not diminish, after 1757 "direct competition within such trades between an Indian merchant and the East India Company or a British private trader was not likely to be advantageous for the Indian merchant." Also, although British trade "probably offered increased employment" in various fields, it was "on terms which left little scope for bargaining for improved living standards."[198] This brings us to my main argument, which is that the world needs to be politically united under the rule of law.

Not only world trade and intercontinental cultural interaction, but the atomic era as well, make a global organization of peace necessary; the new interdependence is the condition of the possibility of such an organization which Nick Robins is calling for to emerge. Authors of the 'little axial period' like Immanuel Kant, William Jones and others had recognized this. It was therefore from the standpoint of historical development only logical that at the beginning of the 19th century the first peace societies were established in England and the United States. From there a straight path leads to the Hague Peace Conferences, with their main goals of disarmament and binding international jurisdiction.[199] The Hague Peace Conferences were the first inclusive political-legal attempt to outlaw war as an institution. Nick Robins perhaps fails to recognize that the trend in that direction had started with the work of the Orientalist pioneers heading purposefully toward the new order.

---

197 N. ROBINS, *The Corporation that Changed the World*, p. 37. The author continues, p. 29: "The direct application of violence by today's corporations is thankfully rare. But the links between successful trade and military force remain as powerful as ever. As Thomas Friedman, the New York Times's ebullient promoter of globalisation, explains, the 'hidden hand of the market will never work without a hidden fist'. In simple terms, 'McDonald's cannot flourish without McDonnell Douglas, the designer of F-15s."

198 P.J. MARSHALL, *East Indian Fortunes*, pp. 261, 265 and 270 respectively.

199 See Peter van den DUNGEN, *The Making of Peace: Jean de Bloch and the First Hague Peace Conference*, Los Angeles, California State University 1983. K. SCHLICHTMANN, Japan, Germany and the Idea of the two Hague Peace Conferences, pp. 377-394.

15. Conclusion

It was hardly possible in this narrative to give a full explanation of the historical circumstances of the events. In South America, too, there was a strong move toward world order, freedom and the equality of man, which led to enlightened and new political constellations. Thus in 1810 Simon Bolivar (1783-1839) occupied the capital Caracas to free his native Venezuela from Spanish colonial rule, and in 1826, in his opening speech at the American Congress in Panama, Don Manuel Lorenzo Vidaurre, Minister from Peru, expressed the hope that the "sad and abject countenance of the poor African, bending under the chains of rapacity and oppression," would soon "no longer be seen in these climes," and that he will "be endowed with *equal privileges with the white man*, whose colour he has been taught to regard as a badge of superiority."[200] No doubt, the French Revolution and "its moral principles—such as open diplomacy and the renunciation of aggressive war—[had] excited the admiration of the people of Europe" and abroad.[201] Similarly Emeric Crucé (1590–1648), author of the *Nouveau Cynée* (1623), "a pioneer work on international relations," wrote at the beginning of the seventeenth century: "Why should I a Frenchman wish harm to an Englishman, a Spaniard, or an Hindoo? I cannot wish it when I consider that they are men like me, that I am subject like them to error and sin and that all nations are bound together by a natural and, consequently, indestructible tie, which ensures that a man cannot consider another a stranger unless he follows the common and inveterate opinion that he has received from his predecessors."[202]

---

200 William LADD, *An Essay on a Congress of Nations*, intr. James BROWN SCOTT, New York, Oxford University Press 1916, Extracts from the 'Speech of Don Manuel Lorenzo Vidaurre, Minister from Peru, at the opening of the American Congress of Panama, on the 22d of June, 1826', p. 111. William LADD had "followed the sea for a number of years" (p. iv), before devising his plan for abolishing war. He considered a Congress of Nations to be "composed of ambassadors from all those ... civilized nations who should ... vote ... [and] organize themselves into a Congress of Nations." (p. 9)

201 Norman HAMPSON, *The Enlightenment*, Penguin: The Pelican History of European Thought, vol.4, 1968, pp. 257-258.

202 Emeric CRUCÉ, *Le Nouveau Cynée ou Discours d'Estat représentant les occasions et Moyens d'establier une Paix générale, et la liberté du commerce par tout le Monde*, 1623, republished in English by Thomas Willing BALCH in 1909, p. 84, quoted in William LADD, *An Essay on a Congress of Nations*, introduced by James Brown SCOTT, New York, Oxford University Press, 1916, p. xiii, note.

Raimund Schwab puts the critical question: What remains?[203] The same question could also be put regarding openings like the original Axial Period or Christianity or the Age of Enlightenment.

In any event, it can be safely said that the 'expanded' universal humanism, embracing the world, which had emerged, created a new awareness of the world as one. Subrata Dasgupta has argued convincingly that through these and subsequent events a new universal "cognitive identity was transmitted into the twentieth century [that was] not just confined to Bengal but was propagated amongst the Indian intelligentsia at large,"[204] and beyond. Toward the end of the nineteenth century two events stand out significantly: the 'World's Parliament of Religions', assembled in Chicago in 1893;[205] and the Hague Peace Conference of 1899.[206] These conventions had *real*-political implications; their message is still heard and its goals are relevant.[207] The Hague Conferences may have appealed

---

203 R. SCHWAB, *The Oriental Renaissance*, p. 473: "SURELY no one will any longer assume that the Oriental Renaissance was a gratuitous dream or a passing fancy. But still it will be asked, what lasting result did it have? In what way are its results comparable to those of the other Renaissance? The obvious fact is this: an immense mental displacement has occurred. The air of the times contained the necessity; Chance created its reality. Will it still be possible to speak of Romanticism, of the nineteenth-century, of the modern soul, without recording the consequences of the Oriental Renaissance in all provinces of the mind? From that time forward complete panoramas of ideological geography expanded with each glance and contracted with each question. In the process of considering humanity, the whole expanse of time had to be traversed, all inhabited space had to be covered, the whole world of speech sounded. Ideas on poetry, revealed religion, and architecture wavered, for neither Homer nor the Bible nor the basilicas were, now, historically unique. The new Renaissance Man was one who no longer approached solutions to eternal problems without adding up the global balance sheet. The Romantic intelligence was no longer satisfied with anything less than totality, and this was, in large part, due to the Oriental past. The ultimate value of the classics was not their totality but rather their traditionality, that is to say their time-honored selectivity. Subsequent to the Oriental Renaissance the study of the masses would prevail: the mind applied its attention to migrations rather than to states. Initially it was origins, which were viewed as widely divergent, that were most exciting, then even origins lost their fixity and one would have eyes only for evolution."

204 S. DASGUPTA, *THE BENGAL RENAISSANCE*, p. 136.

205 John Henry BARROWS (ed.), *The World's Parliament of Religions, An Illustrated and Popular Story of the World's First Parliament of Religions*, held in Chicago in Connection with the Colombian Exposition of 1893, vols. I and II, Chicago 1893.

206 Other events worth mentioning are the creation of the Red Cross, the Inter-Parliamentary Union, the Olympic Games, and the International Postal Union etc.

207 *See* the HAGUE APPEAL FOR PEACE conference in May 1999, commemorating the First Hague Peace Conference.

especially to the participating Asian countries, China, Japan, Persia, Turkey and Thailand, aiming as they did at global agreements including one on disarmament, and administrative measures, based on equity law, that corresponded to the Asian sense of pragmatism and concern over justice. Asian nations were *not* enthusiastic about the 'rules of war', which the conferences also laid down in their conventions, and which—as history has shown—at critical times become largely ineffective, given that laying down the 'rules of war' was to trigger a global arms race. Nonetheless, the Hague Peace Conferences were a choice outcome as well of the Bengal Renaissance and the Age of Enlightenment in Europe and Asia.

PART IV

Modern India, Gandhi and World Peace

Mahatma Gandhi and Rabindranath Tagore at Santiniketan

Mahatma Gandhi with Chiang Kai-shek and Madame Chiang in Kolkata. Source: http://www.flickr.com/photos/pete4ducks/385123329/

Modern India, Gandhi and World Peace: In Search of an International Peace Based on Justice and Order, 1917 to 1947—The Stakes

"Men of great faith have always called us to wake up to great expectations, and the prudent have always laughed at them and said that these did not belong to reality. But the poet in man knows that reality is a creation, and human reality has to be called forth from its obscure depth by man's faith which is creative." (Rabindranath Tagore)[1]

"The point is often made, with evident justice, that it is impossible to have, in the foreseeable future, a democratic global state. This is indeed so, and yet if democracy is seen (as I have argued earlier that it should be) in terms of public reasoning, particularly the need for worldwide discussion on global problems, we need not put the possibility of global democracy in indefinite cold storage. It is not an all or nothing choice, and there is a strong case for advancing widespread public discussion, even when there would remain many inescapable limitations and weaknesses in the reach of the process. Many institutions can be invoked in this exercise of global identity, including of course the United Nations, but there is also the possibility of committed work, which has already begun, by citizens' organizations, many nongovernment institutions, and independent parts of the news media."[2]

Terror and violence dominate the media, while new threats continue to alarm the international community. In view of this situation it may be useful to look back into history, to find or determine various causes and effects, and perhaps, learn how these present problems might be dealt with, by what has been previously offered in the way of solutions. The Westphalian nation-state system established in 1648 after the Thirty Years War in Europe is no longer effective as a model for political order. It was already starting to crumble, when in 1899 and 1907 the nations of the world came together in The Hague for the Peace Conferences to abolish war. Today it is no longer capable of ordering international relations effectively, peacefully and in accordance with the general principles of emerging world law and international humanitarian law. In this time of escalating terrorist threats and brutality manifested through various fundamentalist

---

1   Rabindranath TAGORE, *Creative Unity*, London, Macmillan 1922, p. 25.

2   Amartya SEN, *Identity and Violence. The Illusion of Destiny*, New York and London, W.W. Norton 2006, p. 184.

regimes, continuing social disintegration and destruction of Nature and the Environment, there is urgent need and ideal opportunity for the reforming and restructuring of the United Nations, leading to its eventual replacement by a federal world union, to achieve justice and peace. The question at this point is: do Gandhi's ideas of peace and non-violence still have a message? And furthermore... How can the errors and bad decisions made in the past be remedied and new errors avoided?

Anthony Parel has made a point by referring to Gandhi's ideas and practical philosophy as "Pax Gandhiana" that was meant to become a program of action for the new India:

> Gandhi's nonviolence means different things to different people. To some it means a personal virtue, to others it means pacifism, and to still others it means living in small, isolated, stateless communes. There are those who believe that nonviolence means treating the state as the enemy or at least being ready to agitate against it at every turn. A close examination of the evidence shows that it means something different from all this. It means first, a general principle of reorganizing society, polity and the international order; and secondly, a praxis that translates the principle into action through private and public institutions, most notably the state. Seen in this light, what he wanted to achieve for India was much more than its mere political independence. He wanted to introduce into India a new nonviolent social and political order, one seeking a new equilibrium between consent, coercion, nonviolence, and the state. Let us call this Pax Gandhiana, seeking to replace Pax Britannica.[3]

In this narrative the focus is on Gandhi's ideas on non-violence and world federation.

1. Where We Want to Go

> "I say again that ... World War II has put the cruel science of mass murder into new and sinister perspective. I say again that the oceans have ceased to be moats which automatically protect our ramparts ... flesh and blood now compete unequally with winged steel. War has become an all-consuming juggernaut ... if World War III ever unhappily arrives, it will open laboratories

---

3   Anthony PAREL, Pax Gandhiana: Is Gandhian Non-Violcnce compatible with the coercive State, in Ravi BHATIA (ed.), *Religious Plurality, Gandhian Thought and Environmental Issues*, New Delhi, IMH 2012, p. 197.

of death too horrible to contemplate ... [we must] do everything ... [in our] power to keep those laboratories closed ... they must be kept closed all around the earth because neither time nor space any longer promises to shield the victims of treacherous attack. We must have collective security to stop the next war, if possible, before it starts; and to crush it swiftly if it starts in spite of our organized precautions." (San Francisco, 1945)[4]

Ashoka, the Palas and the protagonists of the (Bengal) Enlightenment were fellow bondsmen signalling a universal leap forward in human history, the outcome of which is still to be determined; like this episode at the end of our narrative regarding the political development on the Indian continent in the first half of the twentieth century; these are precursors and beacons of hope—a hope which culminated centuries later in the life and work of Mahatma Gandhi. Gandhi, his objectives and political principles for realizing a pervasive peace and self-determining inter-dependence in the period 1917-1947, are the focus of the final sections of this narrative. The historical significance which this work seeks to convey compels us to envisage just what India and Mohandas Karamchand Gandhi, the father of the Indian nation, had in view to ensure a safe, non-violent path to world peace, and what precisely this message contains for us. In this way India's 'place in the world' and its mission can be newly appreciated and more accurately defined, for establishing a precedent for a new and universally applicable peace policy.

Gandhi, the "Oriental Saint" (Dieter Conrad), was one of the great political figureheads of the twentieth century, and the most influential advocate of non-violent pacifism. His "theory and practice of non-violent political action revolutionized" the traditional idea of an "irresolvable alliance of law, politics and power."[5] Albert Einstein considered Gandhi "the only truly great political figure of our age," and "the greatest political genius of our time." He "indicated the path to be taken ... [and] gave proof of what sacrifice man is capable once he has discovered the right path."[6] As ethnologist Wilhelm Emil Mühlmann stated in his (in view of his Nazi

---

4   SENATOR VANDENBERG'S REPORT TO THE SENATE ON THE SAN FRANCISCO CONFERENCE, June 29, 1945, printed in the *New York Times*.

5   Jan ASSMANN, Zur Einführung (Introduction), in Dieter CONRAD, *Gandhi und der Begriff des Politischen. Staat, Religion und Gewalt* (Gandhi and the Concept of the Political, State, Religion and Violence), Munich, Wilhelm Fink 2006, p. 17.

6   Albert EINSTEIN, *Einstein on Peace*, edited by Otto Nathan & Heinz Norden, preface by Bertrand Russell, New York, Schocken 1968, pp. 569 and 584).

past) apologetic-sounding book on the Mahatma, Gandhi advocated "with adamant consistency the sentence that the method is more important than the end."[7] The two world wars, which were also constitutive for India and in which it had taken part, were pivotal events that shook the world. The prime occurrence that occupies a special place in this study was the "Quit India Resolution" of the Indian National Congress, adopted in August 1942. The war year of 1942 was a year of preparation, in which the Allies were planning the future peace and thinking how to improve and develop the League of Nations idea further.[8]

In March 1942, after the United States' entry into the war, the British government sent a mission to India that—while it failed in its objective—resulted in the most remarkable movement during the war, culminating in the 'Quit India' Resolution of 8 August. The American sociologist Irving Horowitz in his 1957 *The Idea of War and Peace in Contemporary Philosophy* maintained that at this decisive moment of India's struggle for independence Mahatma Gandhi put forward a novel and striking solution, in order to "revolutionize the world's outlook upon peace and war."[9] To achieve this, India would have to be given its long fought for political freedom. The idea according to Horowitz, entailed "the development of nationalism in underdeveloped nations to a point of equality *as a mode for arriving at a world state.*" This development was considered inevitable

---

7   Wilhelm Emil MÜHLMANN, *MAHATMA GANDHI. Der Mann, sein Werk und seine Wirkung* (Eine Untersuchung zur Religionssoziologie und politischen Ethik) (MAHATMA GANDHI. The man, his work and its impact [An investigation into the sociology of religion and political ethics]), Tübingen, J.C.B. Mohr (Paul Siebeck) 1950, p. 212. MÜHLMANN's own previous conviction, however, seems to have been quite the opposite, i.e. that the end justifies the means.

8   See for example the *Declaration of the United Nations* of January 1, 1942, and the work of the Commission for the Organization of Peace, in particular the article by Quincy WRIGHT, Political Conditions of the Period of Transition, *International Conciliation*, Commission to Study the Organization of Peace—The Transitional Period, No. 379 (April, 1942). See also Margaret MEAD, *And keep your Powder dry*, New York, William Morrow 1942 (new expanded edition 1965 and 2000, Berghahn), p. 248: "When we talk of policing the world, this is meant to be a transition from armies to police, from seeing the world as a set of warring national entities to seeing it as one civic unity." This book was required reading in the U.S. for anthropology students for nearly two decades after the war. (Amazon.com)

9   H. A. JACK (ed.), *Wit and Wisdom of Gandhi*, Boston, Beacon Press 1951, p. 165, quoted in Irving Louis HOROWITZ, *The Idea of War and Peace in Contemporary Philosophy*, with an Introductory Essay by Roy Wood SELLARS, New York, Paine-Whitman 1957, p. 100.

and essential to solve the problems of the world.[10] It is little known that Gandhi in 1942 envisaged, besides independence from colonial rule, an international order transcending the nation-state, or as he himself put it, "a world federation established by agreement"[11]—the key formula—based on non-violence and founded on the United Nations.[12] Obviously, Gandhi and with him the All-India Congress Committee (AICC) had high hopes, as the resolution that was finally adopted clearly demonstrates. In the following pages an attempt is made to investigate and test the above-stated hypothesis, and trace its origins as well as find out what consequences, if any, the 'Quit India' Resolution has had, and what it could mean to us today, more than seventy years after its inception. Again: "Juxtaposing Pax Gandhiana and Pax Britannica makes good historic sense. After all, it was Pax Britannica that created the historical conditions necessary for the possibility of Pax Gandhiana."[13]

2. The Background

Though nominally India had been a founding member of the League of Nations—a fact, which may not be altogether irrelevant — it entered the international community of nations relatively late, unlike other Asian nations such as China, Japan, Persia and Siam, who had all participated in the Hague Peace Conferences in 1899 and 1907.[14] Already before India became a founding member of the League of Nations, in 1917, in a "revolutionary declaration", Edwin S. Montagu, Secretary of State for

---

10 I.L. HOROWITZ, *The Idea of War and Peace*, p. 105: Gandhi "presented a solution involving the development of nationalism in underdeveloped nations to a point of equality *as a mode for arriving at a world state.*" (Emphasis added)

11 *The Wit and Wisdom of Gandhi*, p. 121, in I.L. HOROWITZ, *The Idea of War and Peace*, p. 105.

12 It can be shown that the UN Charter was conceived to eventually accommodate such an aim.

13 A. PAREL, Pax Gandhiana, pp. 197-178.

14 Perhaps understandably from an Indian point of view, Pundit NEHRU dismissed the Hague Conferences, denying their relevance with respect to the development of binding world law and order, and failing to see them as the logical outcome of the age of enlightenment, and the 'oriental renaissance'. In his opinion, they were "a curious attempt at peace", where "[n]othing of the least importance was done." Jawaharlal Nehru, *Glimpses of World History*, Oxford University Press (Jawaharlal Nehru Memorial Fund), 1982, p. 615. And ibid.: "Peace cannot suddenly descend from the heavens. It can only come when the root-causes of trouble are removed."

India, "promised" the country "freedom."[15] Much earlier, in 1858, the year of the dissolution of the East-India Company, the British Queen Victoria (1819-1901) not only "learned Hindi from an Indian tutor"[16] but already "explicitly promised equal treatment to her Indian subjects."[17] Prompted by the First World War, when "India's support of the British war effort was of major importance in terms of men and money,"[18] Montagu declared in the House of Commons on 20 August that British policy aimed at "increasing association of Indians in every branch of the administration, and the gradual development of self-governing institutions, with a view to the progressive realization of a responsible government in India as an integral part of the British Empire."[19] The declaration encouraged the Indians in their quest for independence and democracy. Already before the First World War, Indians had been encouraged in their quest for independence and democracy by the "Russian Revolution of 1905, the Young Turk Revolution of 1909, and the Chinese Revolution of 1911." They "invariably identified political freedom with two things: the absence of an absolute monarch and the presence of an assembly of representatives of the people."[20] With the October Revolution in Russia in the same year, 1917, the Indian cause received a further boost.

Montagu and the Viceroy Lord Chelmsford, who worked out the details of the reform proposals,[21] hoped that "as power was devolved by

15 R.J. MOORE, *The Crisis of Indian Unity, 1917–1940*, Oxford, Clarendon Press 1974, p. vii. Already in 1858 Queen Victoria had "explicitly promised equal treatment to her Indian subjects." Hermann KULKE and Dietmar ROTHERMUND, *A History of India*, Calcutta, Allahabad, Bombay and Delh, Rupa 1991, p. 270.

16 Dietmar ROTHERMUND, *Geschichte Indiens: Vom Mittelalter bis zur Gegenwart*, C.H. Beck 2002, p. 63.

17 H. KULKE and D. ROTHERMUND, *A History of India*, Psychology Press 2004, p. 278. (Calcutta, Allahabad, Bombay and Delhi, Rupa 1991, p. 270.) The German edition does not have this information!

18 H. KULKE and D. ROTHERMUND, *A History of India*, Rupa 1991, p. 280: "India's support of the British war effort was of major importance in terms of men and money." The sentence is missing in the 2004 edition.

19 Judith M. BROWN, *Gandhi Prisoner of Hope*, Bombay, Calcutta and Madras, Oxford University Press 1992, p. 104. "British policy aimed at increasing association of Indians in every branch of the administration, and the gradual development of self-governing institutions, with a view to the progressive realization of a responsible government in India as an integral part of the British Empire."

20 Nirad C. CHAUDHURI, *The Autobiography of an Unknown Indian*, Mumbai, Delhi, Bangalore, Calcutta, Hyderabad and Chennai, Jaico 1998, p. 261.

21 H KULKE and D. ROTHERMUND, *A History of India*, p. 273.

stages Muslim apartness and princely aloofness would diminish sufficiently to enable India to become a single self-governing unit."²² Consequently, from 1917 on India was allowed to participate in the imperial conferences alongside the self-governing dominions.²³ It was thought that eventually a bicameral legislature would replace the old unicameral legislative body at the national level, while the provinces of Madras, Bombay, Bengal, the United Provinces (U.P.), the Punjab, Bihar and Orissa, the Central Provinces, Assam and the North-West Frontier Province remained under direct British rule, with single-chamber legislatures. All this still in spite of the fact that at the time only about 3% of propertied Indians were allowed to vote.

In World War I the Muslims had insisted, as Romain Rolland in his book about the Mahatma related, that "the Turks should remain in Turkey in Europe and that the sultan should retain not only authority over the Holy Places of Islam, but over Arabia as delimited by Mohammedan scholars with the enclaves of Mesopotamia, Syria, and Palestine." This Lloyd George and the Viceroy Lord Chelmsford had "solemnly promised," a pledge that was, however, broken after the war.²⁴ So, when "the rumors of the peace terms to be imposed on Turkey began to circulate in 1919, the Moslems in India began to grow restless, and their discontent finally started the Khilafat or Califat movement."²⁵ Since the British "had always taken advantage of the natural enmity between Hindus and Moslems," Gandhi therefore now tried to use the Islamic Califat movement as a means of achieving and

---

22 R. J. MOORE, *Crisis of Indian Unity*, p. vii.

23 Ibid., p. 7.

24 Romain ROLLAND, *MAHATMA GANDHI. The Man Who Became One with the Universal Being*, transl. by Catherine D. Groth, New York und London, The Century Co. 1924, pp. 78-79: "The European War had placed the Moslems of India in a very painful dilemma. They were torn between their duty as loyal citizens of the empire and faithful followers of their religious chief. They agreed to help England when she promised not to attack the sultan's or the caliph's sovereignty. It was the sense of Moslem opinion in India that the Turks should remain in Turkey in Europe and that the sultan should retain not only authority over the Holy Places of Islam, but over Arabia as delimited by Mohammedan scholars with the enclaves of Mesopotamia, Syria, and Palestine. This Lloyd George and the viceroy solemnly promised. When the war was over, however, all pledges were forgotten."

25 R. ROLLAND, *MAHATMA GANDHI*, p. 79: "It began October 17, 1919 (Khilafat day), with an imposing peaceful demonstration, which was followed, about a month later (November 24), by the opening of an All-India Khilafat Conference at Delhi. Gandhi presided. With his quick glance he had realized that the Islamic agitation might be made into the instrument of Indian unity."

safeguarding Indian unity.[26]

With the Montagu-Chelmsford reforms the Indian members of the executive came to be "in charge of 'transferred subjects' such as education, health and local government, whereas the British members held the 'reserved' portfolios for home, revenue and finance."[27] Foreign affairs and defence, of course, remained in British hands, with the British armed forces as the most effective instrument to ensure continued submission and exploitation of the Indian subjects. As Gandhi stated in 1942: "The present Indian Army is in fact an offshoot of the British Army and has been maintained till now mainly to hold India in subjection."[28] Basically India remained a colony, commercially exploited, so that England could profit.

Nevertheless, the constitutional reforms, introduced by the Montagu-Chelmsford Report in April 1918, became law in December 1919. Yet, the "whole complex process of restructuring the Raj after 1917" envisaged by the Montagu-Chelmsford reforms was slow and created noticeable 'inconsistencies',[29] like retaining separate electorates for the Muslims, which was "actually incompatible with responsible government."[30] Also, the Rowlett Bills in 1919, which "extended the wartime restrictions on individual rights",[31] dampened the impact of the reforms considerably,

---

26 Ibid., pp. 79-80: "The problem of uniting the various races in India was a most difficult one. The English had always taken advantage of the natural enmity between Hindus and Moslems; Gandhi even accused them of having fostered it."

27 H. KULKE and D. ROTHERMUND, *A History of India*, pp. 272 and 273. By a "strange construction of 'dyarchy' ... the provincial executive was split into two halves—an Indian one responsible to the legislature, and a British one which remained irremovable and 'irresponsible'." Ibid., p. 273.

28 Appendix III, Resolution Passed by A.I.C.C., 1 May 1942. CWMG, vol. LXXVI, p. 424.

29 R.J. MOORE, *Crisis of Indian Unity*, p. 10. Of course Bengal, which at that time comprised also Assam, Bihar and Orissa, had already been divided by the Viceroy, Lord Curzon, in 1905, an act that was "obviously meant to strike at the territorial roots of the nationalist elite of Bengal." Also, "Lord Curzon did not hesitate to point out to the Muslims of eastern Bengal that he conceived of this province as Muslim." In 1911 Bengal was repartitioned, now with Bihar and Orissa forming new provinces. H KULKE and D. ROTHERMUND, *A History of India*, p. 280.

30 H. KULKE and D. ROTHERMUND, *A History of India*, p. 273. The Morley-Minto constitutional reform of 1909 had also resulted in separate electorates for Muslims and Hindus, a somewhat "fateful construction." In 1916 the Indian National Congress and the Muslim League agreed to Muslim over-representation in the provincial legislatures where there was a minority, while it was the reverse in the two Muslim majority provinces Bengal and the Punjab, where the Hindus were a minority. *Ibid.*, p. 272.

31 R. J. MOORE, *Crisis of Indian Unity*, p. 4. See H. KULKE and D. ROTHERMUND, *A*

though they were "never actually invoked."[32] The resultant protests provided the first opportunity for Gandhi, who had returned from South Africa in 1915, to test non-violent resistance "on a national scale." Subsequent events like the random shootings in Amritsar on 13 April, by a British Brigadier, General Reginald Dyer, on an unarmed crowd, killing at least four hundred people, among them women, children and old people, carried the protests much further than originally planned.[33]

Nevertheless, in 1919 Indians were present at the Paris Peace Conference, and in 1920 India obtained "diplomatic recognition in London through the appointment of a high commissioner."[34] However, with democracy still a long way off, politicians like Jawaharlal Nehru were critical: "This is nonsense. The so-called representatives (to the League of Nations) cannot be the representatives of India unless the people of India choose them. They are ... the nominees of the Government of India, which, in spite of its name, is just a department of the British Government."[35] Indeed, while the Chinese were led by Wellington Koo, the "voice of India came, then and for too many years thereafter, not from the vast spaces of the subcontinent but from the dusty corridors of Whitehall."[36] However, in 1924, a delegation was for the first time led by an Indian.[37]

Indian politicians continued to face suppression and struggled with the inconsistencies of British policy; in their desire for participation to affect genuine reforms, give shape to their national constitution, and

History of India, p. 283: This meant "No trial, no lawyer, no appeal."

32 Percival SPEAR, *A History of India*, vol. II, Penguin 1978, p. 190.

33 R.J. MOORE, *Crisis of Indian Unity*, p. 4. As a result of the Amritsar Massacre Rabindranath Tagore renounced the knighthood he had obtained in 1915. For the long-term effects of the massacre and subsequent British-Indian failures at rapprochement including racial bitterness see also Ved MEHTA, *Rajiv Gandhi and Rama's Kingdom*, New Haven and London, Yale University Press 1994, p. 48. Luckily, "Gandhi's influence prevented large-scale outbreaks of violence." P. SPEAR, *A History of India*, p. 191.

34 R.J. MOORE, *Crisis of Indian Unity*, p. 7.

35 J. NEHRU, *Glimpses of World History*, p. 463. And ibid., p. 682: "India, curiously enough, became an original member of the League, in flat contradiction of the provision that only self-governing States could be members. Of course by 'India' was meant the British Government of India, and by this clever dodge the British Government managed to get an extra representative."

36 F.P. WALTERS, *A History of the League of Nations*, London, New York and Toronto, Oxford University Press 1960, p. 117.

37 F.P. WALTERS, *A History of the League of Nations*, p. 414.

obtain full independence from colonial rule, they were torn between two opposing forces: co-operation and non-cooperation, including passive resistance and civil disobedience.[38] Yet there was nothing for them to do except continue to call for genuine liberties and full independence.

In Kolkata, in December 1929, the Indian Congress passed a resolution demanding Dominion Status by 31 December the same year, failing which it would embark on a non-cooperation campaign to obtain full independence. Nevertheless, Mahatma Gandhi conceded that "foreign affairs, political relations and defence [could] be reserved in some manner to be defined," to the British government, for the time being.[39] Indeed, the British side appeared willing to negotiate, and preparations were made for a conference to discuss the issues. However, when the first Round Table Conference, as it was called, eventually met in London, in spite of the high expectations, it accomplished little.[40]

Surprisingly perhaps, Gandhi himself did not attach too much importance to 'the constitutional niceties' of Dominion Status, saying: "I can wait for the Dominion Status Constitution, if I can get the real dominion status in action, if … there is a real change of heart … [This] implies [the] ability to sever the British connection if I wish to … *If I choose to remain in the empire, it is to make the partnership a power for promoting peace and goodwill in the world.*"[41] This line of argument corresponds closely to Gandhi's Presidential Address at the Belgaum Congress in December 1924 about independence from the Crown, whilst preserving the British 'connection' "on perfectly honourable and absolutely equal terms."[42] On this occasion Gandhi stated:

> In my opinion if the British Government mean what they say and honestly help us to equality, it would be a greater triumph than a complete severance of the British connection. I would therefore strive for swaraj within the

---

38 Or as Partha CHATTERJEE, *The Nation and its Fragments*, Princeton, N., Princeton University Press 1993, p. 6 has said, quoted in A. SEN, *Identity and Violence*, p. 90: "The greater one's success in imitating Western skills in th material domain, therefore, the greater the need to preserve the distinctiveness of one's spiritual culture."

39 R. J. MOORE, *Crisis of Indian Unity*, p. 46.

40 Ibid., p. 46.

41 R. J. MOORE, *Crisis of Indian Unity*, p. 97 (emphasis added).

42 *Presidential Address at Belgaum Conference*, (Emphasis added.) 26 December 1924, in: CWMG, Vol. XXV, p. 481.

Empire, but would not hesitate to sever all connection, if severance became a necessity through Britain's own fault. I would thus throw the burden of separation on the British people. *The better mind of the world desires today not absolutely independent States warring one against another but a federation of friendly inter-dependent States … I see nothing grand or impossible about our expressing our readiness for universal inter-dependence rather than independence.* [!!!] … I desire the ability to be totally independent without asserting the independence.[43]

It may be that Pundit Nehru, who was perhaps more perceptive in such matters, and may also have been partly responsible for the content, had advised Gandhiji; in any event the general trend in 1924 was to give the League of Nations broader powers than it had possessed until then. The Geneva Protocol for the peaceful settlement of international disputes (later not ratified) was supposed to "give teeth" to the organization, i.e. competencies quite similar to those of a 'limited' world government.[44] In any event it is clear that Gandhi was well aware of India's future status and responsibility in an increasingly smaller and interdependent world. The developments in 1929, the Irwin declaration committing Britain to have "any definition of Dominion Status that the white Dominions might obtain" apply to India, and, with the Round Table Conferences the positive intent to depart "from the paternalism of 'tutorial commissions,'" could well have been regarded as the "tangible beginning" of a "multi-racial Commonwealth."[45] Indeed, the British Commonwealth itself bore the seeds of a global federation, and naturally tended toward such an end.[46] As Anthony Parel states: "There is something common between

---

43 *Presidential Address*, 26 December 1924, CWMG, Vol. XXV, pp. 481-482. (Emphasis added)

44 Harold BUTLER, *The Lost Peace. A Personal Impression*, New York, Harcourt, Brace And Company 1942, pp. 28-30.

45 R. J. MOORE, *Crisis of Indian Unity*, pp. 93, 313 and 94.

46 There are signs that England early on pursued not only "imperial" objectives, but already aspired to a federal world order, especially after the loss of the American colonies. Alfred Lord TENNYSON—the 'Queen's poet'—in his 1842 poem 'Locksley Hall' imparted the following message: "For I dipt into the future, far as human eye could see, Saw the Vision of the world, and all the wonder that would be; Saw the heavens fill with commerce, argosies of magic sails, Pilots of the purple twilight dropping down with costly bales; Heard the heavens fill with shouting, and there rain'd a ghastly dew From the nations' airy navies grappling in the central blue; Far along the world-wide whisper of the south-wind rushing warm, With the standards of the peoples plunging thro' the thunder-storm; Till the war-drum throbb'd no longer, and the battle-flags were

Pax Gandhiana and Pax Kantiana."[47] Quite possibly Gandhi was aware of Immanuel Kant's proposal of a pacific federation, expounded in his treatise on *Perpetual Peace*, which proclaimed that

> without a compact between the nations ... peace cannot be established or assured. Hence, there must be an alliance of a particular kind which we may call a covenant of peace (*foedus pacificum*), which would differ from a treaty of peace (*pactum pacis*) in this respect, that the latter merely puts an end to one war, while the former would seek to put an end to war forever.[48]

This did not mean that Gandhi was so naïve or unrealistic that he wanted to deny the Indian nation the right of self-defense. In a 'formal statement' at the Second Round Table Conference in London in 1931, "the only conference on a constitution for India that he ever attended," he stated:

> I think that a nation that has no control over her own defense forces and over her external policy is hardly a responsible nation. Defense, its army is to a nation the very essence of its existence, and if a nation's defense is controlled by an outside agency, no matter how friendly it is, then that nation is certainly not responsibly governed ... Hence I am here respectfully to claim complete control over the army, over the defense forces and over external affairs ... I would wait till eternity if I cannot get control over defense. I refuse to deceive myself that I am going to embark upon responsible government although I cannot control my defense ... That is my fundamental position.[49]

The outcome of the Round Table conferences—altogether there were three—was the Act of 1935, which gave India a new constitution and anticipated a federal system. The federation would become a reality when a sufficient number of states, i.e. half the state population of India agreed to join. Unfortunately this did not materialize;[50] only some 15 years later, in 1950, important passages pertaining to the federal system were

---

furl'd In the Parliament of man, the Federation of the world. There the common sense of most shall hold a fretful realm in awe, And the kindly earth shall slumber, lapt in universal law."

47 A. PAREL, Pax Gandhiana, p. 211.

48 Immanuel KANT, *Perpetual Peace, A Philosophiacal Essay*, transl. by Campbell Smith. London, George Allen & Unwin 1917 (1903), p. 134.

49 A. PAREL, Pax Gandhiana, p. 209.

50 Sir Atul Chandra CHATTERJEE, *The New India*, London, George Allen & Unwin 1948, pp. 67-68.

implemented into India's post-war Constitution. Critically, Nehru labelled the Basic Law adopted in 1935 the "new charter of slavery," because it did not nearly satisfy the requirement of the Indian National Congress for more far-reaching, 'complete independence'.[51]

The Round Table conferences had in fact not been able to resolve the 'three dualities' that confronted them, the first "between the Raj and its aspirant successor, the parallel government of the Indian National Congress;" further that "between Hindu India and Muslim India;" and finally the one "between British India and the Indian States" that were ruled by the princes. Still, "[b]etween 1917 and 1940 India advanced steadily towards freedom", at the same time however, "it seems, inexorably towards division" as well. The Round Table conferences had "failed to solve the problem of freedom with unity."[52]

3. Times of War

When in September 1939 the war started in Europe, "the British Government unilaterally committed India to the conflict", and this was "without even going through the motions of consulting Indian politicians about it."[53] Not surprisingly, some Congress leaders had doubts whether this was "an anti-fascist war or … just an imperialist war aimed at maintaining the status quo—including colonial rule in India," and had therefore requested that they be given a "declaration of the British war aims with regard to India,"[54] which was turned down.[55] The immediate consequence was a constitutional crisis: all ministers of the Indian National Congress went on strike, immediately cleared their offices and, with Gandhi's backing, resigned from their posts in the provincial governments. As a result of the

51 The NEHRU quote is from the *Area Handbook for India*, Washington D.C., U.S. Government Printing Office, May 1970, p. 80.

52 R.j. MOORE, *Crisis of Indian Unity*, pp. 313 and 317.

53 Paul F. POWER, *Gandhi on World Affairs*, London, George Allen & Unwin 1961, p. 31.

54 In Britain, too, there was a "demand for explicit British War Aims in 1939" that appeared "as a revival of the War Aims controversy of 1917-18," in that it was a "movement to anticipate and avert a repetition of this betrayal," i.e. resulting in an ineffective League of Nations. H.G. WELLS, *Phoenix. A Summary of the Inescapable Conditions of World Reorganisation*, London, Secker & Warburg 1942, p.93.

55 H. KULKE and D. ROTHERMUND, *A History of India*, p. 296. Jawaharlal Nehru, *The Discovery of India*, New Delhi, Bombay, Calcutta and Bombay, Oxford University Press 1990 (Jawaharlal Nehru Memorial Fund), p. 430.

'constitutional crisis' the British governors had to take over their functions.

As the urgency increased to procure greater Indian cooperation in the war effort, because of the advance of the Japanese in Southeast Asia, Great Britain was not only forced to finally make a declaration of its war aims,[56] but also to consider a compromise to accommodate India's political ambitions. The cabinet therefore sent Sir Stafford Cripps, a 'friend' of Jawaharlal Nehru, on a mission to India in 1942, to negotiate a deal. It was known, however, that Prime Minister Winston Churchill was "an uncompromising opponent" of Indian freedom. When Churchill and U.S. president F.D. Roosevelt proclaimed the Atlantic Charter on 14 August 1941, enunciating "certain common principles ... on which they base their hopes for a better future for the world," including "the right of all peoples to choose the form of government under which they will live," Churchill determined that this had "no application to India."[57] As an indication of America's good intentions for a positive outcome to the negotiations, President Roosevelt sent his personal emissary, Colonel Johnson, to New Delhi to support Cripps.[58]

The Indians anyway hardly believed that Britain was willing to concede anything, one obvious reason being that an earlier request by Burma to obtain assurances of dominion status *after* the war had also been denied. Churchill confirmed this view, when in response to the Quit India resolution he said publicly on 10 November 1942:

> We intend to remain the effective rulers of India for a long and indefinite period ... We mean to hold our own. I have not become the King's First Minister in order to preside over the liquidation of the British Empire."[59]

Since the war had started, Gandhi was haunted by the "horror of seeing

---

56 H. KULKE and D. ROTHERMUND, *A History of India*, p. 297: In fact, it was the American Allies who "finally forced the British cabinet to make a declaration of its war aims so as to obtain India's full support for the war effort."

57 J. NEHRU, *The Discovery of India*, pp. 438 and 442.

58 H. KULKE and D. ROTHERMUND, *A History of India*, p. 298: "Roosevelt's personal representative, Colonel Johnson, had actively intervened in New Delhi at the time of the negotiations in order to help Cripps."

59 Statement on 10 November 1942. Francis G. HUTCHINS, *India's Revolution—Gandhi and the Quit India Movement*, Cambridge, Ma., Harvard University Press 1973, p. 143. "Here we are, and here we stand, a veritable rock of salvation in this drifting world." Ibid.

India militarized." As the fighting had "ceased to be a distant spectacle" and came ever closer to the Indian homeland, the debate among the ranks of the A-ICC over the question of the defense of India intensified.[60] Nehru writes: "At no time, so far as I am aware, was the question of non-violence considered [seriously] in relation to the army, navy, or air forces, or the police. It was taken for granted that its application was confined to our struggle for freedom." Yet it was "true that it [non-violence] had a powerful effect on our thinking in many ways, and it made Congress strongly favour world disarmament and a peaceful solution of all international, as well as national disputes."[61] Historically this tradition had previously been formalized in some Buddhist councils, as Amartya Sen has pointed out.[62] Certain discrepancies that surfaced in the discussions on these issues had in 1940 led to "a definite and public break with him [Gandhi] on the issue" of the future applications of the principle of non-violence in India's external affairs. Eventually, however, Gandhi had his way, and the A-ICC resolved that it

> firmly believes in the policy and practice of non-violence, not only in the struggle for Swaraj, but also, in so far as this may be possible of application, in free India. The Committee is convinced, and recent world events have demonstrated, that complete world disarmament is necessary and the establishment of a new and just political and economic order, if the world is not to destroy itself and revert to barbarism. A free India will, therefore, throw all her weight in favour of world disarmament and should herself be prepared to give a lead in this to the world. Such lead will inevitably depend on external factors and internal conditions, but the state would do its utmost to give effect to this policy of disarmament. Effective disarmament and the establishment of world peace by the ending of national wars depend ultimately on the removal of the causes of wars and national conflicts. These causes must be rooted out by the ending of the domination of one country over another and the exploitation of one people or group by another. To that end India will peacefully labour and it is with this objective in view that the

---

60 J. NEHRU, *The Discovery of India*, p. 443.

61 J. NEHRU, *The Discovery of India*, pp. 442-444.

62 A. SEN, *Identity and Violence*, p. 53: "For example, some of the earliest open general meetings aimed specifically at settling disputes between different points of view took place in India in the so-called Buddhist councils, where adherents of different points of view got together to argue out their differences. Ashoka ... tried to codify and propagate ... formulations of rules ..."

people of India desire to attain the status of a free and independent nation. Such freedom will be the prelude to the close association with other countries within a comity of nations for the peace and progress of the world.[63]

This was substantial, undiluted 'spirit of Geneva' (L'esprit de Genève). "When later Sir Stafford Cripps came up with his proposals," however, Nehru wrote, "there was no question of non-violence. His proposals were considered purely from the political point of view."[64]

Incidentally, just prior to Cripps' arrival, in February 1942, Gandhi and Chiang Kai-shek, "a friend of Indian self-determination," had met in Calcutta.[65] At the time it seemed to be "one of those events which may change the course of history," as John Gunther observed in his momentous socio-political documentary *Inside Asia*. Chiang Kai-shek who had only recently been sworn in as Supreme Allied Commander of China, "consulted with British officials and also Gandhi and Nehru. His purpose was to encourage the unity of the 450,000,000 people of China and the 388,000,000 people of India in a common war effort, and to stimulate the Indian nationalist movement."[66] It is needless to say that Gandhi and Nehru in their talks with the Generalissimo had full sympathy with China's cause; it was their aim for India to be recognized as an equal partner in the fight against Japanese aggression, and participate in the decision-making. And for that Gandhi was willing even to compromise by allowing Indians to actually fight (under certain conditions), and letting the Allied Powers under some kind of treaty "keep their armed forces in India and use the country as a base for operations against the threatened Japanese attack."[67]

---

63 J. NEHRU, *The Discovery of India*, pp. 446-447.

64 J. NEHRU, *The Discovery of India*, p. 447. And: "In late months, leading up to August, 1942, Gandhiji's nationalism and intense desire for freedom made him even agree to Congress participation in the war if India could function as a free country. For him this was a remarkable and astonishing change ... The practical statesman took precedence over the uncompromising prophet."

65 P.F. POWER, *Gandhi on World Affairs*, p. 31.

66 John GUNTHER, *Inside Asia* (1942 War edition, completely revised), New York and London, Harper 1942, pp. 219-20. During their five-hours talks Madame Chiang acted as interpreter. Chiang and his wife also visited Rabindranath Tagore's university Shantiniketan in West Bengal and donated 50.000 Rupees to it. A series of meetings also took place between Chiang and Jawaharlal Nehru. Originally, Chiang had planned to visit Gandhi in his village at Wardha. CWMG, Vol. LXXV, pp. 306f. and 313.

67 Letter to CHIANG Kai-shek, Sevagram, 14 June 1942, CWMG, Vol. LXXVI, p. 225. In an interview with Reuter's on 21 June GANDHI stated: "There can be no limit to what

4. The Cripps Mission

On 23 March Sir Stafford Cripps, "a close friend of both Chiang and Nehru," arrived in India. Conditions for the success of his mission were favourable, as there had been a reshuffling of the British cabinet more friendly to the Indian cause. At that time it had been proclaimed that "India would be given a seat in the war cabinet, like the dominions, and on the Pacific War Council." Also, Lord Cranborne, the "new Colonial Secretary, stated in the House of Lords that Britain 'is in favor of India's political freedom.'" Apparently, Cripps had "agreed to enter the government only on this condition." Furthermore, US president Roosevelt in a statement on 2 February had reassured the Indians that the Atlantic Charter was to apply to "the whole world," contradicting Churchill's previous statement.[68]

The Chinese Premier also supported the Indian position, and said:

> I hope Britain, without waiting for any demand on the part of the Indian people, as speedily as possible will give them real political power so they will be in a position to develop further their spiritual and material strength. The Indian people thus would realize that their participation in the war was not merely to aid anti-aggression nations for securing victory but also the turning point in their struggle for their own freedom. For the sake of civilization and human freedom, China and India should give their united support to the principles of the Atlantic Charter and ally themselves against aggression on the ABCD front.[69]

In the course of the discussions with Sir Stafford, however, it became clear that the British government actually had no intention of giving the Indians any responsible positions in the government or the War Cabinet, for the defence of India. As Nehru later recounts, it suddenly "transpired that all our previous talk was entirely beside the point,[70] as there were going to be no [Indian]

friendly Independent India can do. I had in mind a treaty between United Nations and India for the defence of China against Japanese aggression." Ibid., p. 236.

68 J. GUNTHER, *Inside Asia.* p. 506.

69 Quoted in J. GUNTHER, *Inside Asia.* p. 506: "India would be given a seat in the war cabinet, like the dominions, and on the Pacific War Council."

70 See H. KULKE and D. ROTHERMUND, *A History of India*, p. 298: When Cripps had "almost succeeded in getting the Congress leaders into a wartime cabinet with the viceroy acting like a constitutional monarch," the viceroy himself, the ultra-conservative Lord Linlithgow, thwarted the scheme by complaining to the British prime minister that "Cripps intended to deprive him of his constitutional powers. This killed the 'Cripps

ministers with any power." Following the breakdown of the negotiations, Sir Stafford Cripps "returned to England by air. But before he did so, and on his return, he made certain statements to the public which were contrary to the facts and which were bitterly resented in India."[71] However, there were critical voices as well, blaming Congress for the failure:

> Our doubts about the usefulness of the Cripps Mission have been borne out. We warned that the hope of the mission succeeding was a forlorn hope. Even more time has been wasted than originally feared. The danger involved in this delay, therefore, may be proportionately greater, unless bold steps and drastic measures are taken to cope with the situation. It would be hypocritical liberalism to say that there is no use apportioning blame. Because, it is evident that a settlement has been prevented only by the intransigence of the Congress leaders. Had they taken up a positive attitude, the Muslim League would have followed suit. The revised formula regarding the control of the Defence Department should have satisfied all who are really anxious to mobilise the Indian people to resist invasion.[72]

Following his initial 'Quit India' call in April, anyway, Gandhi wrote in a letter to the 'Generalissimo' on 14 June:

> I am anxious to explain to you that my appeal to the British power to withdraw from India is not meant in any shape or form to weaken India's defence against the Japanese or embarrass you in your struggle. India must not submit to any aggressor or invader and must resist him. I would not be guilty of purchasing the freedom of my country at the cost of your country's freedom. That problem does not arise before me as I am clear that India cannot gain her freedom in this way, and a Japanese domination of either India or China would be equally injurious to the other country and to world peace. That domination must therefore be prevented and I should like India to play her natural and rightful part in this. I feel India cannot do so while she is in bondage. India has been a helpless witness of the withdrawals from

---

offer' ... he had obviously offered more than he could deliver." "It transpired that all our previous talk was entirely beside the point, as there were going to be no ministers with any power" writes J. NEHRU, *The Discovery of India*, p. 463.

71 J. NEHRU, *The Discovery of India*, pp. 461 and 463. Both the non-partisan Congress and the Muslim League rejected the Cripps proposals.

72 M.N. ROY, The Atmosphere Clears, Independent India, April 19, 1942, in M.N. ROY, *India and War*, Lucknow, Dr. A.P Singh, Radical Democratic Party (First Edition. December 1942), p. 455.

Malaya, Singapore and Burma. We must learn the lesson from these tragic events and prevent by all means at our disposal a repetition of what befell these unfortunate countries. But unless we are free we can do nothing to prevent it, and the same process might well occur again, crippling India and China disastrously. I do not want a repetition of this tragic tale of woe. Our proffered help has repeatedly been rejected by the British Government and the recent failure of the Cripps Mission has left a deep wound which is still running.[73]

Gandhi was convinced that non-violent resistance against the invading Japanese could be applied and had tried to influence Chiang in on this account. Despite Gandhi's pacifist convictions, at about the same time, in mid-1942, it became possible to close "the gap between Gandhi and most of his Congress colleagues," when "the apostle of total pacifism, came gradually round to a measure of political realism and agreed that India could not in the event of immediate independence do without the assistance of allied soldiers for her defence."[74]

Of course, Gandhi was not so naïve anyway as to believe that Indian security or for that matter, world peace and international relations could be based solely on goodwill and non-violence. Peace, justice and security required organization. As Kenneth Boulding argued some time ago:

> Just as war is too important to leave to the generals so peace is too important to leave to the pacifists. It is not enough to condemn violence, to abstain from it, or to withdraw from it. There must be an organization against it; in other words, institutions of conflict control or, in still other words, government. The case for world government to police total disarmament ... seems to me absolutely unshakeable ... In general, we know the main lines of the kind of world organization that can eliminate the present dangers and give us permanent peace. What we do not know is how to get to it ... Where, then, are the new ideas and the new images of the future that look like upward paths? One is clearly the idea of non-violent resistance associated with the name of Gandhi.[75]

Gandhi had reiterated his stance concerning the necessary conditions

---

73 Letter to CHIANG Kai-shek, Sevagram, 14 June 1942, CWMG, Vol. LXXVI, pp. 223-224.

74 J.M. BROWN, *Gandhi Prisoner of Hope*, p. 323, with sources.

75 Kenneth E. BOULDING, *Conflict and Defense, A General Theory*, New York, Harper & Row 1963, p. 334, 335-336.

for peace and security in an interdependent world in an interview to the *New York Times* on 22 April 1940,[76] saying he would "welcome a world federation of all the nations of the world. However, he considered a "federation of the Western nations only" would be "an unholy combination and a menace to humanity. In my opinion a federation excluding India is now an impossibility. India has already passed the stage when she could be safely neglected."[77]

Gandhi's peace efforts included attempts to convince the Axis powers to put an end to their aggressive pursuits. In a letter to Hitler in December 1940 he stressed: "We would never wish to end the British rule with German aid," and warned the 'Führer':

> You are leaving no legacy to your people of which they would feel proud. They cannot take pride in a recital of cruel deeds, however skilfully planned. I, therefore, appeal to you in the name of humanity to stop the war. You will lose nothing by referring all the matters of dispute between you and Great Britain to an international tribunal of your joint choice. If you attain success in the war, it will not prove that you were in the right. It will only prove that your power of destruction was greater. Whereas an award by an impartial tribunal will show as far as it is humanly possible which party was in the right."[78]

---

76 The question by the interviewer was: "Have you any views about world federation (Streit's scheme of 15 white democracies with India excluded at present) or about a federation of Europe with the British Commonwealth and again excluding India? Would you advise India to enter such a larger federation so as to prevent a domination of the coloured races by the whilte?" CWMG, vol. LXXII, p. 11. With that GANDHI rejected the proposal of Clarence K. STREIT, *Union Now. The Proposal for Inter-democracy Federal Union* (short version), New York and London, Harper 1940. George ORWELL also rejected STREIT's idea, since it would not give the coloured population equal rights. George ORWELL, Not Counting Niggers, *Adelphi*, July 1939, online at http://ebooks.adelaide.edu.au/o/orwell/george/not-counting-niggers.

77 Interview in the *New York Times* of 22 April 1940. CWMG, vol. LXXII, p. 11.

78 CWMG, vol. LXXIII, pp. 254-255. Gandhi had previously also written to HITLER on 23 July 1939, and written to Lord LINLITHGOW on 26 May 1940, that "I am prepared to go to Germany or anywhere required to plead for peace not for this interest or that but for the good of mankind." He added: "This may be a visionary's idea. But as your friend I owe it to pass it to you. Perchance it may be wisdom more than a vision." CWMG, vol. LXXII, p. 101. GANDHI's letter to Hitler is in CWMG, vol. LXXIII, p. 254-255. See also W. E. MÜHLMANN, *MAHATMA GANDHI*, p. 88, who also quoted from Gandhi's letter to Hitler: "Friends have urged me to write to you. I have resisted their request, because I feel that any letter from me would be improper. Something tells me, however, that I must not consider too much, and that I must risk an appeal, whatever might be its

Apparently the letter was never sent. In July 1940 he had written an appeal to 'every Briton', "wherever he may be now," recommending that they "accept the method of non-violence instead of that of war for the adjustment of relations between nations;" 'non-violent non-cooperation', Gandhi stated, was a "matchless weapon:" "I have applied it in every walk of life, domestic, institutional, economic and political. I know of no single case in which it has failed."[79] And now, just prior to the final launching of the Quit India movement, he wrote another appeal, 'to every Japanese'. In this he "took care to make it plain that the demand for the British to quit India signalled no welcome for the Japanese but quite the reverse: they could expect to meet both allied troops and a resisting population if they invaded an India granted its liberty."[80] Gandhi wrote:

> I must confess at the outset that though I have no ill-will against you, I intensely dislike your attack upon China. From your lofty height you have descended to imperial ambition. You will fail to realize that ambition and may become the authors of the dismemberment of Asia, thus unwittingly preventing World Federation and brotherhood without which there can be no hope for humanity ... I was thrilled when in South Africa I learnt of your brilliant victory over Russian arms ... It was a worthy ambition of yours to take equal rank with the great powers of the world. Your aggression against China and your alliance with the Axis powers was surely an unwarranted excess of the ambition ... You have been gravely misinformed, as I know you are, that we have chosen this particular moment to embarrass the Allies when your attack against India is imminent. If we wanted to turn Britain's difficulty into our opportunity we should have done it as soon as the war broke out nearly three years ago. Our movement demanding the withdrawal of the British power from India should in no way be misunderstood."[81]

Here Gandhi warned against what Erik Erikson called "the careless

---

value. It is quite clear that you are the one person in the world today who can prevent a war which would set the human race back to the stage of barbarism. Can you pay such a price for such a purpose, how high in value this may seem to you? Do you want to hear the pledge of a man who has deliberately avoided the method of war, after all, with considerable success?" (My own translation from the German.)

79 CWMG, vol. LXXII, pp. 229-30.

80 J. M. BROWN, *Gandhi Prisoner Of Hope*, p. 323.

81 The letter dated 18 July 1942 was apparently published in Japan by three newspapers, the *Nichi Nichi*, the *Yomiuri*, and the *Miyako*. CWMG, vol. LXXVI, pp. 309-12. However, I have so far not been able to verify this.

perfection of armament paired with that righteous and fanatic kind of moralism which ever again can pivot from peace to war."[82] Concerning world federation, Gandhi replied to the following question in the question box of his *Sevagram Ashram* near Wardha in Maharasthra, where he stayed most of the time: "Instead of striving for India's freedom why would you not strive for a far greater and nobler end—world federation? Surely this will automatically include India's freedom as the greater includes the less." This was Gandhi's answer:

> There is an obvious fallacy in this question. Federation is undoubtedly a greater and nobler end for free nations. It is a greater and nobler end for them to strive to promote federation than be self-centred, seeking only to preserve their own freedom. ... It has become a necessity while the war lasts and it would be good if they voluntarily pledge themselves now, to remain united even after the war. Defeat of any one member should make no difference. The survivors will not rest content till the defeated member is avenged. Still this won't be a world federation. It would be a mere defensive alliance... *The very first step to a world federation is to recognize the freedom of conquered and exploited nations.* Thus, India and Africa have to be freed. The second step would be to announce to and assure the aggressor powers, in the present instance, the Axis powers, that immediately after the war ends, they will be recognized as members of the world federation in the same sense as the Allies. This presupposes an agreement among the members of the world federation as to the irreducible fundamentals. If this is not forthcoming, the federation will fall to pieces under the slightest strain. Therefore *it has to come about voluntarily. I suggest that non-violence is the basis of voluntariness. It is because of all the nations of the world India is the one nation which has a message, however limited and crude it may be, in that direction that it must have immediate freedom to enable it to play its part.* ... I hope you will agree with me that India, in seeking first to be free, is not retarding federation. It wants her freedom for the sake of the nations in distress, especially China and Russia and for the whole of humanity..."[83]

Gandhi's stance regarding his advocacy for world federation, given expression for the first time already shortly after the First World War, is

---

82 Erik H. ERIKSON, *Gandhi's Truth. On the Origins of Militant Nonviolence*, New York and London, W.W. Norton 1969, p. 416. However I doubt that Gandhi, as Erikson presumes, had such a negative opinion of Woodrow Wilson.

83 Written "on or before" 2 August 1942, while still in Sevagram Ashram. CWMG, vol. LXXVI, pp. 350-51 (emphasis added).

astounding.[84] While portions of the AICC greatly sympathized with Nazi Germany, Gandhi seems to have been the one person who resisted the trend of "The enemy of my enemy is my friend," never once considering the British an enemy, only at the most an adversary. Nehru seems to have shared this view, as did others. Manabendra Nath Roy, a Bengali intellectual and political activist,[85] likewise favoured cooperation "with British Democracy, as distinct from British Imperialism, for the common cause."[86] Congress leaders on the other hand, though by far not all of them, seemed to believe that

M.N. Roy (1887-1954). Source: http://en.banglapedia.org/images/d/dd/RoyManabendraNath.jpg

ideally, "defeated by victorious Fascism, the British Government would be compelled to accept the terms dictated to them." Obviously, as M.N. Roy pointed out, with this kind of thinking, the AICC had gone too far.[87] He was of the opinion that

> The issue is that this war is going to decide the fate of the world, including India, for many years to come. We want a revolution, which means, we want to create a new world order. Revolution may be a necessity, but we should

84 A comparison with the Japanese Foreign Minister SHIDEHARA Kijuro may be in place here. SHIDEHARA similarly expressed himself when he was foreign minister between 1924 and 1931. See K. SCHLICHTMANN, *Japan in the World. Shidehara Kijuro, Pacifism and the Abolition of War*, Lanham, Boulder, New York, Toronto etc., Lexington Books 2009.

85 ROY founded the Communist Party of Mexico in 1911, but later became a radical humanist. In 1940 ROY helped set up the Radical Democratic Party, "in which he played a leading role for much of the decade of the 1940s. Roy later moved away from Marxism to become an exponent of the philosophy of radical humanism." https://en.wikipedia.org/wiki/M._N._Roy.

86 Manabendra Nath ROY (ed.), *India and War*, p. 35.

87 M.N. ROY (ed.), *India and War*, p. 38.

not forget that it is not an inevitability. To-day, when we say that the fate of the world is in the balance, we mean that revolution, or a new and better world order is no more likely than a relapse of humanity into barbarism. Therefore, we must throw our weight into the balance on the side of the force fighting barbarism; and that means co-operation; we cannot help it; we must want it.[88]

5. The Quit-India Resolution

The original draft by Gandhi of the 'Quit India' Resolution is dated 27 April 1942, and this was Congress's answer to the British Government's deception that brought about the failure of the Cripps Mission. The resolution[89] strongly disapproved of the British "policy of mistrust",[90] discarded the "plea that they should remain in India for the protection of the Indian princes," and spelled out the "principles of nonviolent non-cooperation;" this, however, was rejected by the All-India Congress Working Committee in favour of a modified version submitted by Pundit Jawaharlal Nehru. In fact, as the revised Resolution, adopted on 1 May pointed out, the British betrayal that had caused the Cripps debacle had "led to greater bitterness and distrust of that [i.e. British] Government and the spirit of non-cooperation with

---

88 M.N. ROY, Should Anti-Imperialism lead us to Welcome Fascism? Speech at the Bengal Provincial Congress of he R.D.P., Jan 18/19, 1941, in M.N. ROY (ed.), *India and War*, p. 282. However, already in June 1942 M.N. ROY, United Nations Day, *Independent India*, June 17, 1942, in M.N. ROY (ed.), *India and War*, p. 508, wrote: "New conventions are developing in the relation between Britain and India. India is gaining a new diplomatic status. She has representatives on all the Commonwealth bodies created for the conduct of the war. She has an Agent-General in China. She will, we trust, have direct diplomatic relations with all the Allied countries soon, including the U.S.S.R. particularly, now after the signing of the Anglo-Soviet Treaty of Alliance. She is going to have something very near a War Cabinet, if only her leaders can make it that. India's freedom is thus evolving in practice. It is in the process of making. If she can throw up the leadership to shape this process, the legal recognition of India's freedom will be only a formal step, the recognition of a fact which will be already a reality."

89 Draft Resolution for A.I.C.C. CWMG, vol. LXXVI, pp. 63-65.

90 It may well be that the British suspected "Bose might bring about reconciliation between China and Japan," and thus "Churchill was particularly apprehensive about it and had a suspicion that China might negotiate a separate peace with Japan and form part of the Pan-Asiatic movement." However, in retrospect it seems to have been a serious mistake of British politics, "offering all possible aid to China to maintain resistance to Japanese aggression," but not to India. Dr. T.R. SAREEN at http://www. uoregon.edu/~iwata/ private/EACS/new_page_7.htm.

Britain has grown."[91] Another resolution emphasized British policy had "resulted in a rapid and widespread increase of ill-will against Britain and a growing satisfaction at the success of Japanese arms" in certain sections among the Indian population.[92] As Gandhi related to Louis Fischer in an interview lasting several days, it was "the Cripps fiasco that inspired the idea" of asking for the "complete and irrevocable withdrawal" of British power from India,[93] because in this way and in this way only could India truly become part of and help in the United Nations' effort to win the war.

The aforementioned Resolution stressed that Congress was "agreeable to the stationing of the armed forces of the Allies in India, should they so desire, in order to ward off and resist Japanese or other aggression and to protect and help China." Furthermore, the call for withdrawal was "never intended to mean the physical withdrawal of all Britishers from India..."[94] Obviously, there was also an awareness that Indian unity was at stake, and a future partition of India could be avoided only if the tacit agreement between Muslims and the British for the creation of non-secular Muslim states could be thwarted. In response to Louis Fischer's question whether he thought that Jinnah was "set on Pakistan" or whether this was 'perhaps' "a bargaining counter with him which he will give up if Hindu-Muslim cooperation can be achieved," Gandhi answered: "As I have told you before, he will only give it up when the British are gone and when there is therefore nobody with whom to bargain."[95] This, too, was a powerful motive for

---

91 Appendix III, Resolution Passed by A.I.C.C., 1 May 1942. CWMG, vol. LXXVI, p. 424.

92 Appendix VI, Resolutions Passed by Congress Working Committee, 14 July 1942. CWMG, vol. LXXVI, p. 452. See also M.N. ROY, Cards on the Table, *Independent India*, May 10, 1942, in M.N. ROY (ed.), *India and War*, pp. 485-486, who reports: "Members of the Forward Bloc parade the streets of Bengal towns and villages with the slogan: 'Let us go forward to hail the rising sun of freedom'. The slogan found its echo in the A. I. C. C. meeting, and it was voiced by the mover of the Working Committee resolution. Nationalism has vindicated Subhas Bose. To-day he is the hero of Indian Nationalism. Those who hounded him out of the Congress are to-day toeing his line, and he has entered into an alliance with the Axis Powers. That explains why, in spite of Pandit Nehru's fulmination, and 'fascination for the idea of guerrilla warfare' the A. I. C. C. placed all the cards on the table, and adopted a resolution to the effect that there could be no resistance to the imminent invasion, and that the Congress leaders should have power only to keep India out of the war."

93 Appendix V, Interview with Louis Fischer, 8 June 1942. CWMG, vol. LXXVI, p. 449.

94 Appendix VI, Resolutions Passed by Congress Working Committee, 14 July 1942. CWMG, vol. LXXVI, p. 453.

95 Appendix V, Interview with Louis FISCHER, 8 June 1942. CWMG, vol. LXXVI, p.

putting forward and adopting the Resolution.

In his speech to the All-India Congress, introducing the final 'Quit India' Resolution, Gandhi on 7 August again stressed the main points, and concluded:

> We do not want to remain frogs in a well. We are aiming at world federation. It can only come through non-violence. Disarmament is possible only if you use the matchless weapon of non-violence. There are people who may call me a visionary, but I am a real bania [shrewd business man] and my business is to obtain swaraj [home rule]. If you do not accept this resolution I will not be sorry. On the contrary, I would dance with joy, because you would then relieve me of tremendous responsibility, which you are now going to place on me. I want you to adopt non-violence as a matter of policy. With me it is a creed, but so far as you are concerned I want you to accept it as policy. As disciplined soldiers you must accept it in toto, and stick to it when you join the struggle."[96]

The Resolution finally adopted on 8 August spelled out with precision and lucidity that "the immediate ending of British rule in India is an urgent necessity, both for the sake of India and for the success of the cause of the United Nations. The continuation of that rule is degrading and enfeebling India and making her progressively less capable of defending herself and of contributing to the cause of world freedom." This measure would "not only affect materially the fortunes of the war, but will bring all subject and oppressed humanity on the side of the United Nations," and fill "the peoples of Asia and Africa ... with hope and enthusiasm."[97] Furthermore, it would

---

450. However, the Muslims obviously pursued their own objectives. Mohammed Ali JINNAH, Gandhi's Muslim counterpart and a colleague, had on 4 September 1939 "met Lord Linlithgow and pledged to Britain the loyalty of Indian Muslim troops—nearly 40 per cent of the British Indian army—and help with Muslim recruitment. The Muslim League resolution of March 1940 demanding 'independent states for the Muslims of India' was passed after Jinnah, through Khaliq-ul-Zaman, obtained the support for Muslim states [i.e. Pakistan] from Lord Zetland, the secretary of state for India." Narendra Singh SARELA, Creation of Pakistan—Safeguarding British Strategic Interests, *Times of India*, 17. März 2000.

96 MOHANDAS K. GANDHI'S SPEECH (EXCERPTS) TO THE ALL-INDIA CONGRESS, Bombay, August 7, 1942, printed in: New York *Times*, August 8, 1942.

97 The resolution, which was finally adopted on 8 August, CWMG, vol. LXXVI, p. 460, determined in no uncertain terms that "the immediate ending of British rule in India is an urgent necessity, both for the sake of India and for the success of the cause of the United Nations. The continuation of that rule is degrading and enfeebling India and

have to be "clearly understood that such of these countries as are under Japanese control now must not subsequently be placed under the rule or control of any other Colonial Power." More specifically, the Committee expressed its

> opinion that the future peace, security and ordered progress of the world demand a world federation of free nations, and on no other basis can the problems of the modern world be solved. Such a world federation would ensure the freedom of its constituent nations, the prevention of aggression and exploitation by one nation over another, the protection of national minorities, the advancement of all backward areas and peoples, and the pooling of the world's resources for the common good of all. On the establishment of such a world federation, disarmament would be practicable in all countries, national armies, navies and air forces would no longer be necessary, and a world federal defence force would keep the world peace and prevent aggression. An independent India would gladly join such a world federation and cooperate on an equal basis with other countries in the solution of international problems. Such a federation should be open to all nations who agree with its fundamental principles. In view of the war, however, the federation must inevitably, to begin with, be confined to the United Nations, such a step taken now will have a most powerful effect on the war, on the peoples of the Axis countries, and on the peace to come. The Committee regretfully realizes, however, that despite the tragic and overwhelming lessons of the war and the perils that overhang the world, the Governments of few countries are yet prepared to take this inevitable step towards world federation ... Lastly, whilst the A-ICC has stated its own view of the future governance under free India, the A-ICC wishes to make it quite clear to all concerned that by embarking on a mass struggle, it has no intention of gaining power for the Congress. The power, when it comes, will belong to the whole people of India.[98]

The eventual failure of the 'Quit-India' Resolution is largely due to the fact that the British mistrusted the Indians, because of Subhas Bose's Indian National Army's advance toward India and the AICC's relative sympathy for Germany, and also because of the occurrence of a "naval mutiny" on

---

making her progressively less capable of defending herself and of contributing to the cause of world freedom." Such a step would "not only affect materially the fortunes of the war, but will bring all subject and oppressed humanity on the side of the United Nations," und "[fill] the peoples of Asia and Africa ... with hope and enthusiasm."

98 CWMG, vol. LXXVI, pp. 460-461.

two British vessels on 22 June 1942 and in September the same year, namely the HMIS *Konkan* and the HMIS *Orissa*, respectively.[99]

As a consequence Gandhi and the entire Congress Party were arrested and detained. "In the early hours of August 9, 1942, only a few hours after the termination of the climactic session of the All-India Congress Committee in Bombay ... shortly after the many leaders gathered there had returned to their residences, police began arriving at the door," arresting all of them,[100] many of whom were taken to Ahmadnagar Fort.[101] Following the arrest of the Mahatma, "a mass struggle on non-violent lines on the widest possible scale" started all over India.[102] Gandhi was taken to Aga Khan Palace near Poona, while subsequently all over the country more arrests were made. As the revolution swept across the country, by October in Bihar province alone, "jails were crammed with 27,000 prisoners."[103] Muslims, however, "kept aloof, offering support neither to the nationalist uprising nor to their supposed British benefactors," and to the surprise of Lord Linlithgow there was no communal violence.[104]

Interestingly, meanwhile, in what seemed like a follow-up to the

---

99 G.D. SHARMA, *Untold Story 1946 Naval Mutiny: Last War of Independence*, New Delhi, Vij Books 2015, pp. 22-26. See also Dipak Kumar DAS, *Revisiting Talwar: a study in the Royal Indian Navy uprising of February 1946*, Ajanta Publications 1993, p. 54: "In June ... there was trouble on board HMIS *Konkan* at Tobermory, UK ... On the night of 16 September 1942 the ratings of HMIS *Orissa* clashed with the manager of Clarendon Hotel, East London, South Africa, over color bar." I thank Romila THAPAR for drawing my attention to this occurrence.

100 F. G. HUTCHINS, *India's Revolution*, p. 217.

101 See for example F. G. HUTCHINS, *India's Revolution*, p. 217.

102 CWMG, vol. LXXVI, p. 463. Gandhi discarded the charge of being responsible for the disturbances following August 1942 since the Viceroy had "not wait[ed] for the letter which [he] ... had declared he would write before starting any action." CWMG, vol. LXXVII, p. v. In a Statement to the Press on 4 May 1945 he said: "I alone was armed with authority to start it when in my opinion the time for it came. But I was arrested before I could take any action or even issue any instructions. Therefore neither the Congress nor I could be saddled with any responsibility for the disturbances of 1942." CWMG, vol. LXXX, p. 65.

103 F. G. HUTCHINS, *India's Revolution*, p. 227. During 1940-41 already, as a consequence of the disobedience campaign Gandhi had announced in October 1940, "30,000 of our leading men and women were sent to prison" having "followed a policy of non-embarrassment ... in the nature of symbolic protest." J. NEHRU, *Discovery of India*, p. 472.

104 F. G. HUTCHINS, *India's Revolution*, p. 237.

world federalist 'Quit India' Resolution, in the United States a Resolution was passed in the House of Representatives on 21 September 1943, stating:

> *Resolved by the House of Representatives (the Senate concurring),*
> That the Congress hereby expresses itself as favoring the creation of appropriate international machinery with power adequate to establish and to maintain a just and lasting peace, among the nations of the world, and as favoring participation by the United States therein through its constitutional processes.[105]

6. The United Nations, Beacon of Hope in an Imperfect World

"Our object is friendship with the whole world. Nonviolence has come to men, and it will remain. It is the annunciation of peace on earth." (M. Gandhi)[106]

"It is only natural that India, which has come a long way since it first joined the UN's founding members as a British colony in 1945, should expect a place at the high table..."[107]

It would have been logical and consistent, if India, having been present at the Paris Peace Conference after World War I, would have participated in the Dumbarton Oaks and San Francisco United Nations Conferences.[108]

---

105 THE FULBRIGHT RESOLUTION (House Concurrent Resolution 25, Seventy-Eighth Congress. September 21, 1943), printed in: Pamphlet No. 4, *PILLARS OF PEACE*, Documents Pertaining To American Interest In Establishing A Lasting World Peace: January 1941-February 1946, Published by the Book Department, Army Information School, Carlisle Barracks, Pa., May 1946. See for example in the U.S.A, *House Joint Resolution 223* of 4 June 1910, which called for the convocation of a Commission, "to consider the expediency of utilizing international agencies for the purpose of limiting the armaments of the nations of the world *by international agreement*, and of constituting the combined navies of the world in an international force for the preservation of universal peace ... to diminish the expenditures of government for military purposes and to lesson the probabilities of war." Quoted in Warren F. KUEHL, *Seeking World Order. The United States and International Organization to 1920*, Nashville, Vanderbilt 1969, pp. 129-130.

106 Quoted in Romain ROLLAND, *Mahatma Gandhi*, p. 245.

107 Shashi THAROOR, *Pax Indica. India and the World of the 21st Century*, New Delhi, Allen Lane (Penguin) 2012, p. 386.

108 In fact there was an Indian delegation dispatched to the San Francisco Conference, consisting of V.T. KRISHNAMACHARI, A. Ramaswami MUDALIAR, and Sir Firoz KHAN NOON, whom the "British Government had nominated." In his Statement to the Press (*The Bombay Chronicle*, 18.4.1945) Gandhi suggested that this "camouflage

In hindsight it appears indeed as a serious handicap that the U.N. should have started off on such a dissonant note, contrary to its avowed purpose of decolonization and self-determination, with European nations continuing to insist on their alleged rights as imperial and colonial powers. It is sometimes said that one of the shortcomings of the UN is that the permanent members of the Security Council represent the victors of the Second World War; this is seen as a handicap, since the colonial powers, keeping up a relic of days long past, thereby have been given special recognition and assigned a 'privilege'. This anachronism is considered by many, especially in developing countries, to be detrimental to the peaceful cooperation and equality of nations. This conclusion, however, is simplistic; the truth is more complicated.[109]

On the eve of the United Nations Conference held in San Francisco, Gandhi issued the following statement:

> There will be no peace for the Allies and the world unless they shed their belief in the efficacy of war and its accompanying terrible deception and fraud and are determined to hammer out real peace based on freedom and equality of all races and nations. Exploitation and domination of one nation over other can have no place in a world striving to put an end to all wars.[110]

War, the Mahatma continued, was the "natural expression of the desire for exploitation and atom bomb its inevitable consequence."[111] Gandhi warned there should be "no armed peace imposed upon the forcibly disarmed,"

of Indian representation through Indians nominated by British imperialism should be dropped. Such representation will be worse than no representation. Either India at San Francisco is represented by an elected representative or represented not at all." CWMG, vol. LXXIX, pp. 390-391. The Statement continued then quoting the world federalist part in the 1942 'Quit India' Resolution.

109 For one thing these are the same nations that already at the Hague Peace Conferences in 1899 and 1907, in anticipation of things to come, were in favour of disarmament and the peaceful settlement of disputes through an international court with binding powers—an objective that was vetoed by a small minority spearheaded by Germany.

110 M. GANDHI's declaration on the eve of the UN Conference, in *Bombay Chronicle*, 18.4.1945, quoted in Ramjee SINGH and S. SUNDARAM (eds.), *Gandhi and World Order*, New Delhi, APH Publishing Corporation 1996 (Gandhian Institute of Studies), pp. 236-237. The Statement to the Press is also found in CWMG, vol. LXXIX, pp. 389-90. The last sentence of the quote is, however, not found in the CWMG. The first mention of the atom bomb in the Collected Works apparently is in vol. LXXXI, p. 5 (Speech at Cuttack, 20 January 1946).

111 *Bombay Chronicle*, 18. 4. 1945.

pleading that "[a]ll will be disarmed." In addition, as indeed the U.N. Charter later stipulated, there "will be an international police force to enforce the highest terms of peace."[112] In his statement Gandhi again quoted those parts of the 'Quit India' Resolution which refer to the world federation and its goals.

As we have already noted, Gandhi had replied to a question in his Ashram's question box that world federation had to come about "*voluntarily*," and suggested that non-violence was

The Hiroshima explosion, recorded at 8:15am, August 6, 1945, is seen on the remains of a wristwatch found in the ruins in this 1945 United Nations photo. The shadow of the small hand on the eight was burned in from the blast, making it appear to be the big hand. Source: AP Photo, United Nations

"*the basis of voluntariness.*" This formula—'by agreement' or 'voluntarily'—comprises the essence of how a federation should be brought about, and was frequently used by pacifists.[113] Similarly, Albert Einstein in answer to a young German refugee and pacifist on 20 March 1951 stressed: "Revolution without the use of violence was the method by which Gandhi brought

---

112 CWMG, vol. LXXIX, p. 390. Also, ibid., "Peace must be just. In order to be that, it must neither be punitive nor vindictive. Germany and Japan should not be humiliated. The strong are never vindictive. Therefore, fruits of peace must be equally shared."

113 E.g. in 1910, in the U.S., H.J. Resolution 223 of 4 June called for the appointment of a commission "to consider the expediency of utilizing international agencies for the purpose of limiting the armaments of the nations of the world *by international agreement*, and of constituting the combined navies of the world in an international force for the preservation of universal peace ... to diminish the expenditures of government for military purposes and to lesson the probabilities of war." In W.F. KUEHL, *Seeking World Order*, pp. 129-130.

about the liberation of India. It is my belief that the problem of bringing peace to the world on a supranational basis will be solved only by employing Gandhi's method on a large scale."[114]

Before 14 August 1947, Gandhi and Nehru worked untiringly to find a formula to keep the subcontinent from being broken up into two separate nations, India and Pakistan. Also at about this time a great number of international pacifists, including Aldous Huxley, Rabindranath Tagore, Reginald Reynolds and Jawaharlal Nehru planned a 'World Pacifist Meeting' for 1948 in Santiniketan, "to provide an opportunity for devoted workers for peace all over the world to meet and discuss with Gandhiji the ways of achieving a pacifist World Order."[115] Before the project could be realized, Mahatma Gandhi was assassinated.

Nehru, as also later the Indian President professor Sarvepalli Radhakrishnan,[116] repeatedly after independence spoke up for a politically unified world, where peace and justice might be preserved. In a broadcast in September 1946, Nehru said:

> The world, in spite of its rivalries and hatreds and inner conflicts, moves inevitably towards closer cooperation and the building up of a world commonwealth. It is for this One World that free India will work, a world in which there is free cooperation of free peoples, and no class or group exploits

---

114 A. EINSTEIN, *Einstein on Peace*, p. 543. EINSTEIN, however, had criticized GANDHI in an interview in August 1935: "I admire Gandhi greatly but I believe there are two weaknesses in his program: while non-resistance is the most intelligent way to cope with adversity, it can be practised only under ideal conditions. It may be feasible to practice it in India against the British but it could not be used against the Nazis in Germany today. Then, Gandhi is mistaken in trying to eliminate or minimize machine production in modern civilization. It is here to stay and must be accepted." Ibid., p. 261.

115 Rajendra PRASAD, Foreword, in Kshitis ROY (ed.), *Gandhi Memorial Peace Number*, Santiniketan, The Vishwa-Bharati Quarterly, 2 October 1949, p. ix. See also Arthur MOORE, World Government, ibid., pp. 196-203.

116 Sarvepalli RADHAKRISHNAN, *Towards a New World*, New Delhi, Bombay, Orient Paperbacks 1980, pp. 45, 52 and 135: "The United Nations is the first step towards the creation of an authoritative world order. It has not got the power to enforce the rule of law ... Military solutions to political problems are good for nothing. Ultimately they will leave bitterness behind ... The challenge that is open to us is survival or annihilation ... but what are we doing to bring about that survival? Are we prepared to surrender a fraction of our national sovereignty for the sake of a world order? Are we prepared to submit our disputes and quarrels to arbitration, to negotiation and settlement by peaceful methods? Have we set up a machinery by which peaceful changes could be easily brought about in this world?"

another.[117]

And on 22 January 1947 Nehru said:

> We wish for peace. We do not want to fight any nation if we can help it. The only possible real objective that we, in common with other nations, can have is the objective of cooperating in building up some kind of world structure, call it One World, call it what you like. The beginnings of this world structure have been laid in the United Nations Organization. It is still feeble; it has many defects; nevertheless, it is the beginning of the world structure. And India has pledged herself to cooperate in its work."[118]

When Nehru travelled in the United States between October and November 1948 he had the opportunity to address the issue not only with US President Harry Truman but with a great number of people including Eleanor Roosevelt, John Dewey, and nuclear physicists J. Robert Oppenheimer and Albert Einstein. In a speech before the Chicago Chamber of Commerce and the Foreign Policy Association he asserted that "World Government must come ... The alternative to a World Government is a disaster of unprecedented magnitude."[119] The basis for this much-needed development was the United Nations.

Before this, in December 1947, Albert Einstein had sent a long letter to the Soviet Academy of Sciences, asking the Soviets to cooperate in bringing the world under the rule of law,[120] a proposal that was initially rejected.[121] While there was disappointment in some quarters about the 'minimalist' U.N. Charter, the movement for abolishing war (and creating

---

117 J. NEHRU, *Jawaharlal Nehru's Speeches*, vol. I, Sept. 1946-May 1949, Delhi, Ministry of Information and Broadcasting, Government of India, Revised Edition, Third Impression, 1967, p. 3.

118 In a debate on the Objectives Resolution in the Constituent Assembly. *Jawaharlal Nehru's Speeches*, p. 21.

119 *Pandit Nehru's Discovery of America*, foreword by Eleanor ROOSEVELT, Madras, The Indian Press Publications (1950?), p. 56. Under the leadership of Chicago University president Robert M. HUTCHINS, the Committee to Frame a World Constitution had published its *Preliminary Draft of a World Constitution* in the same year (1948).

120 A. EINSTEIN, *Einstein on Peace*, pp. 449-455. See also pp. 430ff.

121 See the Moscow *New Times*, edition of 26 November 1947. A. EINSTEIN, *Einstein on Peace*, p. 443. Interestingly, in April 1988, the weekly *New Times*, republished *and approved* Einstein's reply to the Soviets, which had originally appeared in the February 1948 *Bulletin of the Atomic Scientists* in the U.S. *World Peace News* (777 U.N. Plaza, 11th floor, New York, N.Y. 20017, U.S.A.), June-Sept. 1988.

the necessary institutions toward that end), was strong among the Western democracies, as well as India and Japan, and in the early years had many followers.[122] Most of them, however, like the great majority of concerned academics and peace activists today, failed to realize the importance of the concept of the 'Transitional Period' stipulated in the U.N. Charter, which obligates Member States to agree to limitations of their sovereignty with regard to the right to wage war. Two years later Einstein could still say: "I feel that the influence of India in international affairs is growing and will prove beneficent. I have studied the works of Gandhi and Nehru with real admiration. India's forceful policy of neutrality in regard to the American-Russian conflict could well lead to a unified attempt on the part of the neutral nations to find a supranational solution to the peace problem."[123] Perhaps India, by remaining neutral, not only helped contain and restrain the USSR but also indirectly contributed to the eventual dismissal of Communist rule

Rabindranath Tagore and the Mahatma in Santiniketan. Source: https://allthepollys.files. wordpress.com/2012/02/gandhi-andtagore.jpg

---

122 See Klaus SCHLICHTMANN, Helmut Hertling und die Weltbürgerbewegung (Helmut Hertling and the World Citizens' Movement), in Detlev BALD und Wolfram WETTE, *Friedensinitiativen in der Frühzeit des Kalten Krieges 1945-1955* (Peace initiatives in the early days of the Cold War, 1945-1955), Essen, Klartext Verlag 2010, pp. 155-174; idem, H.G. Wells and Peace Education, *Journal of Peace Education*, vol.4, no.2 (September 2007), pp. 193-206; idem, Japan, Germany and the Idea of the two Hague Peace Conferences, *JOURNAL OF PEACE RESEARCH*, vol. 40, no. 4 (2003), pp. 377-394.

123 Letter to a Hindu correspondent on 24 March 1950. A. EINSTEIN, *Einstein on Peace*, p. 525.

from Russia.[124] Has India perhaps, by remaining neutral, not only helped to keep the Soviet Union at bay, but indirectly brought on the collapse of Communist rule in Russia?

Meanwhile, in June and July 1949, identical resolutions were passed in the U.S. by the House and the Senate, proclaiming that "it should be a fundamental objective of the foreign policy of the United States to support and strengthen the United Nations and to seek its development into a world federation open to all nations with defined and limited powers adequate to preserve peace and prevent aggression through the enactment, interpretation and enforcement of world law."[125] In the U.K., in 1945, Ernest Bevin, the British Foreign Secretary, "envisioned the establishing of a World People's Assembly to be seen as a completion of a development of the United Nations,[126] which the German peace delegation at Versailles in 1918 had also called for after the First World War.

Already before the First World War the call had been issued, not to return after the hostilities ended to the pre-war state of armed peace, but in a *transitional period* to establish a peace based on law and order. Entered into the UN Charter, the transitional provision became international law. With that Mahatma Gandhi's requirement was met that following the end

---

124 Ibid., p. 525: "I feel that the influence of India in international affairs is growing and will prove beneficent. I have studied the works of Gandhi and Nehru with real admiration. India's forceful policy of neutrality in regard to the American-Russian conflict could well lead to an unified attempt on the part of the neutral nations to find a supranational solution to the peace problem."

125 H. CON. Rep. 64 of 7 June 1949 and the identical S. CON. Rep. 56 of 26 July1949. An earlier U.S. Resolution proposed the "establishment of an International Federation of the World." H.J.RES.75, 64th Congress, 4 January 1916, Joint resolution proposing the establishment of an International Federation of the World (16 p., VII Articles).

126See http://www.camdun-online.gn.apc.org/meeting.html. Closing Address by Gita Brooke, initiating proposer of the New Zealand's Forum for UN Renewal. CAMDUN (Campaign For A More Democratic United Nations). The call for a world parliament was put forward by the German delegation at the Versailles Peace Conference on the recommendation of the neo-Kantian delegate Professor Walther Schücking. See Ulrich von BROCKDORFF-RANTZAU and Hans DELBRÜCK (eds.), *Dokumente* (Documents), Berlin, Deutsche Verlagsgesellschaft für Politik und Geschichte 1922, pp. 64ff. After the Second World War this initiative was apparently forgotten in Germany. That all of these goals have not yet been implemented seems to be the responsibility of the Europeans and especially the Germans. See Klaus SCHLICHTMANN, 1950—how the opportunity for transitioning to UN collective security was missed for the first time, Global Nonkilling Working Papers #11, Hawaii, Center for Global Nonkilling 2016.

of war there should be "no armed peace."[127]

As journalist Arthur Moore pointed out in his contribution to Shantiniketan's *Gandhi Memorial Peace Number*: "World government can come about in two ways ... by conquest ... [or] by agreement between sovereign states to delegate some of their sovereign powers to a world state, the Government of which would thereafter derive its mandates from the sovereign will of the people of the world. The form in such an event would be a federal Government."[128]

7. Conclusion

Whatever the subjective intent, the objective fact is clear. The rejection of violent means, the faith in the power of love, the rejection of material gain, was a philosophy that promoted the cause of nationalism in the specific historical circumstances modern India found itself. But in so doing, Gandhi revealed an uncomfortable truth, that pacifism became a call to action, to conflict as it were. This fact alone makes it clear that pacifism was in itself not necessarily the only most adequate philosophy of peace, but simply a reflection of more fundamental attitudes to the issue of war and peace in our time. Therefore, just as the individual must transcend his ego, the State must overcome its essentially violent nature, that is, it must abolish itself. In its place is to be 'a world federation established by agreement.' The concrete situation Gandhi faced, however, revealed the existence of sovereign States of unequal power, and nations like his own, without sovereignty altogether. He therefore presented a solution involving the development of nationalism in underdeveloped nations to a point of equality as a mode for arriving at a world state. 'Internationalism is possible only when nationalism becomes a fact, i.e., when peoples belonging to different countries have organized themselves and are able to act as one man.' Nationalism was to be the vehicle of internationalism ... The universal man is thus to be fulfilled in the universal State.[129]

---

127 Alfred Hermann FRIED, *Grundlagen des revolutionären Pazifismus* [Fundamentals of revolutionary pacifism], J.C.B. Mohr (Paul Siebeck), Tübingen 1908. See also Klaus SCHLICHTMANN, Der Friedensnobelpreisträger Alfred Hermann Fried (1864-1921), Pazifist, Publizist und Wegbereiter [Nobel Peace laureate Alfred Hermann Fried (1864-1921), pacifist, publicist and trailblazer], *Jahrbuch des öffentlichen Rechts* (ed. Peter Häberle), Neue Folge, vol. 60 (2012), pp. 105-129; idem, Alfred Hermann Fried (1864-1921)—Transitioning to World Order (forthcoming).

128 A. MOORE, World Government, p. 196.

129 I. L. HOROWITZ, *The Idea of War and Peace in Contemporary Philosophy*, pp. 106 and

As a result of our inquiry we may draw certain definite conclusions. Gandhi's aims in 1942 were manifold and can be summarized as having been to (1) rally all Indians, specifically all Hindus and Muslims, to a single cause; (2) avert Indian partition; (3) guarantee India's full independence from British dominance; (4) make India an example to follow for decolonization; (5) cooperate with Asian and African counterparts and former colonies for world peace and development; (6) ensure genuine Indian participation in the post-war peace conference; (7) make India a champion of world disarmament, and (8) a constitutive member of a future world federation without which disarmament and a permanent peace would be an impossibility. His great accomplishment for all time was to recognize the aspirations and requirements of the times, and to take the action necessary to accomplish his aims. Although he did not succeed in his time, his example remains in the world as one for us to follow. Indeed, as Mahendra Kumar had pointed out in an early book on peace research in India:

> After the attainment of independence by India under Gandhi's leadership, India was regarded for some years as a country placed in a special position to guide the world in achieving permanent peace. ... Research on Gandhi is relevant to peace because Gandhi presented elaborate theories of war and peace and he came to know those theories scientifically [...which he applied "scientifically"]. Thus Gandhi has significance for peace research not only for the content of his philosophy but also for ... his method ... [From this point of view:] There have been two major schools of pacifism in the political thought of the twentieth century—Christian pacifism and Gandhian pacifism ... one of them is the introduction of non-violence in all aspects of life on a world scale. Reginald Reynolds' 'What are Pacifists doing?' enunciates a distinction between western pacifism and Gandhian pacifism and comes to the conclusion that whereas the former only seeks to avoid war mainly by refusing to fight and by carrying on propaganda against war, the latter goes much deeper and aims at the eradication of the seeds of war from the social and economic life of man."[130]

105.

130 Mahendra KUMAR, *Current Peace Research and India*, Varanasi, Gandhian Institute of Studies 1968, pp. 34, 36, and 70. Reginald REYNOLDS, What are Pacifists doing?, *Peace News*, 20 July 1956 (London). M. KUMAR, *Current Peace Research and India*, Varanasi, Gandhian Institute of Studies 1968, pp. 82, 83, and 85: "[Ashakant] Nimbark holds that even Gandhi's political ideas were caught in the dilemma between what Max Weber called 'ethic of ultimate ends' and 'ethic of responsibility' ... Nimbark is right in pointing out that

How would Max Weber, "as a sociologist and economist as well as a political writer, have evaluated Gandhi? This question has been asked in the past by Mühlmann (1966) and Kantowsky (1982) and both have thought that Weber would have been impressed."[131] Andreas Buss goes on to ask "to what extent Gandhi's ideas and proposals can be explained in terms of a Weberian sociology and also to what extent Weber might have been able to interpret Gandhi's successes and failures."[132] Andreas Buss continues:

> Indian passive resistance movements … can be seen in the context of Weber's view that conflict is a phenomenon which cannot be excluded from social life. Not only can political and military struggle be replaced by economic struggle, he said, but "there can be, instead of external struggle of antagonistic persons for external objects, an inner struggle of mutually loving persons for subjective values … Peace is nothing more than a change in the form of the conflict or of the antagonists or in the objects of the conflict, or finally in the chances of selection."[133]

Having cast terror on the world twice in the last century, and being the chief responsible party for a few hundred years of colonial exploitation, the effects of which are still felt today, it may be the Europeans who might want to take steps toward a just and peaceful world order, based on the rule of law and the consent of the governed, by conferring on the UN the necessary sovereign powers to function effectively, as its founders had planned.[134] By their collective weight and will they are bound, also "by law,"

---

on the problem of war Gandhi as an ideologist would advocate 'peace at any price', while as a responsible nationalist leader he would accept 'peace, but not at any price'. Thus the dilemma mentioned above is not an indication of a logical inconsistency but a pointer to the need for carrying the Gandhian experiment further… Gandhi believed in a political method, the chief ingredients of which were compromise, conciliation, and cooperation." Ashakant NIMBARK, Gandhism Re-Examined, *Social Research* (New York), vol.31 (March 1964), pp. 94-125.

131 Andreas BUSS, *Max Weber in Asian Studies*, vol. I, part II, (International studies in sociology and social anthropology, v. 42), Leiden, Brill Archive 1985, p. 16.

132 Ibid., p. 16.

133 Ibid., p. 18, quoting Max WEBER, *Methodology of Social Sciences*, ed. and transl. by Edward SHILS and Henry A. FINCH, New Brunswick, NJ, Transaction Publishers 2011, p. 27. (Orig. 1949)

134 Globalization is not "a contribution of Western civilization to the world … there is a nicely stylized history that goes with this allegedly nonsensical reading. It all happened in Europe: first came the Renaissance, then the Enlightenment and the Industrial Revolution, and this led to a massive rise in living standards … And now those great achievements of the West are spreading to the world. Globalization, in this view, is not

to formally transfer 'security sovereignty' on the United Nations Security Council. Such a supranational order must be based on the principle of the rule of law and the consent of the governed. When and if that happens, India (and Pakistan) should be given a special responsibility in the UN Security Council. On the other hand, it might be possible for India herself to take the initiative and 'force' the Europeans to act, by transferring certain defined sovereign powers to the United Nations "*by law.*" Possibly India and states that maintain no standing army, such as Costa Rica and Switzerland, could demand action and take the initiative to force the Europeans to transfer specific well-defined sovereign powers to the United Nations "by law," to carry out the "transition" from armed to an unarmed peace as stipulated in the UN Charter. [135]

When the Europeans have decided their place in the world,[136] defined their position and purpose in the Security Council and in this process initiated a Charter Review Conference, to inject the necessary changes into the UN's constitution, by removing the anomaly of the anachronistic relic of the colonial past. By establishing a common European permanent representation, the permanent members would be reduced to four, so *now the empty seat can, for the time it takes for the transition, go to the South.* [137]

---

only good, it is also a gift of the West to the world." Amartya SEN, *Identity and Violence. The Illusion of Destiny*, New York and London, W.W. Norton 2006, p. 125.

135 See e.g. Article 24 in the German constitution which stipulates that the country may "*by law* transfer sovereign powers to international organizations" eventually to "bring about and secure a peaceful and lasting order in Europe and among the nations of the world." The drafters of the constitution believed that the 'international organization' to which sovereign powers would be transferred, was the U.N. Accordingly, the French constitution of 1946 similarly stipulated: "On condition of reciprocity, France accepts the limitations of sovereignty necessary for the organization and defence of peace." This commitment was confirmed in the 1958 constitution. The condition of reciprocity refers primarily to Germany, but is also a generally binding legal principle.

136 The Europeans could collectively or individually, under Article 43 of the UN Charter, conclude with the Security Council "special ... agreements ... for the purpose of maintaining international peace and security ... in accordance with their respective constitutional processes." As part of the European transfer of security sovereignty to the Security Council a "Review" of the United Nations Charter should be initiated, in which WE, THE PEOPLES OF THE UNITED NATIONS would also be called upon to provide input.

137 In the past for a long time, the US has rejected an Indian Security Council seat. So Larry M. WORTZEL und Dana R. DILLON, in a publication of the Heritage Foundation, *Improving Relations with India without Compromising U.S. Security, Backgrounder*, No. 1402 (11. Dezember 2000), why "giving India a permanent seat on the United Nations Security Council is not in America's best interest at this time. Given the current

Through the establishment of a common European representation and the handing over of the empty chair to the South, the Council will automatically become more representative and manifestly more effective.[138] If India were willing to take the responsibility and make its armed forces, assistance and facilities available to the Security Council, this—granting at the same time certain privileges to India's neighbours — would greatly enhance stability in South and Central Asia and the world, at this critical time—and for a long time to come.[139]

At the same time UN Member States should start "developing ... a

makeup of the Security Council, India's accession appears highly unlikely. Therefore, consulting with India on matters of mutual interest in the long term may bring India into a closer strategic alignment with the United States and convince its next generation of leaders to view cooperation with America as more important to its future stability and relations than the appearance of independence." This view is no longer upheld today.

138 Efforts by the UN in the 1990s, to revise the Charter and reform the Security Council, to adapt to the new challenges, have failed, for lack of a rational, historically reasoned, rational approach. In an article published in 1999 (A Draft on Security Council Reform, *Peace & Change*, vol. 24, no. 4, October 1999, pp. 505-535) I advocated a "skilful surgeon" approach to Security Council Reform, calculated to get maximum results with minimum effort. I criticized the anomaly that two European countries and none from the South are represented on the Security Council as permanent members, recommending a single European permanent representation—arguing that European integration into the world community was an absolute necessity if we are to effectively face the challenges of the twenty first century. The Europeans can make the United Nations work—and fulfil a great historic purpose (while making up for having started two World Wars in the twentieth century)! Although as a *second step* enlargement of the Council should be supported, the proposal underscores the importance of maintaining the *number 5* for its basic composition as a *first step* because, with the Security Council having the power to decide on war and peace, there should be no chance allowed for such decision to be taken by a *majority vote* among the 'Permanent Five'. Obviously, the *number* "5" is reasonable in an environment that makes it necessary to resolve conflicts by *consensus*.

139 One could start by taking small steps toward a sub-continental confederation, such as liberating "capital market and other economic activities ... from ... all kinds of procedural obstacles of state sovereignty; by creating ... [a] customs union ... Free Trade Area, and next a common market in which non-tariff barriers over territorial boundaries do not exist any more." Motoko SHUTO, Graduate School of International Political Economy (GSIPE), University of Tsukuba, Japan, in a personal correspondence to the author (email of 22 June 2002). Anyway, the international community should encourage India and Pakistan to work for the long-term goal of monetary union (like the one in Europe), linking that with a sub-continental permanent representation in the Security Council (such as the 'continental' permanent representation many Europeans want). The economic issues and the issue of peace and security should be connected, to find a comprehensive and permanent solution to the problem.

parliamentary dimension" of the UNO,[140] i.e. a parliamentary assembly as a principal organ under Article 7 (or Article 22) of the U.N. Charter, consisting of activists and civil society associations such as the *World Federalist Movement*, the *Provisional World Parliament*, *Green Peace* and *Medicins sans Frontiers* and others.

In order to achieve these ends, and obtain the consent of the international community for a permanent Indian representation, a definite time frame should be set in order to, besides convening a Charter Review Conference, achieve comprehensive U.N. reforms, and bring about general and complete disarmament. For the transitional period, pacifist Japan and Germany could be co-opted to assist the five permanent members of the Security Council who are responsible for the peaceful passage toward general and complete disarmament and collective security. Efforts to embark on the transition toward an international peace based on justice and order are to be coordinated between the United Nations and the Provisional World Parliament, which has provided a blueprint for moving forward to replace the present militaristic nation-state system with a peaceful world federal order in which war is outlawed, and the world's social, political and environmental problems can be solved.[141]

The horrifying terrorist attacks on 11 September 2001 and subsequent fundamentalist activities like those of the Islamic State of Iraq and the Levant (ISIL) have clearly demonstrated that the anarchic nation-state system can no longer ensure the safety of its citizens.[142] The world must band together to face transnational crime and terrorism, and deal effectively with social injustices and ecological degradation by forming a genuine political union. The nuclear bombings of Hiroshima and Nagasaki have made the point clear more than 70 years ago that *no government alone can guarantee national security* any more. That is why the UNO was

---

140 See Recommendation 1476 of the Parliamentary Assembly of the Council of Europe, 27 September 2000.

141 See http://worldparliament-gov.org

142 A. SEN, *Identity and Violence*, p. 145 states: "Poverty and economic inequality may not instantly breed terrorism or influence the leaders of terrorist organizations, but nevertheless they can help to create rich recruiting grounds for the foot soldiers of the terrorist camp." There is additional danger: the "tolerance of terrorism by an otherwise peaceful population ... in many parts of the contemporary world, particularly where there is a sense of having been badly treated, for example, because of being left behind by global economic and social progress, or where there is a strong memory of having been politically roughed up in the past."

created. Indeed, there is "a strong case for institutional reforms that would facilitate the kind of change that would be needed to make globalization a fairer arrangement."[143] Governments must give the United Nations the power to do its job effectively.

Naturally, within this larger picture, if steps are taken in the direction indicated, regional conflicts like that between India and Pakistan will be resolved, Kashmir will no longer be an issue, and the fundamentalist threats to world peace can be removed and are likely to subside. Within a democratic world federation the autonomy goals of separatist movements can be realized. Also, India might consider voicing public (and official) support for Article 9 of Japan's pacifist Constitution, while in return Japan should support India in its quest to obtain a permanent seat in the UNSC. [144]

---

143 Ibid., p. 182.

144 Today, countries that "explicitly and openly" support India for a UNSC permanent representation are Armenia, Australia, the Bahamas, Bahrain, Bangladesh, Belarus, Belgium, Belize, Benin, Bolivia, Brunei, Bulgaria, Cambodia, Chile, Croatia, Cuba, Cyprus, Czech Republic, Denmark, Dominican Republic, Ethiopia, Finland, Ghana, Guyana, Hungary, Iceland, Israel, Jamaica, Laos, Lesotho, Liberia, Libya, Kazakhstan, Kyrgyzstan, Malawi, Malaysia, The Maldives, Micronesia, Mongolia, Morocco, Myanmar, Nigeria, Norway, Oman, Palau, Peru, Poland, Portugal, Romania, Rwanda, Qatar, Senegal, Singapore, Slovakia, Suriname, Swaziland, Sweden, Syria, Tajikistan, Tanzania, Trinidad and Tobago, Tuvalu, Ukraine, the United Arab Emirates, Uzbekistan, Vietnam, and Zambia, apart from the African Union, China, Russia, the United Kingdom and the United States. (Wikipedia)

Epilogue

The subject of this book was the positioning of India in the context of peace history. In this development political-ethical and certain legal-philosophical concepts played a dominant part. With the Axial Period, and especially with the missionary activity of the Indian emperor Ashoka (see PART I), *principles of discourse ethics* (as one would put it today) were applied and recognized which substantiated and promoted new rules of how social intercourse and affairs of state were to be conducted and organized. "Human beings merged into self-consciousness," and part of this was the realization that "[w]ar and poverty are not essential to the human condition."[1] Benevolence and generosity marked Ashoka's rule as Emperor.

Legal foundations and ordering principles were being codified and established that would come to fruition worldwide in the subsequently emerging international relations and modern political systems. These developments took shape for the first time with the onset of the Axial Period, and were manifested to an unprecedented degree also in India.

Discourse ethics is defined as "a justification program of normative philosophical moral theory that characterizes communicative reason as the only source that allows a rational definitive justification of generally binding moral obligations under the value-pluralistic and rational-sceptical conditions of modernity" and—we may add—post-modernity.[2]

---

1   Glen T. MARTIN, Introduction, in *The Constitution for the Federation of Earth*, The Institute for Economic Democracy 2016, pp. 9 and 64.

2   Karl-Otto APEL und Matthias KETTNER, Vorwort, in idem (ed.), *Zur Anwendung der Diskursethik in Politik, Recht und Wissenschaft* (On the application of discourse ethics in politics, law and science), Frankfurt, M., Suhrkamp 1992, S. 7. Jürgen HABERMAS, Discourse Ethics: Notes on a Program of Philosophical Justification, in Seyla BENHABIB and Fred Reinhard DALLMAYR, *The Communicative Ethics Controversy*, MIT Press 1990, p. 60, quoting Alasdair MACINTYRE, *After Virtue*, London etc., Bloomsbury 2013 p. 64: "Reason is calculative; it can assess truths of fact and mathematical relations but nothing more. In the realm of practice therefore it can speak only of means. About ends it must be silent." However, J. HABERMAS asserts, ibid.: "Since Kant, this conclusion has been opposed by cognitivist moral philosophies that maintain, in one sense or

This definition presupposes that there are common ethically justifiable laws and obligations, concerning which it is rationally and definitively possible to give a responsible account. *Communicative reason* bridges the gulf between aspiration and reality and—in a world marked by growing interdependence—can bring together and motivate all possible actors—individuals, groups and states—to tackle those problems, which are in urgent need of a solution. As Romila Thapar has asserted with regard to India, there is a necessity for "meaningful discussion on how to organize and reorganize institutions to find new ways of nurturing the values we held as necessary to social advance."[3] A fundamental concept is the variable *peace through law.*[4] The concept of law which was applied under Ashoka comprised rules of the Buddhist moral code that excluded violence and man's domination of others and over nature.

However, as Jürgen Habermas has pointed out, it is necessary to convince "the consistent sceptic" and relieve him of his "opposition to any kind of rational ethics."[5] Paul Taylor provides an argument for the universalization of ethical principles:

> However deeply our own conscience and moral outlook may have been shaped by it, we must recognize that other societies in the history of the world have been able to function on the basis of other codes. . . . To claim that a person who is a member of those societies and who knows its moral code nevertheless does not have true moral convictions is, it seems to me, fundamentally correct. But such a claim cannot be justified on the ground of our concept of the moral point of view. For that is to assume that the moral code of liberal western society is the only genuine morality.[6]

So, the focus today is toward a program of action based on genuine research and analysis, designed to define the historical underpinnings of a modern, theoretically and practically applicable, ethically designed constitution of

---

another, that practical questions 'admit of truth.'"

3   Romila THAPAR with Sundar SARUKKAI, Dhruv RAINA, Peter Ronald DESOUZA, Neeladri BHATTACHARYA, and Jawed NAQWI, *The Public Intellectual in India*, ed. By Chandra CHARI and Uma IYANGER, New Delhi, Aleph Book Company 2015, p. xii.

4   See for example Antony ADOLF, *Peace, A World History*, Cambridge, UK, Polity Press 2009.

5   Jürgen HABERMAS, Discourse Ethics: Notes on Philosophical Justification, p. 61.

6   Paul TAYLOR stated, The Ethnocentric Fallacy, in *The Monist* (1963), p. 570, quoted in Jürgen HABERMAS, Discourse Ethics: Notes on Philosophical Justification, p. 75.

human society as a global community. In other words, we as players in a world game, by our dedicated devotion to the community, and possibly our dedication to the ideal of Creative Unity, bound to one another through a network, through meaningful, free exchange of ideas and action, are destined to find a way to establish a solid social base for peace and justice, good law and politics. Toward this end India may become a model, as it has been in the past—seen from a historical perspective—to lay down maxims for a universal morality. In this way it will be accepting certain responsibilities for the future of the planet.

The method (which was) employed in the present study is historical. That is, it was to be demonstrated, based on historical precedents and events experienced in one part of the world, how a discourse—namely one that pursues the goals and objectives identified above—was able to develop, and was, in fact, inevitable. The method is (specifically) that of peace history, since it has as its subject the living together of people in an order, in which peace and justice and non-violent conflict resolution are basic. For our purpose, the spiritual space where these experiences and events may ideally be located is India, if India can come to "understand the fundamental questions of [its] identity,"[7] and avoid certain extremist views (that seem to be) emerging in some places. The choice of India as an ideal-type location is, as I have tried to show, no coincidence. India has a tradition that is comparable and equal to that of the Mediterranean and of the Far East. As an axial civilization India has exerted significant influence throughout its history; today it can make a valuable contribution, giving evidence that a society oriented toward integration, non-violence, cooperation, education and cultural advancement (Albert Einstein), in which (divine) creation and human dignity are protected and human security, personal development, growth, progress, and peace can be promoted, is possible.

It's a good omen that India is the only axial country whose civilization has lived on and continued since its beginnings five thousand years ago until today, almost without interruption and without losing its cultural characteristics or perishing altogether. In PART IV the case was presented that India could make a positive contribution to world peace if the country were to be given a permanent seat on the UN Security Council.

It can be shown that India is particularly well suited for the present

---

7   Romila THAPAR, Introduction, p. xxiv. This does not mean that there are not spaces elsewhere that are equally significant.

study: in fact, it is 'exemplary'. However, there is a problem in that, while for the European and Mediterranean cultures, and also for China and Japan, literary, cultural and socio-historical studies having peace as an objective exist, general and comprehensive historical studies such as this peace history (however incomplete and meagre) that go beyond a general history in the religious-historical and anthropological context, have been lacking for India—except of course for the numerous studies on Mahatma Gandhi and his practice and teachings. In the field of the history of science the situation is similar, and a comprehensive work comparable to that of Joseph Needham for China, is still missing, as Amartya Sen has rightly criticized.[8] Historian S. N. Mukherjee writes:

> India ... appeared disorderly, chaotic and superstitious. Her heterogeneous culture, her diverse customs and her loosely mined empire were to the *philosophes* difficult to put into a rational order. The cunning and ritual-ridden Brahmins were no match for the Mandarins, the scholar-governors. India never occupied such a position in the European mind as did China. In d'Herbelot's *Bibliotheque Orientale*, in Diderot's *Encyclopedie* and Voltaire's *Essai sur les Moeurs* fewer pages are devoted to India than to China.[9]

On the other hand India does possess a long and versified cultural tradition, which, however, seemed to be historically self-unaware and lacking a historiography in the Western sense.[10] Indian history proceeds in cycles, like the revolution of the stars. Progress in this sense is conceived merely as the personal career of the seeker for truth and enlightenment on the road to selfless annihilation, Nirvana. The world is a means not an end, man mutable and without a home, the body precious, but impermanent and vulnerable. As Hermann Kulke and Dietmar Rothermund have pointed out, India is "an old country with a venerable tradition;" hope and a chance for positive change lie in the fact that it has "at the same time ... a predominantly young population," one that is destined to "shape the future."[11]

---

8   Amartya SEN, *On Interpreting India's Past*, Calcutta, The Asiatic Society 1996, pp. 32-33.

9   S. N. MUKHERJEE, *Sir William Jones. A Study in Eighteenth Century British Attitudes to India*, Cambridge University Press 1968 (Cambridge South Asian Studies No. 6), p. 6.

10 See Romila THAPAR, *The Past Before Us, Historical Traditions in North India*, Bangalore, Calcutta, New Delhi etc., Orient Blackswan 2013.

11 Hermann KULKE und Dietmar ROTHERMUND, *Geschichte Indiens: von der Induskultur bis heute*, C.H. Beck 2010, p. 455.

With the Indus Valley culture of Mohenjodaro and Harappa (not treated in this volume), India is a civilization most likely to question the correctness of the thesis that the emergence of civilized cultural communities, with their city systems, economic planning, trade etc. has necessarily to be accompanied by the development and establishment of military institutions. Gandhi's way,

> as we have seen, is that of a double conversion: the hateful person, by containing his egotistic hate and learning to love the opponent as human, will confront the opponent with an enveloping technique that will force, or rather permit, him to regain his latent capacity to trust and love."[12]

No doubt, in the nuclear age another total war, a Third World War, even if ever so moderately fought, is not an option. It would be suicide. On the other hand, abolishing war and achieving an unarmed peace may seem to be an impossible task. But even Max Weber, though not a pacifist, admitted:

> Certainly all historical experience confirms the truth—that man would not have attained the possible unless time and again he had reached out for the impossible."[13]

In the last five hundred years humanity has made amazing strides forward, affording today the technical means and the manpower to green the deserts, achieve clean energy and transform this world into a veritable garden Eden, if we want to.

---

12 Erik H. ERIKSON, *Gandhi's Truth. On the Origins of Militant Nonviolence*, New York and London, W.W. Norton 1969, p. 437.

13 Max WEBER, *Essays in Sociology*, translated by Hans Heinrich Gerth and Charles Wright Mills, 2009, p. 128.

Bibliography

Emil ABEGG, *Der Messiasglaube in Indien und Iran*, Berlin and Leipzig, Walther de Gryter & Co. 1928

Günter ABRAMOWSKI, *Das Geschichtsbild Max Webers. Universalgeschichte am Leitfaden des okzidentalen Rationalisierungsprozesses*, Stuttgart, Ernst Klett 1966 (Kieler Historische Schriften)

Brooks ADAMS, *The Law of Civilization and Decay*, New York, Vintage 1955 (orig. 1896)

Antony ADOLF, *Peace, A World History*, Cambridge, UK, Polity Press 2009

Charles ALLEN, *Ashoka*, London, Little, Brown 2012

Benedict ANDERSON, *Imagined Communities. Reflections on the Origin and Spread of Nationalism* (revised ed.), London and New York, Verso 1996 (1983)

Karl-Otto APEL and Matthias KETTNER (eds.), *Zur Anwendung der Diskursethik in Politik, Recht und Wissenschaft*, Frankfurt, M., Suhrkamp 1992

Area Handbook for India, Washington D.C., U.S. Government Printing Office, May 1970

Arthur Llewellyn BASHAM, *The Wonder that was India*, Calcutta etc., Rupa 1990 (1954),

Wolfgang BAUER, *China and the Search for Happiness: Recurring Themes in Four Thousand Years of Chinese Cultural History* (transl. Michael Shaw), New York, Seabury Press 1976

W.G. BEASLEY, *The Rise of Modern Japan*, Tokyo, Tuttle 1991

Heinz BECHERT, *Buddhismus, Staat und Gesellschaft in den Ländern des Thervada-Buddhismus*, vol. I, Grundlagen. Ceylon, Frankfurt, M. and Berlin, Alfred Metzner 1966

---- Max Webers Darstellung der Geschichte des Buddhismus in Süd- und Südostasien, in Wolfgang SCHLUCHTER (ed.), *Max Webers Studie über Hinduismus und Buddhismus, Interpretation und Kritik.* Frankfurt, M., Suhrkamp 1983

Stephan V. BEYER, *The Classical Tibetan Language*, Albany, State University of New York Press 1992

D. R. BHANDARKAR, *Some Aspects of Ancient Hindu Polity*, Benares, Benares Hindu University 1929

Swapna BHATTACHARYA, The Ari Cult of Myanmar, in Uta GARTNER und Jens LORENZ (eds.), *Tradition and modernity in Myanmar: proceedings*, LIT Verlag Münster, 1994

---- *Landschenkungen und Staatliche Entwicklung im frühmittelalterlichen Bengalen (5. bis 13. Jh. n. Chr.)*, WIESBADEN, 1985

Frederik David Kan BOSCH, De inscriptie van Keloereak, *Tijdschrift van het Bataviaasch Genootschap van Kunsten and Wetenschappen (TBG)*, vol. 68, nos. 1/2 (1928), pp. 1-64

---- *Selected Studies in Indonesian Archeology*, The Hague, M. Nijhoff 1961

N. S. BOSE, *The Indian Awakening and Bengal*, Calcutta, K.L. Mukhopadhyay 1960

Kenneth E. BOULDING, *Conflict and Defense, A General Theory*, New York, Harper & Row 1963

Thomas BOWREY, *A Geographical Account of Countries Round the Bay of Bengal, 1669 to 1679*, New Delhi, Munshiram Manoharlal 1997 (orig. 1905)

C. R. BOXER, *The Mandarin at Chinsura*, Amsterdam, Koninklijke Vereeniging Indisch Instituut 1949 (Mededeling No. LXXXIV, Afdeling Volkenkunde No. 32)

Ulrich von BROCKDORFF-RANTZAU und Hans DELBRÜCK (eds.), *Dokumente*, Berlin, Deutsche Verlagsgesellschaft für Politik und Geschichte 1922

Judith M. BROWN, *Gandhi Prisoner of Hope*, Bombay, Calcutta and Madras, Oxford University Press 1992

Hans BRÄKER, *Indonesien,* Freiburg i.Br., Walter-Verlag Olten 1987

Martin BRANDTNER, Koloniale Archäologie: Monopolisierte Vergangenheitsdeutung und Herrschaftslegitimation in Britisch-Indien, in: Stephan CONERMANN (ed.), *Mythen, Geschichte(n), Identitäten: Der Kampf um die Vergangenheit,* Hamburg, E.B.-Verlag (Beiträge des Zentrums für Asiatische und Afrikanische Studien (ZAAS) der Christian-Albrechts-Universität zu Kiel) 1999

Fernand BRAUDEL, *A History of Civilisations,* New York etc., Penguin 1995 (orig. French 1963)

———— *On History,* Chicago, University of Chicago Press 1982 (Paris 1969)

———— Georges DUBY und Maurice AYMARD, *Die Welt des Mittelmeers,* Frankfurt, M., Fischer 1990

Carol A. BRECKENRIDGE and Peter van der VEER, Orientalism and the Postcolonial Predicament, in: idem. (eds.), *Orientalism and the Postcolonial Predicament,* Philadelphia, University of Pennsylvania Press 1993

D. Mackenzie BROWN, *The White Umbrella. Indian Political Thought from Manu to Gandhi,* Berkeley and Los Angeles, University of California Press 1958

Kostas BURASELIS, Mary STEFANOU and Dorothy J. THOMPSON, *The Ptolemies, the Sea and the Nile: Studies in Waterborne Power,* Cambridge University Press 2013

Andreas E. BUSS, *Max Weber and Asia. Contributions to the Sociology of Development,* Munich, Weltforum 1985

———— *Max Weber in Asian Studies,* vol. I, part II, (International studies in sociology and social anthropology, v. 42), Leiden, Brill Archive 1985

———— Max Weber's Contributions to Questions of Development in Modern India, in: Andreas E. BUSS (ed.), *Max Weber in Asian Studies,* Leiden, E.J. Brill 1985

Donald MacLaine CAMPBELL, *Java: Past & Present: a Description of the Most Beautiful Country in the World, its Ancient History, People, Antiquities, and Product,* London, W. Heinemann 1915

Lokesh CHANDRA, Borobudur, *Kabar Seberang sulating Maphilindo,*

Nomor Kebudayaan 1986

Sir Atul Chandra CHATTERJEE, *The New India*, London, George Allen & Unwin 1948

Partha CHATTERJEE, *The Nation and its Fragments*, Princeton, N., Princeton University Press 1993

Alaka CHATTOPADHYAYA, *Attisa and Tibet: life and works of Dīpamkara Śrijñana in relation to the history and religion of Tibet with Tibetan sources transl. under Professor Lama Chimpa*, Delhi, Motilal Banarsidass 1999 (orig. 1967)

Brajadulal CHATTOPADHYAYA, Political Processes and the Structure of Polity in Early Medieval India, in Hermann KULKE (ed.), *The State in India, 1000-1700*, New Delhi, Oxford India Paperbacks 1997

Nirad C. CHAUDHURI, *The Autobiography of an Unknown Indian*, Mumbay, Delhi, Bangalore, Calcutta, Hyderabad and Chennai, Jaico 1998

Radha Krishna CHOUDHARI, *Kautilya's Political Ideas and Institutions*, Benares (Varanasi), Choukhamba Prakashan 1971

Collected Works of Mahatma Gandhi (CWMG), online at http://www. gandhiashramsevagram.org/gandhi-literature/collected-works-of-mahatma-gandhi-volume-1-to-98.php

Georges COEDÈS, *The Indianized States of Southeast Asia*, Honolulu, Kuala Lumpur, Singapore etc., University of Malaya Press 1968 (French orig.: *Histoire ancienne des états hindouisés d'Extrême-Orient*, Hanoi 1944)

H. Floris COHEN, The Emergence of Early Modern Science in Europe; with remarks on Needham's "Grand Question," including the Issue of the cross-cultural Transfer of Scientific Ideas, *Journal of the Japan-Netherlands Institute* (Papers of the First Conference on the Transfer of Science and Technology between Europe and Asia since Vasco da Gama (1498-1998), Amsterdam & Leiden, 5-7 June 1991), vol. III (1991)

Henry Thomas COLEBROOKE, Discourse at the Royal Asiatic Society of Great Britain and Ireland, *Miscellaneous Essays*, London, William H. Allen 1837

Dieter CONRAD, *Gandhi und der Begriff des Politischen. Staat, Religion und Gewalt*, München, Wilhelm Fink 2006

Emeric CRUCE, *Le Nouveau Cynée ou Discours d'Estat représentant les occasions et Moyens d'establier une Paix générale, et la liberté du commerce par tout le Monde*, 1623, English reprint and translation Thomas Willing Balch, 1909

Dipak Kumar DAS, *Revisiting Talwar: a study in the Royal Indian Navy uprising of February 1946*, Delhi, Ajanta Publications 1993

Subrata DASGUPTA, *THE BENGAL RENAISSANCE: Identity and Creativity from Rammohun Roy to Rabindranath Tagore*, Bangalore, New Delhi etc., Orient Blackswan 2007

Narendra Kumar DASH (ed.), *Indo-Tibetan Culture*, Kolkata, Visva-Bharati 2003

Ronald M. DAVIDSON, *Indian Esoteric Buddhism: A Social History of the Tantric Movement*, Colombia University Press, New York 2002

Max DEEG, *Das Gaoseng-Faxian-Zhuan als religionsgeschichtliche Quelle. Der älteste Bericht eines chinesischen buddhistischen Pilgermönchs über seine Reise nach Indien mit Übersetzung des Textes*, Wiesbaden, Harrassowitz 2005

S. DHAMMIKA (transl.), *The Edicts of King Ashoka*, Kandy (Sri Lanka), BUDDHIST PUBLICATION SOCIETY 1993

Vinoy DHARWARKAR, Orientalism and the Study of Indian Literatures, in: BRECKENRIDGE und van der VEER, *Orientalism and the Postcolonial Predicament*, Philadelphia, University of Pennsylvania Press 1993

Charles DREKMEIER, *Kingship and Community in Early India*, Stanford, Stanford University Press 1962

Jaques DUMARÇAY, *Borobudur*, Oxford in Asia Paperbacks, 1978

Mpu DUSUN, A. TEEUW, Stuart O. ROBSON, *KUNJARAKARNA DHARMAKATHANA: liberation through the law of the Buddha: an Old Javanese poem, vol. 21 of the Bibliotheca Indonesica*, M. The Hague, Nijhoff 1981

Sukumar DUTT, *Buddhist Monks And Monasteries Of India: Their History And Contribution To Indian Culture*, George Allen and Unwin Ltd, London 1962

Shmuel N. EISENSTADT, *Japanese Civilisation, A Comparative View*, Chicago and London, University of Chicago Press 1996

–––– (ed.), Kulturen der Achsenzeit, vol. II, Frankfurt, M., Suhrkamp 1992

–––– Die Paradoxie von Zivilisationen mit außerweltlichen Orientierungen, Überlegungen zu Max Webers Studie über Hinduismus und Buddhismus, in: Wolfgang SCHLUCHTER (ed.), *Max Webers Studie über Hinduismus und Buddhismus*, Frankfurt, M., Suhrkamp 1984

Vadime ELISSEEFF, *The Silk Roads: Highways of Culture and Commerce*, Oxford and New York, Berghahn 1998

Erik H. ERIKSON, *Gandhi's Truth. On the Origins of Militant Nonviolence*, New York and London, W.W. Norton 1969

Douglas FERNANDO, *Tsunami in Sri Lanka*, Berlin, Tenea Verlag 2005

Alfred Hermann FRIED, *Grundlagen des revolutionären Pazifismus*, J.C.B. Mohr (Paul Siebeck), Tübingen 1908

Hans Norbert FÜGEN, *Max Weber*, Reinbek bei Hamburg, Rowohlt 1985

Gerald FUSSMANN, Central and Provincial Administration in Ancient India: The Problem of the Mauryan Empire, *The Indian Historical Review*, vol. XIV, nos. 1-2 (July 1987 & Jan. 1988, publ. In 1990)

Jacques GERNET, *A History of Chinese Civilization*, Cambridge University Press (2nd edition) 1996

H.H. GERTH and C. Wright MILLS, *From Max Weber: Essays in Sociology*, New York, Oxford University Press 1954

Dilip Coomer GHOSE, *Sir William Jones*, Bicentenary of his Birth. Commemoration Volume, 1746-1946, Kolkata, The Asiatic Society 1948 (reprint 2002)

Keat GIN OOI, *Southeast Asia: A Historical Encyclopedia, from Angkor Wat to East Timor*, vol. 1, ABC-CLIO 2004

Karl-Heinz GOLZIO, *Die Ausbreitung des Buddhismus in Süd- und Südostasien: Eine quantitative Untersuchung auf der Basis epigraphischer Quellen*, Frankfurt, M., Peter Lang 2010

John GUNTHER, *Inside Asia* (1942 War edition, completely revised), New York and London, Harper 1942

Jürgen HABERMAS, Discourse Ethics: Notes on a Program of Philosophical Justification, in Seyla BENHABIB Fred Reinhard DALLMAYR (eds.), *The Communicative Ethics Controversy*, Cambridge, MIT Press 1990

John Whitney HALL, *Das japanische Kaiserreich*, Frankfurt, M., Fischer 1968

Edmund HARDY, *Der Buddhismus nach älteren Pali-Werken*, Münster i.W., Aschendorffsche Buchhandlung 1926 (1890)

G.E. HARVEY, *History of Burma*, London, Longmans, Green and Co. 1925

Robert HEINE-GELDERN, Conceptions of State and Kingship in Southeast Asia, *The Far Eastern Quarterly*, Vol. 2, No. 1 (Nov. 1942), pp. 15-30

Otto HINTZE, Kalvinismus und Staatsraison in Brandenburg zu Beginn des 17ten Jahrhunderts, *Historische Zeitschrift*, No. 144 (1931)

R. HOLTZMANN, Der Weltherrschaftsgedanke des mittelalterlichen Kaisertums, *Historische Zeitschrift*, No. 159 (1939)

Irving L. HOROWITZ, *The Idea of War and Peace in Contemporary Philosophy*, with an Introductory Essay by Roy Wood Sellars, New York, Paine-Whitman 1957

Susan L. HUNTINGTON, Introduction to Southeast Asia and Southern China, in: Susan L. HUNTINGTON and John C. HUNTINGTON, *Leaves from the Bodhi Tree: The Art of Pala India (8th-12th centuries) and Its International Legacy*, Seattle and London, The Dayton Art Institute and University of Washington Press 1990

Samuel P. HUNTINGTON, *The Clash of Civilizations and the Remaking of the World Order*, London etc., Touchstone 1998

Francis G. HUTCHINS, *India's Revolution—Gandhi and the Quit India Movement*, Cambridge, Ma., Harvard University Press 1973

H.A. JACK (ed.), *Wit and Wisdom of Gandhi*, Boston, Beacon Press 1951

D.N. JHA, How History was Unmade at Nalanda, *Kafila*, 9 July 2014, online publication at http://kafila.org/2014/07/09/how-history-was-unmade-at-nalanda-d-n-jha

William JONES, *Al Sirajiyyah: or the Mohamedan Law of Inheritance: with a commentary* (1792), Kessinger Publishing (May 23, 2010)

Roy E. JORDAAN, Tara and Nyai Lara Kidul: images of the divine feminine in Java, *Asian Folklore Studies*, Vol. 56, No. 2 (Oct. 1997)

–––– Why the Sailendras were not a Javanese Dynasty, *Indonesia and the Malay World*, vol. 34, no. 98 (March 2006),

Engelbert KAEMPFER, *The History of Japan, Together with a Description of the Kingdom of Siam, 1609-1692*, 2 vols., London 1727-1728 (Glasgow 1906)

KANG Youwei, *Ta T'ung Sshu. The one-world philosophy of K'ang Yu-wei*, London, Allen & Unwin 1958

Detlef KANTOWSKY, Die Fehlrezeption von Max Webers Studie über "Hinduismus und Buddhismus" in Indien: Ursachen und Folgen, *Zeitschrift für Soziologie*, Jg. 14, Heft 6 (Dezember 1985)

–––– Recent research on Max Weber's studies of Hinduism: papers submitted to a conference held in New Delhi, 1-3 March 1984 (vol. 4 of the publications of the *Internationales Asienforum*)

Katha Sarit Sagara. Die Mährchensammlung des Sri Somadeva Bhatta aus Kaschmir, Erstes bis fünftes Buch, Sanskrit und Deutsch, Leipzig, F. A. Brockhaus 1839

A.J. Bernet KEMPERS, *Ancient Indonesian Art*, Harvard University Press 1959

Abu Taleb KHAN, *The Travels of Mirza Abu Taleb Khan in Asia, Africa, and Europe during the Years 1799, 1800, 1801, 1802, and 1803*, transl. Charles STEWART, London, Longman, Hurst, Rees, and Orme 1810

Peter KHOROCHE (transl.), *Once the Buddha Was a Monkey. Arya Sura's 'Jatakamala'*, University of Chicago Press 1989/2006

Johann Friedrich KLEUKER, *Zend-Avesta, Zoroasters lebendiges Wort*, Riga, J. F. Hartknoch 1776

David KOPF, *The Brahmo Samaj and the Shaping of the Modern Indian Mind*, Princeton, Princeton University Press 1979

–––– *British Orientalism and the Bengal Renaissance. The Dynamics of*

Indian Modernisation, 1773-1835, Berkeley, University of California Press 1969

Ekkehart KRIPPENDORFF, *Staat und Krieg. Die historische Logik politischer Unvernunft*, Frankfurt, M., edition suhrkamp 1985

M.V. KRISHNA RAO, *Studies in Kautilya*, Delhi, Munshi Ram Manohar Lal 1958

Nicolaas Johannes KROM, *Hindoe-Javaansche geschiedenis*, 's-Gravenhage 1931

Warren F. KUELH, *Seeking World Order. The United States and International Organization to 1920*, Nashville, Vanderbilt 1969

Hermann KULKE and Dietmar ROTHERMUND, *Geschichte Indiens* (History of India), Stuttgart, Berlin, Köln, Mainz, Kohlhammer 1982

Hermann KULKE and Dietmar ROTHERMUND, *Geschichte Indiens: von der Induskultur bis heute*, C.H. Beck 2010

Hermann KULKE and Dietmar ROTHERMUND, *A History of India*, London and New York, Routledge 2004

Hermann KULKE, Ausgrenzung, Rezeption und kulturelles Sendungsbewußtsein, in: S. N. EISENSTADT (ed.), *Kulturen der Achsenzeit*, vol. II, Frankfurt, M., Suhrkamp 1992

– – – – From Ashoka to Jayavarman VII: Some Reflections on the Relationship between Buddhism and the State in India and Southeast Asia, in Tansen SEN (ed.) *Buddhism Across Asia: Networks of Material, Intellectual and Cultural Exchange*, Singapore, Institute of Southeast Asian Studies 2014

– – – – Indian Colonies, Indianization or Cultural Convergence? Reflections on the Changing Image of India's Role in Southeast Asia, in H. SCHULTE-NORDHOLT (ed.), *Onderzoek in Zuidoost-Azië* (Semaian 3), Leiden 1990

– – – – *Indische Geschichte bis 1750*, Oldenbourg Verlag 2005

– – – – Orthodoxe Restauration und hinduistische Sektenreligiosität im Werk Max Webers, in Wolfgang SCHLUCHTER (ed.), *Max Webers Studie über Hinduismus und Buddhismus – Interpretation und Kritik*,

M., Suhrkamp 1984

---- (ed.), *The State in India, 1000-1700*, New Delhi, Oxford India Paperbacks 1997

---- Überlegungen zur Begegnung Europas und Asiens bis ins 19. Jahrhundert, *Oriens Extremus*, vol. 33, no. 1 (1990)

Mahendra KUMAR, *Current Peace Research and India*, Varanasi, Gandhian Institute of Studies 1968

William LADD, *An Essay on a Congress of Nations*, intro. James BROWN SCOTT, New York, Oxford University Press 1916

Nayanjot LAHIRI, *The Archaeology of Indian Trade Routes up to c. 200 BC*, Oxford India Paperbacks 1999

Etienne LAMOTTE, *Histoire du Bouddhisme Indien. Des Origines a l'Ere Saka*. Paris, Louvain 1958

A Record of Buddhistic Kingdoms. Being an Account by the Chinese Monk Fa-Hien of Travels in India and Ceylon (AD 399-414) in Search of the Buddhist Books of Discipline, translated and annotated with a Corean Recension of the Chinese Text by James Legge, New Delhi 1986 (orig. Oxford 1886)

Louise LEVATHES, *When China Ruled the Seas. The Treasure Fleet of the Dragon Throne, 1405-1433*, New York und Oxford, Oxford University Press 1994

Frank LEQUIN, *Het personeel van de Verenigde Oost-Indische Compagnie in Azie in de achttiende eeuw, meer in het bijzonder in de vestiging Bengalen*, Diss. Leiden 1982

---- (ed.), *The Private Correspondence of Isaac Titsingh*, vol. I (1785-1811), Amsterdam, J.C. Gieben 1990

Daniel LERNER, *The Passing of Traditional Society*, New York, Glencoe Free Press 1964

J.P. LOSTY, *Calcutta, City of Palaces. A Survey of the City in the Days of the East India Company 1690-1858*, London, The British Library, New Delhi, Arnold Publishers 1990

Helmut LUKAS, THEORIES OF INDIANIZATION. Exemplified by

Selected Case Studies from Indonesia, *Proceedings of Papers. Sanskrit in Southeast Asia: The Harmonizing Factor of Cultures*, International Sanskrit Conference (May 21-23, 2001), Sanskrit Studies Centre and Department of Oriental Languages, Silpakorn University (Mahachulalongkornrajavidyalaya Press), Bangkok 2003

Alfred Comyn LYALL, *History of India*, vol. VIII (9 vols., ed. by A.V. Williams JACKSON), From the Close of the Seventeenth Century to the Present Time, New Delhi, Asian Education Services 1987

Alasdair MACINTYRE, *After Virtue*, London etc., Bloomsbury 2013

Sachindra Kumar MAITY, *Cultural Heritage of Ancient India*, New Delhi, Abhinav 1983

R. C. MAJUMDAR, *Ancient Indian Colonies in the Far East,* vol. ii, Suvarnadvipa, Dacca 1937

–––– *Glimpses of Bengal in the Nineteenth Century*, Calcutta, Firma K. L. Mukhopadhyay 1960

–––– *Hindu Colonies in the Far East*, Calcutta, K.L. Mukhopadhyay 1944

–––– Indian Culture as a factor in the World Civilization, in *Sir William Jones*, Bicentenary of his Birth. Commemoration Volume, 1746-1946, Kolkata, The Asiatic Society (published by Professor Dilip Coomer Ghose) 1948 (reprint 2002)

–––– *India and South East Asia*, B.R. Pub. Corp., 1979

–––– *Suvarnadvīpa: Cultural history*, New Delhi, Gian 1986

G. P. MALALASEKARA, *The Pali Literature of Ceylon*, Colombo, Colombo 1958 (orig. M. D. Gunasena 1928)

Glen T. MARTIN, Introduction, in *The Constitution for the Federation of Earth*, The Institute for Economic Democracy 2016

Karl MARX, Die künftigen Ergebnisse der britischen Herrschaft in Indien, ["New-York Daily Tribune" No. 3840 of 8 August 1853] London, Friday, 22 July 1853

Karl Marx-Friedrich Engels – Werke, Band 9, Dietz Verlag, Berlin/DDR 1960

John Watson McCRINDLE (transl.), Ancient India as described by Megasthenes and Arrian, a tr. of the fragments of the Indika of Megasthenes collected by dr. Schwanbeck and of the 1st part of the Indika of Arrian, by J.W. McCrindle. With intr., notes. Repr., with additions, from the ‚Indian antiquary‘, Calcutta, Bombay and London, Thacker, Spink & Company 1877

Ved MEHTA, *Rajiv Gandhi and Rama's Kingdom*, New Haven and London, Yale University Press 1994

Wolfgang MOMMSEN, *Max Weber. Gesellschaft, Politik und Geschichte*, Frankfurt, M., Suhrkamp 1974 (Suhrkamp-Taschenbuch Wissenschaft 53)

G. MOORHOUSE, *Calcutta. The City Revealed*, New Delhi etc., Penguin 1994 (1971)

Radha Kumud MOOKHERJI, *Indian Shipping. A History of the Sea-Borne Trade and Maritime Activity of the Indians from the Earliest Times*, New Delhi 1999 (orig. 1912)

R. J. MOORE, *The Crisis of Indian Unity, 1917–1940*, Oxford, Clarendon Press 1974

Arthur MOORE, World Government, in Kshitis ROY (ed.), *Gandhi Memorial Peace Number*, Santiniketan 1949

Wilhelm Emil MÜHLMANN, *MAHATMA GANDHI. Der Mann, sein Werk und seine Wirkung* (Eine Untersuchung zur Religionssoziologie und politischen Ethik), Tübingen, J.C.B. Mohr (Paul Siebeck) 1950

N. MUKHERJEE, *Sir William Jones. A Study in Eighteenth Century British Attitudes to India*, Cambridge University Press 1968 (Cambridge South Asian Studies No. 6),

Kuldip NAYAR, *India, The Critical Years* (Revised and Enlarged Edition), Delhi, Bombay, Bangalore and Kanpur, Vikas 1971

Joseph NEEDHAM, *Science and Civilisation in China*, Cambridge etc., Cambridge University Press 1975 (1954), vol. 1, Introductory Orientations

Joseph NEEDHAM, *Wissenschaftlicher Universalismus, Über Bedeutung und Besonderheit der chinesischen Wissenschaft*, ed., intro. and transl. by

Tilman SPENGLER, Frankfurt, M., Suhrkamp 1979

----- *Within the Four Seas, The Dialogue of East and West*, London etc., George Allen & Unwin 1979 (1969)

Jawaharlal NEHRU, *The Discovery of India*, New Delhi, Jawaharlal Nehru Memorial Fund and Oxford University Press 1990 (orig. Calcutta, Signet Press 1946)

----- *Glimpses of World History*, Oxford University Press (Jawaharlal Nehru Memorial Fund). 1982

Pandit Nehru's Discovery of America, foreword by Eleanor ROOSEVELT, Madras, The Indian Press Publications n.d. (1950?)

Jawaharlal Nehru's Speeches, vol. I, Sept. 1946-May 1949, Delhi, Ministry of Information and Broadcasting, Government of India, Revised Edition, Third Impression 1967

N.A. NIKAM und Richard McKEON (eds. and transl.), *The Edicts of Asoka*, Bombay etc. New York, Asia Publishing House 1962 (University of Chicago 1959),

Ashakant NIMBARK, Gandhism Re-Examined, *Social Research* (New York), vol. 31 (March 1964), pp. 94-125

George ORWELL, Not Counting Niggers, *Adelphi*, July 1939

K. M. PANIKKAR, *Asia and Western Dominance. A Survey of the Vasco Da Gama Epoch of Asian History 1498-1945*, London, George Allen & Unwin 1961

Gregor PAUL, *Philosophie in Japan. Von den Anfängen bis zur Heian-Zeit, Eine kritische Untersuchung*, München, iudicium 1993

Sheldon POLLOCK, Deep Orientalism? Notes on Sanskrit and Power Beyond the Raj, in: BRECKENRIDGE and van der VEER, *Orientalism and the Postcolonial Predicament*, Philadelphia, University of Pennsylvania Press 1993

Gregory L. POSSEHL (ed.), *Harappan Civilization*, 2nd ed., New Delhi, Oxford & IBH 1993

Paul F. POWER, *Gandhi on World Affairs*, London, George Allen & Unwin 1961

Om PRAKASH, *European Commercial Enterprise in Pre-Colonial India*, New Delhi, Cambridge University Press 2000

Rajendra PRASAD, Foreword, in Kshitis ROY (ed.), *Gandhi Memorial Peace Number*, Santiniketan, The Vishwa-Bharati Quarterly, 2 October 1949

Charan PRASAD, *Foreign Trade and Commerce in Ancient India*, New Delhi, Abhinav Publications 1977

Roderich PTAK, *Die maritime Seidenstraße*, München, C.H. Beck 2007

Sarvepalli RADHAKRISHNAN, *Towards a New World*, New Delhi, Bombay, Orient Paperbacks 1980

Stamford RAFFLES, *History of Java*, London, Black, Parbury, and Allen 1817

Nihar-Ranjan RAY, *Sanskrit Buddhism in Burma*, Orchid Press, 2002 (Amsterdam – H.J. Paris, 1936)

Reginald REYNOLDS, What are Pacifists doing?, *Peace News*, 20 July 1956 (London)

Thomas William RHYS DAVIDS, Caroline Augusta Foley RHYS DAVIDS, *Buddhist Birth Stories (Jataka Tales)*: the commentarial introduction entitld Nidāna-kathā, The story of the lineage, London, Routledge 1925

Nick ROBINS, *The Corporation that Changed the World. How the East India Company Shaped the Modern Multinational*, Hyderabad, Orient Longman 2006 (orig. London, Pluto Press)

Heiner ROETZ, *Die chinesische Ethik der Achsenzeit*, Frankfurt, M., Suhrkamp 1992

Romain ROLLAND, *MAHATMA GANDHI. The Man Who Became One with the Universal Being*, transl. Catherine D. Groth, New York and London, The Century Co. 1924

Norbert ROPERS, *Annäherung, Abgrenzung und friedlicher Wandel in Europa*, Bonn-Bad Godesberg, DGFK-Hefte 8 (1975)

Jakob RÖSEL, *Die Hinduismusthese Max Webers: Folgen eines kolonialen Indienbildes in einem religionssoziologischen Gedankengang*, Munich etc., Weltforum-Verlag 1982

Francis ROSENSTIEL, *Supranationalität – Eine Politik des Unpolitischen*, Köln und Berlin, Kiepenheuer & Witsch 1964 (franz. Orig. 1962),

Dietmar ROTHERMUND, *Geschichte Indiens: Vom Mittelalter bis zur Gegenwart*, Munich, C.H. Beck 2002

Manabendra Nath ROY, *India and War*, Lucknow, Dr. A.P Singh, Radical Democratic Party (First Edition. December 1942)

Edward W. SAID, *The World, the Text, and the Critic*, Harvard University Press 1983

George SANSOM, *A History of Japan, 1615-1867*, Stanford University Press 1978 (1963)

T.R. SAREEN, Subhas Chandra Bose, Japan and British Imperialism, *European Journal of East Asian Studies*, vol. 3 (Brill 2004)

Narendra Singh SARELA, Creation of Pakistan—Safeguarding British Strategic Interests, *Times of India*, 17 March 2000

E. SARKISYANZ, *Buddhist Backgrounds of the Burmese Revolution*, The Hague, Nijhoff 1965

–––– *Rußland und der Messianismus des Orients*, Tübingen, J.C.B. Mohr 1955

Haraprasad SASTRI (ed.), *Ramacaritam of Sandhyakaranandin,* Memoirs of the Asiatic Society of Bengal, vol. 3, no. 1 (1910); revised with English translation by Radhagovinda BASAK, Calcutta, The Asiatic Society 1969

K.J. SAUNDERS, *The Story of Buddhism*, Oxford University Press 1916

Pauline C. M. Lunsingh SCHEURLEER and Marijke J. KLOKKE, *Ancient Indonesian Bronzes: A Catalogue of the Exhibition in the Rijksmuseum Amsterdam with a General Introduction*, Brill Archive 1988

Klaus SCHLICHTMANN, *1950—How the Opportunity for Transitioning to UN Collective Security was Missed for the First Time*, Hawaii, Center for Global Nonkilling (Global Nonkilling Working Papers, # 11 2016, in print)

–––– A Draft on Security Council Reform, *Peace & Change*, vol. 24, no. 4, October 1999, pp. 505-535

---- Friede als Rechtsordnung. Der Beitrag von Alfred Hermann Fried (1864–1921) zur Entwicklung des Völkerrechts, *Die Friedens-Warte*, vol. 87, No. 2-3 (2012)

---- Der Friedensnobelpreisträger Alfred Hermann Fried (1864-1921), Pazifist, Publizist und Wegbereiter, *Jahrbuch des öffentlichen Rechts* (ed. Peter HÄBERLE), Neue Folge, vol. 60 (2012), pp. 105-129

---- Helmut Hertling und die Weltbürgerbewegung, in Detlev Bald und Wolfram Wette, *Friedensinitiativen in der Frühzeit des Kalten Krieges 1945-1955*, Essen, Klartext Verlag 2010

---- India, Japan and Western Influence around 1800, *Sophia International Review*, vol. 21 (1999), pp. 31-38

---- Japan, Germany and the Idea of the two Hague Peace Conferences, *JOURNAL OF PEACE RESEARCH*, vol. 40, no. 4 (2003), pp. 377-394

---- *Japan in the World. Shidehara Kijuro, Pacifism and the Abolition of War*, Lanham, Boulder, New York, Toronto, Lexington Books 2009

Ulrich SCHNEIDER, *Die großen Felsen-Edikte Asokas, Kritische Ausgabe, Übersetzung und Analyse der Texte*, Wiesbaden, Otto Harassowitz 1978

Wilfred Harvey SCHOFF and Arrian ARRIAN, *The Periplus of the Eritraean Sea: Travel and Trade in the Indian Ocean*, BiblioLife 2015

Wolfgang SCHUMACHER, *Die Edikte des Kaisers Asoka*, Konstanz, Weller 1948

Raymond SCHWAB, *The Oriental Renaissance. Europe's Rediscovery of India and the East, 1680-1880*, New York, Columbia University Press 1984 (Paris 1950)

---- *Vie d'Anquetil-Duperron suivie des Usages Civils et religieux des Parses par Anquetil-Duperron*, Paris, E., Leroux 1934

Gertrude C. SCHWEBELL, *Die Geburt des modernen Japan in Augenzeugenberichten*, München, dtv 1981 (Düsseldorf 1970)

Shailendra Nath SEN, *Ancient Indian History and Civilization*, Second Edition, New Delhi 1999 (orig. 1988)

Jyotirmay SEN, Asoka's mission to Ceylon and some connected problems,

The Indian Historical Quarterly, Vol. 4, No. 4 (1928)

Amartya SEN, *Identity and Violence. The Illusion of Destiny*, New York and London, W.W. Norton 2006

–––– *On Interpreting India's Past*, Calcutta, The Asiatic Society 1996

Sudarsan SENEVIRATNE, The Mauryan State, in Henry J.M. CLAESSEN and Peter SKALNIK (eds.), *The Early State*, The Hague, Mouton 1978

G.D. SHARMA, *Untold Story 1946 Naval Mutiny: Last War of Independence*, New Delhi, Vij Books 2015

Walter SIMON, A Note on Tibet, *Asia Major*, new series vol. 5 (1955-1956)

Ramjee SINGH and S. SUNDARAM (eds.), *Gandhi and World Order*, New Delhi, APH Publishing Corporation 1996 (Gandhian Institute of Studies)

D.C. SIRCAR, *Inscriptions of Asoka*, Government of India Press, Revised edition 1967

–––– (ed.), *The Sakti Cult and Tara*, Calcutta, University of Calcutta 1967

A. SMITH, *The Oxford History of India*, Oxford, the Clarendon Press 1961

David L. SNELLGROVE, *The Nine Ways of Bon*, Oxford University Press 1980 (orig. 1967)

Percival SPEAR, *A History of India*, vol. II, Penguin 1978

John STEVENSON D.D., *The Kalpa Sutra, and Nava Tatva: Two Works illustrative of the Jain Religion and Philosophy*, Varanasi, Bharat-Bharati 1972 (1848)

Clarence K. STREIT, *Union Now. The Proposal for Inter-democracy Federal Union* (short version), New York and London, Harper 1940

K. R. SUBRAMANIAN, *Buddhist remains in Andhra and The history of Andhra between 224 & 610 A. D.*, Vepery, Diocesan press 1932

Daisetsu SUZUKI, *Outlines of Mahayana Buddhism*, London, Luzac & Co., publishers to the University of Chicago, 1907

Rabindranath TAGORE, *Creative Unity*, London, Macmillan 1922

Stanley Jeyaraja TAMBIAH, *World Conqueror & World Renouncer. A Study of Buddhism and Polity in Thailand against a Historical Background*, Cambridge, London, New York, Melbourne, Cambridge University Press 1976

Jean-Baptiste TAVERNIER, *Travels in India*, London and New York, Macmillan and Co. 1889

Paul TAYLOR, The Ethnocentric Fallacy, *The Monist*, vol. 47 (1963), pp. 563-584

Romila THAPAR with Sundar SARUKKAI, Dhruv RAINA, Peter Ronald DESOUZA, Neeladri BHATTACHARYA, and Jawed NAQWI, *The Public Intellectual in India*, ed. by Chandra CHARI and Uma IYANGER, New Delhi, Aleph Book Company 2015

Ramila THAPAR, *Asoka and the Decline of the Mauryas*, London, Oxford University Press 1961

–––– *From Lineage to State, Social Formations in Mid-first Millennium B.C. in the Ganga Valley*, Delhi etc., Oxford University Press 1984

–––– *The Past Before Us, Historical Traditions in North India*, Bangalore, Calcutta, New Delhi etc., Orient Blackswan 2013

–––– *The Past and Prejudice*, New Delhi, National Book Trust 2000 (orig. 1975)

–––– State Formation in Early India, *Indian Social Science Journal*, vol. XXXII, no. 4 (1980)

Shashi THAROOR, *Pax Indica. India and the World of the 21st Century*, New Delhi, Allen Lane (Penguin) 2012

Thomas R. TRAUTMANN, *Kautilya and the Arthashastra, a Statistical Investigation of the Authorship and Evolution of the Text*, Leiden, E.J. Brill 1971

Edward UPHAM (ed.), *The Mahavansi, the Raja-ratnacari, and the Raja-vali: forming the sacred and historical books of Ceylon; also, a collection of tracts illustrative of the doctrines and literature of Buddhism: translated from the Singhalese*. London, Parbury, Allen, and Co. 1833 (3 vols.)

John VILLIERS, *Südostasien vor der Kolonialzeit*, Frankfurt, M., Fischer

Weltgeschichte 1990 (orig. 1965), Bd.18

Elisabeth-Chalier VISUVALINGAM, Bhairava's Royal Brahmanicide: The Problem of the Mahabrahmana, in Alf HILTEBEITEL (ed.), *Criminal Gods and Demon Devotees: Essays on the Guardians of Popular Hinduism*, SUNY Press 1989

Caesar VOÛTE, The Restoration and Conservation Project of Borobudur Temple, Indonesia. Planning – Research – Design, *Studies in Conservation*, vol. 18, No.3 (1973), pp. 113–130.

F.P. WALTERS, *A History of the League of Nations*, London, New York and Toronto, Oxford University Press 1960

Max WEBER, *Essays in Sociology*, translated by Hans Heinrich GERTH and Charles Wright MILLS, New York, Routledge 2009

Max WEBER, *Gesammelte Aufsätze zur Religionssoziologie*, vols. I & II, Tübingen, J.C.B. Mohr

———— *Gesammelte Aufsätze zur Sozial- und Wirtschaftsgeschichte*, ed. Marianne WEBER, Tübingen, J.C.B. Mohr 1988

———— in *Gesammelte Politische Schriften*, Tübingen, J.C. B. Mohr (Paul Siebeck) 1980 (orig. Munich 1921)

Max WEBER, *Methodology of Social Sciences*, ed. and transl. by Edward SHILS and Henry A. FINCH, New Brunswick, NJ, Transaction Publishers 2011

———— *Wirtschaft und Gesellschaft*: *Grundriss der verstehenden Soziologie*, Tübingen, Mohr Siebeck 2002

H.G. WELLS, *Phoenix. A Summary of the Inescapable Conditions of World Reorganisation*, London, Secker & Warburg 1942

André WINK, *Al-Hind: Early medieval India and the expansion of Islam*, vol. 1, The India Trade, Brill 1990

———— *Al-Hind: Early medieval India and the expansion of Islam*, vol. 1, The kingdom of Dharma (Palas of Bengal), Brill 1990

Larry M. WORTZEL und Dana R. DILLON, Improving Relations with India without Compromising U.S. Security, *Backgrounder*, No. 1402 (11 December 2000)

Quincy WRIGHT, Political Conditions of the Period of Transition, *International Conciliation*, Commission to Study the Organization of Peace—The Transitional Period, No. 379 (April 1942)

Theodor ZACHARIAE, Zur Geschichte vom weisen Haikar, *Zeitschrift des Vereins für Volkskunde*, 17. Jg. (1907)

Gerda ZELLENTIN (ed.), *Annäherung, Abgrenzung und friedlicher Wandel in Europa*, Boppard am Rhein, Harald Boldt 1976

Erik ZÜRCHER, *The Buddhist Conquest of China—The Spread and Adaptation of Buddhism in Early Medieval China*, Leyden, E.J. Brill 1959

Index